D1629153

Canada
APR 10 2002
D.A.I 65
Vancouver B.C.
IMMIGRATION

TRAVELER'S
WESTERN
CANADA
COMPANION

DEPARTMENT OF IMMIGRATION
PERMITTED TO ENTER
AUSTRALIA.
on 24APR1996
For stay of 12 Month
SYDNEY AIRPORT 54

IMMIGRATION BANGKOK THAILAND
DEPARTED
- 6 FEB 1998
SIGNED

IMMIGRATION
ETHNIC AFFAIRS
...........Person
30 OCT 1999
DEPARTED
AUSTRALIA
SYDNEY 32

上陸許可
ADMITTED
15. FEB. 1996
Status: 4-1- 4
Duration: 90 days
NARITA(N)
Immigration Inspector
日本国

ADMITTED
20 OCT. 1998
Status: 4-1-16
Duration 180 days
Port: HANEDA
Signature

№ 011278

THE UNITED STATES
OF AMERICA
NONIMMIGRANT VISA
ISSUED AT
PASSED Air Port
U.S. IMMIGRATION
170 HHW 1710
JUL 20 1998

HONG KONG
(1038)
- 7 JUN 1997
IMMIGRATION
OFFICER

The Traveler's Companions
ARGENTINA • AUSTRALIA • BALI • CALIFORNIA • CANADA • CHINA • COSTA RICA •
CUBA • EASTERN CANADA • ECUADOR • FLORIDA • HAWAII • HONG KONG • INDIA •
INDONESIA • JAPAN • KENYA • MALAYSIA & SINGAPORE • MEDITERRANEAN FRANCE •
MEXICO • NEPAL • NEW ENGLAND • NEW ZEALAND • PERU • PHILIPPINES • PORTUGAL •
RUSSIA • SOUTH AFRICA • SOUTHERN ENGLAND • SPAIN • THAILAND • TURKEY •
VENEZUELA • VIETNAM, LAOS AND CAMBODIA • WESTERN CANADA

Traveler's Western Canada Companion

First Published 1998
Second Edition 2003
The Globe Pequot Press
246 Goose Lane, PO Box 480
Guilford, CT 06437 USA
www.globe-pequot.com

© 2003 by The Globe Pequot Press, Guilford CT, USA

ISBN: 0-7627-2333-5

Created, edited and produced by
Allan Amsel Publishing, 53, rue Beaudouin
27700 Les Andelys, France.
E-mail: AAmsel@aol.com

Editor in Chief: Allan Amsel
Editor: Anne Trager
Picture editor and book designer: Roberto Rossi

This Edition updated and revised by Melissa Shales

Authors' Acknowledgments
A multitude of individuals and organizations contributed to this book with their generosity,
hospitality and expert advice. This list is far too long to include here, but the authors remember
and thank each one of them. Special thanks goes to Carol Sykes for all her hard work and dogged
determination to hunt down obscure facts, and to the national, provincial and local Canadian
tourist-information providers.

Printed by Samwha Printing Co. Ltd., Seoul, South Korea

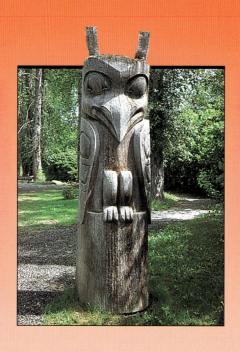

TRAVELER'S
WESTERN
CANADA
COMPANION

by Laura Purdom and Donald Carroll

Photographs by
Robert Holmes and Nik Wheeler

Second Edition

The
Globe
Pequot
Press

GUILFORD
CONNECTICUT

Contents

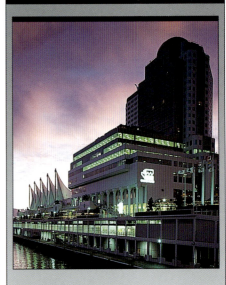

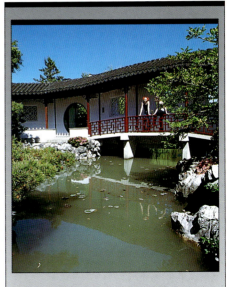

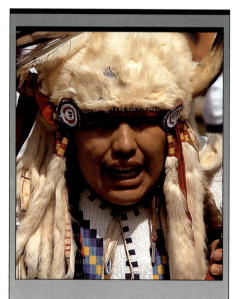

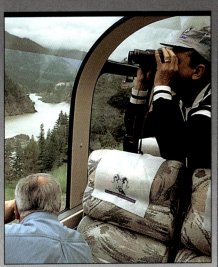

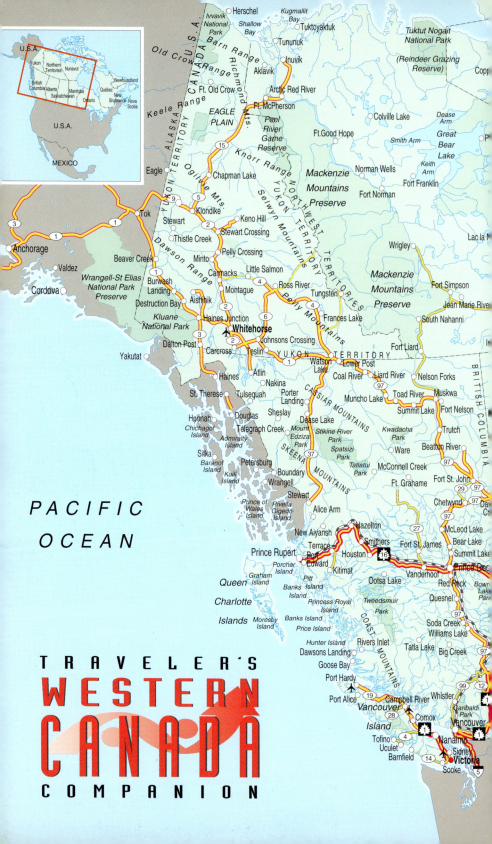

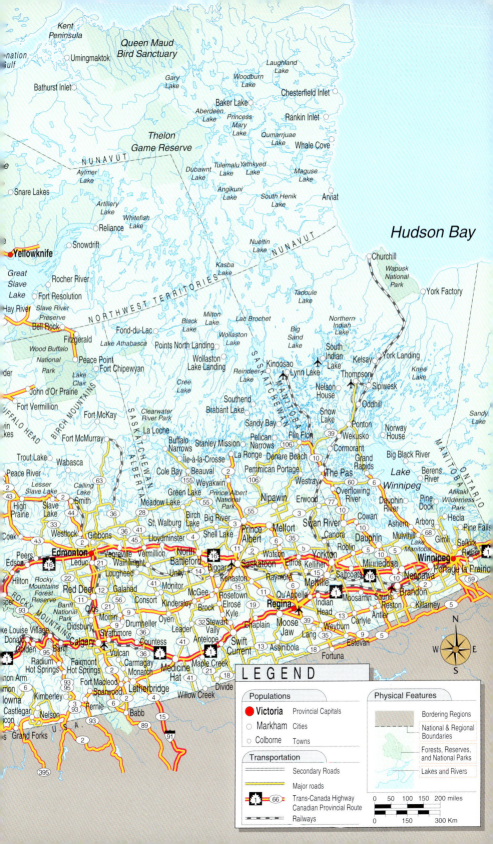

TOP SPOTS

for the next two days, as you climb towards Banff, jaw-dropping panoramas just get better and better. Every mention of a photo opportunity by the train crew is like a call to battle: cameras and binoculars bristle on one or the other side of the car — training their sights on blue-streaked glaciers and mile-high mountains, aerial bridges slung over thundering rivers with names like Jaws of Death and Suicide Rapids, and silent arcades of 1,000-year-old cedars. Over the course of the trip, wildlife sightings send passengers into yet higher ecstasies: a beaver paddling across a pond, Canada geese in V-formation, osprey fledglings in their aerie, a black bear curious about the hulking giant that's passing through its berry patch.

The *Rocky Mountaineer* runs from early May to mid-October, with two winter specials a year. For information, contact Rocky Mountaineer Railtours ((604) 606-7200 TOLL-FREE (800) 665-7245 WEB SITE www.rockymountaineer.com.

There is only one true transcontinental train left in Canada, VIA Rail's *TransCanada* service, from Vancouver to Toronto, via Jasper and Edmonton, Saskatoon and Winnipeg (three days). Everyone has access to domed observation cars; Silver and Blue Class passengers are given comfortable cabins and excellent dining facilities. VIA Rail also runs the scenic *Skeena Train* from Jasper to Prince George and Prince Rupert. For information contact VIA Rail ((514) 871-6000 TOLL-FREE (888) 842-7245 WEB SITE www.viarail.ca. In the United Kingdom, contact Leisurail ((0870) 750 0222 WEB SITE www.leisurail.co.uk which is the agent for VIA Rail and the *Rocky Mountaineer*.

Ride the Legendary Rails

Until the completion of the Trans Canada Highway in the 1960s, it was the railways that stitched Canada together as a nation. Although many miles of track have closed, some historic and wildly scenic routes remain, reminders of a romantic era in Canadian history.

"We're going to be highballing for the next few miles, folks, so hang on to your champagne glasses!" Thus begins a classic Canadian journey: the two-day train ride (daytime only, you overnight in Kamloops so as not to miss any of the splendor) through the Rockies from Vancouver to Calgary or Jasper, aboard the *Rocky Mountaineer*. After a toast to the journey ahead, you settle into plush digs. *Red Leaf* is a particularly posh ordinary train, while *Gold Leaf*, a spacious two-level coach, has a glass-domed roof and a dining room crisp with white linen. Both have outside observation decks.

Right out of Vancouver, you are into the magnificent scenery of the Fraser Valley, and

The *Rocky Mountaineer* passing through Glacier National Park OPPOSITE on its way from Alberta to the Pacific coast; a bridal veil cascade ABOVE captures the attention of passengers.

Once you've crossed the Continental Divide by rail, the next adventure lies further north, where the White Pass & Yukon Railway crosses the 60th parallel, that latitudinal marker that for Canadians designates the transition from "north" to "true north." Anyone familiar with the history of the Klondike will know that this was the treacherous route to the gold fields that thousands attempted to cross on foot in the mad rush of 1898–99. One of the most famous images of that era is of an endless stream of humanity toiling up the snow-covered incline to White Pass.

Most people said a railroad over the pass was impossible, but with English capital, Canadian contractors and American engineers, the "Stampede Rail" was completed in 1900 under extreme weather conditions. Now the WP&YR is the last of the Canadian narrow-gauge passenger service railways, an intensely romantic steam train that follows a glacially fed river through the Tongass National Forest from Skagway, Alaska, to Fraser, British Columbia, gaining 900 m (3,000 ft) in elevation. Along the 32-km (20-mile) route you cross through Glacier Station, Slipping Rock, Inspiration Point and Deadhorse Gulch, names that convey both the magnificence and misery of the route. The tiny train wraps itself around each bend, running by waterfalls that churn under half-melted snow bridges — so close that you could touch them. At Fraser, you can transfer to a bus for the rest of the 176-km (110-mile) journey to the Yukon.

The WP & YR runs four to six trips per day, from mid-May to late September, with several available routes. For information, contact the White Pass & Yukon Railway ℂ (907) 983-2217 TOLL-FREE (800) 343-7373 WEB SITE www.white passrailroad.com.

If none of this provides enough splendor — or time on a train — consider the super-luxurious *Royal Canadian Pacific*, built from a series of beautifully restored 1900s Canadian Pacific business cars, which operates out of Calgary, Alberta. Passengers sleep onboard and sightsee, play golf, walk or fish by day. The *Royal Canadian Pacific* runs a series of four to six day tours through the scenic heart of the Rockies. With only 24 guests per train, attention is personal and comfort a sumptuous five-star plus. For information on their tours, contact Royal Canadian Pacific Tours ℂ (403) 508-1400 TOLL-FREE (877) 665-3044 WEB SITE www.cprtours.com.

Walk with the Dinosaurs

When you hear the ominous "boom… boom… boom," you've entered the Royal Tyrrell Museum's extreme theropod exhibit, which relates the gory tale of the *velociraptor* and other meat-eating dinosaurs that once roamed Alberta's badlands. The *Jurassic Park* connection is exploited to the fullest at this world-class paleontology museum that attracts 350,000 visitors each year.

Situated in Alberta's Midland Provincial Park, 140 km (90 miles) northeast of Calgary, the Royal Tyrrell Museum collects, conserves and exhibits paleontological history through to the appearance of man. That means dino bones, and lots of them. On display are 35 complete dinosaur skeletons — including the dramatic *Albertosaurus*, a fully articulated skeleton in death pose — along with some very impressive bits and pieces (like the rare "Black Beauty" *Tyrannosaurus rex* skull and a T-rex leg bone as thick as a tree trunk). Many of these specimens were found right in the extraordinary landscape of the Red Deer Valley, where erosive conditions — nature's ongoing archeological dig — expose more petrified wood, fossils and dinosaur bones with every gully-washing storm.

But, as museum staff like to point out, "It's not just bones!" Visitors with an aesthetic eye linger at display cases sparkling with million-year-old seed ferns in endless patterns and shades. There are fragile crystallized leaves imprisoned in stone, zebra-patterned blocks of Jurassic Period limestone, and rare multicolored ammolite gemstones, unique to the province.

Kids, needless we say, have a blast here. At the museum entrance, youngsters crawl over the life-size dinosaur models, hanging from giant teeth and sliding down sloping backs. Inside they find plenty of interactive computers and touchable displays. A black-light puppet show featuring the PaleoPlayers presents the story of the "Weird Wonders":

the strange marine animals of the Burgess Shale — the first multi-cellular animals in the fossil record. The Weird Wonders are also the subject of one of the museum's permanent exhibits, a three-dimensional Burgess Shale diorama that explores these extraordinary creatures and their underwater environment before they were buried 515 million years ago (see YOHO NATIONAL PARK, page 125, for information on hiking trips to the Burgess Shale fossil beds in British Columbia, or contact the Tyrrell Museum).

At the museum's preparation-lab viewing area, visitors can watch technicians meticulously releasing fossilized remains from massive chunks of stone. Surrounding the museum, Midland Provincial Park's trails give explorers a chance to investigate the badlands on one- and two-hour loops. You can even pitch in and excavate alongside trained technicians with the museum's Day Digs program. At nearby Dinosaur Provincial Park, the Tyrrell Museum operates an important field station where volunteers can sign up for a more intensive field experience, working for stints of a week or longer in the park's fossil rich fields.

In recognition of its rich fossil deposits, representing nearly 300 species of plants and animals, Dinosaur Provincial Park ☏ (403)

OPPOSITE: Passengers peruse the British Columbia scenery from the *Rocky Mountainer's* "dome car."
ABOVE: At Alberta's Royal Tyrrell Museum, *Tyrannosaurus rex* towers over a visitor.

378-4342 or (403) 378 4344 (tour reservations) FAX (403) 378-4247 WEB SITE www.discoveryweb .com / aep / parks / dinosaur, was designated a UNESCO World Heritage Site in 1979. It is located a half-hour northeast of Brooks, Alberta. Take Route 56 to Brooks then Highway 873 and follow the signs.

The Royal Tyrrell Museum ((403) 823-7707 TOLL-FREE (888) 440-4240 WEB SITE www.tyrrell museum.com, Drumheller, Alberta, is open in summer daily 9 AM to 9 PM, and in winter Tuesday to Sunday 10 AM to 5 PM.

Paddle the Pacific Rim

Hugging the fjord-pitted coastline of Vancouver Island in southwestern British Columbia, Pacific Rim National Park encompasses one of the most extensive temperate rainforests in the world. Kayakers paddle here in the calm waters surrounding the Broken Islands, alighting on tiny islets framed with white-sand beaches. Day hikers out of Tofino roam the rainforest under a canopy of red cedars and through a damp profusion of sword fern. Beachcombers emerge from the muted colors of the forest to the sparkling tidal pools of the coast, where green sea anemones feed and fat orange starfish cling to the rocks. Here, zealous backpackers follow the challenging West Coast Trail carrying all of their supplies for the six- to eight-day trip from Port Renfrew to Bamfield.

This infamous trail covers the southern third of the park, weaving through 77 km (48 miles) of woods and waterfalls, scaling slippery slopes and tracing the shoreline that has been the death of many a ship. Killer and gray whales, sea otters and black bears are commonly seen along the route.

Pacific Rim National Park is also the setting for a somewhat more genteel adventure experience. In the midst of the rainforest, a small lodge nestles in a notch carved out of the granite hillside along the emerald waters of Barkley Sound. Eagle Nook Ocean Wilderness Resort offers a taste of the rich variety of flora and fauna to be found in the Pacific Rim National Park, but here guests rough it in style, enjoying a true wilderness experience — hiking and heli-hiking, sea-kayaking, salmon fishing, whale-, seal- and bird-watching — and returning to the comforts of a warm hearth, a gourmet meal, a moonlit dip in the hot tub, a sauna and a soft bed.

One constant in the park is the weather, whether you're trekking or taking it easy. Some days the sky seems to hang within yards of the water. The air is liquid. "Classic West Coast weather," you'll be told by Vancouver Islanders, who seem to thrive on the misty atmosphere as much as the cedars and ferns do. But rain or shine, rough or relaxed, Pacific Rim National Park is splendid. No roads lead

Pacific Rim National Park — OPPOSITE: Starfish and sea anemones. ABOVE: Kayaking.

to the secluded resort (see PACIFIC RIM NATIONAL PARK, page 98).

Only experienced hikers should attempt to hike the West Coast Trail, and never alone. There is a strict quota system regulating the number of people who hike the trail. Reservations are strongly recommended (see PACIFIC RIM NATIONAL PARK, page 96).

Cruise the Inside Passage

With a deep groan and a whistle, the ferry swings round its bow and sails north along the British Columbian coast towards Prince Rupert. For the next three days, it will make its way along the southern stretch of the Inside Passage, Canada's historic inland waterway. The full route stretches far to the north, usually ending in Skagway, Alaska.

We're following in the wake of hundreds of thousands of prospectors who blazed this route in 1898, when gold was discovered in the Klondike region of the Yukon. Just over 100 years later, this is one of North America's most scenic and popular journeys, taking voyagers through and beyond the Pacific rainforest and into the glacier-locked Coast Mountains of the north. The scenery is astounding, and opportunities for spotting wildlife, especially marine mammals, are unparalleled.

The voyage runs along British Columbia's northern coast and the Southeast Alaskan panhandle — which shares British Columbia's rainforest flora of Sitka spruce, western hemlock and tall cedars. Further north still, the landscape changes dramatically. The onboard naturalist explains that Alaska has glaciers the size of Rhode Island and then ticks off a list of the wildlife you may see in this icy wilderness: grizzlies, black bears, bald eagles, orcas (killer whales), humpback whales, Steller's sea lions and Pacific white-sided dolphins.

Evening invariably finds many of the passengers enjoying the waning day on the ship's port side. It's the orca watch. A few false alarms: a log floats by ... then a resounding, "There they are!" comes from an upper deck, and everyone rushes to the rail. It's a large school of Pacific white-sided dolphins. Magnificent! But where are the whales? Finally, at dusk, they appear — a pod of five orcas, with their unmistakable tall black fins. It's not difficult to understand why the Pacific West Coast natives so revered these creatures, calling them sea wolves, incorporating them into their art and endowing them with supernatural powers.

In addition to a stopover in Prince Rupert, the ship may dock briefly at the Alaskan ports of Ketchikan, Wrangell, Petersburg, Juneau and Haines. It's possible to ferry-hop along the coast, debarking at these picturesque towns, some of which can only be reached by boat. The journey usually ends at Skagway, Alaska, the very place where thousands of gold seekers erected a muddy tent-city a century ago in preparation for their trek over the White and Chilkoot Passes to the Yukon.

In addition to the ferries, the choice of cruise vessels ranges from floating cities, carrying thousands of passengers and offering a variety of entertainment, to smallish ships with the emphasis firmly on seeing as many natural attractions as possible. These can get close to shore when such creatures as bears are spotted or glaciers are shedding some of their load. The duration of the voyage and the ports visited vary. Take your time selecting the version that will best suit your tastes.

The main Canadian operator is BC Ferries ((604) 669-1211 TOLL-FREE IN BRITISH COLUMBIA (888) 223-3779 WEB SITE www.bcferries.com, for trips between Vancouver, Vancouver Island, Port Hardy and Prince Rupert, British Columbia. In the USA, try the Alaska Marine Highway System ((907) 627-1744 or (907) 627-1745 TOLL-FREE (1-800) 642-0066, for ports of call between Bellingham, Washington, and Skagway, Alaska. If you take the Alaska Marine Highway out of a Canadian port of call, don't forget to bring along United States dollars.

Cruise West ((416) 444-2410 TOLL-FREE (800) 580-0072 WEB SITE www.cruisewest.com is a small-ship cruise specialist that continues from Skagway to Juneau, Alaska.

Listen to Ancient Voices

It's an hour's boat ride out of Dawson up the Yukon River — a short trip, but a long journey, taking visitors back many years as they sail into the Ancient Voices Wilderness Camp. Throughout the year, Dawson City visitors who want a change from the gold-rush hullabaloo gladly embark on this quiet river journey, where they can visit the descendants of the region's original inhabitants and learn about life in this valley before the gold seekers came and changed their lives forever.

This place in the woods may have originally been a Hän native hunting bivouac. Towards the turn of the last century it became a logging camp, providing fuel for the riverboats that

The Inside Passage — ABOVE: The village of Petersburg in the Alaska panhandle. BELOW: Snowcapped mountains from the deck of the ferry ship MV *Matanuska*.

steamed up and down the Yukon at the height of the gold-rush era. Now Marge and Peter Kormendy, along with their family, friends and colleagues, are fulfilling a lifelong dream to reclaim and preserve their native heritage. They're part of an immensely exciting movement in the Yukon, and throughout Canada, of First Nations people regaining their land and their culture after a century of marginalization.

On the boat ride to the camp, Marge explains how she and Peter chose the camp's name. "We call this place Ancient Voices because it's a place of spirits. We're here because we want to keep alive our past. The voices are calling to tell us to come back to the past, because it is simple and true. The land is alive with our ancestors' voices."

Though it is a sacred place, Ancient Voices welcomes everyone. Some people come in winter to see *naoka*, the Northern Lights; some come for the summer women's retreat, knife-making workshops, wilderness survival courses or leather- and bead-craft seminars. Others just want to be here among the voices — to sleep in rustic cabins, to learn the skills of building a lean-to out of spruce boughs, to bask in the *makivik*, the traditional steam-house, and to share a meal at the outdoor fire pit. While some visitors come for week-long stays, many come just for a few hours to see demonstrations of the traditional crafts being practiced: the fish wheel, moose-hide curing, storytelling, drumming and singing. After the demonstrations, a picnic of traditional foods is served: *bannock*, a delicious fried biscuit, is eaten with high-bush cranberry jam and dried caribou. A barbecue of moose steaks and salmon follows.

For information about Ancient Voices Wilderness Camp, contact Marge Kormendy ((867) 993-5605 FAX (867) 993-6532 WEB SITE www.ancientvoices.ca, Box 679, Dawson, Yukon Y0B 1G0. Day visits operate through the summer; workshops and conferences are offered throughout the year; package trips and customized vacations are also available year-round.

First Nations tourism is growing rapidly throughout Canada. These native-owned and run enterprises range from historical villages to tour companies to camps to lodges. What they offer in common is a chance to meet and talk to some of Canada's First Nations peoples, and to learn about their culture first hand, often in a participatory manner. These are not living history museums with costumed interpreters, but real encounters with living cultures — and ones others have much to learn from.

For lists of contacts, get in touch with associations such as the Yukon First Nations Tourism Association ((867) 667-7698 FAX (867) 667-7527, Box 4518, Whitehorse, Yukon Y1A 2R8; the Québec Aboriginal Tourism Corporation ((418) 843 5030 TOLL-FREE (877) 698-7827 WEB SITE www.staq.net; the Northern Ontario Native Tourism Association ((807) 623-0497 FAX (807) 623-0498 E-MAIL nonta@norlink.net, Rural Route 4, Mission Road, Thunder Bay, Ontario P7C 4Z2; or the Nunavut Tourism Association ((867) 979-6551 TOLL-FREE IN CANADA (800) 491-7910, Box 1450, Iqaluit, Nunavut X0A 0H0, an excellent source of information for all things Inuit.

British Columbia is also an excellent place to encounter First Nations cultures. In the Vancouver area there is the Hiwus Feasthouse ((604) 980-9311, on Grouse Mountain, with a program of Coast Salish dancing and dining. On Vancouver Island there are a number of cultural centers, including the U'Mista Cultural Centre at Alert Bay; the Quw'utsun Cultural and Conference Centre, Duncan; and the Kwagiulth Museum and Cultural Centre on Quadra Island. At Cape Mudge you can stay at the Tsa-Kwa-Luten Lodge and dine in a longhouse on traditional native cuisine. Further north in British Columbia, Prince Rupert is steeped in Tsimshian history and culture (30 percent of the population is aboriginal), and there is much to see and do in and near the city. From here, you can sail to the Queen Charlotte Islands, ancestral home of the Haida, or head east to the Hazelton area to visit the 'Ksan Historical Village, a restored Gitksan native village.

Finally, annual events and festivals are a good way to encounter First Nations culture (see FESTIVE FLINGS, page 35 in YOUR CHOICE). Ask the local tourism office or native tourism association for details.

Ancient Voices Wilderness Camp, Yukon — ABOVE : After a barbecue of salmon and moose steaks, Nova Scotian visitors "jam" BELOW with native Canadians.

YOUR CHOICE

The Great Outdoors

Extending from the densely populated 49th parallel into the empty reaches of the north, Canada — the world's second largest country — encompasses not only a stunning breadth of wilderness, but also a mind-boggling variety of terrains. Western Canada in particular spans from treeless far northern tundra to dense Pacific Coast rainforest, from the boundless prairie wheat fields to the pocket deserts and towering mountains of Alberta and British Columbia.

Established throughout western Canada are some of the continent's grandest national parks. Most are accessible to travelers, and most offer an array of facilities and activities. Boating, biking, skiing, dog sledding … take your pick. But a stout pair of hiking boots is all that is really required to experience many of western Canada's wide-open spaces.

HIKING IN THE NATIONAL PARKS

Top of the list are the Rocky Mountain parks, which straddle the provinces of Alberta and British Columbia. **Banff** alone has more than 1,500 km (900 miles) of marked trails. **Jasper**, larger than Banff, Yoho and Kootenay combined, is the third-most visited park in Canada (after Banff and Kootenay), with some 800 lakes and mountain trails to satisfy every type of hiker. In both Banff and Jasper, many trailheads are close to the townsites themselves, though for a true wilderness experience you'll want to climb to higher pastures. **Yoho** and **Kootenay** draw mountaineers and rock climbers from around the world, but also have trails for all levels of ability and interest.

Coastal British Columbia is the home of one of the world's most fabled long-distance treks, the West Coast Trail in **Pacific Rim National Park**. Originally used as a lifesaving route for shipwrecked sailors along Vancouver Island's sparsely populated coastline, this is a challenging 77-km (46-mile) trek that can take five to nine days to complete, and is only for experienced hikers. The **Chilkoot Trail**, a grueling three- to five-day hike between Dyea, Alaska, and Lake Bennett, British Columbia, was the poor man's route to the Klondike gold fields in 1898. From Lake Bennet it's just a short hop to some of the best true-wilderness hiking in Canada in the Yukon Territory's **Kluane National Park**. Canada's highest peak, Mount Logan (6,050 m / 19,844 ft) looms over vast ice fields in Kluane's back ranges, drawing alpinists from around the world. The park's front ranges are accessible to all, offering spectacular scenery and opportunities for spotting wildlife.

Springtime in the Canadian Rockies, Alberta — OPPOSITE: A glacial lake mirrors its towering neighbor. ABOVE: A ground squirrel peers out from the rocks surrounding Lake Louise.

Some of Canada's parks are remote indeed, but well worth the effort and expense to reach. Bisected by the Arctic Circle, on Baffin Island in Nunavut, **Auyuittuq National Park Reserve** is an international draw for climbers and hikers, who follow traditional Inuit routes marked by *inukshuks*, rock cairns resembling human figures.

Most people don't think of Saskatchewan as a hiker's paradise, but **Prince Albert National Park**, where the prairie meets the forested northern region of the province, offers backpackers a 400,000-hectare (million-acre) playground, with hiking and trekking trails for all abilities. **Riding Mountain National Park** has 40 hiking and cycling trails traversing Manitoba's highlands — where bison, moose, elk and white-tailed deer roam.

In addition to local tourist information centers, park centers are often equipped with adequate trail maps. If you are venturing into the backcountry, you'll need a topographical map. The **Canada Map Office** produces an excellent series, available from all good map retailers.

WILDLIFE

Canada's tundra, mountains, forests and prairies support a profusion of wildlife. On Vancouver Island, **tidal pools** fascinate hikers who can gaze through clear waters at golden starfish and green sea anemone, while kayakers paddling the Broken Island Group drift through sparkling schools of sardines. Coastal British Columbia teems with **marine mammals**; from the majestic humpbacks to graceful orcas (killer whales), Steller's sea lions and Pacific white-sided dolphins. In the northern interior of British Columbia, the rare white **kermode bear** is sometimes spotted around Terrace. The Tsimshian natives called these white bears "ghosts," and they figure prominently in their folklore. The kermode is cousin to the **black bear**, which roams Canada's boreal forest and can sometimes be seen foraging for berries along highways.

Grizzly bears (called brown bears in Canada) are found in greater numbers in the Yukon Territory's Kluane National Park than anywhere else in Canada. **Caribou**, **elk**, **timber wolves** and **thin horn sheep** are abundant in the Kluane Range, which also has the world's largest population of **Dall sheep**.

In April, Yukon bird watchers flock to M'Clintock Bay for the annual migration of the **trumpeter swan**, and in the Northwest Territories some 300,000 **snow geese** migrate annually to the Mackenzie Delta and other areas of the Arctic mainland and islands. In Wood Buffalo National Park, North America's

largest herd of **bison** — commonly called buffalo — roam.

Visitors to Alberta are delighted at the sight of **elk** grazing the medians and yards in Banff and Jasper townsites. Outside the towns, a drive through the parks in summer virtually guarantees sightings of **bighorn sheep**, **black bears** and **mountain goats**.

Saskatchewan is an important migratory stop for the endangered **whooping crane**, and in late August, Last Mountain Lake, northwest of Regina, is the place to watch cranes and **pelicans**. Churchill, Manitoba, is the **polar bear** capital of the world, and polar bears are abundant along Nunavut's Arctic coast as well as at Herschel Island in the Yukon.

Sporting Spree

Whatever your sporting passion, be it curling or croquet, watching a beer-soaked hockey match or skiing solo down a pristine mountainside, Canada is likely to offer a time and a place for it.

CANOEING, KAYAKING AND RAFTING

Canada is the world's most watery land, with lakes and rivers that contain half of the world's

OPPOSITE: The glacier-fed Lake Annette in Jasper National Park, Alberta. ABOVE: A bald eagle perched like a totem on Queen Charlotte Island, British Columbia.

supply of fresh water, and with more than 240,000 km (151,000 miles) of coastline. With so much H$_2$O, it's no surprise that Canada's shores and inland waterways are an irresistible draw for paddlers from all over the world.

British Columbia is well known for its water routes. In the Okanagan region, rafts bob and weave through the whitewater rapids of **Fraser Canyon**. The 116-km (72-mile) trip on the Cariboo River to **Bowron Lake Provincial Park** is a classic. Sea kayaking is splendid along the Vancouver Island shoreline, especially around the **Broken Islands** and in the **Gwaii Haanas National Park** (part of the Queen Charlotte Islands), where most people hire a guide to help them navigate the archipelago's 180-odd islands.

In the Northwest Territories, the Mackenzie system presents a variety of challenging voyages, including a 300-km (180-mile) stretch of the **South Nahanni River** near Fort Simpson, where the Nahanni National Park, a UNESCO World Heritage Site, has its headquarters. The Yukon river system has it all, from the gentle currents of the **Takhini** to the Class III rapids and spectacular river-level glaciers of the **Tatshenshini** and **Alsek** Rivers.

SKIING

In this land of legendary winters, where snow covers hill and vale for five months (or more!) of the year, skiing is a good way to stay warm. Good skiing can be had in just about every province and territory, but it is in British

Columbia and the Rockies that you find ski slopes of a variety and grandeur unsurpassed anywhere in the world.

The world-famous ski resort of **Whistler/ Blackcomb** is two hours north of Vancouver along the spectacular Sea-to-Sky Highway. Whistler Mountain has a rise of 1,530 m (5,020 ft) and the longest ski season: November to early June. Blackcomb Mountain has the greatest vertical rise in North America at 1,609 m (5,280 ft), and its Horstman Glacier offers some skiing and snowboarding even in summer. Both are well served by high-speed lift systems and between them they have 2,800 hectares (7,000 acres) of skiing, a third of it above the treeline. The area has some particularly beautiful cross-country skiing, with over 200 marked trails, three glaciers and heli-skiing, for intermediate or advanced skiers, with Whistler Heli-Skiing TOLL-FREE (888) 435-4754 WEB SITE www.heliskiwhistler.com, The Crystal Lodge, 3-4241 Village Stroll, Whistler.

In the Canadian Rockies' Banff National Park, there are three world-class ski resorts within easy reach of Banff townsite and Lake Louise: **Mount Norquay**, **Sunshine Village** and the **Lake Louise Ski Area**. These three resorts combined offer 2,400 hectares (6,000 acres) of ski terrain with everything from groomed runs to pure powder. Over in Jasper National Park, **Marmot Basin** lays on another 400 hectares (1,000 acres) of snow.

Perhaps the best part of the Canada ski report is that skiing doesn't have to be an expensive undertaking. Many resorts, hotels and bed-and-breakfast inns offer affordable packages. In British Columbia and Alberta, some hostels offer ski packages. Hostelling International Southern Alberta ((403) 283-5551 TOLL-FREE (866) 762-4122 FAX (403) 283-6503 WEB SITE www.hihostels.ca, Suite 203, 1414 Kensington Road NW, Calgary, Alberta T2N 3P9, will send you a brochure with the details.

SPECTATOR SPORTS

Though many North American professional spectator sports are dominated by United States leagues, on the ice Canada reigns supreme. There are six Canadian teams in the **National Hockey League** (NHL), whose season lasts from October to May. Three of them are in Western Canada. The Vancouver Canucks play at GM Place. The Edmonton Coliseum is home to the Edmonton Oilers, several times winners of the Stanley Cup, while one-time Stanley Cup winners, the Calgary Flames, play at home in the splendid Saddledome in Stampede Park. For an **NHL season schedule**, contact the National Hockey League ((416) 981-2777 (Toronto) or (212) 789-2000 (New York) WEB SITE www.nhl.com.

The Open Road

Al Capone once said, "I don't even know what street Canada is on." Everyone laughed, but old Scarface had put his chubby finger on one of Canada's most pressing needs: transportation. Nor could he have known that after his death Canada would come to live on one principal street, the **TransCanada Highway (TCH)**.

Completed in 1962, the TCH is only two lanes for much of its 6,978-km (4,361-mile) length from St. John's, Newfoundland, to Victoria, British Columbia. With more than 90 percent of all Canadians living within 80 km (50 miles) of this road, it truly is the country's main street. What's more, most of the major tourist attractions are within easy reach of the TransCanada Highway.

Adventurous vacationers and those with more time to spend will want to get off this well-beaten track to experience the country's more remote regions, including its incomparably beautiful national parks in the central and northern regions of the provinces.

In Winnipeg, Manitoba — at about the halfway point of the TCH — cross-continental drivers can opt to veer northwest onto the **Yellowhead Highway**, the "other TransCanada highway." Named after the blonde guide known as Tête Jaune (Yellow Head) who showed early

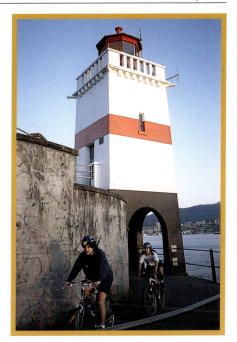

fur traders a pass through the mountains, this road follows a First Nations trading route running 3,185 km (1,911 miles) from the prairies over the Rockies through Jasper National Park to the Pacific coast of British Columbia.

From Edmonton, Alberta, the Yellowhead Highway runs northwest to link up with the **Alaska Highway** (Mile 0 is at The Forks in Winnipeg). Running 1,500 km (900 miles) through often-spectacular scenery. This historic route has beckoned four-wheeled adventurers since the United States government flung it hastily across the northern reaches of Canada during the early stages of World War II, when fears of a Japanese invasion via Alaska ran high. The Alaska Highway is no longer the rough-and-tumble affair that it was a decade or more ago. These days vehicles of every description, notably of the recreational type, zip along the highway at a rate of one per minute. One of the most beautiful stretches of this road runs along Kluane National Park in southwest Yukon, where blue-green glacier-fed lakes and alpine scenery flank the road.

The Alaska Highway is just the tip of the iceberg when it comes to Yukon road adventures. From south of Dawson City, the **Dempster Highway** leads intrepid travelers into the wilder side of the north on an 18-hour drive

OPPOSITE: Preparing a kayak at Eagle Nook Wilderness Lodge, Vancouver Island, British Columbia. ABOVE: Cyclists cruise the seawall in Stanley Park, Vancouver, British Columbia.

that ends in Inuvik, Northwest Territories. Opened in 1979, the Dempster was Canada's first all-weather road to cross the Arctic Circle. It's a gravel surface all the way, but is well maintained. Autumn travelers are often rewarded with the sight of huge herds of caribou.

If you're not bent on making one of Canada's many epic-length road trips, plenty of scenic loops and Sunday drives remain to be enjoyed. You will find many of them described in the regional chapters.

Backpacking

Perhaps it is the length and harshness of northern winters, but when summer rolls around, Canadians just can't stay indoors. Alberta's and British Columbia's **Rocky Mountain parks** are obvious destinations, with 14 Hostelling International sites, inexpensive hikers' shuttle buses and endless trails that are free for the taking. **Interior British Columbia** draws backpacking travelers with its miles of empty roads and spectacular waterways — perfect for long-distance biking and paddling. The **Yukon**

ABOVE: Train tracks head west out of Banff, Alberta, bound for the Pacific Coast. OPPOSITE TOP: Basset hound and a Ford Edsel, Jasper National Park. BOTTOM: A truck is covered with dust after the drive up the Dempster Highway to Inuvik, Northwest Territories.

Territory has similar attractions, as well as offerin g the far north's only HI hostel — at Dawson City, in the land of the midnight sun.

In short, penny-pinching travelers find much to like in Canada.

ACCOMMODATION

Canada's **hostels** are usually the least expensive places to lay your head down — especially for solo travelers — costing from $13 to $25 per night, per person. They also provide good company, a refreshing change from the isolation of hotels. Many of them have cooking facilities for self-catering, offering additional savings on food cost.

Those who plan to do a fair amount of hostelling will benefit by becoming members of **Hostelling International** WEB SITE www.hihostels .ca. There are 12 regional offices across Canada, as well as branches in many other countries around the world. Membership of your home association offers full benefits in Canada, including reducing nightly fees at hostels and discounts at many local businesses. Ask when joining for a copy of the *Official Guide to Hostels in Canada and the United States of America*.

YMCA and **YWCA** residences can be found in many Canadian cities. They are often quite comfortable, with extras such as inexpensive cafeterias, fitness facilities and swimming pools. Though some residences offer dormitory accommodation for as little as $20, others can cost as much as a budget hotel. **YMCA Canada** ((416) 967-9622 FAX (416) 967-9618 WEB SITE www.ymca.ca, 42 Charles Street East, Sixth Floor, Toronto, Ontario M4Y 1T4, will send you the *YMCA-YWCA Residence Directory*, a complete list of all YMCA-YWCA residences in the country.

Some **university campuses** open their dormitories to travelers from May to August. Anyone can use the facilities, though preference is often given to students. Rates for single and double rooms start at $35 to $40. Most universities have an office that handles reservations, and it's a good idea to book well in advance. You'll find university accommodation contact numbers listed under WHERE TO STAY in the regional chapters.

GETTING AROUND

Have we mentioned that Canada is big? The largest part of your traveling budget will undoubtedly be transportation. Distances are vast; gasoline is expensive in comparison to United States prices, although much cheaper than in Europe; and trains can be outrageously expensive, although there are some excellent value passes available. Internal airfares are generally fairly high. **Greyhound Canada**

YOUR CHOICE

TOLL-FREE (800) 661-8747 WEB SITE www.grey hound.ca and the other bus lines ply just about every route in the country and are almost always cheaper than rail, air or driving, unless you are traveling in a group of three or more. Greyhound offers a wide range of discounts, so don't buy a ticket until you've explored the possibilities (see TRAVELERS' TIPS, page 236).

Living It Up

While some vacationers come to Canada to test themselves against the great outdoors, others come to soak up the scenery at the country's luxury hotels and resorts. And, short of palm-shaded tropical beaches, Canada has just about everything the sybaritic swinger could want.

EXCEPTIONAL HOTELS

There is a common theme running through the best hotels in Canada. Many, although by no means all, are the historic railway hotels now run by Fairmont WEB SITE www.fairmont.com. Their prices are not cheap, but there is a level of elegance and service matched by few other large hotels.

When we're in Vancouver and in the mood for pampering, we stay at the **Wedgewood Hotel**. This intimate 89-room hotel has everything the large luxury chain hotels have, as well as what they lack: a personal touch. Owner Eleni Skalbania decorated this gorgeous property using her own antiques and works of art to embellish the lobby and halls. Her elegant taste and characteristic warmth are evident everywhere in this charming hotel. The suites are spacious and many include fireplaces and/or balconies that look out over leafy Robson Square. Staff is friendly, as well as helpful and efficient.

It is virtually impossible to think of Victoria without the image of the **Fairmont Empress Hotel** springing instantly to mind. This ivy-clad dowager, once a Canadian Pacific property, dominates the Inner Harbour and remains a bastion of Englishness and old-style glamour. Popular with honeymooners are the secluded rooms in the attic, which have four-poster beds and window seats for enjoying the beautiful views of the harbor.

No roll call of Canada's top hotels would be complete without mention of the historic **Fairmont Banff Springs Hotel**, opened in 1888 by the Canadian Pacific Railway Company. Its architecture, inspired by the baronial castles of Scotland, is now a revered Rocky Mountain landmark, with 770 river- or mountain-view rooms and a European-style beauty and health spa. The equally luxurious **Rimrock Resort Hotel**, near Banff's hot springs, immerses its guests in modern opulence. Smaller than its venerable neighbor, yet equally refined, the Rimrock is our pick for the best place to stay in Banff — a more restful retreat than its too popular neighbor. Nearly all rooms have views of the lovely Bow Valley.

But why stay in busy Banff when there is the laid-back Lake Louise, where our favorite Rocky Mountain retreat is nestled along the Pipestone River? The **Post Hotel**, owned by Swiss brothers André and George Schwarz, adds a European twist to mountain lodge accommodation, with its spacious and airy suites decorated in hunter green hues and Canadian pine. Some suites have cozy lofts and all have fireplaces with river-stone hearths. This Relais & Châteaux property is situated along the Pipestone River and ski lifts are just five minutes away by the hotel's complimentary shuttle service. Miles of cross-country trails start at the hotel's front door.

Further north, the **Fairmont Jasper Park Lodge** is another distinctive Canadian Pacific property, noted not only for its excellent and varied accommodation in luxurious log cabins which sprawl across huge gardens and wilderness, but also for its plethora of recreational offerings: year-round swimming in a heated pool, tennis, golf, horseback riding, boating, cycling, ice skating, in-line skating, sleigh rides and more.

EXCEPTIONAL RESTAURANTS

The Pacific Rim-influenced **Lumiere** has been voted the best restaurant in Vancouver for the last three years, but many still swear by **Diva at the Met**, where the open kitchen serves "art you can eat." Others prefer the **Chartwell** at the Four Seasons Hotel, with its inspired international cuisine. But never fear, this is one toss-up you can't lose. Vancouver also has some excellent French *haute cuisine* with the upscale bistro **Le Crocodile** and the **Bacchus** at the Wedgewood Hotel, where the Savoy/ Dorchester/Roux-trained chef turns out innovative dishes to titillate the most jaded palate. Piloted by a Cordon Bleu Award-winning chef, **Floata** is the largest Chinese restaurant in Canada. Lunchtime dim sum is fresh and tasty, while dinners are lavish, featuring such delicacies as shark's fin and bird's-nest soups.

On Vancouver Island, the internationally acclaimed **Sooke Harbour House**, west of Victoria, has wonderfully inventive Pacific Northwest cuisine. The couple who run the restaurant grow their own vegetables and herbs, and use only locally caught seafood and the meat of animals raised on nearby farms.

In the Rocky Mountains, the **Dining Room at Buffalo Mountain Lodge** is one of Banff's favourite gourmet treats, with main courses centered on expertly prepared caribou, rack of Alberta lamb, and sea bass. The **Banffshire Club** at the Fairmont Banff Springs has baronial splendor, complete with tapestries and

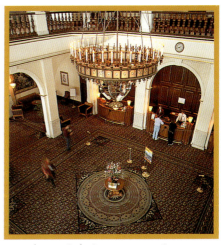

wrought-iron light fittings to complement chef Daniel Buss's sumptuous menus, using Canadian products from Alberta bison to caribou and Alaskan sable fish.

Not to be missed is the **Post Hotel** in Lake Louise Village, which offers warm hospitality in their renowned dining room. Start with one of the delightful soups, such as squash with caramelized apples, and move on to a main course of grilled salmon on a bed of mashed potatoes mixed with heavenly chunks of boiled lobster. Ask for a window seat and enjoy a view of the Victoria Glacier as you dine. Breakfast is a treat here also: there's a generous cold buffet, or you can tuck into eggs Benedict with Pacific smoked salmon from the à la carte menu.

Family Fun

The bad news is: there is no Disneyland Canada. Or is this the good news? Whatever your opinion, this fact points to an essential, if subtle, difference between Canada and the United States when it comes to family vacations. The United States may have bigger thrill rides, glitzier cartoon characters, better-known superstars, but Canada has a small-town warmth and friendliness that we believe makes it just right for kids. It's safer, too. Canada, claims one of our American friends, reminds him of the United States of the 1950s. So, put Beaver and Wally in the car …

As long as there is snow on the ground, children seem to be impervious to the cold. So, why not take a winter vacation in Canada?

OPPOSITE: The Post Hotel in Lake Louise Village is noted for its excellent cuisine. ABOVE: The lobby of the Château Lake Louise in Alberta.

Many cities across Canada have terrific winter carnivals (see FESTIVE FLINGS, page 38).

Skiing, as you might expect, is very big in Canada. Families love British Columbia's Whistler/Blackcomb ski resort, a short drive north of Vancouver, which has ski lessons for children and other supervised children's programs. If your tastes run to adventure, your Canadian winter break might include **dog sledding** and **snowmobiling** in the Yukon, a **canyon ice walk** in Jasper National Park, or **backcountry skiing** and **winter camping** in one of the country's national parks.

When the snow melts, Canada's vacation offerings multiply. Teenagers are thrilled by **rafting** trips in British Columbia's Fraser Valley or the Athabasca River in the Alberta Rockies. Whether you join a tour or go it on your own, possibilities for **hiking** and **backpacking** are virtually endless and can be easily combined with **off-road biking** and **paddling** in Canada's lakes, rivers and along its seashores. **Ranch vacations** and **farm stays** in southern Alberta, the Okanagan Valley (British Columbia) and the Qu'Appelle Valley (Saskatchewan) give everyone in the family a chance to share in the day-to-day operations of working ranches and farms: guests help with chores, ride horses, and round up cattle, along with a variety of leisure activities (see SPECIAL INTERESTS, below).

Children (and adults) are always delighted with **animal encounters**. There are zoos in most major cities — Calgary has a particularly good one, while Vancouver has a superb aquarium in Stanley Park — but one of Canada's great assets is its abundant wildlife. Each of Canada's provinces and territories has its characteristic populations (see THE GREAT OUTDOORS, page 21), and an entire family vacation can easily be planned around wildlife watching.

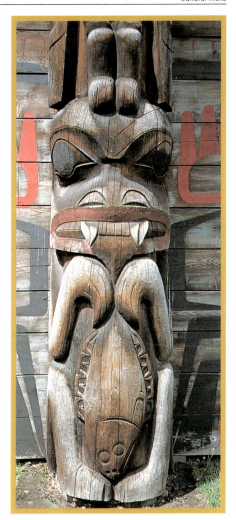

Cultural Kicks

Canada is a mosaic of cultures, an assembly of immigrant groups and native peoples, many of whom have maintained their uniqueness rather than merging into a national Canadian identity. This makes Canada in many ways a more exciting cultural destination than its southern neighbor, where ethnic origins have been obscured by the "melting pot."

Vancouver is the place to unwind in the tranquil Dr. Sun Yat-Sen Classical Chinese Garden, browse a Japanese grocery store, or watch a Punjabi parade. You can cultivate your cowboy image in Calgary with its world-class rodeos, country-and-western music and Wild West bars. In Manitoba, Winnipeg's historical district of St. Boniface, with the largest French-speaking community in western Canada, will have you conjugating your verbs, while the prairies still have Scandinavian, Ukrainian and German speaking communities.

Canada's **First Nations** peoples are as culturally varied as the country's immigrant groups. In this spectrum of native bands, it is the Inuit and the Pacific Northwest Coast natives whose art first garnered international attention. The **Inuit** are known for their carvings on soapstone, ivory, antler and whalebone, as well as for their printmaking. With the rising popularity of Inuit art, there are frequent temporary shows in galleries and museums throughout Canada. The **Pacific**

OPPOSITE: A boy checks out the orthodontics at the Royal Tyrrell Museum, Alberta. ABOVE: Another toothy creature clutches its catch of halibut at the 'Ksan Historical Village, British Columbia.

Northwest Coast tribes developed a complex culture and a distinctive artistic style which can be seen today in the works of Haida, Tsimshian, West Coast (Nootka), Kwagiutl, Coast Salish and 'Ksan artists. Animals such as the killer whale, the wolf and the raven feature in prints, sculptures and ceremonial objects such as Chilkat blankets, totem poles and masks. Like the Inuit, the Pacific Northwest Coast native artists are rising stars in the Canadian arts constellation, and every major city shows these magnificent works in a variety of venues. In Alberta and Saskatchewan, the **Blackfoot** and **Cree** are demanding their rightful place in the country's identity. For tourists, this translates into fascinating museums, shows and cultural centers.

Canadian painters began to distinguish their art from its continental influences at the beginning of the twentieth century, when the Group of Seven emerged as an artistic force, creating a uniquely Canadian school of landscape painting. Western Canada's outstanding museums include the **Vancouver Art Gallery** for its collection of works by Emily Carr, the **Provincial Museum of Alberta** in Edmonton, the **Glenbow Museum** in Calgary and the **Manitoba Museum** in Winnipeg.

Of Canada's three international **ballet** companies only one lives in the west: the Royal Winnipeg Ballet. Most major cities have a professional company, however, along with an **opera** company, symphony orchestra and smaller ensembles, and several theatres with resident and touring **theater** companies. Vancouver and Winnipeg have **symphony orchestras** of international status. Edmonton's Fringe theater festival is now the largest in North America.

First Nations individuals and groups are also active in the performing arts. One of the best ways to see and learn about native art and artists is to go to the **Great Northern Arts Festival** that takes place in Inuvik, Northwest Territories, each July. Native drumming and dancing, exhibitions, sales of arts and crafts, and participatory workshops are part of this growing festival.

Shop till You Drop

The rule to remember is: look out for local specialties. In the **Prairie Provinces**, especially in Alberta, you will find every sort of cowboy attire you could possibly want. In the **Rockies**, look for rainbow-colored ammolite, a magnificent fossil gemstone only found here and used in jewelry and objets d'art. In **British Columbia** look for the elaborately carved handicrafts of

the West Coast natives, including Cowichan sweaters from Vancouver Island and Haida carvings from the Queen Charlotte Islands. In the **Yukon**, gold-nugget jewelry is still in style. Fossilized mastodon ivory, most often seen beautifully carved, polished and set in earrings, is unique to the region.

In the **Northwest Territories** and **Nunavut**, in addition to wonderful Inuit carvings, seek out Dene specialties: snowshoes, baskets and drums as well as traditional clothing such as parkas, mitts and moccasins. Also in the north, Fort Liard is noted for its birch-bark baskets, and Fort Simpson for the now-rare art of moose-hair tufting.

There are two caveats to bear in mind when shopping for native Canadian arts and crafts. Although these items, when genuine, are among the loveliest things to buy in Canada, shops are often swamped by cheap imitations. Be suspicious of any handcrafted article that strikes you as a bargain. To be certain that you are getting the real thing, buy from the artist, a crafts guild or cooperative, or from a museum shop.

Also keep in mind that one of the specialties of the region is salmon, which you can buy smoked and gift-packed. Maple syrup and maple products come in every conceivable form and make good, if sticky, presents.

OPPOSITE: The Dr. Sun Yat-Sen Classical Chinese Garden, Vancouver. ABOVE: West Coast native art on sale in Vancouver.

Short Breaks

Few visitors attempt to take Canada in as a whole. Nor is there a single entry-point at which all international flights arrive. In the west, Vancouver and Calgary serve as **transportation hubs**. Both of these cities have their own unique attractions, and both have the distinct advantage of being within easy striking distance of the great outdoors, making them excellent choices for short vacations. They are also both within an hour's drive of the United States border — over which vast numbers of Americans flock to Canada each year.

You could easily spend five days in **Vancouver** city limits without fear of boredom. For those who wish to venture further afield, great side-trips abound. **Whistler**, North America's premier ski resort, is a two-hour drive away. If it's cloudy in Vancouver, take the ferry (a 40-minute trip) or charter a floatplane to the laid-back **Sunshine Coast**, where swimming on beaches, hiking in Canada's oldest forest, visiting charming villages and bird watching are among the attractions. Although most British Columbia **wineries** are too far away from Vancouver to include in a day trip, Domaine de Chaberton ((604) 530-1736 is just an hour's drive east in the rural Fraser Valley. This winery offers tours, tastings, a bistro open for lunch Thursday to Sunday, and a wine shop where you can pick up a bottle of their award-winning Chardonnay.

It would be a pity to visit Vancouver without a trip to British Columbia's provincial capital, **Victoria**. Using the "superferries" that link Tsawwassen and Schwartz Bay, it's possible to see Victoria on a day trip from Vancouver (see HOW TO GET THERE, page 93 under VICTORIA). Allow time to explore the city's Inner Harbour, the Royal British Columbia Museum, Bastion Square and Chinatown. The fabulous Butchart Gardens is a half-hour drive away.

Calgary is the jumping off point for trips into Alberta's **badlands**, where paleontology buffs can get their fill of Tyrannosaurus-Rex bones and trilobite fossils. There's much to explore here, including Dinosaur Provincial Park, the Royal Tyrrell Museum and Midland Provincial Park. There are also several **guest ranches** in the vicinity for those who fancy trying their hand as a cowboy. The **Rocky Mountains** are easily accessible from Calgary. Regular shuttles run direct from the Calgary International Airport to Banff townsite in under an hour. Here, you are in the heart of

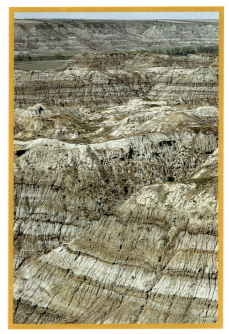

one of the world's greatest scenic wonderlands and the field is wide open for all sorts of vacation pleasures, from skiing and dog sledding in spring and winter to rafting and hiking in summer. Five days allows you enough time to do some hiking and take in a few of the area's museums. Note that if your destination is Jasper rather than Banff, you should consider flying into Edmonton International Airport.

Festive Flings

No matter what the season, Canadians love a party. In addition to those listed, there are literally hundreds of other festivals around the year. Ask the local tourist office for an up-to-date calendar of events.

WINTER
In **Alberta**, Jasper-in-January ((403) 852-3858 means nine days of alpine skiing, canyon crawling, parades, ski workshops and live entertainment. The Calgary Winter Festival (February) ((403) 543-5480 emphasizes the city's Olympic spirit with bobsledding and ski-jumping events.

OPPOSITE TOP: The "Snocoach" shuttles passengers to the Athabasca Glacier, Alberta. BOTTOM: A cruise ship is docked at Canada Place, Vancouver. ABOVE: Alberta's badlands are an open book on the region's geological history.

Manitoba celebrates the region's early French fur-trading history in Winnipeg during the Festival du Voyageur (February) ((204) 237-7692 WEB SITE www.festivalvoyageur.mb.ca, staged in Fort Gibraltar. Although it's not compulsory, many participants dress the part. It's all great fun, with such events as the creation of gigantic snow sculptures and motorcycle races on the iced-over river.

Way up north in the **Yukon Territory** when cabin fever reaches its height, the Yukon Sourdough Rendezvous in Whitehorse (February) ((867) 667-2148 WEB SITE www.rendezvous.yukon.net is the cure. Featured events include the crowning of the Rendezvous Queen as well as feats of strength such as the Tug-a-Truck Contest.

The Yukon Quest International Sled Dog Race (February) ((867) 668-4711 WEB SITE www.yukonquest.org is called the toughest in the world. Mushers and their dog teams travel more than 1,600 km (1,000 miles) through frozen wilderness between Whitehorse and Fairbanks (the starting point alternates from year to year between the two cities), with revelers cheering them on.

SPRING

British Columbia welcomes spring with the Okanagan Wine Festival (April–May) ((250) 861-6654, which takes place in the Okanagan Valley and features wine tasting, tours and gastronomic and sporting events.

In the **Northwest Territories**, the Caribou Carnival (late March) ((867) 873-4262 or (867) 873-3408 WEB SITE www.cariboucarnival .com, in Yellowknife, is a three-day event with traditional

northern First Nations games, snowmobile races, an ice-sculpting contest, a dog Derby, music, dancing and crafts.

SUMMER

Edmonton, **Alberta**, swings into summer with Jazz City International (June) ((403) 432-7166, 10 days of concerts and free outdoor events, the Edmonton Heritage Festival ((780) 488-3378 WEB SITE www.edmontonheritagefest.com and the Edmonton Folk Music Festival ((780) 429-1899 WEB SITE www.edmontonfolkfest.org. Calgary hosts the "greatest outdoor show on earth," the Calgary Exhibition and Stampede (July) ((403) 261-0101, the highlight of which is the chuck wagon race and rodeo, while Edmonton's Klondike Days (July) ((403) 479-3500 relive the gold rush with a week of festivities. Edmonton wraps up the summer with its Fringe Theatre Event (August) ((403) 448-9000 WEB SITE www.fringealberta.ca, one of the major festivals for alternative theater in North America.

Vancouver, **British Columbia**, hosts the Alcan Dragon Boat Festival (June) ((604) 688-2382, which features Asian cuisine and the colorful ritual of the dragon boats.

In **Manitoba**, the Winnipeg Folk Festival (July) ((204) 231-0096 WEB SITE www.winnipeg folkfestival.ca, held in Birds Hill Provincial Park, features over 80 concerts, with all forms of popular music. Eclectic crafts, many weird, are also on show and there are some 30 or 40 restaurants serving good quality food from around the world. The National Ukrainian Festival (August) ((204) 622-4600, in Dauphin, presents costumed

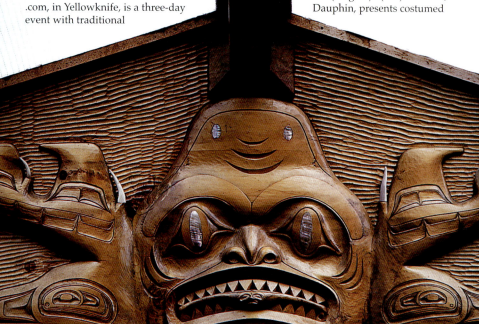

interpreters, fiddling contests, dancing and workshops. Winnipeg celebrates its rich ethnic heritage with the colorful two-week-long Folklorama (August) ℂ (204) 982-6210 WEB SITE www.folklorama.ca, the largest multi-cultural festival in the world. Very authentic.

The **Northwest Territories'** premier cultural event is the Great Northern Arts Festival (July) ℂ (867) 777-3536 WEB SITE www.greatart.nt.ca, when visitors and northerners gather in Inuvik to participate in a variety of visual arts events including exhibitions, workshops, live performances and crafts demonstrations.

Regina, **Saskatchewan**, presents the Mosaic Festival of Cultures (June) ℂ (304) 757-5990, celebrating the province's ethnic heritage. Regina returns to the days of the Wild West for a week of celebration known as the Buffalo Days Exhibition (end of July) ℂ (306) 781-9200. Citizens dress themselves and the town up in pioneer style to enjoy entertainment, livestock exhibitions, music and parades. The Saskatoon Exhibition (July) ℂ (306) 931-7149 is a week of agriculturally based events also featuring livestock shows, tractor pulls, music, parades and dances; while the Shakespeare on the Saskatchewan Festival (July to August) ℂ (306) 653-2300 brings the Bard to the bottomland.

The **Yukon** International Storytelling Festival (May / June) ℂ (867) 633-7551 WEB SITE www.yukonstory.com, in Whitehorse, draws storytellers from throughout the world to the North for four days of yarn-spinning.

Everyone looks forward to the Dawson City Music Festival (July) ℂ (867) 993-5584 WEB SITE www.dcmf.com, when Dawsonites break forth with three days of country and western and folk concerts, dances and workshops.

FALL
British Columbia swings with the Whistler Jazz & Blues Weekend (middle weekend in June) ℂ (604) 932-2394. The Vancouver International Film Festival (late-September / early-October) ℂ (604) 685-0260 WEB SITE www.viff.org, lasts 16 days and presents hundreds of films from dozens of countries. The lively Okanagan Fall Wine Festival (October) ℂ (250) 861-6654 is an annual 10-day celebration of fine wine and gourmet food.

Galloping Gourmet

It must be said that Mobil-star-spangled restaurants are few and far between in Canada. But that is not to say that you can't eat wonderfully well in every part of the country. The key is to concentrate on the regional specialties and local produce.

In western Canada, you will want to go for the Pacific salmon, shrimp and king crab in British Columbia. For a change from all the wonderful seafood, you should try the lamb from Salt Spring Island or the moose steaks from the Yukon. Throughout the far north, fish, such as Arctic char, and game are particular specialties. You'll find such delicacies as caribou or musk-ox jerky, and scallops and giant shrimp fresh from the frozen Arctic waters.

In Alberta, steak is the thing. Even if you are not normally a beef eater, you may well be won over by Alberta's beef. Only in Argentina have I ever tasted steaks to compare with the ones you can get here. In fact, across all the Prairie Provinces the beef is exceptional — as is the freshwater fish from the thousands of lakes and rivers carved into the prairies. In Saskatchewan, I would urge you to order wildfowl — especially the partridge and wild duck — and even the prosaic farm birds, which are tastier here than almost anywhere else, reputedly because they eat better here. In Manitoba, you should try bison: lean and flavorful, preferably accompanied by the local wild rice, which is grown by First Nations peoples. Watch out, too, for the Saskatoon berry, unique to western Canada, which

Queen Charlotte Islands — OPPOSITE: A carving adorns the house of Haida artisan Alfie Collins. ABOVE: Traditional Haida foods.

resembles a small blueberry — it's full of flavor and generally used for desserts rather than being eaten as fruit. In these provinces, too, you will come across a sort of Borscht Belt, where the large Ukrainian population has left its mark on the menus in the form of spicy sausages, dumplings and a variety of cabbage dishes.

On the other hand, if you are just looking for a pit stop where you can refuel quickly, you will find coffee shops, diners and fast-food places just about everywhere you go.

As in the United States, Canadian restaurants tend to be informal and welcoming. They also tend to serve meals at earlier hours than Europeans are used to, so if you are counting on having a late dinner you would be wise to check on kitchen closing times first.

DRINKING

The first time I visited Canada I asked a shopkeeper where I might find a bottle of liquor. This simple question caused utter consternation, followed by endless consultations, followed by — blank. The reason was, it turned out, that spirits may only be purchased from specially licensed liquor stores. To buy liquor by the bottle in many parts of the country, you have to go to one of these official stores — of which there are maddeningly few, which are maddeningly out of the way, and maddeningly closed at night and on Sundays and holidays — and there, but only there, are you allowed to conduct your thirsty transaction. Why this should be the case I cannot say. What I can say is that it interferes with one's budgeting more than with one's drinking, because even the happiest of Happy Hours is not as economical as a couple of self-catered cocktails, and a Rémy in your room is better

value than any postprandial drink in a restaurant. Fortunately most hotels and restaurants are licensed.

Even the most convivial imbibing is complicated by local laws, which come in various shades of blue. In some places you can get a drink if you're 18, in other places you have to be 19. In some places the bars close at midnight, in other places they stay open as late as 4 AM. In most places, on Sundays you can only order a drink at a restaurant or a hotel dining room, and then only if you order a meal. In a few places you can't buy a drink — period — whatever day it is. Minors (in British Columbia, Northwest Territories, Nunavut and Yukon, that's defined as anyone under 19; in Manitoba it's 18) are not admitted into licensed nightclubs.

Equally strange, Canadians are not great whisky drinkers, even though they make some

excellent whiskies. But they are great beer drinkers, although until recently the beer they made had been at best mediocre, at worst comparable to what passes for beer south of the border. Happily, Canadian beer has improved immeasurably with the growth of microbreweries, and now good local brews are available from Toronto to Whitehorse.

Though it is true that Canadian wines don't have an international reputation, there are many which are coming up to world standard. Quails' Gate is one of the best. Cedar Creek Wineries have an excellent Chardonnay, as well as a widely respected Merlot. Mission Hill is another winery with a good reputation. In British Columbia, very sweet "ice wine" made from grapes that are left on the vine until frozen is rapidly becoming a Canadian speciality, enjoyed as a dessert wine or liqueur.

Special Interests

LEARNING VACATIONS
Outward Bound Canada Western School ((604) 737-3093 TOLL-FREE (888) 688-9273 FAX (604) 737-3109 WEB SITE www.outward bound.ca offers challenging 7– to 21–day courses in **mountaineering** along British Columbia's Interior Coast Range. Ice, snow and rock climbing, backcountry navigation, off-trail hiking, first aid and minimum-impact camping are all part of the curriculum.

With Voyageur Outward Bound School ((612) 338-0565 TOLL-FREE (800) 328-2943 E-MAIL vobs@vobs .com, canoers and kayakers can perfect their

OPPOSITE: A canoe is waiting for you high in the Yukon's Kluane Range at St. Elias Lake. ABOVE: Coal Harbour Yacht Club, Vancouver.

Eskimo roll on Madawaska Kanu Centre's ☎ (613) 594-KANU weekend and five-day whitewater **paddling** courses in the warm waters of the Madawaska River in southern Ontario.

Ecological study tours are the specialty of Earthwatch ☎ (617) 926-8200 TOLL-FREE (800) 776-0188 E-MAIL info@earthwatch.org, whose volunteers get a chance to contribute to ongoing studies by assisting researchers in the field.

Elderhostel ☎ (613) 530-2222 TOLL-FREE (877) 426-8056 offers learning vacations for the 55-and-older set. Their "Take a Closer Look at Canada" series encompasses a variety of weeklong tours that explore the **culture and history** of the country from Saskatchewan's Mounties to

Nova Scotia's maritime communities. Also offered are tours to the Arctic where you can learn about Inuktitut history and modern Arctic life. Elders of these First Nations communities often take part in providing the experience. Costs are very reasonable.

Anishinabe Village ☎ (204) 925-2026 FAX (204) 925-2027 E-MAIL avi@mts.net WEB SITE www.wredco.com, 36 Roslyn Road, Winnipeg, operates Shawenequanape Kipichewin Camp, ☎/FAX (204) 848-2815 from mid-May through mid-September, offering visitors the opportunity to learn, first-hand, the **culture and crafts of the Ojibway aboriginals**, by living as they did (but with a few extra amenities). Three days is enough to learn the how (and why) of erecting a tipi, preparing hides, making weapons and cooking traditional dishes. If you can extend your stay, optional excursions to First Nation villages add to the overall experience.

FARM AND RANCH VACATIONS

Everybody say, "Yeehaw!" for Canada's guest farms and ranches. These vacation spots range from working cattle ranches, where guests can try their hand at cattle drives or branding, to remote lodges in pristine backcountry, and to luxury resorts complete with room service.

Alberta Outfitters Association TOLL-FREE / FAX (800) 742-5548 represents independent ranch and farm families located throughout the southern and central province. You can contact the **British Columbia Guest Ranchers' Association** ☎ (250) 374-6836 TOLL-FREE (800)

435-5622 FAX (250) 374-6640 WEB SITE www.bc guestranches.com for a list of the province's guest ranches. There are a few places around Regina, Saskatchewan, that offer farm accommodation, mainly in the Qu'Appelle Valley. For details, contact the **Saskatchewan Country Vacation Association** ((306) 931-3353, which lists farm vacations as well as bed-and-breakfast accommodations.

Manitoba vacation farms can be found through the **Manitoba Country Vacations Association (MCVA)** (/FAX (204) 776-2176 E-MAIL ffamfarm@escape.ca WEB SITE www. countryvacations.mb.ca.

WINE TASTING AND TOURS
The Okanagan Similkameen Valley is British Columbia's wine country, and wine-touring opportunities abound here. Contact **Thompson Okanagan Regional Tourism** ((250) 860-5999 FAX (250) 860-9993 WEB SITE www.thompson okanagan.com, 1332 Water Street, Kelowna, British Columbia.

Motorists can follow the well-marked wine route through hill and valley, tasting the fruits of the season as they go (be sure to appoint a designated driver). Among the wineries to contact for details are: **Sumac Ridge Estate Winery** ((250) 494-0451 WEB SITE www.sumac ridge.com, 17403 Highway 97, Summerland; **Kelowna's Calona Vineyards** ((250) 762-3332 WEB SITE www.calona.kelowna.com, 1125 Richter Street, Kelowna; **Mission Hill Family Estate** ((250) 768-7611 WEB SITE www.missionhillwinery

.com, 1730 Mission Hill Road, Westbank; and **Quails' Gate Estate Winery** ((250) 769-4451 TOLL-FREE (800) 420-9463 WEB SITE www.quails gate.com, 3303 Boucherie Road, Kelowna.

Taking a Tour

Ready for adventure? Whether your idea of a thrill is dog mushing through the Arctic or riding a luxury bus through wine country, Canada has a tour for you.

ADVENTURE
Ecosummer Expeditions ((250) 674-0102 TOLL-FREE (800) 465-8884 WEB SITE www.ecosummer .com, has one- to two-week kayaking trips through the misty archipelago of the Queen Charlotte Islands, and rafting trips on the Tatshenshini and Alsek Rivers of the Yukon and northern British Columbia.

Nature Trek Canada (/FAX (250) 653-4265 WEB SITE www.naturetrek.ca, 220 Hillcrest Drive, Salt Spring Island, organizes trekking expeditions in Canada's Pacific Northwest.

Butterfield & Robinson's ((416) 864-1354 TOLL-FREE (800) 678-1147 FAX (416) 864-0541 WEB SITE www.butterfield.com, 70 Bond Street, Suite 300, Toronto, Ontario, offers backcountry

OPPOSITE TOP: Life in the tidal pools fascinates a golden retriever. A beluga whale BELOW at the Vancouver Aquarium. ABOVE: Downtown Calgary gleams from the Calgary Tower.

walks and biking in British Columbia and hikes in the Rockies, among various other tours.

Backroads ((510) 527-1555 TOLL-FREE (800) GO-ACTIVE FAX (510) 527-1444, 801 Cedar Street, Berkeley, California, specializes in active adventures in an irresistible framework of luxury lodging and gourmet dining. Trips include bicycling walking tours of Banff and Yoho national parks. There are also multi-sport trips in the Rockies that can include mountain biking, hiking and rafting, heli-hiking, cross-country skiing and snowshoeing.

In summer (June to August) **G.A.P Adventures** ((416) 260-0999 TOLL-FREE (800) 465-5600 FAX (416) 260-1888 E-MAIL adventure @gap.ca WEB SITE www.gapadventures.com offers a selection of week-long sailing trips around the Queen Charlotte Islands, and bear- and whale-spotting off the northern coast of British Columbia. G.A.P operates small environmentally and culturally aware tours, with basic accommodation and grassroots-style traveling. This active-participation company also offers multi-activity trips in the Canadian Rockies.

In the Yukon Territory, **Walden's Guiding and Outfitting** ((867) 667-7040 TOLL-FREE (877) 925-3367 WEB SITE www.waldensguiding.com, Whitehorse, Yukon, offers dog-mushing adventures in winter and, in summer, canoeing on the Big Salmon River.

AAA – Big Bear Adventure Tours ((867) 633-5642 FAX (867) 633-5630 WEB SITE www .helloyukon.com, Whitehorse, has canoeing, kayaking, hiking, rafting, fly / drive and bicycle tours, plus bicycle and camper rental. English, Dutch and German are spoken.

You can follow the trail of the old fur traders on a six day kayaking trip on Georgian Bay with **Black Feather Wilderness Adventures** ((705) 746-1372 TOLL-FREE (800) 574-8375, Rural Route 3, Parry Sound, Ontario. Black Feather also offers canoeing on the Nahanni River in the Northwest Territories combined with a four- to five-day alpine hike in the Cirque of the Unclimbables, as well as rugged 16-day kayaking and hiking trips on Ellesmere Island — the top of the world.

There are a number of excellent First Nations-owned and run tour companies. One of the longer-established of them is the **Arctic Tour Company** ((867) 977-2230 FAX (867) 977-2276 E-MAIL atc@auroranet.nt.ca, Tuktoyaktuk, Northwest Territories, which offers various winter and summer tours, including dog-team and snowmobile excursions, wildlife viewing and bird watching, Northern Lights viewing, camping, hiking and community tours, along with native cultural and traditional tours.

GUIDED BUS AND CRUISE TOURS

Globus Tours ((303) 797-2800 TOLL-FREE (800) 851-0728 EXTENSION 7518 WEB SITE www.globus journeys.com, is a Swiss-owned company offering deluxe bus tours. Their sister company, **Cosmos** (contact Globus) WEB SITE www.cosmos vacations.com offers bargain-priced bus tours with accommodation in modest hotels. **Maupintour** ((913) 843-1211 TOLL-FREE (800) 255-4266 FAX (913) 843-8351 WEB SITE www .maupintour.com and **Tauck Tours** ((203) 226-6911 TOLL-FREE (800) 468-2825 FAX (203) 221-6828 WEB SITE www.taucktour.com are two more well-established luxury bus-tour operators with many Canadian destinations.

The city-sized ships of **Holland America** WEB SITE www.hollandamerica.com ply the North Atlantic and North Pacific coastlines. Otherwise there is an abundance of cruises that chug along the gorgeous glacier-bound west coast of British Columbia, typically making their way to Alaska. The cruise season is generally late May through early September (see CRUISE THE INSIDE PASSAGE, page 16 in TOP SPOTS).

The Canadian Rockies — OPPOSITE: Along Alberta's Icefields Parkway, Athabasca Falls roars through a canyon created by eons of erosion. ABOVE: Atop Athabasca Glacier.

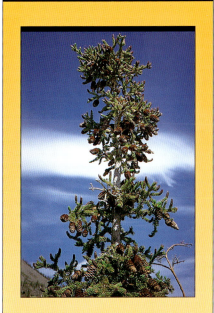

Welcome
to
Western
Canada

If you like the idea of a gigantic country that can be enjoyed without a gigantic wallet, a New World nation that has taken care not to squander its Old World inheritance, a place where the dazzle of the landscape is matched by the kaleidoscopic mix of peoples who inhabit it, then you will like Canada — a lot.

And there is a lot of it to like. Covering almost 10 million sq km (or nearly 3.9 million sq miles), Canada is the second largest country in the world (after Russia). Unlike Russia, however, or its next-door neighbor to the south, Canada has only 30.3 million inhabitants — slightly more than California. While the land extends northward well into the Arctic Circle, the vast majority of the population is concentrated in a narrow band along the long border with the United States.

From a strictly demographic point of view, the two most striking things about this population are that it is overwhelmingly urban — over 75 percent of Canadians live in cities or towns — and surprisingly heterogeneous. Unlike their American counterparts who have been historically quick to jettison their cultural baggage in the rush to become assimilated, immigrants to Canada have tended to cherish and safeguard their distinctive traditions, preserving the old in order to civilize the new. Thus it is not uncommon to see signs in Finnish by Lake Superior or to hear Ukrainian spoken on the Manitoban prairies. Likewise, members of various other nationalities and ethnic groups in Canada have created cheery enclaves without creating dreary ghettos.

It's a pity that United States president John F. Kennedy appropriated the phrase "a nation of immigrants" to describe the United States, because it applies more accurately to Canada. Whereas the United States may have been founded by immigrants, and substantially populated by them for a century or more, Canada is still being shaped by immigration. At the beginning of the nineteenth century the country had a population of barely five million people; since then two tidal waves of immigrants — the first before World War I and the second following World War II — have washed up on Canada's shores, helping to boost the population to its present level and helping to determine what kind of nation has entered the twenty-first century. Even today, people continue to pour in, including recently many Hong Kong Chinese. Canada, with land to spare and a great heart, is not only a generous contributor of aid to the developing world, but one of few countries genuinely welcoming to refugees.

There are, of course, problems. Many First Nations people are still fighting through the courts and parliament for the return of their traditional lands — or suitable compensation. The creation of the territory of Nunavut ("Our Land" in Inuit) in 1999 was one triumph. Meanwhile Friction still exists between Canada's two predominant cultures, the British and the French, although calls for Québec to tear itself away from the Confederation seem to have died back to a murmur, for the moment. And, inevitably, the arrival of new, often poor and ill educated, people from the world's developing countries has put a drain on social resources and blue-collar jobs in some cities. However What is remarkable is that with most other Western countries foaming at the mouth about economic migrants, in Canada, there really are relatively few serious racial tensions.

Perhaps the achievement the Canadians themselves rate most highly has been their ability to share a continent with the United States without becoming totally Americanized, something that is not always easy, particularly given the imbalance in population numbers and the sheer volume of American media that floods across the longest unguarded national boundary in the world. Canadians seem to be forever worrying about their national identity being obliterated by the long shadows cast by the colossus to the south. As former Prime Minister Pierre Trudeau, in a celebrated quip, told Americans on a visit to Washington in 1969, "Living next to you is in some ways like sleeping with an elephant. No matter how friendly and even-tempered the beast, one is affected by every twitch and grunt."

Most Canadians live within reach of American radio and television stations, a major concern of Canadian intellectuals for the better part of the twentieth century. The worry first surfaced in the 1920s, when Canada was absorbed into the American radio system at a time when the United States was beginning to flex its imperial muscles. Then, after the end of World War II, when America was at the zenith of its power and influence, there came the new threat of cultural annexation by television.

So seriously was this threat viewed that no fewer than three royal commissions were set up between 1949 and 1961 to address "the problem of American culture in Canada," and specifically to seek ways of organizing "resistance to the absorption of Canada into the general cultural pattern of the United States." There was little the commissioners could do, however, apart from encouraging the Canadian Broadcasting Corporation (CBC) to feature home-

OPPOSITE TOP: A farm off Highway 1 in southern British Columbia. The Fraser Valley is western Canada's breadbasket. BOTTOM: A mountain lake on the remote Queen Charlotte Island in northern British Columbia.

grown material. Even this rearguard action, faithfully pursued by the CBC since its creation in 1936, has never received wholehearted government support. Recent surveys show that 80 percent of total television viewing in the big metropolitan areas near the border is of American programs; even in Edmonton, which receives only Canadian stations, the figure reached 66 percent.

Nor is the cross-border invasion limited to the airwaves. American films occupy most of the cinema screens, American magazines dominate the newsagents, and American clothes line the shelves of the stores. Even Canadian sports have not escaped American colonization. All of the top ice hockey teams — the one sport Canadians are passionate about — play in America's National Hockey League, and Canada's major baseball teams compete in the American major leagues. Perhaps the only sport that Canadians have managed to remain somewhat aloof about is American football, but that's only because they enthusiastically embraced the game, made a few minor adjustments, and renamed it Canadian football.

Sporting rivalry is just one way Canadians find of coping with being considered by the world as nicer, quieter versions of the Americans, their accent rarely differentiated when overseas, and their dollar treated as a slightly discounted version of the real thing. There was countrywide ecstasy when the United States and Canada met head-to-head in the Olympic ice hockey finals in 2002 — and Canada took the gold!

When I told a prominent Canadian businessman over lunch (truthfully) that I had never met a Canadian I didn't like, he reacted with exasperation bordering on disgust. "That's precisely our problem," he said. "Nobody dislikes us, because nobody knows us."

It is true that most Canadians are incredibly friendly, welcoming and hospitable people, and many Canadians have chosen to reach back, sometimes way back, into their colonial past for a suitable identity. There are parts of the country where stylized versions of the British and French ways of life have been lovingly, not to say fanatically, preserved.

Canada's multi-ethnic population, British monarch, ongoing ties to Europe and active role in the Commonwealth all play a decisive role in shaping the national psyche, making them more outward looking and worldly wise than many Americans. Canada has a strong European-style social security and health system, which it guards jealously against the American capitalist model. The homegrown media is markedly different from the United States version. Not only is there a strong French-language broadcast culture, but much of the news and

discussion on CBC TV and radio is set up on decidedly British lines, coverage of international events is broader and more objective, humor is gently sophisticated and ironic.

In the end, for all the agonizing over their soft-focus national profile, the great majority of Canadians sensibly realize that they quite probably live in the best of all possible worlds. After all, their country has only one neighbor — and that one is so friendly that neither of them has ever bothered to put up a fence. They have the luxury of living in cities that are not only handsome and comfortable, but come equipped with the world's largest backyard, in the form of wilderness areas of awe-inspiring beauty. Their society has the civilizing patina of history while enjoying all the benefits of modern technology.

In this book we explore western Canada, one of the best-loved travel destinations in the world. Since the great preponderance of major tourist attractions in western Canada are within easy reach of the TransCanada Highway, we journey along the nation's "Main Street" from far western Victoria and Vancouver on British Columbia's Pacific coast as far east as Winnipeg, Manitoba, the cultural capital in the heart of the prairies. En route, we make those classic detours that are necessary to experience the incomparable beauty of the great Rocky Mountain national parks, the wilderness of northern British Columbia, and the chilly grandeur of the Yukon and the remote Northwest Territories and Nunavut in the far north. To cover every town and every site in a country as rich as this would be impossible without writing a 24-volume encyclopedia. Here we attempt to bring you the best of what is on offer. As you travel, local visitors' centers can provide more detail on what else is available.

As the country's Chinatowns attest, Canadians have managed to create cheery enclaves rather than dreary ghettos.

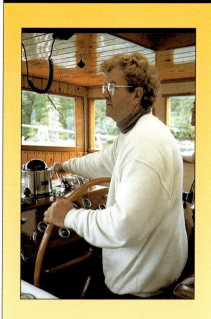

The Country and Its People

HISTORICAL BACKGROUND

Just when people first came to Canada is a matter of considerable debate among the experts — some say it could have been up to 40,000 years ago, while others insist that it was no more than 11,000 years ago — but there is no argument over who they were or where they came from. They were nomadic tribes from Asia, principally Siberia and Mongolia, who came into North America across a land bridge that crossed the Bering Strait during successive ice ages. This migration, often imagined as a mass exodus like Moses crossing the Red Sea, in fact happened gradually as bands

named Vinland ("land of grapevines"), they established a settlement at the site of present-day L'Anse aux Meadows. Unfortunately, the archeological remains don't tell us how long the settlement survived or what finished it off, but it is generally assumed that a combination of the harsh winters and clashes with the region's indigenous populations drove the settlers away before they had a chance to establish a viable colony.

Thing then went quiet for nearly five centuries. In the fourteenth century, Portuguese, Basque and Breton fishermen discovered the Grand Banks fishing grounds off the coast of Newfoundland to be among the richest in the world. Then, in 1497, the Venetian John Cabot (*né* Giovanni Caboto)

of hunters traveled east in search of game. And the land bridge from Asia, now referred to as Beringia, was actually hundreds of miles wide, more like a small continent.

Over thousands of years, these bands and their descendants fanned out across North America, establishing different Amerindian societies and civilizations, which in some cases became highly developed as early as the eighth millennium BC.

THE FIRST EUROPEANS

There is evidence, although inconclusive, that the first European to set foot in North America was a sixth-century Irish monk who, according to legend, landed briefly on the coast of Newfoundland. Vikings sailing from Greenland around AD 1000 made the earliest verified landing. Arriving at the northwestern tip of Newfoundland, which they

arrived in Newfoundland, and then Nova Scotia, to claim these new-found lands for England and Henry VII. The next claimant to what was already shaping up as another stage for the longstanding Anglo-French rivalry was the Breton Jacques Cartier, who in 1534 sailed into the Gulf of St. Lawrence, landing at Prince Edward Island (which he named Île St-Jean) and the Gaspé Peninsula before sailing down the St. Lawrence as far as a native village in the shadow of an impressive hill, which he named *Mont Réal* (royal mountain). He claimed the entire area for France, referring to it by the Algonquin word for "settlement": Kannata.

NEW FRANCE

Since Cartier didn't return to France laden with the hoped-for gold and gems, French interest in Canada quickly waned, only to be revived at the start of the seventeenth century by, of all things, the demands of haute couture. In a word, furs.

In 1605 French explorer Samuel de Champlain established the first permanent European settlement in Canada at Port Royal, Nova Scotia, on the Bay of Fundy, in hopes of trading with the natives for beaver pelts. Three years later Champlain founded another settlement on a plateau overlooking the St. Lawrence River at the bend where the river suddenly narrows. He named the village Québec, and as the center of the fur trade, it rapidly grew into the most important city in New France.

Following in the footsteps of the explorers and the fur traders, the Jesuits swiftly began the

because it may have held the long-sought Northwest Passage to the Orient. Gradually, however, it began to dawn on them that Canada, or New France, possessed its own treasure trove of riches — and Britain had the key to the back door.

In 1610 the English navigator Henry Hudson sailed into the giant bay that now bears his name. Sixty years later Hudson Bay in turn gave its name to a commercial enterprise, the Hudson's Bay Company, which was to leave an indelible mark on the history of Canada. Formed by British fur merchants to provide an alternative to Québec as an outlet for the fur trade, it was granted by Charles II right to all the lands drained by rivers flowing into Hudson Bay. Thus backed by a

spiritual and intellectual colonization of the region. Their more contemplative lay counterparts, the Société de Notre-Dame, moved in on Cartier's "royal mountain" and founded the settlement of Montréal in 1642. Before long it had supplanted Québec as the center of the fur trade in New France.

The two decades spanning the middle of the seventeenth century were difficult ones for the French settlers, as they became inexorably drawn into the bitter tribal conflicts between the Hurons, their principal trading partners, and the warlike Iroquois. But the real threat to their colonial supremacy came, as always, from the British. The British had watched uneasily as New France expanded, but their primary concerns remained settling and securing their American colonies and exploiting the fertile fishing grounds off the Canadian coast. Canada itself was of interest only

solicitous sovereign and a powerful navy, it was to become the largest fur trading company in North America, and today is still a force to be reckoned with in Canadian retailing.

Although British military activity in Canada was minimal during the War of the Spanish Succession (1701–13), under the Treaty of Utrecht France was forced to relinquish all claims to Hudson Bay and Newfoundland, and to give up Acadia, which the British promptly renamed Nova Scotia ("New Scotland"). The Catholic French farmers, who refused to swear an oath of loyalty to the British crown, were evicted. Some later returned, but many made their way south to Louisiana, where they became known as Cajuns.

OPPOSITE: A bridal party of Kwakiutl Indians, photographed by Edward Curtis in 1914, arrives at the groom's village. ABOVE: Yukon native women and their children.

There was a period of relative peace and tranquility for the next 40 years, broken only in 1744 by the British seizure of the French fortress of Louisbourg on Cape Breton Island. It was handed back four years later under the Peace of Aix-la-Chapelle.

The Seven Years' War, known in America as the French and Indian War, was to be the decisive turning point in Canadian history. The war began well for the French and their native allies, as in battle after battle the British forces showed themselves to be tactically unprepared for what amounted to quasi-guerrilla warfare. But the tide began to turn in 1758 with the arrival of British land and naval reinforcements. A successful siege

had fallen. Both Wolfe and Montcalm were killed. The battle had lasted 20 minutes.

Although it was one of the shortest battles on record, its consequences ultimately reverberated around the world. The fall of Québec effectively marked the fall of New France, and when the French handed over all of Canada under the terms of the Treaty of Paris in 1763, the British were left as undisputed masters of the entire North American continent. Some historians argue, however, that it was a Pyrrhic victory in that the British were also left overconfident and overstretched, not to mention out-of-pocket, while the many American colonists who fought on the British side, including one George Washington, had gained

of the fortress at Louisbourg led to its recapture, giving the British control of the entrance to the Gulf of St. Lawrence, while at the Lake Ontario end of the St. Lawrence River the British took the vital Fort Frontenac. Then, in the summer of 1759, an assault force under the command of 32-year-old General James Wolfe, the youngest general in the British army, sailed from the Atlantic down the St. Lawrence to Québec. All summer long Wolfe's artillery pounded the city, reducing it to rubble, but without budging the French forces under the Marquis de Montcalm in their citadel atop the steep cliffs above the town. Then, on the night of September 12, Wolfe tried a daring maneuver. He led a force of 5,000 infantrymen in boats to a point behind the city, where they silently scaled the cliffs and assembled on the Plains of Abraham. The next morning, the startled French forces, flushed out of their fortified redoubt, were slaughtered. Québec

wartime experience as well as insights into British military strategy that would prove invaluable a few years later when the Americans launched their War of Independence.

BRITISH CANADA

The conquest of Canada brought another problem for Britain: what to do about the predominantly French population in the new territory over which they now ruled. In the end, they did the decent thing — and paid dearly for it. By passing the Québec Act of 1774, the British gave the French Canadians the right to continue using their own language, the secure ownership of their property, the primacy of French civil law, as well as the freedom to practice the Roman Catholic religion (including the Church's right to collect tithes). This did not go down at all well with the overwhelmingly Protestant population in the 13 American colonies, who were already incensed over what they considered unjust taxes imposed by Britain to help pay for the war against France. When the boundaries of the province of Québec were extended to protect the French Canadian fur traders operating in the Ohio and Mississippi River valleys, the American colonists decided that they had had enough.

The colonial rebellion became the American Revolution late in 1775 with attacks on Montréal and Québec City which, had they been successful, would almost certainly have heralded a fairly swift victory for the Americans. In fact, the attack on Montréal was successful, but so brutish was the behavior of the "liberators" that most French Canadians decided they would prefer not to be thus liberated and went on to fight fiercely alongside the British, thus denying the Americans an early knockout.

By the time the war ended in 1783, Canadians had a new neighbor, the United States of America, and also a lot of new Canadians, for about 50,000 Americans who remained loyal to the British Crown had fled northwards. Most of them settled in Nova Scotia and what is now New Brunswick, although about 7,000 made their way to present-day Ontario. More still arrived at the end of the war claiming to be Loyalists, but their devotion to George III might possibly have been influenced by the offer of free land to Loyalist immigrants. In any case, as a result of the American Revolution, Canada received a large transfusion of English-speaking immigrants, many of whom were well-educated and had occupied positions of responsibility and influence under the old colonial regime. The balance of power shifted abruptly away from the French to the Anglo Canadians.

In the years following the war Canada was transformed both politically and territorially. In 1791 the province of Québec was divided into Upper Canada (mainly English-speaking: now Ontario) and Lower Canada (mainly French-speaking: now Québec), each with its own Lieutenant Governor and parliament. Meanwhile, the vast and hitherto neglected lands to the west were gradually being opened up in the wake of the pioneering explorations of Alexander Mackenzie, who in 1793 became the first white man to cross Canada all the way to the Pacific coast, and Simon Fraser and David Thompson, who were the first to map the great mountains and rivers from the Rockies to the Pacific.

The War of 1812 was the last neighborhood brawl before the United States and Canada settled down to live together more or less happily ever after. The war had a number of causes: border disputes, British interference with American shipping, fierce rivalry in the lucrative fur trade,

American claims that the British were behind native raids on American border settlements, British claims that Americans were trying to export republicanism to Canada, and so forth. Whatever the justice of any of these claims, they added up to war. Although both sides suffered some telling blows — the Americans captured Toronto (or York, as it was then called) and burned it to the ground, whereupon the British retaliated by capturing Washington and burning the White House — neither side really seemed to have much appetite for the fight. The Americans wanted to get on with nation-building and the British wanted to get on with countering the Napoleonic threat at home, while the Canadians wanted to be left in peace. In 1814 they got together and declared the war over.

Not surprisingly, considering the enormous size of the two countries, the border issue was not resolved immediately. The first major step was taken in 1818 when they agreed on the 49th parallel as their mutual border from the Great Lakes to the Rockies, but it was not until 1842, after much haggling and a little skirmishing, that the Canadian border with the New England states was established. The last link, the border with the Oregon Territory west of the Rockies, was established along the 49th parallel in 1846.

As increased immigration swelled the population, French Canadians became convinced that the British were deliberately trying to dilute their power by swamping them with English-speaking newcomers. As a result, in 1837 French Canadians under the leadership of Louis-Joseph Papineau demanded autonomy for Lower Canada (Québec) so that they could establish an independent republic. When the British refused, a violent rebellion broke out which was not finally defeated until 1838. It was the first time that the call for an independent Québec had been heard. It would not be the last.

Nor were the French Canadians the only ones growing impatient with British rule around this time. In Upper Canada (Ontario) a rough and ready coalition of economic have-nots led by newspaper editor William Lyon Mackenzie rose up against the oligarchic Tory establishment and demanded that the government be remodeled along American lines. When these demands, predictably, were not met, Mackenzie too resorted to armed rebellion, with even less success than Papineau whom he soon joined in exile in the United States.

Although both insurrections had been easily put down, they succeeded in lighting an anti-colonialist fuse that would prove unquenchable.

Nevertheless, Canada at mid-century was a picture of expansion and growth. New waves of immigrants boosted the population of the Mari-

Expo '86 in Vancouver.

time Provinces, which were beginning to prosper as a result of their flourishing lumber, fishing, and shipbuilding industries. The population explosion also led to the creation of settlements further westward, in addition to providing the labor needed to build the canals, roads and railways that made the westward expansion possible. In less than 20 years, over 3,000 km or 2,000 miles of railroad tracks were laid. All that was needed for Canada to become a truly coast-to-coast country was for some sort of tug to be exerted from the other side of the Rockies. That tug, when it came, turned out to be a powerful yank: in 1858 gold was discovered in the Fraser River valley.

The gold rush that followed was so frenetic, and so dominated by Americans rushing northwards to stake their claims, that Britain quickly proclaimed a new Crown colony, British Columbia, to control the stampede into the territory.

British colonies now straddled the continent from the Atlantic to the Pacific.

THE DOMINION OF CANADA

With the old Anglo-French tensions still causing problems, and the turmoil to the south caused by the American Civil War, not to mention the ordinary growing pains brought on by rapid population growth and territorial expansion, it was widely felt that the colonies should come together and forge a stronger union among themselves. So in 1864, delegates from the various colonies convened in Charlottetown, Prince Edward Island, to begin laying the groundwork for a new confederation. Three years later, the British North America Act of 1867 created the Dominion of Canada, in which the colonies of Nova Scotia, New Brunswick, and Québec became provinces in a confederated union with self-rule under a parliamentary system of government. Manitoba joined the Confederation in 1870, British Columbia in 1871 and Prince Edward Island in 1873. The Yukon, formerly a district of the Northwest Territories, was made a separate territory in 1898 at the height of the Klondike gold rush. Alberta and Saskatchewan, also carved out of the old Northwest Territories, joined in 1905; Newfoundland, typically, held out until 1949, when it finally became Canada's tenth province.

As important as this political union was to Canada's development, it was more symbolic than real so long as there was no corresponding physical link between the provinces. In fact, three of the provinces — Nova Scotia, Prince Edward Island, and British Columbia — only agreed to join the Confederation on condition that a transcontinental railway was built to tie the new nation together. Work on this mammoth project began in 1881 and, incredibly, was completed in only four years. In 1885, at Rogers Pass in the Selkirk Mountains,

the last spike was driven: the Canadian Pacific Railway was in business.

As was to be expected, however, this mighty triumph of engineering was not achieved without casualties. The coming of the Iron Horse meant the virtual disappearance of the buffalo, the driving of natives from their ancestral homelands, and the deaths of hundreds of (mostly Chinese) laborers on the railroad itself. It also precipitated a bloody uprising in 1885 on the part of the Métis, who were the descendants of French trappers and Cree women, aided and abetted by several tribes of Plains natives, all of whom felt threatened by the armies of new settlers swarming over their land.

Already driven out of Manitoba as far west as the southern banks of the Saskatchewan River, the Métis and their native allies, under the leadership of Louis Riel, overwhelmed the Mounted Police post at Duck Lake, attacked the town of Battleford, and captured and burned Fort Pitt. But

their successes were short-lived. Before long they were subdued by the superior firepower of the Canadian forces, and Riel was hanged. His execution became another source of resentment both among First Nations people and French Canadians, who felt that he would not have been treated so harshly had he not been a Roman Catholic of French ancestry.

With the country now linked literally and politically from sea to sea, the final years of the nineteenth century saw Canada blossom dramatically as a nation. As thousands upon thousands of new immigrants arrived, new lands were settled and cultivated, hydroelectric projects were initiated, new manufacturing industries were started up alongside the already-thriving industries of lumbering, fishing, mining, pulp and paper. Above all, agriculture boomed as the Prairie Provinces became one of the great grain-producing areas of the world. And, for icing on the national cake, in

1896 gold was discovered in the Klondike, setting off one of the biggest gold rushes in history as 100,000 (mainly American) fortune-seekers poured into the Yukon. These were heady times.

The Twentieth Century

Thus Canada entered the twentieth century in a buoyant mood. It was also blessed from 1896 to 1911 with one of its greatest prime ministers, Sir Wilfrid Laurier, a French Canadian and Roman Catholic who set himself the Herculean task of ending the antagonism and suspicion between Canada's English and French communities. But World War I came along and deepened the rift: French Canadians violently objected to military conscription, which was introduced in 1917 after the Canadian volunteer forces fighting along-

The entrance to Ottawa's Confederation Building.

side the British in the trenches had suffered such appalling losses that there were no volunteers left to fight. The French Canadian point of view — that the war had nothing to do with them, and therefore they shouldn't be drafted to fight in it — left much residual bitterness on both sides after the war was over.

A happier legacy of the war was an economy enriched by a vastly increased manufacturing capacity, streamlined industrial development, expanded mining activity and burgeoning exports of wheat. Along with Canada's postwar prosperity came growing independence from Britain, acknowledged by the British at the Imperial Conference of 1926 when Canada was granted the right

to conduct its own international affairs without reference to London, and sealed by the Statute of Westminster in 1931, which made Canada an independent nation.

Then came the Depression, which was even worse in Canada than in the United States. Suddenly the Promised Land was a ravaged land, as drought erased the wheat fields and unemployment stalked the cities. The misery of the "Dirty Thirties," as the Canadians called the decade, lasted until September 1939, when Hitler marched into Poland. Canada, following Britain's lead, immediately declared war on Germany, whereupon the economy coughed, spluttered, then roared back to life.

Also revived, sadly, was the bitter Anglo-French debate over military conscription, which once again split the country, even though one of the aims of the war was to liberate occupied

France. Again, Canada suffered battlefield losses out of all proportion to its population. On the other side of the ledger, the Canadian economy prospered out of all proportion to its prewar capacity, as almost 10 percent of the population were engaged in war-related industries. Thanks to the war, Canada became one of the world's major industrial nations as well as an important military power, a cofounder of the United Nations, and a member of NATO.

Peace was as good to Canada as the war had been. A huge oil field was discovered near Edmonton, Alberta, in 1947. Giant uranium deposits were discovered in Ontario and Saskatchewan, and its extraordinary mineral riches made Canada the world's leading producer of nickel, zinc, lead, copper, gold and silver. Its inexhaustible water resources made countless hydroelectric projects possible, its forests made it the world's foremost exporter of newsprint, and its oceans made it the world's foremost exporter of fish. As if that weren't enough, Canada was fortunate in having the world's best customer for raw materials right on its doorstep.

Another milestone in Canada's rise among the world's top industrial nations was the opening in 1959 of the St. Lawrence Seaway, a joint United States–Canadian project that made possible shipping from the Great Lakes to the Atlantic. Three years later the TransCanada Highway was completed, a concrete link spanning all 10 provinces.

In 1967 Canada celebrated its hundredth birthday by throwing itself a big party in the form of a World's Fair — Expo '67 — in Montréal. Canadians had much to celebrate: a vigorous and rapidly expanding economy, one of the highest standards of living in the world, advanced social welfare programs providing health care and other benefits for all citizens, virtually unlimited natural resources, and a history of international conduct such that Canada had managed to join the front rank of the world's nations without making any enemies. What better reasons to have a party?

QUÉBEC AND THE CANADIAN FEDERATION

Alas, there was a ghost at the birthday party. The old specter of separatism, which had haunted the federation during the entire century of its existence, was suddenly summoned up in a speech by visiting French President de Gaulle. Speaking to a large throng outside the Montréal City Hall, he declared, "*Vive le Québec libre!*" Considering that he was present in Canada as a guest of a nation celebrating its "unity through diversity," this was mischief-making on an epic scale.

With their clamoring having thus been endorsed by the President of France, Québec's separatists found new heart for the struggle to wrench the province away from the rest of the nation. With the ultimate goal of full independence, the Parti Québécois (PQ) was formed under the leadership of René Lévesque. The PQ won 23 percent of the vote in the 1970 provincial elections. That same year the separatist movement turned nasty around its fringes, as the *Front de Liberation du Québec* (FLQ) kidnapped and murdered the province's Minister of Labor, Pierre Laporte. Prime Minister Pierre Trudeau responded by invoking the War Measures Act and sending 10,000 troops into the province, an unpopular action that ultimately benefited the PQ, who came to power in 1976. They set about developing the province's economy, instituting educational reforms, and making Québec monolingual, all the while pressing for a referendum

and secession from the Canadian federation. But, in 1980, when the referendum came, 60 percent of the province voted "*non*" to secession.

At the next election Lévesque's separatists were voted out of office. In 1987 the Conservative government of Brian Mulroney made a significant gesture towards the Québécois when the prime minister signed a document recognizing them as a "distinct society." The following year, in what seemed like a reciprocal gesture of appreciation, Québec gave Mulroney's Conservatives a large part of their majority in the national elections. It seemed, at last, that the flames of separatism had finally been extinguished.

Not so. As before, the desire for separation among the Québécois simply smoldered unnoticed, waiting to be re-ignited into the burning issue it had so often been in the past. Sure enough, it blazed back into prominence at the start of

the 1990s. This time, however, nobody was able to say precisely what set it alight. The best explanation we heard came from Don Johnson, a columnist for the Toronto *Globe and Mail*. "We are merely advised that Québeckers feel humiliated, the status quo is unacceptable and unhappiness prevails," he said with a helpless shrug. He then went on to compare it to the breakdown of a marriage — "where neither party can point to a specific cause, but there is a general feeling that a divorce would be preferable."

In 1992 and again in 1995, referenda for sovereignty were held in Québec. In both cases, the electorate rejected the idea. But the 1995 vote was nearly a dead heat with 51 percent against. It is almost certain that at some point in the future, another "neverendum" — as Canadians have named them — will be called. For the moment, the stuffing has been knocked out of the cause and most Québécois seem happier with the status quo. Independence is on the backburner, and the small Maritime Provinces, desperately worried that an independent Québec would cut them off physically from the rest of Canada, too small and poor to survive alone, can rest that bit more easily.

CANADA TODAY

While the future of the federation is one of Canada's prime political issues, economics are seen as a more burning issue. In 1989, the free trade agreement with the United States (NAFTA) was pushed through parliament by Prime Minister Brian Mulroney, causing the loss of thousands of jobs and exposing the country's industries to American competition. The collapse of the North Atlantic cod fishing industry brought hard times to Newfoundland and Nova Scotia, where unemployment now runs very high. In 2002, a series of political scandals rocked the administration, leaving an increasingly cynical population struggling to believe in any of their politicians.

One thing, however, is clear: after centuries of exploitation and marginalization, Canada's native peoples are beginning a new and happier era. Having gained political strength throughout the late 1960s and early 1970s, the First Nations of the north launched a series of land claims against the Canadian government in the late 1970s, demanding financial compensation, funding for social programs, hunting rights and a greater role in wildlife management and environmental protection. The success of these land claims has led to a native cultural revival and, finally, to redrawing the very map of Canada. On April 1, 1999, Canada — formerly comprised of 10 provinces and two territories — gained a new territory, when the North-

OPPOSITE: Canada — a land called Winter.
ABOVE: Formed by eons of erosion, a hoo doo towers over the sweltering Alberta badlands.

west Territories was divided in two. The eastern half is now known as Nunavut, "Our Land" in the Inuit language. The western lands are still called the Northwest Territories.

Both in the north and throughout the rest of the country, native Canadians (excluding the Inuit) number around 282,000 and are members of 574 separate communities, called "bands." Ethnically, many of Canada's native peoples have the same heritage as certain United States tribes: Cree, Sioux and Blackfoot, for example, are found in both countries. In Canada, native people belong to 10 linguistic groups, each of which has many local dialects.

Since 1973, when the Canadian government accepted a proposal by the National Indian Brotherhood, increasing numbers of bands manage their own schools. These schools have introduced new curricula, which often include the history of native Canadians and native-language courses.

GEOGRAPHY AND CLIMATE

William Lyon Mackenzie King, Canada's longest-serving prime minister (1921–30, 1935–48), observed at the beginning of his third term of office in 1936: "If some countries have too much history, we have too much geography."

It's hard to argue with that. Spread over almost 10 million sq km (3.6 million sq miles), Canada stretches more than 5,500 km (3,400 miles) from Cape Spear, Newfoundland, in the east, to the Alaskan border in the west, and 4,600 km (2,900 miles) from Lake Erie's Pelee Island in the south to Cape Columbia on Ellesmere Island in the north (which is only 800 km or 500 miles from the North Pole).

Within this vastness one finds stunning topographical extremes. Almost half the country, for example, is forested — one single forest zone of conifers extends for 6,000 km (3,730 miles) in a wide sweep from Newfoundland to the far north — while similarly enormous tracts of land are empty, treeless prairies. There are millions of acres of flood plains and marshy lowlands, and there are the majestic Rocky Mountains, though Canada's highest peak, Mount Logan (6,050 m / 19,844 ft), is not in the Rockies but in the St. Elias Mountains of southwestern Yukon.

And then there is the water. Canada is awash in lakes and rivers; they account for over seven percent of the country's total area. There are 400,000 of them in Ontario alone. Three of the 20 longest rivers in the world are to be found in Canada. In all, the country has a staggering 25 percent of the world's fresh-water resources.

Geologically, Canada can be divided into five distinct regions, not counting the archipelago of islands inside the Arctic Circle. The Appalachian region is that hilly, wooded part of the country

bounded on the west by the St. Lawrence River and on the east by the Atlantic. It includes the Maritime Provinces, Newfoundland, and the Gaspé Peninsula, and belongs to an ancient mountain system, now eroded to modest elevations, that reaches as far south as Alabama.

The St. Lawrence Lowlands comprise the swath of land from the mouth of the St. Lawrence River to the Great Lakes. This fertile floodplain is home to most of Canada's people, industry and commerce.

The prairies spread across the provinces of Manitoba, Saskatchewan and Alberta, and on up into the Northwest Territories. The rich soil in the southern reaches, where the prairies join the Great Plains of the United States, yields great golden seas of wheat, which gradually dry up in Alberta, giving way to huge cattle ranches.

The Western Cordillera is bounded on the east by the Rocky Mountains and on the west by the Coast Mountains. In between is the spectacular diversity of British Columbia, a province of soaring mountain peaks, alpine lakes and meadows, large boreal forests, intricate networks of rivers, deep blue lakes, hot springs and long green valleys.

The fifth region, the Canadian Shield, encompasses everything else: the immense, horseshoe-shaped land mass that surrounds Hudson Bay, and stretches from the coast of Labrador down to the St. Lawrence Lowlands, over to the prairies, and up to the Arctic. Covering some 4.7 million sq km (1.8 million sq miles), about half the entire area of Canada, this rough-hewn, rock-strewn, lake-pitted wilderness is one of the oldest sections of the earth's crust.

The flora and fauna naturally vary from region to region. There are, however, some animals that can be found just about everywhere: squirrels and chipmunks, rabbits and hares, porcupines and skunks. Equally widespread throughout the country's forests and woodlands are deer, moose, black bears, beavers, wild geese and ducks. The richest fishing grounds in Canada — possibly in the world — are to be found in the Gulf of St. Lawrence and the waters of the continental shelf off Newfoundland: though cod stocks have been wiped out by over-fishing, the area still teems with herring, mackerel, tuna, oysters, clams, lobsters and scallops, along with some 800 other species of edible marine life.

In the St. Lawrence Lowlands the coniferous forests of spruce, firs, and pines that sweep from Labrador to the Rockies begin to be infiltrated by aspen, birch, oak, elm, beech, hemlock and ash. In southern Québec the sugar maples appear, and in southwestern Ontario the walnut and tulip trees, the hickories and dogwoods. As for its animal life, the region is better known for its bipeds than its quadrupeds.

In the prairies, one animal in particular is conspicuous by its absence: the plains buffalo (also called bison). The few that have survived are now in national parks or specialist ranches, while their place has been taken by great herds of cattle. Denizens of the semiarid grasslands of the southern prairies include kangaroo rats, hares, pronghorn antelopes, and the ranchers' nemesis, coyotes.

In the mountain ranges of the Western Cordillera one can find, if one tries hard enough, brown bears, elk, mountain goats, bighorn sheep and the bosses of the upper slopes, grizzly bears. In the lakes and rivers there is some of the best trout and salmon fishing to be found anywhere in the world.

In the great expanse of forests across northern Canada are the largest concentrations of fur-bearing animals: mink, ermine, marten, muskrat,

that guarantees Vancouver milder winters than, say, Dallas. True, the eastern coast takes a beating from the Atlantic, but parts of it are also caressed by the Gulf Stream, creating swimming beaches equal to any in the Mediterranean.

Having said that, one has to admit that for much of the year Canada is a theme park called Winter. Harold Town, one of Canada's leading artists, once said: "We are a nation of thermometers monitoring cold fronts. We jig to the crunch of snow." Indeed, over a third of the annual precipitation in Canada falls as snow, compared to a worldwide average of five percent. The only national capital city colder than Ottawa is Ulan Bator, in Mongolia; Winnipeg is the coldest city

beaver, river otter, weasel, lynx, bobcat, wolves and wolverines. Further north, in the tundra, are arctic foxes, lemmings, musk oxen and caribou, as well as snow geese and trumpeter swans. Still further north, where the frigid waters are full of whales, seals, and walrus, the mighty polar bear patrols the ice packs of the Arctic.

Because words like "frigid," "polar," "ice" and "Arctic" — and even the subtly prejudicial "north" — are all words that we readily associate with Canada, most foreigners think that Canada's climate can probably be summed up in one word: cold. This is a mistake. True, Canada occupies the northern — and therefore colder — part of the continent, but this ignores the fact that Pelee Island, Ontario, is on the same latitude as Rome. True, the dominant images of western Canada are the snow-capped peaks of the Rockies, but this obscures the fact that those same Rockies form a protective wall

in the world with a population of more than half a million; and residents of Montréal shovel more snow every year than residents of any other city.

But there is a bright side. It's just that: brightness. Canada may be refrigerated half the time, but it is sunlit most of the time. Which means that it is beautiful all the time, brilliantly white in winter, infinitely and variously green the rest of year — except for the fall in the southeast and maritime provinces, which are cloaked in a gaudy display of reds and golds to rival the best in New England. What's more, its meteorological diversity mirrors its geographical diversity, so that the visitor has the luxury of choosing not only the scenery and activities that most appeal, but also the precise climate in which to enjoy both. In Canada there is truly a time and place for everything.

The Canadian prairies in bloom.

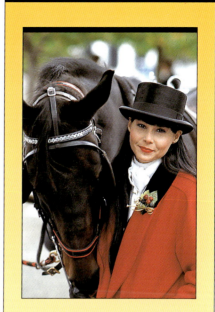

British Columbia

Canada's third largest and most westerly province stretches from the Pacific to the Rockies and from the 49th to the 60th parallel. It is bordered by the states of Washington, Idaho and Montana at its southern edge, the Yukon and Northwest Territories to the north, Alaska at its northwest corner, and Alberta to the east, beyond the Rockies. The rugged, snowcapped Coast Mountains rise above the deeply indented Pacific coastline, and beyond them mountain ranges run northwest to southeast, giving way to valleys and wide rolling prairies carpeted with ancient forests and dotted with lakes.

The climate is as varied as the landscape. The coast, shadowed by the high Coast Mountains and

warmed by the Pacific current, has mild, wet winters and cool to warm summers. The more exposed interior is generally drier, with more extreme temperatures, while northeastern winters are the coldest of all and have the heaviest snowfall.

The province covers an enormous area — 947,800 sq km (366,255 sq miles) — big enough to hold a handful of European countries. However, the entire province has a population of only a little over four million inhabitants, the majority of whom live in the southwestern corner — around half of them can be found in Greater Vancouver. With so many people huddled in its bottom corner, and with the great barrier created by the Rockies, it is not surprising that British Columbia seems separated from the rest of the country. It has often been said that its lifestyle and easygoing attitudes owe more to California than to Canada. Elsewhere, there is an awful lot of space.

There are literally hundreds of parks covering millions of acres of wilderness, making ideal habitats for all kinds of wildlife and a heaven for outdoor enthusiasts.

The First Nations tribes who once populated the West Coast enjoyed prosperity and had a highly developed culture, expressed in art forms still much in evidence. Stunning examples of woodcarving are carefully preserved, most strikingly in the form of totem poles. Many First Nations communities still exist in British Columbia and, like the bands of the far north, they are in the midst of an exciting cultural renaissance.

Europeans were slow to arrive here because of the enormous physical barriers presented by the terrain. It was 1774 when tentative Spanish exploration began, and 1778 when Captain James Cook landed on Vancouver Island, where he traded with natives for furs, which he later sold to the Chinese at a large profit. News of this began to speed things up, and the inevitable skirmishes ended with the Spanish conceding control to the British. In 1792, Captain George Vancouver was dispatched by the British to map the coast. In the meantime, intrepid fur traders were exploring overland routes to the Pacific and establishing trading posts.

The Hudson's Bay Company established its headquarters on Vancouver Island. In 1849 the English colonized the island in the name of the Crown, and Victoria was declared its capital. The discovery of gold along the banks of the Fraser River brought a rush of prospectors, and to secure its hold on their territories the British Government made the mainland (then known as New Caledonia) a British colony, renaming it British Columbia in 1858. In the 1860s the construction of the Cariboo Highway opened up the area. Lumber mills and canneries began to spring up, and in 1866 the colonies of Vancouver Island and British Columbia joined together. When the United States acquired Alaska, a further attack of nerves prompted British Columbia to consider joining the Canadian confederation as a security measure against American invasion, but it was with caution and only upon the promise that a transcontinental railway would reach its coast that, in 1871, British Columbia finally joined.

This promise was fulfilled by 1885, and industries based on the province's natural resources were able to develop. A further boost came with the opening of the Panama Canal, which made transportation easier and cheaper. Today the economy still rests largely on natural resources such as fishing, forestry, mining, energy, agriculture (particularly in the lower Fraser Valley and the irrigated Okanagan) and tourism — an upshot

ABOVE: Vancouver's Marine Building with its art deco façade. OPPOSITE: A fjord parts the mountains in the Queen Charlotte Islands.

of the area's extraordinary natural beauty. Timber remains the bedrock of the local economy, although it is currently at the center of a battle between conservationists, First Nations activists and the British Columbia government, with the province's image of caring environmentalism being severely challenged by the destruction of the rainforests and the pollution resulting from logging activities.

VANCOUVER

Magnificent in setting, sophisticated and cosmopolitan in character, Vancouver must rate as one of the world's most livable and beautiful cities. The air is fresh, the atmosphere is vibrant and youthful, and being little more than a century old, this youngster is suitably seated in the lap of nature. The Coast Mountains shadow it to the north; Vancouver Island peaks lie to the west. Water is all around: Burrard Inlet separates the city core from the residential North Shore area, while the Strait of Georgia lies to the west and the Fraser River to the south. Water of another kind also figures largely in the life of Vancouverites — the city averages 145 cm (57 inches) of rain a year. However, protected by the bulk of Vancouver Island and warmed by the Japan Current, Vancouver has a gentle climate and, unlike so much of Canada, has very little snowfall. May to September are the warmest months, with the least rainfall, although even in July and August there may be days when the mountains are shrouded in mist.

Vancouver is Canada's third largest city and its busiest port. It is British Columbia's business center, but with a metropolitan population of only two million in Greater Vancouver (roughly 555,000 in the city itself), and being so close to nature, it can afford a laid-back attitude to life and is far less hectic than most major cities. There are over 14 km (nine miles) of beaches within the city limits, a rainforest within walking distance of the business core, and ski slopes only 20 minutes away.

With the high rate of foreign investment here and the latest wave of immigration from Hong Kong, in some quarters the city has been dubbed "Hongcouver." However, tourism is now the city's number one industry and timber the second (these positions are reversed in the province as a whole), while the fastest-growing sector appears to be filmmaking — the Vancouver area is often called "Hollywood North." Mining, power and international finance are also of great importance, and the sea plays a vital role in the city's economy. Vancouver has the largest port on the North American Pacific coast, and fishing remains a crucial industry. It's from here that grain, timber and minerals are exported, and valuable trade links with Japan have been forged.

BACKGROUND

When the Spanish explorer José María Narváez sailed up the Georgia Strait in 1791, the shores on which Vancouver now stands were densely carpeted with trees and inhabited by Salish natives who fished the waters. The following year, Captain George Vancouver quite literally put the area on the map when he explored and charted Burrard Inlet on behalf of the British Navy. The next white man to explore the area was Simon Fraser who, in 1808, reached the Pacific by means of an overland route. This brought him to the mouth of the river now named after him, and in his wake fur trading posts were set up.

The site was largely ignored until the 1860s, when sawmills started to appear around Burrard Inlet. Alcohol was not allowed on company land, so when a Yorkshireman named Jack Deighton turned up with a keg of whisky, he answered the

prayers of the thirsty workers. He persuaded the men to help him build a saloon, and that was when things really began to happen. The year was 1867, and the rough-and-ready community that quickly sprang up around the bar was named Gastown after its loquacious saloonkeeper, known by then as "Gassy Jack." The town kept on growing, and in 1869 the provincial government officially renamed it Granville.

The next major development came in 1884 when William Van Horne, builder of the Canadian Pacific Railway (CPR), decided to make Granville the site of the West Coast terminus. He also suggested the town be renamed; and in 1886 it was incorporated as the city of Vancouver. Within months fire destroyed the city, but with speed and determination it was rebuilt by the time the first CPR passenger train chugged into town in 1887.

Many Chinese had arrived to work on constructing the railroad, and a series of clashes between them and the white community spurred Vancouver authorities to deport them to Victoria. The incensed provincial government intervened to right this injustice, and the Chinese community continued to live in the area that developed into the city's Chinatown. Racism did not end there, however, and, to the city's further shame, until the late 1940s the Chinese were denied many of the rights granted to other citizens.

The twentieth century saw Vancouver's rapid growth: the port grew in importance as trade with the Far East developed, and the fishing and timber industries thrived. The opening of the Panama Canal in 1914 facilitated export of grain to Europe, thus increasing the port's importance, and the demands created by World War II further boosted

The Vancouver skyline at dusk seen from Stanley Park. On the left is the city's most recognizable landmark: Canada Place with its white sails.

the mining and timber industries. Urban development hurtled onwards, making Vancouver the envy of many older cities.

Where once a wilderness of 1,000-year-old trees greeted the eyes of the first explorers, shiny high-rise buildings glitter against the background of the Coast Mountains. The city gently tends the little history it has: old buildings have been restored and First Nations art carefully preserved.

GENERAL INFORMATION

For information, the excellent **Vancouver Tourist Information Centre** ((604) 683-2000 FAX (604) 682-1717 WEB SITE www.tourismvancouver.com, 200 Burrard Street, carries a full range of information about the province. Pick up the leaflet *Discover Vancouver on Transit*, and public transportation schedules and maps. There are information kiosks at the airport and scattered around Greater Vancouver. **Tourism British Columbia** ((604) 435-5622 TOLL-FREE (800) 435-5622 WEB SITE WWW .HelloBC.com is not open to walk-in visitors.

BC Transit ((604) 953-3333 (6:30 AM to 11:30 PM) WEB SITE www.translink.bc.ca, issues all-day passes, available from convenience stores and visitor information centers, and good on the city buses, SkyTrain and SeaBus. Bus stops are clearly marked and often list the route numbers serving the stop. If you purchase tickets on board you must put the exact amount in a machine in coins.

The **SkyTrain** is an automated light rail that follows a 28-km (18-mile) route with 20 stations, running from downtown east to the suburb of Surrey. The **SeaBus** takes passengers and their bicycles (but not cars) to the North Shore via a scenic 15-minute harbor crossing, departing from the SkyTrain Waterfront station downtown, and from the south foot of Lonsdale Avenue at Lonsdale Quay on the North Shore.

The **Vancouver Trolley** ((604) 801-5515 TOLL-FREE (888) 451-5581 WEB SITE www.vancouver trolley.com has a hop-on hop-off narrated circuit, with stops close to most of the city sights.

WHAT TO SEE AND DO

Downtown

One of the city's most distinctive landmarks is **Canada Place** ((604) 647-7390, which projects boldly into the harbor north of Burrard Street. With its unmistakable roof of white Teflon-coated "sails" that whiten in the sunlight, it has inevitably been referred to as "Vancouver's answer to the Sydney Opera House" and, like the Opera House, it has become an emblem of the city. Originally built as the Canada Pavilion for the 1986 World's Fair, the complex now encompasses the World Trade Center, the Vancouver Trade and Convention Center, an IMAX cinema ((604) 682-4629, a

luxury hotel, restaurants, shops and a major cruise-ship terminal. An outdoor promenade runs around the structure.

Also of architectural note is the nearby **Canadian Pacific Railway Station** on West Cordova Street. This splendidly restored structure was built in the 1880s as the Canadian Pacific Railway terminus; both the SkyTrain and the SeaBus now operate from here.

To fully appreciate the city's glorious setting you should take a trip 167 m (555 ft) up **The Lookout!** ((604) 689-0421 WEB SITE www.vancouver lookout.com, Harbour Centre Tower, 555 West Hastings Street. The views from the top will take your breath away, if you have any left to take after the 45-second journey up the outside of the building in the glass elevator. Go by day and ask for a (free) ticket to return after sunset.

Three blocks south of the Harbour Centre and then a couple east along Georgia Street, **Robson Square** covers the area between Howe and Hornby Streets. This complex, built in 1979, contains government buildings, a seven-story law court building with a vast sloping glass roof, restaurants, multi-level terraces and waterfalls.

The dignified old neoclassical courthouse still stands across from the modern complex, and now houses the **Vancouver Art Gallery (VAG)** ((604) 662-4700 or (604) 662-4719 WEB SITE www.vanart gallery.bc.ca, 750 Hornby Street (10 AM to 5:30 PM, Thursday to 9 PM). The building was designed in 1907 by British Columbia's foremost architect of the time, Francis Rattenbury, and it seems fitting that the interior of the building was redesigned in the 1980s by Arthur Erickson, the internationally renowned Vancouver architect who was responsible for the square's modern complex. The gallery holds temporary exhibitions of (mainly) contemporary, frequently bizarre, art. Its permanent collection (approximately 7,000 works) includes more accessible art forms. One of its main attractions is the large collection of works by the acclaimed British Columbia artist Emily Carr.

You can soak up a bit of European atmosphere when you stroll along Robson Street between Howe and Broughton streets. Once a primarily German neighborhood, this stretch is known locally as **Robsonstrasse**. You can sample all varieties of European food in the restaurants, cafés and delicatessens that line the street, or take a look at the high fashion shops.

Gastown

East of the Harbour Centre, between Richards and Columbia Streets lies Gastown, the birthplace of Vancouver and the oldest part of the city. In 1867 it was here that Englishman John "Gassy Jack" Deighton built his saloon with the willing help of thirsty mill workers. The shantytown that sprung up around it grew eventually to become

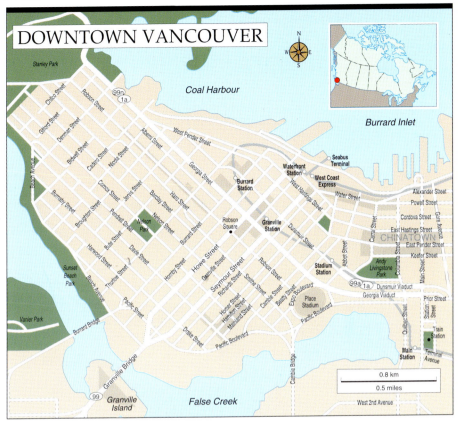

DOWNTOWN VANCOUVER

Stanley Park

Coal Harbour

Burrard Inlet

CHINATOWN

False Creek

0.8 km

0.5 miles

Granville Island

Vancouver, and although the 1886 fire destroyed the town, it was quickly rebuilt using more robust materials. By the 1960s these buildings had degenerated into slums, and during the 1970s Gastown underwent the familiar rags-to-riches story of gentrification. The nineteenth-century buildings were restored, modern but matching additions were built, streets were cobbled, imitation nineteenth-century streetlights popped up, and the area filled with bistros, restaurants, galleries and shops. Gastown is now a major tourist draw both by day and night. At its center is Maple Tree Square, where the original Globe Saloon once was and where a statue of Gassy Jack and his barrel of whiskey now stands in memory. At the corner of Cambie and Water Streets stands what is proudly proclaimed to be the first **steam-powered clock** in the world. It pipes out its very own version of the Westminster chimes on the quarter-hour and truly lets off steam on the hour.

Gastown has the city's largest selection of cheap souvenirs, but also offers good shopping for quality Canadian crafts. **Frances Hill's** ((604) 685-1828 WEB SITE www.franceshills.com, 151 Water Street, has excellent Canadian-made crafts, clothing and gifts. Water Street is also the place for Northwest Coast and Inuit arts and crafts, including Cowichan sweaters, moccasins and carved silver jewelry, which can be purchased at the government-licensed **Inuit Gallery of Vancouver** ((604) 688-7323 WEB SITE www.inuit.com, 206 Cambie Street, which will ship purchases. Another good source, literally round the corner, is **Images for a Canadian Heritage** ((601) 685-7046, 164 Water Street.

Chinatown

Just south of Gastown, in the area demarcated by Hastings and Keefer / Abbott and Gore, and centered on Pender Street, is Chinatown, home to North America's third-largest Chinese community (after San Francisco and New York). Many of Vancouver's Chinese citizens have also settled in the suburb of Richmond. The neighborhood developed in the 1880s and some of the original buildings still stand. It's a bustling area filled with the noises and smells of Hong Kong, and it brims with restaurants, bakeries, herbalists and shops selling all kinds of Chinese goods, from ginseng, green tea and exotic fresh produce to embroidered linens and silk robes.

Behind the Chinese Cultural Center on East Pender Street is a peaceful sanctuary from the city bustle, the **Dr. Sun Yat-Sen Classical Chinese Garden** ((604) 689-7133 or (604) 662-3207 WEB SITE www.vancouverchinesegarden.com, 578 Carrall Street. The first of its kind outside China, it was designed in Ming Dynasty style by a team from the city of Suzhou, in honor of the revolutionary Sun Yat-Sen, who visited Vancouver while planning the overthrow of China's last dynasty. Everything in the garden was manufactured in China and brought over for the 1986 World's Fair, the hundredth anniversary of the founding of Vancouver. (That same year was an important anniversary for the city of Suzhou — its two thousand five hundredth.) The garden is a peaceful composition of sculptural limestone rocks, plants, trees, bridges and water; a tour explains the principles behind the design.

of people of all colors, creeds and customs for all time." There are tennis courts, a biking/in-line skating/running track (anything on wheels must travel anti-clockwise), a separate walking path (a full circuit takes about two hours), miniature golf courses, cricket pitches, lawn bowls, a children's water park, a miniature train, restaurants, snack bars, an open-air theater and numerous picnic sites.

At the Georgia Street entrance, the marshy **Lost Lagoon** is a bird sanctuary where you'll see Canada geese, Trumpeter swans, great blue heron and other wildfowl. Stanley Park is home to many animal species, but the most noticeable are black squirrels, originally imported from New York's

In the area, do not miss the **Sam Kee Building**, reputedly the world's narrowest building, which stands at the corner of Pender and Carrall Streets, one block wide and a mere 1.8 m (six feet) deep at street level; the upper stories overhang.

Stanley Park

The city's pride and joy, Stanley Park's 404 hectares (1,000 acres) cover the whole western tip of the downtown peninsula that juts out into Burrard Inlet, and consists of some 280 hectares (700 acres) of lush rainforest. Two-thirds of the park is in its natural state. The other third is given over to gardens, beaches and public facilities. There are information centers in the park and a Special Events line ℂ (604) 473-6204 WEB SITE www.parks.vancouver.bc.ca.

In 1886 Ottawa granted this land to Vancouver, and in 1889 Canada's governor-general Lord Stanley dedicated it "to the use and enjoyment

Central Park. The 10.5-km (6.5-mile) scenic **seawall** that encircles the park is popular with cyclists and strollers, and for the less energetic there's a **scenic drive**, which starts from the Georgia Street entrance. Stanley Park is within easy reach of downtown on foot or via city buses 35/135. A free shuttle bus runs around the park from May to mid-September 10 AM to 6:30 PM every 15 minutes, with 14 strategically sited stops. Information is available from the **Park Board** ℂ (604) 257-8438 or (604) 257-8440. There's also a one-hour horse-drawn 20-passenger "bus" operating fully narrated tours ℂ (604) 681-5115, mid-March to October.

At **Brockton Point** there are great views across Burrard Inlet of the North Shore mountains, and nearby is a display of totem poles. At **Prospect Point**, the Lions Gate Bridge forms the only land link between the downtown area and the North

Shore, and from here you get a good view of the ships passing through First Narrows to and from the port. At the southwest tip of the park peninsula, **Ferguson Point** looks over to Third Beach and the peaks of Vancouver Island.

Also in the park is the superb **Vancouver Aquarium** ((604) 659-3474 or (604) 659-3511 WEB SITE www.vanaqua.org. This award-winning exhibition of marine life has displays of over 8,000 aquatic specimens. It staggers feeding times so that you can enjoy the playful beluga whales, acrobatic Pacific white-sided dolphins and endearing sea otters. You can take a turn in the Amazonian jungle, recreated under cover with sloths, snakes, piranhas, turtles and birds.

where stalls sell seafood, produce and foods of many countries. On the west of the island you'll find the **Maritime Market**, a block of shops selling just about everything needed for pleasure boating. There is also the **Kids Market**, a collection of games, play areas and shops stocking things for children.

To the west of Burrard Bridge in Vanier Park (downtown buses 2 or 22 or False Creek Ferry) stands the **Vancouver Museum** ((604) 736-4431 WEB SITE www.vanmuseum.bc.ca, 1100 Chestnut Street (10 AM to 5 PM, Thursday to 9 PM). The museum has a gallery devoted to West Coast native culture, with some stunning native art and artifacts, and exhibits on Vancouver's history.

Further Afield

Over on the south side of False Creek, **Granville Island** is a small peninsula connected to the downtown core by Granville Bridge. It's a fun place to have lunch and enjoy the harbor. Take a bus from downtown, the False Creek passenger ferry from Sunset Beach near the Aquatic Centre, or the Aquabus from Hornby Street. Once the center of Vancouver's shipbuilding industry, by the 1960s the area had degenerated into a grim spot full of dingy factories and warehouses. Renovation began in the 1970s, and it is now a lively neighborhood of businesses, craft studios, industry, theaters, galleries, restaurants, markets, shops and a three-in-one **museum** ((604) 683-1939, 1502 Duranleau, covering model ships, game fishing and model trains. A huge converted warehouse underneath Granville Bridge houses the popular **Public Market**,

Sharing the same building is the **H. R. Macmillan Space Centre** ((604) 738-7827 WEB SITE www.hrmacmillanspacecentre.com (10 AM to 5 PM, March to June, Tuesday to Sunday; July to early September daily, which underwent major renovation in 1997 and is now as high-tech as its subject, with dozens of hands-on space-themed exhibits. It incorporates a **Planetarium**, which has up to five shows daily, including a "ride" to save a settlement on Mars, and laser shows set to rock music at night. Next to the museum is the small **Gordon Southam Observatory** ((604) 738-2855 (Friday and Saturday 7 PM to 11 PM, but subject to weather conditions).

OPPOSITE: Vancouver's Chinatown not only has the largest Chinese community in Canada, but many of its buildings were erected by the original settlers. ABOVE: The Dr. Sun-Yat Sen Classical Chinese Garden is an oasis of calm.

Nearby, the **Vancouver Maritime Museum** ((604) 257-8300, 1905 Ogden Avenue, (10 AM to 5 PM daily May to August; September to April Tuesday to Saturday, and Sunday from noon) traces the history of shipping in the region and the development of the port of Vancouver. The centerpiece is the *St. Roch*, a fully restored Royal Canadian Mounted Police ship, which became the first vessel to navigate the Northwest Passage in both directions, during World War II. Outside you can see some of the museum's restored boats in **Heritage Harbour**.

Moving west (downtown buses 4 and 10), the **University of British Columbia** sits on the headland of Point Grey, which is tipped with forest

NW Marine Drive, a serene Japanese garden with a ceremonial teahouse. The entrance is at the corner of Memorial Road and Lower Mall; open summer daily 10 AM to 6 PM, winter Monday to Friday to 2:30 PM.

At the southwest end of the campus, highlights of the **UBC Botanical Gardens** ((604) 822-4208 WEB SITE www.ubc.botanicalgardens.org, 6804 Sixteenth and SW Marine Drive, include the **Asian Garden** and the **Physick Garden**, a sixteenth-century-style garden of medicinal plants. Open daily 10 AM to 6 PM.

In the eastern corner of False Creek, the silver geodesic dome that was built for the 1986 World's Fair is now home to **Science World** ((604) 443-

and overlooks the Georgia Strait and English Bay. The **UBC Museum of Anthropology (MOA)** ((604) 822-5087 or (604) 822-3825 WEB SITE www .moa.ubc.ca, 6393 NW Marine Drive, is a concrete-and-glass building worthy of its dramatic setting. Designed by Vancouver architect Arthur Erickson, the building's huge glass windows embrace views of cliffs, mountains, sea and trees, giving context to one of the world's finest exhibits of Pacific Northwest Coast First Nations art. There are also works of art and artifacts from many other cultures. Totem poles and reconstructed Haida dwellings are set in the rainforest in the museum grounds.

From here you can follow the marked trails that lead down to **Wreck Beach**, a popular six-kilometer-long (four-mile) nudist beach. Or you can enjoy nature in a more cultivated form at the **UBC Nitobe Memorial Garden** ((604) 822-6038, 6565

7443 or (604) 443-7440, 1455 Quebec Street at Terminal Avenue, where visitors come to grips with science through imaginative hands-on displays. The SkyTrain runs to the nearby Main Street Station; weekdays 10 AM to 5 PM, weekends to 6 PM.

Keen gardeners and those who enjoy floral displays will love **Queen Elizabeth Park** ((604) 257-8570, 33rd Avenue and Cambie Street. At 153 m (501 ft) it's the city's highest point, with wonderful views and magnificent gardens. Inside the domed **Bloedel Conservatory** ((604) 257-8584 (admission fee), exotic plants grow and brightly colored tropical birds fly free.

A few blocks away is yet another manifestation of Vancouver's love affair with nature, the **VanDusen Botanical Gardens** ((604) 878-9274 WEB SITE www.vandusengarden.org, 5251 Oak Street at Thirty-seventh Avenue. In this 22-hectare (55-acre) garden there are geographical and botanical groupings of plants, a fragrance garden, a maze and a children's topiary garden with bushes cut into animal shapes.

The North Shore

On Vancouver's North Shore, the Coast Mountains rise steeply out of the sea, cut deeply by inlets and canyons. On the lower slopes are the smart residential suburbs of North and West Vancouver, and beyond them peaks and parks beckon hikers in the summer, skiers in the winter, and lovers of the great outdoors all the year round. The spectacular **Lions Gate Bridge** links the Stanley Park to Western Vancouver. Alternatively, take the Second Narrows Bridge or the SeaBus.

Next to the SeaBus terminal is the **Lonsdale Quay Market** ((604) 985-6261 WEB SITE www .lonsdalequay.com, 123 Carries Cate Court, a lively waterfront development of shops and eateries centered on a busy public market selling produce. There are lovely views of the city across Burrard Inlet.

At the north end of Capilano Road, the **Skyride** ((604) 980-9311 WEB SITE www.grouse mountain.com, 6400 Nancy Green Way, runs 1,100 m (3,700 ft) up **Grouse Mountain**. The ride takes about eight minutes, and on a clear day panoramic views take in Washington's Olympic Peninsula. In the winter this is one of the most popular ski resorts, being the closest to the city. It also offers a range of summer attractions, from a well-established lumberjack show to a birds-of-prey show, guided nature walks, helicopter tours and mountain biking. Thirty-five-meter-high (16-ft) chainsaw sculptures are scattered round the mountain, and there's an eagle-viewpoint movie. The **Grouse Mountain Refuge for Endangered Wildlife**, a combined conservation, education and research center, focuses on wildlife native to British Columbia. There's a choice of eateries up here, while the **Híwus Feasthouse** offers a sunset program combining traditional First Nations song and dance with explanations of totem carvings and a dinner of native foods. For information on the restaurants call ((604) 984-0661.

Near the foot of Grouse Mountain, the dramatic **Capilano Suspension Bridge** ((604) 985-7474 WEB SITE www.capbridge.com, 3735 Capilano Road (summer 8:30 AM to 8/8:30 PM; winter 9 AM to dusk) offers thrills for those with a head for heights. It's very commercialized, but beautiful and awe-inspiring. The plank-and-cable bridge is 137 m (450 ft) long and sways 70 m (230 ft) above the Capilano River, which rushes through a canyon full of Douglas firs and Western Red cedars. The park contains other attractions, including the (small) Big House where you can watch traditional craftspeople at work. From downtown, pick up the Capilano Road from Lions Gate Bridge.

You can enjoy a similar, but less commercial experience without charge at **Lynn Canyon Park and Ecology Centre** ((604) 981-3103. Here, nature trails run through thick rainforest and a suspension bridge crosses Lynn Creek. Like the bridge at Capilano, though only half as long, it crosses the creek at a height of 80 m (240 ft). Cross at Second Narrows Bridge, take Lynn Valley Road, and then head east along Peters Road.

Sixteen kilometers (10 miles) from Vancouver, the **Mount Seymour Provincial Park** ((604) 986-2261 WEB SITE www.mountseymour.com, 1700 Mount Seymour Road, overlooks the waters of Indian Arm, offering opportunities for hikers, horse riders, picnickers, view-seekers and, during

the winter months, skiers. Walking trails and a road climb eight kilometers (five miles) up the mountain to a lookout where there are a café, an information center, more walking paths and views of eastern Vancouver. From June to September, the **Bear Necessities Tour** offers a varied trip providing an understanding of bears, with sightings in the wild. Take the Mount Seymour Parkway from Second Narrows Bridge, then turn off to the north on Mount Seymour Road.

To see the impressive coastal scenery of **Howe Sound**, take a trip in the *Royal Hudson's* refurbished carriages, towed by stately old Canadian Pacific Railway steam locomotive 3716, which pulled trains across Canada in 1912. With a shrill whistle, a hiss and the squealing of wheels, the

OPPOSITE: The seawall in Stanley Park attracts cyclers, skaters and a lone runner.
ABOVE: Downtown Vancouver.

train pulls away from North Vancouver Station at 10 AM and begins its 66-km (41-mile) journey northwest to the small logging community of Squamish, along a route that runs through forests, up mountains, by waterfalls, all at a leisurely 32 km/h (20 mph). The train arrives at Squamish at approximately noon and passengers have two hours to explore — enough time to get to **Shannon Falls**. You can return to Vancouver by sea aboard the **MV *Britannia***. The rail operates May to mid-September Wednesday to Sunday and holiday Mondays; you must book in advance. Contact **West Coast Rail Tours** ((604) 524-1011 TOLL-FREE (800) 722-1233 WEB SITE www .wcra.org.

Hudson's Bay Company, the fort dates from 1839, and it was here, in the Big House, that British Columbia was officially proclaimed a crown colony in 1858. The fort with its wooden palisade has been restored, and the buildings are open to the public, some with costumed guides.

SPORTS AND OUTDOOR ACTIVITIES

Outdoor pursuits are very much part of the Vancouver lifestyle and, from late November through Easter, it's a paradise for **skiing**. Just 15 minutes from downtown, Grouse Mountain ((604) 980-9311 WEB SITE www.grousemountain .com, 6400 Nancy Greene Way, offers runs suit-

Canada's second-largest collection of railway equipment is housed at the **West Coast Railway Heritage Park** ((604) 898-9336, Squamish, which has vintage rail cars filled with artifacts, photos and information about the history of railroading in British Columbia.

Southeast of Vancouver

To the east of Vancouver lies the fertile **Fraser Valley**, an area of parklands shadowed by mountains all around, and a popular weekend escape for Vancouverites. The TransCanada Highway follows the Fraser River along its south shore, while Highway 7 runs along the north side. **Fort Langley National Historic Park** ((604) 513-4777 WEB SITE www.parkscanada.gc.ca/langley, 23433 Mavis Avenue (March to October daily 10 AM to 5 PM), is 56 km (35 miles) from Vancouver on the south side of the river. Once a trading post for the

able for all abilities. An aerial tramway takes skiers to the top; runs are lit at night. With a daily Skyride ticket, you can also enjoy **snowshoeing, snowboarding, cross-country skiing, ice skating** and **sleigh rides**.

Neighboring Mount Seymour Resorts ((604) 986-2261, 1700 Mount Seymour Road, and Cypress Mountain ((604) 926-5612, end of Cypress Bowl Road, Exit 8 off Highway 1 westbound, also have good skiing and nighttime illumination. In lieu of sleigh rides and skating, they both offer snow-tubing, and Cypress has tobogganing.

For ski information and conditions in the Vancouver area call the **Snowphone** ((604) 687-7507 or (604) 932-4211.

About 120 km (72 miles) north of Vancouver is the fashionable Whistler Resort, named for the indigenous whistling marmot and claiming to be North America's No. 1 ski resort, with 200 ski runs, a season that lasts about 10 months a year, and over 60 hotels and lodges. Information and accommodation bookings are available from Tourism Whistler ((604) 932-2394 FAX (604) 932-7231 WEB SITE www.tourismwhistler.com, 4010 Whistler Way, Whistler. The large, and rapidly growing, pseudo-European Whistler Village nestles between Blackcomb and Whistler Mountains, and caters to every need. It is primarily famous for its skiing, but also offers all manner of summer recreational activities that include **fishing**, **hiking**, **water sports**, **heli-hiking**, **mountain biking** and simply sightseeing.

A terrific overview is provided by a **helicopter flight** with Blackcomb Helicopters ((604) 938-

Heritage Park in Squamish (see under THE NORTH SHORE, page 74), one of the larger towns in British Columbia, with a population of around 15,000; or at the **British Columbia Museum of Mining** at Britannia Beach (there is no beach) and visit the small group of somewhat ramshackle buildings (don't be put off by the appearance), where you can get excellent-value First Nations crafts and good snacks. West Coast City & Nature Sightseeing ((604) 451-1600 WEB SITE www.vancouver sightseeing.com, 3945 Myrtle Street, Burnaby, operates a daytrip to Whistler that incorporates stops at Shannon Falls, Britannia Beach, Brandywine Falls and Squamish (though it's too short to visit the museums).

1700 TOLL-FREE (800) 330-4354 WEB SITE www .blackcombhelicopters.com, 8621 Fissile Lane, Whistler V0N 1B8, which also offers a glacier landing when conditions are right. In summer there's a daily floatplane service between Vancouver and Whistler, weather permitting; a number of companies offer floatplane tours of the Whistler area.

You can also get there along Highway 99, the Sea to Sky Highway, which provides beautiful views of Howe Sound for much of the way. There are Greyhound buses several times a day; the Perimeter Whistler Express bus from Vancouver Airport drops-off / picks-up at most of the Whistler hotels.

If you're driving, it's worth stopping to view the beautiful 335-m-high (1,100-ft) **Shannon Falls**, signposted on the highway. You may also like to make a stop en route at the **West Coast Railway**

Two more of Vancouver's popular pastimes are **cycling** and **in-line skating**, and there's no problem with rentals. Bayshore Bicycles & Rollerblade Rentals ((604) 688-2453, 745 Denman Street, and Spokes Bicycle Rental ((604) 688-5141, 1798 West Georgia Street, are two possibilities.

If you fancy **sailing**, there are schools to teach you how to do it, and plenty of places where you can charter something, particularly around the Coal Harbour area and on Granville Island. **Windsurfing** classes and equipment rentals are available at Kitsilano, Jericho and English Bay beaches. Fraser Canyon is a good area for **canoeing** and **whitewater rafting**, while nearer downtown there's canoeing at False Creek. Ocean West Expeditions ((604) 898-4979, English Bay Bath

OPPOSITE: B.C. Place Stadium in Vancouver.
ABOVE: Sails interrupt Vancouver's shoreline and skyline.

House, 1755 Beach Avenue, are among the companies organizing **sea-kayaking** tours, rentals and lessons (spring to fall).

The Vancouver area has some excellent **scuba diving**, particularly in Howe Sound. The Diving Locker ((604) 736-2681 WEB SITE www.diving locker.ca, 2745 Fourth Avenue West at MacDonald, rents out equipment, offers instruction and organizes scuba trips.

With 11 bathing beaches within the city limits, **swimmers** are also spoiled for choice. The closest to downtown are the beaches in Stanley Park, all of which are good for swimming. Beaches are open Victoria Day to Labor Day, and are guarded daily, usually from 11:30 AM to 8:30 or 9 PM, but if a red light is showing, nobody's on duty. To know more mid-May to mid-September, call the Vancouver Board of Parks and Recreation (swimming information) ((604) 738-8535. At other times of year, call the Aquatic Centre ((604) 665-3424, 1050 Beach Avenue, Sunset Beach, which has a heated indoor Olympic pool and a diving tank. There's also the Kitsilano Pool ((604) 731-0011, an outdoor saltwater pool at Kitsilano Beach.

The Vancouver area has exceptionally good freshwater and saltwater **fishing**, with a good choice of lakes, rivers, streams, bays and a variety of fish, being particularly well known for its salmon. Tackle shops sell the required licenses (to their customers) and can provide a list of current regulations, which you should check carefully. Bonnie Lee Fishing Charters ((604) 290-7447 WEB SITE www.bonnielee.com, 104-1676 Duranleau Street, Granville Island, and Granville Island Boat Rentals ((604) 682-6287, 1696 Duranleau Street, Granville Island, are two reputable outfitters.

NIGHTLIFE AND THE ARTS

Gastown has a vibrant nightlife that draws visitors and residents alike. **Granville Island** has a concentration of theaters and art centers, as well as trendy microbreweries, while **Yaletown** is a fashionable historic district of pool halls, art galleries and cafés.

Ask the Tourist Information Centre for their *Art Map of BC*, a useful guide to cultural events and galleries throughout the province. To check the listings you can pick up a free copy of the weekly arts and entertainment paper, the *Georgia Straight*, or check the *Vancouver Sun*'s entertainment section on Thursday. Contact the **Arts Hotline** ((604) 684-2787 WEB SITE www.alliance forarts.com, 100-938 Howe Street, for the latest on performing and visual arts events and the city's numerous festivals. Tickets for most cultural events are available through **Ticketmaster** ((604) 280-3311 or (604) 280-4444 WEB SITE www.ticketmaster.ca, which has many outlets around the city.

The traditional cultural heart of Vancouver is the renamed and reopened **Centre in Vancouver for Performing Arts** (formerly called the Ford Centre) ((604) 602-0616, 777 Homer Street, which presents an eclectic mix of music, dance and theater from around the world.

The modern 3,000-seat **"Queen E"** ((604) 665-3050, Hamilton at West Georgia, is the place to see ballet, opera, Broadway musicals and celebrity performers. Part of the same complex, the **Vancouver Playhouse** ((604) 872-6622 is home to a theater company of the same name, presenting a mix of new drama and classic theater.

The **Arts Club Theatre Company** stages major theatrical productions and contemporary Canadian works at the **Stanley Theatre**, a heritage building at West Twelfth and Granville Street, and at the **Granville Island Stage**, 1585 Johnston Street, Granville Island. For all three, contact ((604) 687-1644. In Gastown, the **Firehall Arts Centre** ((604) 689-0926, 280 East Cordova Street, offers innovative theater and dance, reflecting Canada's cultural diversity. The **Vancouver Theater Sports League** ((604) 738-7013 WEB SITE www.vtsl.com, New Review Stage, 1601 Johnston Street, Granville Island, is renowned for improvisational theater and often performs television specials. **Bard on the Beach** ((604) 737-0625, 1101 West Broadway, is summer Shakespeare under canvas in Vanier Park, while various musical performances are staged at the **Theatre Under The Stars** ((604) 687-0174, Malkin Bowl in Stanley Park.

Second only to Montréal as a major Canadian dance center, Vancouver's dance scene is as diverse as its cultural makeup, and ranges from traditional Japanese and Chinese dance to classical ballet. The **Vancouver East Cultural Centre** ((604) 254-9578, in a renovated church, is home to the innovative Kokoro Dance Company. The **Ballet British Columbia** can be seen at the Queen Elizabeth Theatre (see above), where world-class companies can also be seen.

Another cultural mainstay, the **Orpheum Theatre** ((604) 665-3050, 601 Smithe Street, is a splendidly restored 1920s building that is home to the widely acclaimed **Vancouver Symphony Orchestra** ((604) 684-9100 WEB SITE www.vancouver symphony.ca, and is the major venue for musical events. If you arrive an hour early you can usually hear a free lecture on the forthcoming performance. Every season the **Vancouver Opera** ((604) 682-2871 WEB SITE www.vanopera.bc.ca presents four productions at the Queen Elizabeth Theatre.

Vancouver has quite a mixture of jazz venues. The **Coastal Jazz and Blues Society** has a hotline ((604) 872-5200 WEB SITE www.jazzvancouver.com, with listings and directions to regular venues. **Hot Jazz Society** ((604) 873-4131, 2120 Main Street, features the Big Band sound. The **Purple Onion Cabaret** ((604) 602-9442, 15 Water Street, offers an eclectic mix of music: almost everything except jazz and blues. The spot for serious blues is **The Yale** ((604) 681-9253, 1300 Granville Street, at the north end of the Granville Bridge.

WISE Hall ((604) 254-5858, 1882 Adanac Street, offers a variety of music, but is a particularly good venue for Celtic and other folk music, while big rock concerts are often held at **GM Place** ((604) 899-7469, 150 Pacific Boulevard East at Abbott Street. The **Commodore Ballroom** ((604) 739-4550, 868 Granville Street, is another major venue for rock and many other kinds of music.

On the dance club circuit, the classy-yet-cool **Richard's on Richards** ((604) 687-6794, 1036 Richards Street, is one of the longest-running ven-

WHERE TO STAY

Expensive

One of the city's top hotels, and winner of the AAA Five Diamond Award for 25 consecutive years, is the **Four Seasons** ((604) 689-9333 TOLL-FREE (800) 332-3442 or (800) 268-6282 FAX (604) 684-4555 WEB SITE www.fourseasons.com, 791 West Georgia Street. This hotel embodies excellent service, ultimate comfort and good taste, with beautifully furnished rooms and suites, two excellent restaurants — the informal Garden Terrace (essentially an indoor garden) and the award-winning Chartwell. It has an all-season indoor/

ues in the city; it has DJs on Friday and Saturday and often at other times, but also frequent live music. The very hip **Babalu** ((604) 605-4343 WEB SITE www.babalu.com, 654 Nelson at Granville, serves martinis while the house band plays Latin rhythms in the Cuban Lounge. Currently closed because of a fire, it is due to reopen shortly.

The dark and shiny **Luvafair** ((604) 685-3288, 1275 Seymour, is one of Vancouver's see-and-be-seen spots, very popular with the younger set.

The club scene depends largely on age. Granville Island is the hub for places likely to appeal to the younger crowd (up to 30ish), while those a little older should try the more upmarket Yaletown — aimed primarily at 30-somethings. A good spot for the more sedate is the **Georgia Street Bar & Grill** ((604) 602-0994, 801 West Georgia, which has a comfortable jazz lounge and serves good drinks. Sometimes there's dancing.

outdoor swimming pool, adjoining a pleasant sun deck cum roof garden.

Immediately across the street, the **Crowne Plaza Hotel Georgia** ((604) 682-5566 TOLL-FREE (800) 663-1111 FAX (604) 642-5579 WEB SITE www.hotelgeorgia.bc.ca, 801 West Georgia Street, is more old-fashioned in style, reflecting its status as an official heritage site — it's been in operation since 1927. Afternoon tea in the Casablanca Lounge is recommended, while the restaurant As Time Goes By has a wide-ranging menu. There's a 24-hour business center and an exercise room, but no pool. Rooms on the Club Floor have access to the Crowne Plaza Club, with a selection of complimentary goodies.

Across from Robson Square, the **Wedgewood Hotel** ((604) 689-7777 TOLL-FREE (800) 663-0666

A stunning sculpture greets visitors to the University of British Columbia's Museum of Anthropology.

FAX (604) 688-5348 WEB SITE www.wedgewood hotel.com, 845 Hornby Street, is a smaller, privately owned hotel with 89 elegant rooms and suites, with every amenity one could wish for. Owner Eleni Skalbania's dedication to excellence and personal touch make this hotel a favorite among knowledgeable travelers. Executive facilities are available, and there's an award-winning restaurant, The Bacchus, with its cozy fire-lit room decorated in cherry wood, silk and velvet.

For old-fashioned grandeur look to the **Fairmont Hotel Vancouver** ((604) 684-3131 TOLL-FREE (800) 441-1414 FAX (604) 668-8335 WEB SITE www.hotelvancouver.com, 900 West Georgia Street, one of the great railway hotels with over 500 rooms. With a classical façade crowned with a steep green copper roof, this hotel is a Vancouver landmark. Its spacious public areas are furnished in grand style with chandeliers, antiques, an ocean of marble, and comfortable old-fashioned sofas and armchairs. The rooms are also spacious, but decorated in a more low-key fashion. The service here is impeccable.

The **Metropolitan Hotel** ((604) 687-1122 TOLL-FREE (800) 667-2300 FAX (604) 643-7267 WEB SITE www.metropolitan.com, 645 Howe Street, is another leading hotel, with 197 individually designed rooms and suites, many with marble bathrooms. The hotel boasts one of the city's best restaurants, Diva at the Met, as well as an indoor swimming pool, a health center and squash courts.

Rising above the Royal Centre mall, the recently renovated **Hyatt Regency Vancouver** ((604) 683-1234 TOLL-FREE (800) 633-7313 FAX (604) 689-3707 WEB SITE www.vancouver.hyatt.com, 655 Burrard Street, had 645 spacious rooms and state-of-the-art facilities.

Magnificently situated in the remarkable Canada Place waterfront complex is the **Pan Pacific Hotel Vancouver** ((604) 662-8111 TOLL-FREE (800) 937-1515 FAX (604) 662-3815 WEB SITE www.panpac.com, 300-999 Canada Place. This hotel really does have everything. All the rooms and suites are luxurious and its excellent restaurants offer Japanese, Italian and Pacific Rim cuisine, along with spectacular harbor views.

The **Sutton Place Hotel** ((604) 682-5511 TOLL-FREE (800) 961-7555 FAX (604) 682-5513 WEB SITE www.suttonplace.com, 845 Burrard Street, has a distinctly European accent. This is a relatively new hotel (1986), furnished in classical French style with marble, antiques and great elegance. The rooms, although on the small side, match the public areas for style and grace, and the service is superb and personal. Also European in style, the **Georgian Court Hotel** ((604) 682-5555 TOLL-FREE (800) 663-1155 FAX (604) 682-8830 WEB SITE www.georgiancourt.com, 773 Beatty Street, is located opposite the BC Stadium, only a block away from the Queen Elizabeth Theatre. Antiques adorn

the elegant lobby, the airy rooms are beautifully furnished, well equipped and many offer splendid views.

Opus Hotel ((604) 642-6787 TOLL-FREE (866) 642-6787 FAX (604) 642-6780 WEB SITE www.opushotel.com, 322 Davie Street, is the city's latest boutique hotel, combining creativity, elegance and comfort. Hotel amenities include a cocktail / tapas bar, the nouvelle cuisine Elixir Restaurant, health and business centers, a spa, and rental of bicycles, boats and in-line skates.

In the city's west end, the **Westin Bayshore Resort & Marina** ((604) 682-3377 TOLL-FREE (800) 938-8461 FAX (604) 687-3102 WEB SITE www.westinbayshore.com, 1601 Bayshore Drive, is beautifully positioned near the edge of Stanley Park and set in grounds overlooking Coal Harbour. Rooms have large windows and lovely views, and the hotel offers a wide range of services including a kids' club, restaurants and outdoor and indoor pools. The *pièce de résistance* is the private marina, which brings floatplanes, fishing trips and cruises to the doorstep. Moving a few blocks away from Coal Harbour, the high-rise **Pacific Palisades Hotel** ((604) 688-0461 TOLL-FREE (800) 663-1815 FAX (604) 688-4374 WEB SITE www.pacificpalisadeshotel.com, 1277 Robson Street, offers all-suite accommodation, with balconies overlooking Coal Harbour and Stanley Park. It's particularly well adapted for business travelers, but leisure travelers also enjoy the amenities, which include an indoor pool.

In North Vancouver, the **Lonsdale Quay Hotel** ((604) 986-6111 TOLL-FREE (800) 836-6111 FAX (604) 986-8782 WEB SITE www.lonsdalequayhotel.com, 123 Carrie Cates Court, is located next to the SeaBus Terminal on the top floors of the lively Lonsdale Quay Market. Its rooms and suites are attractively decorated, and there are some good views across Burrard Inlet. South of downtown, the **Granville Island Hotel** ((604) 683-7373 TOLL-FREE (800) 663-1840 FAX (604) 683-3061 WEB SITE www.granvilleislandhotel.com, 1253 Johnston Street, is a lively waterfront place that tends to attract a sporty crowd who take advantage of the tennis courts and the various charters that operate from the marina. The building has the warehouse-like appearance characteristic of Granville Island, but no two rooms are the same and all are well equipped, most with waterfront views.

Mid-range

The **Barclay Hotel** ((604) 688-8850 FAX (604) 688-2534 WEB SITE www.barclayhotel.com, 1348 Robson Street, is within walking distance of Stanley Park and offers some of the best value around. It has 90 rooms, a French restaurant and a piano lounge. Just north of Lions Gate Bridge, you'll find the lovely **Park Royal Hotel** ((604) 926-5511 FAX (604) 926-6082 WEB SITE www.parkroyalhotel.com,

540 Clyde Avenue, West Vancouver, set in attractive grounds on the banks of the Capilano River, well-situated for beaches and mountains, and close to the Park Royal shopping center. The 30 rooms are all attractive and airy.

At the edge of Stanley Park, on English Bay, stands the much-loved **Sylvia Hotel** ((604) 681-9321 FAX (604) 682-3551 WEB SITE www.sylviahotel .com, 1154 Gilford Street. This delightful Virginia creeper-covered heritage building has 119 rooms and suites, some located in a modern extension. The decor throughout is simple, each room is different, and both restaurant and bar have beautiful views of the bay. Book well in advance.

Inexpensive

The **Kingston Hotel Bed & Breakfast** ((604) 684-9024 TOLL-FREE (888) 713-3304 FAX (604) 684-9917 WEB SITE www.kingstonhotelvanouver.com, 757 Richards Street, is a European-style place with continental breakfast included in the rate. The rooms are small but clean; some have private bathrooms, others have hand basins. The hotel has a sauna and coin laundry. East of downtown, the **Budget Inn-Patricia Hotel** ((604) 255-4301 FAX (604) 254-7154 E-MAIL patriciahotel@telus.net WEB SITE www.budgetpathotel.pc.ca, 403 East Hastings Street, has 195 simply furnished rooms with private bathrooms.

There's a wide range of **bed and breakfast** accommodation in metropolitan Vancouver. Among the agencies are the **Old English Bed and Breakfast Registry** ((604) 986-5069 FAX (604) 986-8810 E-MAIL relax@oldenglishbandb.bc.ca, 1226 Silverwood Crescent, North Vancouver, and **Canada-West Accommodation B&B Registry** ((604) 990-6730 TOLL-FREE (800) 561-3223 FAX (604) 990-5876 WEB SITE www.b-b.com, who cover the whole of British Columbia.

Vancouver has two large Hostelling International hostels WEB SITE www.hihostels.bc.ca. **Vancouver Downtown** ((604) 684-4565 FAX (604) 684-4540 E-MAIL van-downtown@hihostels.bc.ca, 1114 Burnaby Street, with 223 beds and some family rooms, and **Vancouver Jericho Beach** ((604) 224-3208 FAX (604) 224-4852 E-MAIL van-jericho @hihostels.bc.ca, 1515 Discovery Street, where there are 285 beds and 10 private rooms.

University accommodation is available May to August at the Simon Fraser University, 20 km (12 miles) east of downtown. For details contact Simon Fraser University Conference Accommodations ((604) 291-4503 FAX (604) 291-5598 WEB SITE www.sfu.ca / conference-accommodation, Room 212, McTaggart-Cowan Hall, 8888 University Drive, Burnaby, Vancouver V5A 1S6.

The University of British Columbia at Point Grey 16 km (10 miles) southwest of the center also offers year-round accommodation; information is available from Conferences & Accommodation at

UBC ((604) 822-1000 FAX (604) 822-1001 WEB SITE www.conferences.ubc.ca, 5961 Student Union Boulevard, Vancouver V6T 2C9.

WHERE TO EAT

Vancouver's large number of restaurants reflects the city's rich ethnic mix in the wide variety of food they offer. You'll also find the region's own brand, Pacific Northwestern cuisine, here, based on plentiful supplies of salmon and other seafood, game, herbs and flowers. *City Food* is a free publication that comes out monthly and can be picked up at restaurants and bookstores. It's a good source of up-to-date information on the Vancouver area dining scene.

Expensive

The top-notch **Diva at the Met** ((604) 602-7788, Metropolitan Hotel, 645 Howe Street, is known for its open kitchen and imaginative international cuisine. Seasonal ingredients are emphasized, and flavors are bold. The terraced room offers atmospheres ranging from lively to intimate. **Chartwell** ((604) 689-9333, Four Seasons Hotel, 791 West Georgia Street, is named after the English country home of Winston Churchill, and the restaurant imitates that ambiance with its warm walnut paneling, subdued lighting and blazing fire. Amid these gracious and tasteful surroundings, diners enjoy a wide-ranging progressive French menu with Pacific Rim influences. Their excellent pretheater dinner slot will let you get to your show on time.

Frank Dodd, the executive chef at the **Bacchus Restaurant** ((604) 608-5319, Wedgewood Hotel, 845 Hornby Street, is an Englishman who learned his trade at London's renowned Savoy and Dorchester hotels, then with Albert Roux, and now combines his skill with Pacific Rim ingredients to award-winning effect. The elegant surroundings, attentive service and extensive wine list all add to the pleasurable experience.

Vancouver has some excellent French restaurants, of which **Lumière** ((604) 739-8185, 2551 West Broadway, has been voted the best for the past three years. French cuisine with influences from the East and West are served amidst minimalist furnishings of polished chrome and wood. A long-running favorite, **Le Gavroche** ((604) 685-3924, 1616 Alberni Street, is set in a lovely old house in the city's west end. This restaurant has a mouth-watering menu, a democratic wine list and excellent service.

For a Chinese experience, try **Floata Seafood Restaurant** ((604) 602-0368, 400-180 Keefer Street, located near the Dr. Sun Yat-Sen Park, in the third floor of a bright-red shopping plaza. It is the western flagship of a renowned Hong Kong restaurant and, despite its cavernous size, it's usually packed with diners enjoying dim sum served from steaming carts and lavish dinners of award-winning delicacies.

Fleuri ((604) 682-5511, Sutton Place Hotel, 845 Burrard Street, has varied fare. The rich and famous can often be seen chatting over traditional English tea, Sunday brunch is *the* place for a special occasion, and the Chocoholic Bar is a must for anyone with a sweet tooth. Innovative French cuisine is the norm for evenings, with the emphasis on seafood on Friday and Saturday. **CinCin Ristorante & Bar** ((604) 688-7338, 1154 Robson Street, opens for lunch Monday to Friday and dinner daily, offering homemade noodles and excellent Mediterranean food, primarily French and

At a beautiful location on Granville Island's waterfront, **Bridges** ((604) 687-4400, 1696 Duranleau Street, has a good seafood restaurant and a large terrace where you can enjoy beautiful mountain views. East of downtown, **The Cannery** ((604) 254-9606, 2205 Commissioner Street, has an extensive seafood menu, a superb wine list, and great harbor views. **O'Doul's** ((604) 661-1400, Listel Vancouver Hotel, 1300 Robson Street, offers sizzling Canadian Triple Beef — accompanied by jazz Thursday to Saturday evenings.

For excellent and moderately priced French food, few places better the bistroesque **Le Crocodile** ((604) 669-4298, 100-909 Burrard Street, while the **Teahouse Restaurant** ((604) 669-3281, in

Italian, produced in wood-burning ovens. The lounge, which offers a limited menu, is open until 11:30 PM.

Moderate

South of the downtown peninsula, **Tojo's** ((604) 872-8050, 202-777 West Broadway, offers Japanese food in sleek, sophisticated surroundings with an outdoor terrace and mountain views. You can choose to dine in a traditional tatami room, at a conventional dining table, or at the small sushi bar. Over in West Vancouver, **Salmon House on the Hill** ((604) 926-3212, 2229 Folkstone Way, is another good place to sample Pacific Northwest cuisine. Perched high above Vancouver, the restaurant commands wonderful views of Stanley Park and the city across the inlet. It's renowned for what is known as Indian Candy: hot smoked salmon.

Stanley Park at Ferguson Point, serves fine continental fare in a delightful Victorian house overlooking the bay.

The **Pacific Institute of Culinary Arts** ((604) 734-4488, 1505 West Second Avenue, at the entrance to Granville Island, the final training ground for Vancouver's up-and-coming chefs, offers the chance to eat top food at moderate prices.

Celebrated Italian chef Umberto Menghi has several restaurants in Vancouver, the most popular being **Il Giardino** ((604) 669-2422, 1376 Hornby Street. Here Italian classics reign, with game featuring prominently on the menu and great garden dining. Reservations are recommended for both lunch and dinner. For imaginative Italian country cooking, go to **Piccolo Mondo** ((604) 688-1633, 850 Thurlow Street, where you'll find a limited but well thought-out menu. The setting's elegant and the food superb.

Some of the best Cantonese food can be found at the **Pink Pearl** ((604) 253-4316, 1132 East Hastings Street, a large restaurant where the emphasis is on seafood. A favorite for Northern Chinese cuisine is **Kirin Mandarin** ((604) 682-8833, 102-1166 Alberni Street, where the menu is diverse, the surroundings sophisticated, and lobster and crab come fresh from the tanks. The drunken live spot prawns are famous.

Inexpensive

Chinatown has a wealth of restaurants. The cheerful and unpretentious **Gain Wah** ((604) 684-1740, 218 Keefer Street, has authentic Cantonese fare including good *congee*. Steaming noodles are

((604) 682-2622, 1301 Robson, has the decor its name suggests and serves monster ice creams.

HOW TO GET THERE

Vancouver International Airport ((604) 207-7077 WEB SITE www.yvr.ca, is 15 km (nine miles) from downtown and a 25- to 40-minute drive from town. The **Airporter Bus** ((604) 946-8866 TOLL-FREE (800) 668-3141 runs shuttles from the airport every 30 minutes, stopping at major downtown hotels, Canada Place and Pacific Central Station (the train and bus terminal), and operates 6:30 AM to midnight. Taxi stands can be found in front of the terminals.

served at the stainless steel counter of **Ezogiku Noodle Café** ((604) 685-8606, 1329 Robson Street, a favorite lunch spot.

For East Indian food, try the **Heaven and Earth India Curry House** ((604) 732-5313, 1754 West Fourth Avenue, in the Kitsilano area. **La Bodega Tapas Bar** ((604) 684-8815, 1277 Howe Street, has Spanish decor and intriguing specials emphasizing creatively prepared meat dishes. **Pezzo** ((604) 669-9300, 106-1100 Robson, has cheap and good pizzas and pastas, local beer and a stereo featuring the tenor voice of Mario Lanza. The inexpensive **WaaZuBee Café** ((604) 253-5299, 1622 Commercial Drive, serves good food all the time, with a good bar in the evening.

If ice cream's your thing, make sure you visit **La Casa Gelato** ((604) 251-3211, 1033 Venables, where you may choose from 388 flavors — and you won't believe some of them, while **Cows Vancouver**

When leaving Vancouver by air, you must pay an "Airport Improvement Fee" (AIF) of $5, $10 or $15 (depending on destination). The issuing machines take cash and cards.

VIA Rail TOLL-FREE (888) 842-7245 WEB SITE www.viarail.ca operates the *Canadian* three times a week each way between Toronto and Vancouver, via Kamloops, Jasper, Edmonton, Saskatoon, Winnipeg and Sudbury Junction. Other points in the province connected to Vancouver by rail include Prince Rupert and Prince George (Vancouver Island is accessed via bus-ferry to Victoria, which is linked by rail to Nanaimo and Courtenay). **Amtrak** TOLL-FREE (800) 872-7245 WEB SITE www.amtrak.com operates one train daily from Seattle to Vancouver's Pacific Central Station, 1150 Station Street, and **BC Rail** ((604) 984-5246

OPPOSITE: Salmon on ice at Granville Market. ABOVE: Produce for sale in Chinatown.

TOLL-FREE (800) 339-8752 WEB SITE www.bcrail.com has daily services into North Vancouver from Squamish, Whistler, Lillooet and points in between, as well as regular services to 100 Mile House, Williams Lake, Quesnel and Prince George. Its station is at 1311 West First Street, North Vancouver. **Rocky Mountaineer Railtours** ((604) 606-7245 TOLL-FREE (800) 665-7245 FAX (604) 606-7250 WEB SITE www.rockymountaineer.com, Pacific Central Station, First Floor, 1150 Station Street, operates April to October between Calgary/Banff/Jasper and Vancouver (see RIDE THE LEGENDARY RAILS, page 11 in TOP SPOTS).

BC Ferries ((250) 386-3431 TOLL-FREE (888) 223-3779 WEB SITE www.bcferries.com, run from the Tsawwassen Ferry Terminal, 30 km (19 miles) south of downtown Vancouver, to Victoria (Swartz Bay), Nanaimo on Vancouver Island, and to the Southern Gulf Islands. They also operate a ferry from Horseshoe Bay, west of Vancouver, to Nanaimo, Bowen Island and the mainland's Sunshine Coast.

Long-distance buses arriving at Pacific Central Station, Main Street, include **Pacific Coach Lines** ((604) 662-7575 TOLL-FREE (800) 661-1725 WEB SITE www.pacificcoach.com, which provides a regular scheduled service (via ferry) between Vancouver and Victoria, as well as a variety of sightseeing tours, and **Greyhound** ((604) 482-8747 TOLL-FREE (800) 661-8747 WEB SITE www.greyhound.ca, which links most mainland cities with regular services. Their offshoot, **Gray Line**, runs tours throughout Canada.

Motorists coming from the east will want to take the TransCanada Highway (Highway 1), while those coming from Seattle, Washington, will take Highway 5, which becomes Highway 99 at the British Columbia border. The drive from Seattle to Vancouver takes about three hours.

VANCOUVER ISLAND

Moored alongside the west coast of the British Columbia mainland, and separated from it by the Georgia Strait, Vancouver Island stretches 520 km (323 miles) and covers an area of 32,000 sq km (12,000 sq miles). It is thus the largest island off North America's Pacific coast, and violates the 49th parallel, much to the annoyance of some. A chain of snow-tipped mountains runs north–south through the center of the island, splitting its personality between a rugged and sparsely populated west with an exposed Pacific coastline cut by deep inlets, and a sheltered eastern shore of a much tamer character with white sandy beaches, gentle slopes, farmlands and seaside towns.

The island is blessed with a gentle climate throughout the year, although rainfall varies dramatically from place to place. The lowest rainfall and mildest temperatures are found at the southern end of the island, which is sheltered by the

Olympic Mountains across the Juan de Fuca Strait. It is not surprising therefore that about half the island's population of around 700,000 lives in the Victoria area and most of the rest in the southeast, leaving the west side inhabited only by a few small fishing communities.

The rainforests, with their soaring red cedars, and the lonely West Coast shores seem a far cry from the neat lawns of Victoria and the snug towns of the southeast. This combination of ruggedly beautiful scenery, the sedate charm of Victoria, and people as gentle as the climate itself makes Vancouver Island appealing to vacationers. The culture is diverse, for the British Empire was not the only society to leave its mark. The Haida, Kwagiutl, Cowichan and Sooke indigenous populations, who lived in fishing villages here long before the arrival of Europeans, have scattered the island with their totem poles, their crafts and legends, while their fishing skills seem to have found their way into the blood of the inhabitants. Together with fishing, mining and logging are the island's main industries.

BACKGROUND

In 1774, Juan Pérez Hernández of Spain visited Vancouver Island. Captain Cook landed at Nootka Island on the west coast in 1778 and conducted a little trade. In 1792, Captain George Vancouver put the island on the map when he charted the waters of Johnstone Strait. However these visits had little effect on the lives of the island's native tribes and it wasn't until 1843, when the Hudson's Bay Company took control and founded a trading post on the island's southeastern tip, that things started slowly to change.

In 1849, Vancouver Island was declared a crown colony, with the Hudson's Bay Company administering it from Fort Victoria. But apart from some company farms established by the subsidiary Puget Sound Agricultural Company, little happened by way of colonization, and the main concern remained fur trading.

The discovery of gold in the Fraser River during the 1850s and 1860s brought prospectors to Victoria, British Columbia's only port and source of provisions. As a result, the area developed into a typical boomtown. When the gold fields were exhausted, Victoria continued as an administrative center. The island united with British Columbia in 1866, and in 1871, Victoria was declared the provincial capital. It was intended to be the western terminus of the Canadian Pacific Railway, but this did not come to pass and the railroad stopped at Vancouver. Industrialization also stopped at Vancouver, and Victoria was left free to build itself a reputation as a center of genteel society.

Coal Harbour divides Stanley Park from downtown's forest of highrise apartment buildings.

VICTORIA

Victoria developed into a graceful city, both conservative and relaxed. Baskets of flowers adorn the lampposts, nineteenth-century buildings have been carefully renovated, tidy lawns and flowerbeds abound. Victoria was transformed from a raucous gold rush town into a colonial fantasy of a British seaside resort.

British Columbia's capital and, with a population of nearly 350,000, the province's second-largest city, Victoria is situated around a beautiful natural harbor at the southeastern tip of the island, sheltered by the mountains of Washington

tal and tweeds in the shops, or take refreshment in one of the many pubs or tearooms.

This "forever England" image stems partly from a population that is largely of British extraction, and the mild weather and low rainfall continue to make Victoria an attractive retirement home for the British. The main employers here are government and tourism, and to keep the latter industry thriving, the Britishness is carefully preserved and reinforced wherever possible.

GENERAL INFORMATION

Victoria's **Visitor Information Centre** ((250) 953-2033 TOLL-FREE (800) 663-3883 FAX (250) 382-6539

State, which lies only 32 km (20 miles) to the south across the Juan de Fuca Strait. It boasts Canada's mildest climate, with only 68 cm (27 inches) of rainfall a year and plenty of sunshine. While the rest of Canada is struggling through snow, Victoria is busy taking its official blossom count and advising the mainland of the number of flowers already in bloom.

The love of beautiful gardens is not the only feature that Victoria has inherited from its British roots. It is a place that revels in, and capitalizes upon, its image as a last bastion of the British Empire. Traditions are fiercely preserved. In parks, people play croquet, cricket or English bowls. You can ride around the city on a red double-decker bus, stock up on Wedgwood china, Waterford crys-

WEB SITE www.tourismvictoria.com, 812 Wharf Street, on the waterfront of Inner Harbour, is open daily, mid-June to September 8:30 AM to 7:30 PM and the rest of the year 9 AM to 5 PM.

WHAT TO SEE AND DO

Downtown

Downtown Victoria is compactly laid-out within a small area, so walking is the easiest and most pleasant way of exploring it. The hub of the city is the **Inner Harbour** area, where Victoria's most majestic buildings overlook the lively little harbor's constant comings and goings of ferries, fishing boats and yachts. There are a number of ways to explore the harbor itself. The simplest is to take one of the dinky little boats that act as ferries. Ask for a voucher to hop on and hop off. They start at the piers in front of the Empress

The First Narrows leads out from Vancouver into the Strait of Georgia.

and have two routes. More spectacular are the floatplane harbor flights (or longer excursions) booked from Hyack Air/Harbour Air, who have an office on the waterside (off Wharf Street, at the bottom of Fort Street). These floatplanes will also take you to Nanaimo and Vancouver, while Kenmore Seaplanes (from the same terminal) do flights to Seattle.

A large portion of the Inner Harbour is filled with the ivied grandeur of the **Fairmont Empress Hotel** ((250) 384-8111, a resplendent castle-like building that is the heart and soul of Victoria. Designed by Francis Rattenbury and built by the Canadian Pacific Railway in 1908, the Empress became the place where Victorian polite society

501 Belleville Street, a Gothic extravaganza of towers and domes that also overlooks the harbor. Completed in 1898 and designed by the irrepressible Francis Rattenbury, these buildings remain the home of the provincial legislature. A statue of Queen Victoria dignifies the lawn to the front, statues of eminent Victorians stand on either side of the elaborate arched entrance, and the central copper-covered dome is crowned with a gilt statue of Captain George Vancouver. At night, the buildings are outlined by over 3,000 little lights. Open 8:30 AM to 5 PM, June to early September daily, the rest of the year weekdays only.

On the corner between the Empress and the Parliament Buildings stands the superb **Royal**

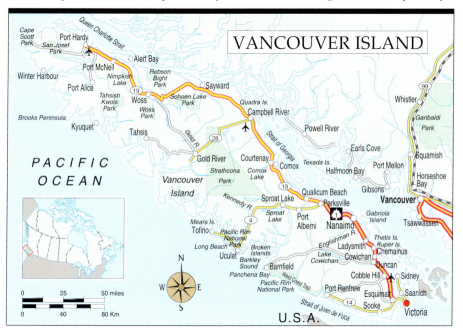

came to take tea. Today visitors flock here for afternoon tea of cucumber sandwiches and scones with jam and clotted cream, served among silver teapots and cake stands in the desperately British ambiance of the Tea Lobby. Tea at the Empress is very popular (and very expensive), so make a reservation.

Behind the hotel stands the **Crystal Garden** ((250) 953-8816 WEB SITE www.bcpcc.com/crystal, 713 Douglas Street, a large glass structure that was designed by Rattenbury and built in 1925. It once held an enormous saltwater pool, and its elegant ballroom was the scene of many social events. It is now an exotic conservatory with fish, free-flying butterflies, colorful tropical birds, lemurs and other creatures among the greenery.

Across from the Empress, neatly clipped lawns and carefully arranged flowerbeds surround the stately **Parliament Buildings** ((250) 387-3046,

British Columbia Museum ((250) 387-3701 WEB SITE www.royalbcmuseum.bc.ca, 675 Belleville Street. This is one of Canada's very best museums, devoted to all aspects of British Columbia's natural and cultural history. One floor is devoted to the natural environment, past and present, with dioramas depicting the flora and fauna of the rainforest, marshlands and seashore. The other floor covers the province's human history, using sight, sound and smell to evoke vivid impressions of the past. A reconstructed street includes a functioning cinema (with silent films) and a walk-through mine with a working waterwheel. There's a reconstruction of Captain George Vancouver's cabin on *Discovery*, and an excellent section about First Peoples that includes a reconstructed pit house and contrasts the lifestyles of the coastal and inland tribes. There's also a display of traditional and modern First Nations art and artifacts.

To the rear of the museum, **Thunderbird Park** has modern totem poles carved with the image of the legendary thunderbird. First Nations artists work in the Carving Shed from mid-May to September, weekdays 10 AM to 4 PM, weekends from noon. At the edge of the park is **Helmcken House** ((250) 361-0021 WEB SITE www.heritage.gov.bc.ca, 10 Elliot Street Square, a heritage building dating from 1852 that was originally the home of Fort Victoria's surgeon. Inside you can see period furnishings and a display of the doctor's medical equipment.

Victoria has its share of commercialized attractions, especially in the area around the Empress. One of the better ones is the **Pacific Undersea Gardens** ((250) 382-5717 WEB SITE www.pacific

can see Victoria's original City Hall, while at **Bastion Square**, site of the original Fort Victoria in 1843, the old criminal courthouse now houses the **Maritime Museum of British Columbia** ((250) 385-4222 WEB SITE www.mmbc.bc.ca, 28 Bastion Square. On display here are model ships, nautical paraphernalia and the *Tili Kum*, a Native American dugout canoe rigged for sails that voyaged from Victoria to England 100 years ago. On the top floor, the Vice-Admiralty courtroom shows a startling 25-minute film taken on one of the last square riggers to achieve a voyage round Cape Horn, in 1929. From Thursday to Sunday, Bastion Square fills with market stalls selling a variety of excellent-quality homemade goods.

underseagardens.com, 490 Belleville Street, where you descend to the bottom of the harbor to look, through glass, at a large collection of local marine life. Beside it, the **Royal London Wax Museum** ((250) 388-4461, 470 Belleville Street, has some 250 wax figures of celebrities, past and present.

For a pleasant waterfront stroll continue westwards along Belleville Street past the ferry terminals and follow the coast to **Fisherman's Wharf**, a lively spot where fishing boats come and go and houseboats are moored: a good place for (excellent) alfresco fish and chips — at **Barb's**.

The **Old Town** section of Victoria lies to the north of the Empress, along Wharf Street and the nearby streets and alleys. This area of narrow streets, squares, gaslights, cobbles and buildings dates from the 1860s. Extensively renovated, many of the old buildings now house chic cafés, restaurants and shops. At **Centennial Square** you

Government Street, particularly where it runs through the Old Town, has some of the city's most interesting stores. Here are shops that have remained unchanged for the best part of a century, stocking everything from imported tea and coffee to bone china, Irish linen and handmade cosmetics. Also along the street are outlets for Canadian arts and crafts, including hard-wearing Cowichan sweaters. Known as "Antique Row," the 500-1100 block of Fort Street is a good place for stamps, coins, rare books, antique silver and art.

On the corner of Fisgard Street and Government Street, an ornate arch known as the **Gate of Harmonious Interest** marks the entrance to Victoria's old **Chinatown**. Once a flourishing community, it was established in 1858, when many Chinese arrived to construct the Canadian Pacific Railway. Over the years Chinatown has dwindled in size and is now somewhat insignificant, but it still boasts the narrowest street in Canada, Fan Tan Alley (between Fisgard and Pandora), and has a few interesting buildings, along with restaurants and shops selling souvenirs, crafts and exotic groceries.

At the southeastern edge of downtown, behind the British Columbia Provincial Museum, **Beacon Hill Park** offers a delightful retreat and a lovely spot to picnic. This hilly parkland of gardens, wildflower meadows, trees, ponds and views stretches southwards to the Juan de Fuca Strait. At its southwestern corner a plaque marks mile 0 of the TransCanada Highway.

A couple of blocks west of the park is **Carr House ℂ** (250) 383-5843 WEB SITE www.emilycarr .com, 207 Government Street (late-May to October daily 10 AM to 5 PM), the birthplace of Emily Carr, British Columbia's best-known painter, who drew a great deal on the First Nations peoples and their cultures. The house contains some of her works as well as exhibits about her life.

Outside Downtown

About one and a half kilometers (a third of a mile) east of downtown, in the Rockland area, a nineteenth-century mansion houses the **Art Gallery of Greater Victoria ℂ** (250) 384-4101 WEB SITE www.aggv.bc.ca, 1040 Moss Street. It exhibits art from around the world and spans several periods, with many works by Emily Carr and a particularly fine collection of Japanese art, including a Shinto shrine.

Nearby stands the imposing **Craigdarroch Castle ℂ** (250) 592-5323 WEB SITE www.craigdarroc hcastle.com, 1050 Joan Crescent, a turreted baronial-style restored mansion of palatial proportions (39 rooms). It was built in 1887 by Robert Dunsmuir, a wealthy Scottish coal tycoon, in order to persuade his wife to leave her home in Scotland. The interior is richly decorated with wood paneling, stained glass and period furniture. Be prepared for 87 steps if you climb the tower.

Moving across the harbor to Victoria West, **Craigflower Farmhouse ℂ** (250) 387-4627, Admirals and Craigflower Roads, is one of Victoria's earliest buildings, dating from 1856. With original furnishings and household appliances, it makes for an interesting visit. Nearby stands the **Craigflower Schoolhouse** (daily mid-May to September noon to 4 PM), of the same era.

Also to the west is the **English Village ℂ** (250) 388-4353, 429 Lampson Street, a collection of replicated old English buildings. The highlight is the accurately reconstructed full-size **Anne Hathaway's Cottage**, furnished with sixteenth- and seventeenth-century antiques and standing in two hectares (five acres) of gardens at the **Olde England Inn**, which offers accommodation and a restaurant serving English-style meals.

Excursions from Victoria

Twenty-one kilometers (13 miles) north of downtown Victoria, on Brentwood Bay, are the outstanding **Butchart Gardens ℂ** (250) 652-4422 WEB SITE www.butchartgardens.com, 800 Benvenuto Avenue. Jenny Butchart was the wife of a wealthy cement manufacturer who, in the process of beautifying their large estate, decided to do something about the unsightly hole left by her husband's abandoned limestone quarry. In 1904 she began setting lawns, planting trees, creating beautiful arrangements of flowers, and covering the sides of the pit with ivy. The success of this sunken garden inspired the Butcharts to continue their horticultural activities, and now the public gardens

cover an area of some 22 hectares (55 acres). They include a magnificent rose garden (best seen in July); a Japanese garden with lacquered bridges, summerhouses and waterfalls; and a formal Italian garden with topiary hedges, a lily pond and statuary. In the summer you can enjoy music on the Concert Lawn and take a nighttime tour of the illuminated gardens. These are pleasure gardens, so you won't find botanical labels among the flowerbeds, but there are illustrated guides, and the Horticultural Centre can answer any questions. To drive there from downtown Victoria, take Highway 17 to the Keating Cross Road turnoff and continue west, or take the 17A direct. From the Swartz Bay ferry, take Highway 17

OPPOSITE: Dignified survivors from a previous century: a horse and carriage and the Parliament Buildings in Victoria. ABOVE: A Morris dancer.

south and turn west onto 17A at McTavish Road. For non-drivers, a regular bus (No. 75) and a frequent, more expensive (but much faster) Gray Line express shuttles run from the downtown bus station. Gray Line also operates a narrated tour, which leaves from the Empress and includes the Saanich Peninsula.

For the coastal scenery northwest of Victoria, travel north out of the city on the TransCanada Highway, and after 16 km (10 miles) you'll hit **Malahat Drive**. The road skirts Finlayson Arm and then climbs Malahat Ridge where you have views across Saanich Inlet of the Gulf Islands, the mainland, and the distant peak of Mount Baker in Washington State.

taking — runs from here to Bamfield and forms a section of the famous Pacific Rim National Park. Numbers on the trail are limited and pre-booking is essential. From here you can either retrace your steps along Highway 14 back to Victoria, or you can take the logging road to Lake Cowichan, where you have a choice of two roads, both of which connect with the TransCanada Highway at Duncan.

Northeast of Victoria, in the Strait of Georgia, lie the lovely and temperate **Southern Gulf Islands**. Artists, retirees and others drawn by the peace or the prospect of an alternative lifestyle inhabit some of the islands, which offer the visitor exceptional arts and crafts, quiet beaches,

To explore some of the beaches and forests of the southwest corner of Vancouver Island, pack your picnic hamper, maybe your tent as well, and head out of Victoria picking up Highway 14 bound for **Sooke**, some 42 km (26 miles) west of Victoria. In this logging town you'll find the **Sooke Regional Museum and Visitor Information Centre** ((250) 642-6351 TOLL-FREE (866) 888-4748 E-MAIL info@sooke.museum.bc.ca, 2070 Phillips Road, with its displays of local native craft. You can also pick up supplies for the rest of your journey in town.

North of Sooke along Highway 14, stop and follow a forest trail to one of the lovely beaches that line the coast here. The highway ends at the one-horse settlement of Port Renfrew, where you can observe some marine life in the tidal pools at **Botanical Beach** when the tide is low. The rugged **West Coast Trail** — a serious hiking under-

beautiful vistas, accommodation, fishing, diving and a host of other opportunities.

From Swartz Bay, **BC Ferries** ((250) 386-3431 TOLL-FREE (888) 223-3779 run several times daily to Salt Spring Island and to most of the other islands, although Gabriola (the most northerly) is only accessible from Nanaimo. In summer, arrive well in advance of your chosen departure time.

SPORTS AND OUTDOOR ACTIVITIES

A prime attraction of the area is **whale watching**, which is possible April to October, when the salmon are migrating through the Georgia Strait, pursued by several pods of resident orcas and some minke whales — occasionally joined by grays in mid-summer. Organizing three-hour trips is Five Star Whale Watching Adventures ((250) 388-7223 TOLL-FREE (800) 634-9617 WEB SITE www

.5starwhales.com / contact.html, 706 Douglas Street, Victoria. You can travel on a small catamaran or an even smaller custom-made Blackfin: less comfortable, but more fun.

There are plenty of places offering **boating** or **sailing** charters, with or without crew. If you'd like to learn how to do it, there are a few schools around the Oak Bay Marina ((250) 598-3369 WEB SITE www.obmg.com, 1327 Beach Drive. There are plenty of opportunities for **canoeing** and **kayaking** in the Victoria area and sports outfitters can often supply information on package trips.

There's **freshwater fishing** at Elk and Beaver lakes (particularly good for bass), about 15-minutes' drive north of Victoria, and several other

There are several **recreation centers** with pools in the Victoria area. One of the best is the Crystal Pool Recreation Centre ((250) 361-0732, 2275 Quadra Street. A bit further out, Saanich Commonwealth Place ((250) 727-5300 or 24-hour information (250) 727-7108, 4636 Elk Lake Drive, was built for the 1994 Commonwealth Games, so has excellent facilities for high-board diving and the like.

Windsurfing is quite a popular pursuit in these parts, and there are plenty of places that give lessons. Some popular spots are Cadboro Bay, east of downtown near the university, Willows Beach (Oak Bay) and Elk Lake, which is a 15-minute drive north of Victoria.

lakes and streams can be found a little further out. The waters surrounding Victoria are renowned for salmon and offer some excellent **deep-sea fishing**, so many companies in town offer charter trips. **Fishing licenses** are required, and regulations are complicated and constantly in flux; call ((604) 666-5835 for information. Licenses are available province-wide from marinas, sporting goods stores, charter boat operators and department stores.

The waters, particularly in the Georgia Strait, are excellent for **diving**, and are inhabited by a wide variety of marine life. Thetis Lake Park is a very pleasant spot for **swimming**. It is only a short drive northwest of downtown, and has a popular beach as well as more secluded spots. You'll also find some beautiful beaches on the southwest coast along the stretch of Highway 14 between Sooke and Port Renfrew.

There are good **hiking** trails around some of the parklands northwest of Victoria, and lots more along the southwest coast between Sooke and Port Renfrew. At Port Renfrew, about 107 km (66 miles) from Victoria, you could join the very challenging West Coast Trail to Bamfield (see PACIFIC RIM NATIONAL PARK, page 96).

NIGHTLIFE AND THE ARTS

Several free magazines carry entertainment listings for the area. The *Monday Magazine*, comes out on Thursday and can be found on street stands.

The **Royal Theatre**, 805 Broughton Street, and the **McPherson Playhouse**, 3 Centennial Square, are both renovated older theaters that stage plays

Victoria — OPPOSITE: Highland dancers step out. ABOVE: Rugby is another Old World activity that thrives here.

and concerts. The **University Centre Auditorium**, Finnerty Road, also stages plays and dance events. For information on all three, call ((250) 386-6121. The intimate **Belfry Theatre** ((250) 385-6835, 1291 Gladstone Street, tends towards contemporary drama.

The **Pacific Victoria Opera** ((250) 382-1641 stages three productions a year at the McPherson Playhouse, while the **Victoria Symphony** ((250) 385-9771, performs year-round, mainly at the Royal Theatre, but sometimes at the University Centre Auditorium. Their most popular event, held on the first Sunday in August, is **Symphony Splash**: they play on a barge in Inner Harbour and conclude with the *1812 Overture*, accompanied by cannons and fireworks.

Victoria holds its own 10-day annual **Jazzfest International** in late June; information from the **Victoria Jazz Society** ((250) 388-4423 TOLL-FREE (888) 671-2112 WEB SITE www.vicjazz.bc.ca.

Downtown, **Hermann's** ((250) 388-9166, 753 View Street, has lots of atmosphere, hearty food and varied live music Thursday to Monday. Priding itself on its Englishness, Victoria has several pubs that serve British-style beer. **Spinnakers Brewpub** ((250) 386-2739, 308 Catherine Street, overlooks the harbor to the west of downtown, and is a pleasant place where you can sample some of the ten or so types of ale brewed on the premises, take a brewery tour, relax with a game of darts or pool and eat well.

WHERE TO STAY

Expensive

The château-like **Fairmont Empress Hotel** ((250) 384-8111 TOLL-FREE (800) 441-1414 FAX (250) 381-4334 WEB SITE www.fairmont.com, 721 Government Street, is the island's largest and most famous hotel, built by Canadian Pacific in 1908, with 476 rooms and suites, all beautifully decorated with traditional prints. Formal dining is in the lovely Empress Room, while Kiplings' Restaurant is a more family-oriented setting. The famous afternoon tea is served in the 1920s elegance of the Tea Lobby. There is an indoor pool and the Willow Stream facility offers full spa treatments.

A member of the prestigious Preferred Hotels & Resorts Worldwide group, and undoubtedly one of the best in town, the **Hotel Grand Pacific** ((250) 386-0450 TOLL-FREE (800) 663-7550 FAX (250) 380-4475 WEB SITE www.hotelgrandpacific.com, 463 Belleville Street, has 304 rooms with views of the Olympic Mountains on one side and the Inner Harbour on the other. All the rooms and suites are comfortable, attractive and well equipped, with balconies. Local calls and Internet access are complimentary. The hotel provides delicious food in a choice of eateries, fully equipped meeting rooms and Victoria's top athletic club.

The 5-star **Abigail's Hotel** ((250) 388-5363 TOLL-FREE (800) 561-6565 FAX (250) 388-7787 WEB SITE www.abigailshotel.com, 906 McClure Street, is a heritage Tudor-style mansion with a great deal of charm, set in colorful English gardens. It has 23 rooms, all with telephones, but no television in the older rooms. The library serves as a delightful social center, with hors d'oeuvres offered in the early evening. A gourmet breakfast is included in the rate.

In complete contrast is the modern high-rise **Executive House Hotel** ((250) 388-5111 TOLL-FREE (800) 663-7001 FAX (250) 385-1323 WEB SITE www.executivehouse.com, 777 Douglas Street. One block away from the Inner Harbour, it has 179 large accommodations, including suites with self-catering facilities, a restaurant, pub and oyster bar. Pets are welcome.

The **Laurel Point Inn** ((250) 386-8721 TOLL-FREE (800) 663-7667 FAX (250) 386-9547 WEB SITE www.laurelpoint.com, 680 Montreal Street, stands on a headland overlooking the Inner Harbour, surrounded by gardens. The coolly elegant, light-wood rooms all have balconies with harbor views. Other facilities include an indoor swimming pool, sauna, Jacuzzi, free local calls and two restaurants.

The **Victoria Regent Hotel** ((250) 386-2211 TOLL-FREE (800) 663-7472 FAX (250) 386-2622 WEB SITE www.victoriaregent.com, 1234 Wharf Street, stands at the water's edge and has excellent harbor views. It has 49 well-appointed accommodations, mainly one- and two-bedroom suites, some with fireplaces and most with kitchens. Continental breakfast is included in the rate, and there is a waterside restaurant and marina facilities.

Conveniently placed for sightseeing, the **Chateau Victoria Hotel** ((250) 382-4221 TOLL-FREE (800) 663-5891 FAX (250) 380-1950 WEB SITE www.chateauvictoria.com, 740 Burdett Avenue, is a high-rise building with 178 rooms and suites, each with cable television and a data port. From the sixth floor up, each has a balcony and kitchenette. Hotel facilities include indoor pool, whirlpool, exercise room and Internet access. On the eighteenth floor, the Vista 18 restaurant provides panoramic views. At street level, Jane's Lobby Lounge bar and restaurant provides good food in a comfortable setting.

If you go to the South Gulf island of Salt Spring, consider staying at **Hastings House** ((250) 537-2362 FAX (250) 537-5333 WEB SITE www.hastingshouse.com, 160 Upper Ganges Road, Salt Spring Island, which belongs to the prestigious Relais & Châteaux chain and has 18 lovely rooms and suites well stocked with life's little luxuries. The half-timbered main house resembles an old English country manor; the other buildings are conversions from a barn, farmhouse and trading post, all set in lovely grounds with views of Ganges Harbour. First-class gourmet food is served in the graceful dining room. The price includes full English breakfast and afternoon tea. Book well in advance.

Just outside Victoria (about 40 km or 24 miles from Victoria International Airport), the **Aerie Resort** ((250) 743-7115 FAX (250) 743-4766 WEB SITE www.aerie.bc.ca, 600 Ebedora Lane, Malahat, is another lovely Relais & Château property, with a superb location offering breathtaking views across the fjords and Olympic Mountains. The sumptuous Mediterranean-style mansion with 29 rooms is surrounded by acres of parkland. Activities abound, with tennis, fishing, sailing and hiking on site, golf and wineries close by. When the day is done, the pool, spa, sauna, massages and whirlpool soothe the body.

birthplace, Anne Hathaway's cottage and the like; they are just a short drive west of downtown, in the Esquimalt district. Genuine sixteenth- to eighteenth-century antiques, including some canopy beds, furnish the rooms. The bathrooms are not, thankfully, sixteenth-century replicas.

Mid-range

Some five kilometers (three miles) east of downtown the delightful seaside, Tudor-style **Oak Bay Beach Hotel** ((250) 598-4556 TOLL-FREE (800) 668-7758 FAX (250) 598-6180 WEB SITE www.oakbay beachhotel.com, 1175 Beach Drive, has antiques in the lovely lobby, and rooms that all differ in size and design. The hotel operates dinner cruises,

On the southwest coast of the island, try the **Sooke Harbour House** ((250) 642-3421 FAX (250) 642-6988 WEB SITE www.sookeharbourhouse.com, 1528 Whiffen Spit Road, Sooke, about 42 km (26 miles) from Victoria. Primarily an internationally famous gourmet restaurant, this large white house, perched high above a bay, also has 28 luxurious guestrooms, each with original artworks and antiques. All rooms have fireplaces, most have balconies or sun decks, some have four-poster beds and two-person Jacuzzis. Rates include breakfast and lunch, and special honeymoon packages are available.

For some fantasy accommodation try the **Olde England Inn** ((250) 388-4353 FAX (250) 382-8311 WEB SITE www.oldeenglandinn.com, 429 Lampson Street. It is part of a group of reconstructed sixteenth-century English buildings (some only façades) that include replicas of Shakespeare's

whale-watching tours and fishing charters from the nearby marina, and has an English-style pub and seaside dining room.

Close to Parliament, the **James Bay Inn** ((250) 384-7151 TOLL-FREE (800) 836-2649 FAX (250) 385-2311 WEB SITE www.jamesbayinn.bc.ca, 270 Government Street (inexpensive to mid-range), is a large old house with character that offers good value and is thus very popular. The 43 rooms vary in amenities and size — all have private baths and some have kitchenettes.

The **Strathcona Hotel** ((250) 383-7137 TOLL-FREE (800) 663-7476 FAX (250) 383-6893 WEB SITE www.strathconahotel.com, 919 Douglas Street, is an old building bursting with character, which also houses a pub, a restaurant, a rooftop patio and

The beautiful Butchart Gardens on Tod Inlet outside Victoria.

Legends — one of the hottest nightspots in town. It's very good value for a downtown location.

The **Cherry Bank Hotel (** (250) 385-5380 TOLL-FREE (800) 998-6688 E-MAIL cherrybank@pacific coast.net, 825 Burdett Avenue, is a late nineteenth-century building with new extensions. The rooms are simply furnished, without phones and some have no television, but they are clean and adequate. There's a restaurant and bar, and a full English breakfast is included in the rate.

The **Accent Inn (** (250) 475-7500 TOLL-FREE (800) 663-0298 FAX (250) 475-7599 WEB SITE WWW .accentinns.com, 3233 Maple Street, is part of a family-oriented chain that is solidly mid-range but good quality and has an attached restaurant.

Victoria has an abundance of **bed and break-fasts**, ranging from basic to luxurious (see WHERE TO STAY, page 79 under VANCOUVER). For B&Bs on Salt Spring Island, contact the **Visitor Information Centre (** (250) 537-5252 FAX (250) 537-4276 WEB SITE www.saltspringtoday.com, 121 Lower Ganges Road, Salt Spring Island (daily 10 AM to 3 PM with longer hours in peak season).

WHERE TO EAT

Expensive

Sooke Harbour House ((250) 642-3421, 1528 Whiffen Spit Road, 42 km (26 miles) west of Victoria, is one of Canada's best restaurants and offers some truly

Inexpensive

Paul's Motor Inn ((250) 382-9231 FAX (250) 384-1435 WEB SITE www.paulsmotorinn.com, 1900 Douglas Street, is a 78-room award-winning motel, located downtown, with a 24-hour restaurant.

Hostelling International-Victoria ((250) 385-4511 TOLL-FREE (888) 883-0099 FAX (250) 385-3232 E-MAIL victoria@hihostels.bc.ca, downtown at 516 Yates Street, is a large (110 beds), modern place with both mixed and single-sex dormitories, as well as some private rooms, and good kitchen facilities. Reservations are essential in peak season.

The University of Victoria, six kilometers (four miles) east of downtown, offers **campus accommodation** (May to August only). For details contact the **University of Victoria Housing and Conference Services (** (250) 721-8395, Box 1700, Victoria V8W 2Y2.

memorable dining. This large white house, perched on a bluff overlooking a bay, has a spectacular view of the Juan de Fuca Strait and the Olympic Mountains. The menu changes daily, but expect to find flowers liberally used (in delightful salads and as garnish), the freshest of fish and free-range chicken. The presentation is pure artistry, the service knowledgeable and the atmosphere informal.

Dinner is a far more formal affair (tie required) at the distinguished **Empress Room (** (250) 384-8111 in the Fairmont Empress Hotel, 721 Government Street. Wooden ceilings, pillars and chandeliers create a setting that is splendidly traditional, while the menu features Pacific Northwest cuisine and holds some pleasant surprises.

Moderate to Inexpensive

Il Terrazzo ((250) 361-0028, 555 Johnson Street (off Waddington Alley), serves first-class Italian food in an old-style courtyard setting. The wood-oven roasted meats and pizzas, homemade pastas and fresh seafood consistently win awards, as does the wine list; reservations are recommended.

Pagliacci's ((250) 386-1662, 1011 Broad Street, serves dependable Italian food and prides itself on the desserts. There's usually a line outside and it is cramped inside, but everyone is very friendly.

Vegetarians (including vegans) and non-vegetarians alike will adore **Re-Bar** ((250) 361-9223, 50 Bastion Square. It's a plain, but bright and cheerful, place with excellent innovative dishes — so popular they now publish a recipe book. There's a slightly Bohemian air about the **Herald Street Caffe** ((250) 381-1441, 546 Herald Street,

For authentic Japanese food try the **Japanese Village Steak & Seafood House** ((250) 382-5165, 734 Broughton Street. If English-style is more to your taste, go to **Old Vic Fish & Chips** ((250) 383-4536, 1316 Broad Street, or, on a rather more dignified note, take afternoon tea at the **James Bay Tea Room and Restaurant** ((250) 382-8282, at 332 Menzies Street.

Ferris' Oyster Bar & Grill ((250) 360-1824, 536 Yates Street, is a casual place that specializes in oysters but does not neglect other good seafood — and meat. For a really filling and delicious snack, look no further than **Sam's Deli** ((250) 382-8424, 805 Government Street, where sandwiches are made to order.

where you can inspect the work of local artists and enjoy some extremely good New World-refined French food and an extensive wine list. For East Indian food, try the **Taj Mahal** ((250) 383-4662, 679 Herald Street, an award-winning MSG-free zone that caters well to vegetarians. Along Fisgard Street in Chinatown, a good number of restaurants serve Sichuan, Hunan and Cantonese food.

Swans Brewpub ((250) 361-3310, 506 Pandora Avenue, occupies a heritage building and supplies home-brewed ales, along with live music Sunday to Thursday nights. A little away from downtown, but still overlooking Inner Harbour, **Spinnakers Brewpub & Guesthouse** ((250) 386-2739, 308 Catherine Street, is Canada's oldest in-house pub brewery, offering over a dozen ales, as well as home-baked bread and a wide-ranging menu that blends contemporary and traditional fare. Reservations are recommended.

HOW TO GET THERE

Victoria International Airport is about 26 km (16 miles) north of downtown. The **Airporter shuttle** ((250) 386-2526 meets all incoming flights and delivers passengers to hotels and some B&Bs. The trip to downtown takes around half an hour.

Victoria is served by more than 50 flights each day from Vancouver International Airport and Seattle-Tacoma Airport, in addition to numerous direct flights from other major cities. Regular floatplane services to downtown Victoria are available from a number of operators in Vancouver and Seattle.

Helijet ((250) 382-6222 or (604) 273-1414 TOLL-FREE (800) 665-4354 WEB SITE www.helijet.com, 5911 Airport Road South, operates fairly frequent

OPPOSITE: The Victoria Eaton Centre.
ABOVE: Afternoon tea in the Empress Hotel.

Sikorsky helicopter flights between Victoria (Inner Harbour, with minibus shuttle to hotels) or Vancouver (close to Canada Place, the airport, Langley, Grouse and Abbotsford) and Seattle. Both journeys take about 35 minutes, and the flying altitude is low, so the views are splendid.

The *Victoria Clipper* is a jet-propelled catamaran, for foot passengers only, that crosses between Victoria (Inner Harbour) and Seattle (Pier 69) in two to three hours, daily year-round — there are frequent sailings in summer, one per day in winter. Contact **Clipper Vacations** ((250) 382-8100 or (206) 448-5000 TOLL-FREE (800) 888-2535 WEB SITE www.victoriaclipper.com, 2701 Alaskan Way, Pier 69, Seattle, for details and reservations.

BC Ferries ((250) 386-3431 TOLL-FREE (888) 223-3779 WEB SITE www.bcferries.com, 1112 Fort Street, operate between Vancouver and Vancouver Island. From Tsawwassen, south of Vancouver on the mainland, ferries sail several times daily to both Victoria and Nanaimo. They also operate between Horseshoe Bay (30 minutes north of Vancouver) and Nanaimo and provide services to the Gulf Islands, Sunshine Coast, Inside Passage, Queen Charlotte Islands and Discovery Coast Passage.

Pacific Coach Lines ((250) 385-3348 or (604) 662-7575 TOLL-FREE (800) 661-1725 WEB SITE www.pacificcoach.com, 660-1070 Douglas Street, Victoria, or 210-1150 Station Street, Vancouver, operates a bus link from the Vancouver bus station, airport or ferry terminal to Victoria (downtown or the airport). PCL also provide a variety of sightseeing tours throughout the province.

Black Ball Transport ((250) 386-2202 or (206) 457-4491, 430 Belleville Street in Port Angeles, runs a ferry between Victoria's Inner Harbour and Port Angeles on Washington's Olympic Peninsula; it operates four times daily in summer, twice in winter, taking an hour and 35 minutes. **Washington State Ferries** ((250) 656-1531, (250) 381-1551 or (206) 464-6400 TOLL-FREE (888) 808-7977 2499 Ocean Avenue, Sidney, operate year-round at least once daily, between Sidney, just north of Victoria, and Anacortes, Washington, with ports of call in the San Juan Islands (crossing time is approximately three hours).

Island Coach and Gray Line, both owned by Greyhound and based at the 700 Douglas Street terminal, provide the island's bus services. **Island Coach Lines** ((250) 385-4411 TOLL-FREE (800) 318-0818 handles all the scheduled runs, linking Victoria and Nanaimo several times a day (with stops at all major points between them) and running from Nanaimo to most other towns on the island. **Gray Line of Victoria** ((250) 388-5248 TOLL-FREE (800) 663-8390 arranges tours of Victoria and excursions to all the island's major points of interest. Information about both can be found at WEB SITE www.victoriatours.com and www.grayline.ca/victoria.

ELSEWHERE ON THE ISLAND

DUNCAN AND VICINITY

The rural town of Duncan, 60 km (38 miles) north of Victoria on the TransCanada Highway, is the gateway and supply center to the **Cowichan Valley**. The valley is still home to many Cowichan, and indigenous craftsmen have collaborated with the town to produce over 80 totem poles, clustered along the roadside. This is a good place to buy one of the famous Cowichan sweaters, as well as other native arts and crafts. Duncan's premiere attraction is the **Quw'utsun' Cultural and Conference Centre** ((250) 746-8119 TOLL-FREE (877) 746-8119 WEB SITE www.quwutsun.ca, 200 Cowichan Way, on a five-hectare (13-acre), tree-lined stretch of the Cowichan River. At the Longhouse Story Centre, a film explains the history and legends of the Cowichan people. At the carving house, you can see artisans at work, and attempt to do some handicrafts.

Highway 18 takes you 31 km (19 miles) westwards to **Lake Cowichan**, the largest freshwater lake on the island. Known mainly for good fishing, it also has good swimming, camping and canoeing, and the surrounding forest is laced with hiking trails.

About two kilometers (just over a mile) north of Duncan, the **BC Forest Discovery Centre** ((250) 715-1113 WEB SITE www.bcforestmuseum.com, 2892 Drinkwater Road, covers 40 hectares (100 acres) and offers a fascinating look at the history of the forestry industry in the province. Here you can take a ride on a narrow-gauge steam railway, visit a reconstructed logging camp, see old equipment, and walk through the surrounding forest.

Twenty kilometers (12 miles) north along the highway from Duncan lies the interesting town of **Chemainus**. To avert the disaster that threatened when the town's sawmill closed down in 1983, the community set out to find itself a new source of revenue by commissioning murals, often with historic themes, to grace the town's buildings. The idea worked: visitors came to look, shops and restaurants opened, and murals depicting the town's history have spread like wildfire, covering not only walls but also litter bins and anything else that stands still long enough. BC Ferries operates frequently from here to nearby **Thetis Island**, part of the Southern Gulf archipelago.

A little further north, the attractive waterfront town of **Ladysmith** sits right on the 49th parallel, which divides the mainland between Canada and the United States (aside from Vancouver Island). The old buildings here have been nicely renovated, and it makes a pleasant place to stop.

The **Best Western Cowichan Valley Inn** ((250) 748-2722 TOLL-FREE (800) 927-6199 FAX (250) 748-

2207 E-MAIL bwcvi@island.net, 6474 TransCanada Highway, Rural Route 4, Duncan, opposite the BC Forest Discovery Centre (mid-range), offers 42 comfortable rooms and suites, a dining room and a pub.

At Ladysmith, the **Yellow Point Lodge** ((250) 245-7422 FAX (250) 245-7411 WEB SITE www.yellowpointlodge.com, 3700 Yellow Point Road, Rural Route 3, is set in delightful parkland overlooking the sea. Accommodation is either in the main lodge or in rustic cottages. Facilities include a saltwater pool, bicycles, kayaks and tennis courts. Rates are mid-range to expensive, but include three full meals. Guests must be at least 14 years of age.

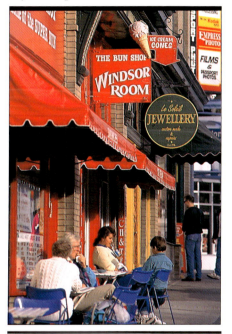

NANAIMO

Nanaimo, 110 km (68 miles) north of Victoria, is the second-largest city on Vancouver Island and a major deep-sea fishing port. Several First Nations tribes lived in peaceful coexistence here until the Hudson's Bay Company discovered coal in the 1850s. Nanaimo remained a thriving coal mining area until demand dwindled with the coming of the oil-burning ships, at which point it turned to logging and fishing. Now an important BC Ferries terminus with a direct link to the mainland, the town has adapted itself to the tourist industry. Renovated buildings, smart boutiques, jolly festivals and inhabitants renowned for their friendliness draw many visitors and facilities are increasing.

The **Visitor Information Centre** ((250) 756-0106 TOLL-FREE (800) 663-7337 WEB SITE www.tourismnanaimo.com, Beban House, 2290 Bowen Road, is just one kilometer (half a mile) off Highway 19. In summer there's a more convenient office in the Bastion. **Tourism Vancouver Island** ((250) 754-3000 WEB SITE www.islands.bc.ca or www.SeeTheIslands.com has an office at 203-335 Wesley Street.

In 1853 the Hudson's Bay Company built the fortified **Bastion**, Front Street, in case of attack. Now the symbol of Nanaimo, this stout fort serves as a museum (July and August, Wednesday to Sunday 9 AM to 5 PM), and during the summer months there's a ceremonial cannon firing each day at noon. If you're curious to find out a little more about Nanaimo's history, visit the **Nanaimo District Museum** ((250) 753-1821, 100 Cameron Street.

For the more active, the **Bungy Zone Adrenalin Centre** ((250) 753-5867 TOLL-FREE (800) 668-7771 WEB SITE www.bungyzone.com, 35 Nanaimo River Road, 13 km (eight miles) from Nanaimo, offers bungy jumping as well as other activities, adventurous and otherwise.

The wealth of parks and lakes in and around Nanaimo gives anglers, boaters, canoeists, kayakers, windsurfers, divers and hikers plentiful opportunities to pursue their sports. Departure Bay at the north end of town is a popular windsurfing spot. If island-hopping appeals to you, there's a regular BC Ferry service to nearby **Gabriola Island**, which, although home to a small artistic community, remains unspoiled and peaceful, with some lovely beaches. **Newcastle Island**, accessible by foot-passenger ferry from May to September, is a provincial park inhabited only by wildlife, park keepers and campers.

Just south of Nanaimo look for **Petroglyph Provincial Park**, where you can see prehistoric carvings on the sandstone rock that were made by native people some 10,000 years ago.

The best place to stay is the **Coast Bastion Inn** ((250) 753-6601 TOLL-FREE (800) 663-1144 FAX (250) 753-4155 WEB SITE www.coasthotels.com, 11 Bastion Street, a large hotel on the waterfront, with pleasant views from all of its rooms (mid-range). Many rooms and suites at the **Best Western Dorchester Hotel** ((250) 754-6835 TOLL-FREE (800) 661-2449 FAX (250) 754-2638 WEB SITE www.dorchesternanaimo.com, 70 Church Street, have harbor views, while all rooms have a wide range of facilities (mid-range). Pets are welcome. The always reliable **Howard Johnson Harbourside Hotel** ((250) 753-2241 TOLL-FREE (800) 146-4656 FAX (250) 753-6722 E-MAIL hojonanaimo@home.com, 1 Terminal Avenue, offers full facilities, including an à la carte restaurant, a comfortable lounge area, nightclub and outdoor swimming pool (mid-range).

Vancouver Island's mild weather favors outdoor cafés.

PARKSVILLE TO PORT ALBERNI

About 38 km (24 miles) north of Nanaimo, Parksville lies along a coastal stretch popular for its lovely sandy beaches and waters said to be the warmest in Canada. To the west of Parksville lie wooded slopes threaded with nature trails, and the nearby Mount Arrowsmith biosphere reserve, which attracts outdoor enthusiasts. This is also where the scenic Highway 4 cuts westwards, crossing the island's central mountain range and leading to its star attraction — the magnificent Pacific Rim National Park, 154 km (96 miles) away.

After about five kilometers (three miles) along Highway 4A, a deviation of about eight kilometers (five miles) to the left will bring you to **Englishman River Falls Provincial Park**, where the Englishman River rushes over waterfalls down into lush, ferny forest, and brims with rainbow trout and steelhead. On Highway 4A, **Coombs** is noteworthy for a market with goats grazing on the grass-topped roof. It's worth stopping here to see the **Butterfly World & Gardens (** (250) 248-7026 WEB SITE www.nature-world.com, home to hundreds of free-flying butterflies, tropical finches (12 species) and hummingbirds.

A further 20 km (12 miles) along Highway 4, the **Little Qualicum Falls Provincial Park** has a

ABOVE: The fearsome image of the thunderbird sits atop a totem pole in Victoria's Thunderbird Park. OPPOSITE: The handsome caboose of a vintage Canadian Pacific Railroad train.

forest trail leading to a series of waterfalls and ice-cold pools. Nearby tree-fringed **Cameron Lake** teems with fish. About nine kilometers (five and a half miles) along the road, in **MacMillan Provincial Park**, the magnificent **Cathedral Grove** is an awesome sight that is not to be missed. Some of the Douglas firs and Western red cedars in this grove are 800 years old and reach heights of 76 meters (250 ft).

Halfway across the island, **Port Alberni** sits at the head of the deep-cutting Alberni Inlet that widens into the West Coast's Barkley Sound. It is a large town founded on the lumber industry. Its other main revenue comes from fishing, as anglers come here for the excellent salmon. From the harbor, the stately **MV** *Lady Rose* and the larger *Frances Barkley* **(** (250) 723-8313 WEB SITE www.ladyrosemarine.com take passengers down the inlet to Bamfield (year-round) and Ucluelet (summer only) via the Broken Islands. Those intending to canoe or kayak around the Broken Islands are allowed to take their vessel aboard. You can rent whatever equipment you need for canoeing, kayaking or diving from outlets in Port Alberni.

From Port Alberni, Highway 4 continues towards the West Coast by **Sproat Lake**, which attracts many water-sports enthusiasts and anglers, through some beautiful mountain scenery, marred only by evidence of extensive logging. The road follows the Kennedy River to Kennedy Lake, and then reaches the junction with the Ucluelet road, where it bends sharply to the right and continues to Tofino.

There's a wide choice of motels and resorts in Parksville; Port Alberni offers several motels. On the east coast there's some interesting accommodation at **Qualicum Heritage Inn (** (250) 752-9262 TOLL-FREE (800) 663-7306 FAX (250) 752-5144 WEB SITE www.qualicumheritageinn.com, 427 College Road, Qualicum Beach (mid-range). This historic landmark building, once a boys' school, overlooks the sea and has 70 rooms, including a few honeymoon suites. Fishing and golfing packages are available.

PACIFIC RIM NATIONAL PARK

The ruggedly beautiful coastal strip that constitutes Pacific Rim National Park Reserve **(** (250) 726-7721 WEB SITE www.parkscan.harbour.com/pacrim stretches for a dramatic 72 km (45 miles) between Tofino and Port Renfrew and is made up of three sections, all very different in character and equally rich in wildlife. The most northerly section, known as **Long Beach**, lies between the villages of Tofino and Ucluelet and is a driftwood-strewn stretch of white sand and rock pounded by Pacific breakers. The Wickaninnish Centre is found at south end of Long Beach (mid-March to mid-October daily 10:30 AM to 6 PM).

This interpretive center focuses on the natural and human aspects of the region, as well as providing information about current happenings; it also has a restaurant.

The weather is generally cold and wet here, but undeterred sportsmen and women don wetsuits to enjoy some superb surfing, swimming, canoeing and kayaking. Hikers wrap up warmly and explore the magnificent trails through the rainforest. Porpoises, sea lions and seals inhabit the waters. Gray whales can be spotted here, most frequently during the spring when they return from their breeding grounds in the south. **Radar Hill** offers a good viewing point, but for closer views there are whale-spotting boat trips from Tofino. Humbler marine life can be seen in the tidal pools along the beach — you can look, but you are not allowed to remove any of the little creatures. Another interesting trip from Tofino runs to **Meares Island**, where you can follow trails through unspoiled rainforest that has some ancient trees of majestic proportions.

The middle section of the park consists of the **Broken Islands group**, 100 or so islands in Barkley Sound that can be reached (April to September) by the MV *Lady Rose* passenger ship (see PARKSVILLE TO PORT ALBERNI, above), by charter from Port Alberni, or by boat from Ucluelet. The islands are popular with canoeists and kayakers, and the area also offers some wonderful scuba diving with plenty of shipwrecks to be seen (the area is known as the "Graveyard of the Pacific"), not to mention the world's largest species of octopus.

Many visitors come to Pacific Rim for the third section of the park, the **West Coast Trail**, a tough hiking path stretching 77 km (48 miles) between Bamfield and Port Renfrew. The trail follows a historic lifesaving route for shipwrecked mariners. It requires stamina and endurance, and hikers must carry all food and supplies for the six-to eight-day trek. This trail has become so popular that a quota system limits the number of walkers to 52 per day. Trailheads are at Gordon River and Pachena Bay. Advance reservations are recommended and can be made by calling ((250) 387-1642 or (604) 663-6000 TOLL-FREE (800) 435-5622. There is a non-refundable reservation charge. For more information on the West Coast Trail, call the **Bamfield (Pachena Bay) Infocentre** ((250) 728-3234 or the **Port Renfrew (Gordon River) Infocentre** ((250) 647-5434.

At the entrance to Barkley Sound, the little town of **Bamfield** is notable because its main highway is the inlet that divides it into two. A boardwalk two kilometers (one mile) long links East and West Bamfield.

Most of the accommodation in the area is to be found in Tofino and Ucluelet. In recent years, fishing charters, lodges, resorts and other kinds of accommodation have appeared in Bamfield

in response to the growing demands of tourism, but during the high season the town still groans under the influx of tourists, mainly fishermen, so everything fills up quickly. Reservations are usually essential for all three places — and for camping at Green Point in the Pacific Rim National Park.

You can explore Pacific Rim and the Broken Islands in high style from the secluded **Eagle Nook Ocean Wilderness Resort** ((250) 723-1000 TOLL-FREE (800) 760-2777 FAX (250) 723-6609 or (425) 771-4518 WEB SITE www.wildernessget away.com, Vernon Bay, Barkley Sound, Port Alberni (mid-May to mid-October; expensive). Eagle Nook is accessible only by floatplane, the resort's own water taxi or ferry from Port Alberni (the MV *Lady Rose* calls).

Clayoquot Wilderness Resort ((250) 726-8235 TOLL-FREE (888) 333-5405 FAX (250) 726-8558 WEB SITE www.wildretreat.com, Quait Bay (expensive), is a similar set-up, with a helipad, 30 minutes from Tofino by water, less by floatplane. It's a real wilderness outpost, set in temperate forest, with three private lakes, a floating lodge, riding horses, a spa and a variety of facilities.

QUALICUM BEACH TO CAMPBELL RIVER

Ten kilometers (six miles) north of Parksville, **Qualicum Beach** is a popular spot for anglers, sunbathers and swimmers, with plenty of accommodation and facilities. Alternatively, there are the quiet beaches of **Denman** and **Hornby Islands**, home to small communities and accessible by BC Ferries.

A little further north, the towns of **Comox** and **Courtenay** sit in the lovely **Comox Valley**. Both are commercial centers that also serve as bases for the surrounding recreational areas. Golf courses, fishing lodges, mountain trails and campsites abound, and during the winter skiers flock to the nearby slopes of **Mount Washington** and Strathcona Park's **Forbidden Plateau**.

Campbell River, the gateway to Strathcona Park, is another town dedicated to outdoor sports, with skiing, hiking, mountaineering and canoeing. The scuba diving here is very highly rated, but above all it is famous for its salmon fishing, which is probably the best anywhere. Its first-class fishing lodges attract enthusiasts from all around the world. It is hardly surprising, therefore, that the town's central attraction seems to be the **Discovery Pier**, a boardwalk that has shelter and facilities for anglers.

If you want to get a real feeling for the area, contact **Island Adventure Tours** ((250) 812-7103 WEB SITE www.islandadventuretours.com, 1032 Oliphant Street, Campbell River, which runs a series of tours combining First Nations culture with wildlife.

From Campbell River it is well worth a trip on the ferry to historic **Quadra Island** to see the **Kwagiulth Museum and Cultural Centre** ((250) 285-3733, Cape Mudge, which displays some fascinating carvings and ceremonial objects, many of which were seized by the authorities during the banning of potlatches — elaborate ceremonies involving ritual and feasting that were deemed heathen by the church. The Canadian government outlawed potlatches in 1884 as part of a forced-assimilation program. The ban was lifted in 1951.

From Campbell River, Highway 28 runs west to **Strathcona Park**, the largest on Vancouver Island. It is a magnificent preserve of wilderness and wildlife that contains the **Golden Hinde**, the

main lodge, its wings or in cottages. The lodge organizes just about any kind of package you could want.

At the **Strathcona Park Lodge** ((250) 286-3122 FAX (250) 286-6010 WEB SITE www.strathcona.bc.ca, 45 km (28 miles) west of Campbell River on Highway 28, there are campsites, hostels, apartments, cottages and chalets (mid-range). The lodge organizes packages for every kind of outdoor sport, including rock climbing, canoeing and sailing.

Tsa-Kwa-Luten Lodge ((250) 285-2042 TOLL-FREE (800) 665-7745 FAX (250) 285-2532 E-MAIL tkllodge@connected.bc.ca, Lighthouse Road, Quadra Island is owned and operated by the Cape Mudge First Nations band (open May to

island's highest peak, as well as the magnificent **Della Falls**. Highway 28 cuts westwards across Strathcona Park to the small town of **Gold River**, where a converted mine sweeper, the *Uchuck III* ((250) 283-2515 WEB SITE www.mvuchuck.com will take you along Nootka Sound to **Friendly Cove** (year-round), the place where Captain Cook first landed and met with the indigenous population in 1778.

Comox and Courtenay both have a full range of accommodation, and at Campbell River there are plenty of fishing lodges and other accommodation. One of the most distinguished lodges in town is the **Painter's Lodge Holiday and Fishing Resort** ((250) 286-1102 TOLL-FREE (800) 663-7090 FAX (250) 286-0158 WEB SITE www.painterslodge.com, 1625 MacDonald Road, Campbell River (April to October; mid-range to expensive). It overlooks the ocean, and guests can stay in the

September; mid-range). Here guests can enjoy authentic Pacific Coast native architecture, relax in an environment steeped in native history, culture and architecture, and dine in the Big House where traditional West Coast fare is served. Accommodation is in the comfortable main lodge or waterfront cottages. All the typical island activities can be pursued here, including hiking, mountain biking, paddling, scuba diving, fishing and beach-combing.

NORTH ISLAND

The best reason for a stop at **Port McNeill** is to take the ferry to the island of **Alert Bay**, home of the **U'Mista Cultural Centre** ((250) 974-5403, a

On Vancouver Island's Barkeley Sound eagles are so numerous that locals joke, "They're like crows to us."

two-kilometer (1.2-mile) walk from the dock. Excellent films on Northwest Coast aboriginal culture are shown, and there's a display of confiscated ceremonial masks once used for potlatch ceremonies.

The island is also a good place for **whale watching** June to October. **Seasmoke/Sea Orca Whale Watching** (/FAX (250) 974-5225 TOLL-FREE (800) 668-6722, Alert Bay, has been leading killer-whale watching educational tours since 1986. You can choose a five-hour tour aboard their sailing yacht or a four-hour motor cruise. Another long-established outfit is a family affair: **Mackay Whale Watching** ((250) 956-9865 TOLL-FREE (877) 663-6722 WEB SITE www.whaletime.com. From

www.ph-chamber.bc.ca, 7250 Market Street (8:30 AM to 5 PM, daily in summer, weekdays in winter). They offer a free reservation service. If a hotel is more your style, the locally owned and operated **Airport Inn** ((250) 949-9434 TOLL-FREE (888) 218-2224 WEB SITE www.airportinn-porthardy.com, 4030 Byng Road, is a reliable choice.

HOW TO GET THERE

A few regular airlines link Vancouver Island cities with Vancouver. There are also regular float-plane flights between Nanaimo and the mainland. Floatplanes are the best way to reach the more remote places.

June to October daily they operate from Port McNeill, with hydrophone-equipped vessels.

Telegraph Cove makes an interesting stop. It began in 1912 as a one-room telegraph station and is now a magnet for fishermen, kayakers, ornithologists, and grizzly bear and orca watchers.

Further north the highway ends at **Port Hardy**, where BC Ferries ply the scenic Inside Passage to and from Prince Rupert, a 441-km (274-mile) journey (see CRUISE THE INSIDE PASSAGE, page 16 in TOP SPOTS). For the intrepid, trails run from Port Hardy to the splendidly isolated **Cape Scott Provincial Park** and **San Josef Bay**.

The Inside Passage ferry leaves from **Port Hardy** early in the morning, so most passengers spend the night somewhere in the vicinity. Always reserve on nights before ferry departures. For bed-and-breakfast listings, contact the **Port Hardy Visitor Information Centre** ((250) 949-7622 WEB SITE

BC Ferries ((250) 386-3431 TOLL-FREE (888) 223-3779 run between Port Hardy in the northern part of the island and Prince Rupert on the mainland. This scenic trip along the Inside Passage takes 15 hours, with ferries operating every second day in the summer and once a week in winter. Reservations are required. BC Ferries also connects Vancouver with Nanaimo's Duke Point: two hours from Tsawwassen or one and a half hours from Horseshoe Bay.

Island Coach Lines ((250) 385-4411 TOLL-FREE (800) 318-0818 WEB SITE www.victoriatours .com is the scheduled bus service linking the towns on Vancouver Island.

ABOVE: A kayaker's view of Barkeley Sound near Pacific Rim National Park — the roots of an ancient tree are claimed by the salt water. OPPOSITE: Sea anemones in a Pacific Rim tidal pool.

If you're traveling by car, the road that connects Victoria to the North Island is Highway 1 to Nanaimo, then Highway 19 all the way to Port Hardy. To reach Ucluelet and Tofino on the West Coast you need to take Highway 4 from Parksville. For rail and bus links, see HOW TO GET THERE, page 93 under VICTORIA).

THE OKANAGAN VALLEY

The Okanagan Valley is a beautiful ribbon of valleys, lakes and beaches in south-central British Columbia, stretching roughly 180 km (112 miles) from Osoyoos near the United States border to Vernon in the north. It is centered on the Okanagan River and a long string of lakes; the largest is the magnificent 144-km (90-mile) Lake Okanagan. According to First Nations legend, this is the home of the serpent-monster N'ha-A-Itk, or "Lake Demon," called Ogopogo in English, after the popular nineteenth-century music hall tune, "The Ogopogo Song." The lakes are surrounded by arid, rolling hills, lakeside provincial parks, smooth beaches and, inevitably, vacation resorts. Highway 97 runs the length of the valley; those who travel it can appreciate the fascinating Okanagan landscape that changes from a "pocket desert" around Osoyoos, where cactus thrives and rainfall is lightest, to the green farmlands in the north. Throughout the valley orchards flourish, and many believe the Okanagan is at its most seductive during April and May, when blossoms cover the trees and their scent fills the air.

The valley averages some 2,000 hours of sunshine a year, summers are hot, winters are mild and rainfall is low. This congenial climate, together with the vast tract of water, has turned the area into a major fruit-producing region. Vineyards cover the hillsides and 36 of the province's 68 licensed wineries are here (many others have licenses pending), extending a warm welcome to the visitors. The various fruit harvests are celebrated with events and festivals and the whole valley joins in the biggest and jolliest of all — the 10-day **Okanagan Fall Wine Festival** in October. For full details contact ((250) 861-6654 WEB SITE www.owfs.com.

The valley has the largest concentration of population in the interior, centered on the towns of Kelowna, Penticton and Vernon. It has also become a popular vacation spot and attracts Canadians from colder regions, who come to soak up some of the abundant sunshine. In and around the main towns, vacation resorts line the lakes and spread over the hillsides. There are waterslide parks and theme parks for the kids, or if you are in search of quieter beauty spots, rent a car, so you can stop where you please to appreciate the variation in the scenery.

GENERAL INFORMATION

Thompson Okanagan Regional Tourism ((250) 860-5999 TOLL-FREE (800) 567-2275 WEB SITE www.ThompsonOkanagan.com, 1332 Water Street, Kelowna, offers information on the whole region. For more localized information contact **Tourism Kelowna** ((250) 861-1515 TOLL-FREE (800) 663-4345 WEB SITE www.kelownachamber.org, 544 Harvey Avenue, Kelowna, or **Penticton Visitor Information Centre** ((250) 493-4055 TOLL-FREE (800) 663-5052 WEB SITE www.penticton.org, 888 Westminster Avenue West. Vernon has a year-round **Travel Infocentre** ((250) 542-1415 TOLL-FREE (800) 665-0795

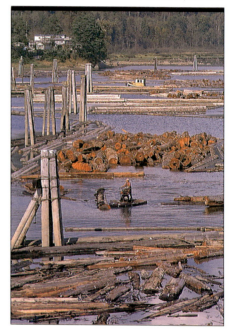

WEB SITE www.vernontourism.com, 701 Highway 97 South, and a seasonal (May–October) center stationed on the main highway at the northern edge of town (6326 Highway 97N).

There are masses of motels, resorts and campgrounds that usually fall within the inexpensive and mid-range price brackets. Many can be found through **Western Canada B&B Innkeepers Association** WEB SITE www.wcbbia.com, Box 74534, 2803 West Fourth Ave, Vancouver V6K 4P4. The local representatives are Jack and Mary Reynolds ((250) 768-5926, Garden Ridge B&B.

OSOYOOS

At the southern end of the Okanagan Valley, just north of the United States border, the little town of Osoyoos sits on the shore of Osoyoos Lake. The town has cultivated a South Western theme to suit its dry, sunny climate and, as is characteristic of the Okanagan Valley, it is a fruit-growing area that celebrates its harvests with colorful festivals. Sandy lakeside beaches and warm trout-filled waters make this a popular spot for sunbathing, swimming, angling, windsurfing, boating and the site for a variety of water sports events. Although fruit-laden orchards cluster around the lake, cacti and sagebrush grow on the arid hills beyond. This sandy area, which extends northwards to Skaha Lake, is often referred to as Canada's "pocket desert." The region supports horned lizards, rattlesnakes, burrowing owls and other life forms associated with the desert. Take Highway 3 slightly east of Osoyoos to **Anarchist**

PENTICTON

Penticton lies along Highway 97, 395 km (245 miles) east of Vancouver, between Skaha Lake and the southern shore of the larger Okanagan Lake. Its name is derived from Salish words meaning "place to stay forever," and the combination of a warm, dry climate and the lovely beaches of two lakes make it as appealing today as it obviously was to the natives who named it. The town is very popular with vacationers, with water parks, motels and other facilities lining Highway 97 as it cuts through the center of the town. The lakes are ideal for all kinds of water sports.

Mountain for views that allow you to appreciate fully the varied landscape.

West of the town, Highway 3 leads into the neighboring Similkameen Valley. Highway 97 continues northwards, following the Okanagan Valley past Vaseux and Skaha Lakes, a route that is lined with orchards and, in the summertime, with stands selling succulent fruit. The cottage wine industry is mushrooming.

There are some 20 hotels and motels around the lakeside in Osoyoos, several with their own private beach and shaded lawns. Contact the local **Chamber of Commerce** ((250) 495-7142 FAX (250) 495-6161 WEB SITE www.osoyooschamber.bc.ca.

The **Desert Centre** ((250) 495-2470 WEB SITE www.desert.org, three kilometers (just under two miles) north of Osoyoos, off Highway 97, occupies 27 hectares (66 acres) of the endangered Antelope Brush ecosystem.

The first orchards were planted here in 1874 and the town is now famous for its peaches. In late-July, early August the week-long **Penticton Peach Festival** TOLL-FREE (800) 663-5052 celebrates the harvesting of the crop with sports events, music, dancing and the extensive drinking of peach brandy. Penticton participates in the Okanagan Wine Festivals in spring and fall, but you don't have to wait until then to enjoy a taste of the local wine (see SPECIAL INTERESTS, PAGE 39 in YOUR CHOICE). Visit **Sumac Ridge Estate Winery** ((250) 494-0451 WEB SITE www.sumacridge.com, 17403 Highway 97, Summerland (daily 9 AM to 6 PM, shorter hours in winter).

Along the Okanagan lakefront, the pleasant **Art Gallery of Southern Okanagan** ((250) 493-

ABOVE: Trees of British Columbia's great forests are reduced to timber OPPOSITE to feed the printing presses of several nations.

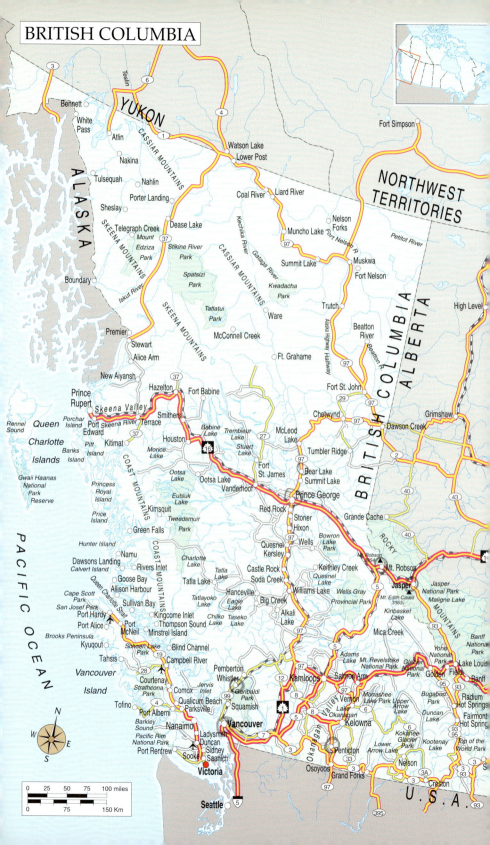

BRITISH COLUMBIA

2928, 199 Front Street, exhibits local and Canadian works. **SS *Sicamous* (** (250) 492-0403, 1099 Lakeshore Drive West, is a dry-docked sternwheeler that operated on the lake from 1914 to 1936, and is now restored, with exhibits of the old days. Beside it, the **Penticton Rose Garden** (free) provides a wonderful stroll in rose season. The **Penticton Museum** (((250) 490-2451, 785 Main Street, offers eclectic exhibits, including a large section on British Columbian fauna.

About a 30-minute drive west of Penticton along Green Mountain Road, the **Apex Resort** (((250) 292-8222 TOLL-FREE (877) 777-2739 E-MAIL info@apexresort.com has a well-equipped ski center, the emphasis in summer shifting to bicycles, walking and horses.

At Penticton, a few hotels stand out above the rest. The **Penticton Lakeside Resort and Conference Centre** (((250) 493-8221 TOLL-FREE (800) 663-9400, 21 Lakeshore Drive West, stands on the shores of Lake Okanagan (expensive). The rooms are attractively furnished, all have balconies, and it offers a good restaurant, cocktail lounge, indoor pool, fitness center and casino. The **Best Western Inn** (((250) 493-0311 TOLL-FREE (800) 668-6746 WEB SITE www.bestwestern.bc.ca, 3180 Skaha Lake Road, has 67 rooms, including family and honeymoon suites, plus housekeeping units, an indoor pool/whirlpool, a heated outdoor pool, a playground, a barbecue and a restaurant (mid-range). The beach is nearby.

Just across the road from Okanagan Lake Beach, the **Tiki Shores Condominium Beach Resort** (((250) 492-8769 FAX (250) 492-8160 WEB SITE www.tikishores.com, 914 Lakeshore Drive, has one-, two- and three-bedroom housekeeping units, some with rooftop patios (mid-range). There's an outdoor heated pool, an indoor hot tub, and (May to September) a restaurant and barbecue area.

The **Days Inn** (((250) 493-6616 TOLL-FREE (888) 999-6616, 152 Riverside Drive, close to Okanagan Lake and only a short walk from the beach, is a family-oriented motel with a heated outdoor pool (inexpensive to mid-range).

Granny Bogner's (((250) 493-2711, 302 Eckhardt Avenue West, is widely held to be one of the best restaurants in the Okanagan. The theme is homey; the fare is European. It's open for dinner only, and reservations are essential. You can sample Greek specialties in pleasant surroundings at **Theo's Restaurant** (((250) 492-4019, 687 Main Street. In 2001 they were voted best Greek restaurant in Penticton. For some hearty good-value food you can't do better than at the **Elite Restaurant** (((250) 492-3051, 340 Main Street, where they do burgers, soups and puddings. For authentic Mexican food you should try the newly renovated **Vallarta Bistro**, **BBQ & Grill** (((250) 492-5610, on 610 Main Street.

KELOWNA

About halfway along Lake Okanagan, Highway 97 crosses a floating bridge to Kelowna, the largest city in the Okanagan Valley, with a population in the region of 98,000, and the center of this fruit-growing and wine-producing region. This attractive lakeside city, with its many vineyards, parks, gardens and orchards, is an island of greenery set among rolling semi-arid hills. It has pleasant, sandy beaches and the lake provides plenty of scope for just about every water sport. The largest of Kelowna's parks is the lovely **City Park**, which has busy beaches, shady retreats, lawns

and tennis courts. In summer it is often the site of free outdoor concerts.

At the **Father Pandosy Mission** (((250) 860-8369, 3685 Benvoulin Road, you can see some of the restored mission buildings that the Oblates founded in 1859 as the first white settlement in the valley. The original church and school still stand and some other buildings of similar age have been brought to the site to give the visitor a fuller picture of life in those pioneering days.

The province's oldest winery is Kelowna's **Calona Wines** (((250) 762-3332, 1125 Richter Street, where visitors are welcome to look around and taste the wine. The recently refurbished **Kelowna Centennial Museum** (((250) 763-2417 WEBSITE www .kelownamuseum.com, 470 Queensway and Ellis, concentrates on the region's people, flora and fauna.

A steamer on Lake Okanagan calls at Kelowna.

During the winter there's plenty of skiing around Kelowna. Near the town on the other side of the lake, **Crystal Mountain** has chairlifts, a ski school and runs for skiers of all abilities. About 57 km (35 miles) east of Kelowna, the **Big White Ski Resort** ((250) 765-3101 TOLL-FREE (800) 663-2772 WEB SITE www.bigwhite.com is Canada's largest ski-in ski-out resort village and offers full facilities, including a helicopter transfer from Kelowna airport. Accommodation ranges from basic condominiums to luxury hotels, and prices vary from cheap to very expensive.

The **Kettle Valley Steam Railway** TOLL-FREE (877) 494-8424 WEB SITE www.kettlevalleyrail.org/ Summerland, provides a ride in an old steam train

Avenue, offers all the creature comforts you could want, with a heated outdoor pool, poolside grill, award-winning restaurant and pub/bistro (mid-range to expensive). There are comfortable units and suites, all with television, telephone and modem jacks. The **Big White Motor Lodge** ((250) 860-1095 TOLL-FREE (800) 663-8603, 1891 Parkinson Way, has a warm, friendly atmosphere, and 16 one- and two-bedroom housekeeping units, all with television (inexpensive).

For dining, Kelowna has the popular **Earl's on Top Restaurant** ((250) 763-2777, 211 Bernard Avenue, a smart, modern-looking place with a rooftop garden. It serves just about everything — tapas, pasta, ribs, steak, seafood and salads. There

over a preserved 10-km (six-mile) stretch of the early 1900s line, which affords fantastic views of the Myra Canyon.

Seventeen kilometers (11 miles) outside Kelowna lies the **Lake Okanagan Resort** ((250) 769-3511 TOLL-FREE (800) 663-3273 FAX (250) 769-6665 WEB SITE www.lakeokanagan.com, 2751 Westside Road. This attractive lakeside resort set in landscaped gardens has luxurious condominiums, chalets, rooms and suites, and two dining rooms. It is an ideal haven for sports enthusiasts with tennis courts (some of which are floodlit for night games), a par-three golf course, horse riding, heated outdoor pools and a marina where guests can water-ski, windsurf and sail. Prices cover the spectrum, according to type of accommodation.

In Kelowna the **Coast Capri Hotel** ((250) 860-6060 TOLL-FREE (800) 663-1144 FAX (250) 762-3430 WEB SITE www.coasthotels.com, at 1171 Harvey

are all kinds of interesting snack items on the menu at **Kelly O'Bryans** ((250) 860-8449, 262 Bernard Avenue, where you can enjoy lake views and, on weekends, late opening hours.

At the attractive **Carmellie's Restaurant** ((250) 762-6350, 101-1836 Underhill Road, a wide choice of sweet and savory crêpes awaits, while the eclectic **Doc Willoughby's** ((250) 868-8288, 353 Bernard Avenue, has western decor and fare from basic hamburgers to sun-dried-tomato pizza.

VERNON

At the northern end of the Okanagan Valley, Vernon is surrounded by Kalamalka, Okanagan and Swan Lakes, and has more of those pleasant Okanagan beaches that draw the vacationers. Where Twenty-fifth Avenue crosses Highway 97 at the southern approach to town, **Polson Park**'s delightful oriental gardens offer a haven of shade and tranquility, and a floral clock. At the **Vernon Museum and Archives** ℭ (250) 542-3142, Thirty-second Avenue and Thirty-first, you can see old photographs of the town, costumes, carriages, telephones, displays on the pioneering days and a collection of native artifacts.

For a fascinating peek at the past take Highway 97 for 12 km (seven and a half miles) north of Vernon to the **O'Keefe Historic Ranch** ℭ (250) 542-7868 (mid-May to mid-October daily 9 AM to 5 PM), one of the first ranches in the area and one of the biggest in the entire province at the turn of the century. You can see O'Keefe's original log house, a general store, blacksmith's shop, early

Sunday), you can book in advance to spend a day digging in the mines; there is a participation charge, but you keep anything you find.

Summer and winter, the **Silver Star Mountain Resort** ℭ (250) 542-0224 TOLL-FREE IN THE UNITED STATES (800) 663-4431 FAX (250) 542-1236 WEB SITE www.silverstarmtn.com, 22 km (14 miles) northeast of town, has much to tempt outdoor lovers. From June to September it has some very pleasant hiking, cycling or horseback riding trails, with views of surrounding mountain ranges. The resort, built to look as though it's straight out of the Victorian era, has accommodation, restaurants and entertainment. In winter the bikes, boots and horses are replaced by

Roman Catholic church, and a fully furnished mansion house. The O'Keefes lived at the ranch from 1867 until 1977, and many of their furnishings and possessions remain here. An annual **Cowboy Festival and Wild West** show is staged at the ranch in August.

The **Allan Brooks Nature Centre** ℭ (250) 260-4227 WEB SITE www.allanbrooksnaturecentre.org, 250 Allan Brooks Way (off Mission Road), is named after a wildlife artist who once lived in Vernon (May to October daily 10 AM to 6 PM). The centre has interactive displays about the area's ecosystems and indigenous species, some of which are endangered.

Okanagan Opal ℭ (250) 542-1103 WEB SITE www.opalscanada.com, 7879 Highway 97, eight kilometers (five miles) north of Vernon, has showrooms where you can admire (and buy) local opals. From early June to September (Friday to

skis and skates, dogsleds and snowmobiles. The two mountain faces provide runs for every grade of skier, two half-pipes for snowboarders and a kids-only area.

At Silver Star, try the **Vance Creek Hotel** ℭ (250) 549-5191 FAX (250) 549-5177 (low mid-range to very expensive). Like a set out of a spaghetti Western, the Vance Creek has a choice location in the center of the resort. Rooms on the first floor have kitchenettes, bunk beds and private entrances. Fireplaces and willow furniture add a touch of additional comfort to suites in the newer annex.

The **Craigellachie Dining Room** ℭ (250) 542-2459, Putnam Station Inn, serves hearty meals, including soups and sandwiches for lunch and

Profiles in the Okanagan Game Farm: a mountain goat OPPOSITE and a bighorn sheep ABOVE.

traditional favorites such as barbecued spare ribs, lasagna, steaks and pastas in the evening. The **Silver Lode Restaurant** ((250) 549-5105, located in the Silver Lode Inn, 146 Silver Lode Lane, serves authentic Swiss raclettes and fondues in a cheerful atmosphere.

HOW TO GET THERE

There are regular flights to Kelowna from Vancouver, Victoria, Calgary, Edmonton, Toronto and Seattle (USA). These are mainly provided by: **Horizon Air** TOLL-FREE (800) 547-9308 WEB SITE www.horizonair.com; **WestJet Airlines** TOLL-FREE (800) 538-5696 WEB SITE www.westjet.com; and **Air Canada** TOLL-FREE (888) 247-2262 WEB SITE www.aircanada.com. Air Canada also serves Kamloops and Penticton.

Greyhound TOLL-FREE (800) 661-8747 WEB SITE www.greyhound.ca links Vancouver with Kam-

loops, Penticton, Kelowna, Vernon and all the smaller communities. In Penticton the bus station is at 307 Ellis Street ((250) 493-4101. In Kelowna there is a station at 2366 Leckie Road ((250) 860-3835. Regular services run to Vancouver, Banff, Calgary, Vernon, Kamloops and Prince George. In Vernon it's at 3102 Thirtieth Street at Thirty-first Avenue ((250) 545-0527.

If you're driving, head for Highway 97, which begins at the United States border just south of Osoyoos and runs northwards through the whole Okanagan Valley. From Spokane area, take Highway 395 to Grand Forks, then Highway 3 to the border south of Osoyoos.

From Seattle area, take Highway 5 to Vancouver, then head east. If you don't want to visit Vancouver, avoid its traffic by leaving the highway at Bellingham, heading northeast to cross at Sumas border then going towards Abbotsford until you turn east.

KAMLOOPS

The largest town in the Thompson Valley, with a population of 85,000, Kamloops has been a major crossroads ever since the Secwepemc Nation first used the waterways as highways. They were followed by fur trappers, missionaries, prospectors and farmers, and when the highways arrived, the strategic position of Kamloops was maintained, as the TransCanada went through it east–west and the Yellowhead north–south. Although not a particularly attractive town, there is a great deal here of interest to visitors, and it is surrounded by glorious scenery.

GENERAL INFORMATION

Kamloops Visitor Information Centre ((250) 374-3377 TOLL-FREE (800) 662-1994 WEB SITE WWW .adventurekamloops.com, 1290 West TransCanada

Highway (exit 368) is open daily in the summer from 9 AM to 6 PM, weekdays only to 5 PM in fall and spring.

WHAT TO SEE AND DO

The *Kamloops Heritage Walking Tour* leaflet provides a good guide to the many late-1800s buildings in town. **Kamloops Museum (** (250) 828-3576, 207 Seymour Street at Second Avenue, covers the history of the area and its wildlife, with videos as well as standard exhibits. **Kamloops Art Gallery (** (250) 828-3543 WEB SITE www.gallery@kag .bc.ca, 465 Victoria Street, has an excellent selection of works by local and other Canadian artists.

Kamloops Wildlife Park ((250) 573-3242 WEB SITE www.kamloopswildlife.org, 17 km (10.5 miles) east on the TransCanada Highway, has a good assortment of wild creatures (not all indigenous), a miniature train to get around in summer and the Zippity Zoo Zone playground.

Well worth the effort, although it's a little north of town and not served by city buses, is the **Secwepemc Native Heritage Park (** (250) 828-9801, 355 Yellowhead Highway. A museum combines with a full-scale reproduction of a traditional village to give a fascinating look at the old lifestyle of the Secwepemc people: a word too difficult for the white men to pronounce, so they settled for "Shuswap." The annual **Pow Wow**, held the first weekend in August, is a major event.

The *Wanda Sue* **(** (250) 374-7447 departs from the Old Yacht Club, 1140 River Street at the foot of Tenth Avenue (June–September). She is a restored sternwheeler offering daytime and dinner cruises on the Thompson River.

WHERE TO STAY

Sun Peaks Resort ((250) 578-7232 TOLL-FREE (800) 807-3257 WEB SITE www.sunpeaksresort.com, 53 km (33 miles) northeast of Kamloops, is a year-round Tyrolean-style family-oriented vacation spot, with 80 ski runs spread over three different mountains (many of the runs are suitable for beginners), and a good choice of restaurants and shops.

The **Sun Peaks International Hostel (** (250) 578-0057 WEB SITE www.sunpeakshostel.com, 1140 Sun Peaks Road (inexpensive), is a ski-in ski-out location across the road from a chairlift and within easy walking distance of the main village. It's the only cheap place to stay at the resort, but still offers such facilities as Internet access, laundry and free movies.

In town the cheapest options are the **HI Kamloops (** (250) 828-7991 FAX (250) 828-2442 E-MAIL kamloops@hihostels.bc.ca, 7 West Seymour Street, and **bed-and-breakfast** places (details from the

Eventide along the South Thompson River at Kamloop's riverfront park.

Visitor Information Centre). This old courthouse, converted into a hostel in 1992, retains such features as the original stained-glass windows and jury box. Facilities include Internet access and laundry facilities.

HOW TO GET THERE

Kamloops is served by daily flights from Vancouver, operated by **Air BC** TOLL-FREE (888) 247-2262. The **VIA Rail** station TOLL-FREE (888) 842-7245 WEB SITE www.viarail.ca is 11 km (about seven miles) north of town and open only when there are departures: three a week to Vancouver and three a week heading for Jasper, Edmonton and points further east. The Rocky Mountaineer train also stops here overnight.

From the **Greyhound** depot ((250) 374-1212, 725 Notre Dame Drive, off Columbia Street West, there are regular services in all directions. The building contains luggage lockers and a café; it closes only between 3 AM and 5 AM.

WELLS GRAY PROVINCIAL PARK

Off the Yellowhead Highway (Highway 5), roughly halfway between Kamloops and Jasper, Wells Gray Provincial Park is British Columbia's fourth largest park, covering 541,000 hectares (1,337,000 acres). It contains five large lakes, two large river systems and a mass of beautiful waterfalls — notably the spectacular Helmcken Falls, which have a 137-m (445-ft) drop. The first white man to settle here was John Ray, a fur trapper, and the remains of his home can still be seen in the park, where you can drive, hike, ski, ride horses and canoe.

There are three entrances, but we recommend the south gate on Clearwater Valley Road, 36 km (22 miles) north of Clearwater, where you can collect information and maps from the **Visitor Information Centre** ((250) 674-2646 WEB SITE www.ntvalley.com / clearwaterchamber, Yellowhead Highway and Clearwater Valley Road. Clearwater is on the Greyhound route between Vancouver and Jasper / Kamloops.

If you want to stay inside the park, there are four campgrounds with basic facilities. Otherwise the best option is the **Helmcken Falls Lodge** ((250) 674-3657 FAX (250) 674-2971 WEB SITE www .helmckenfalls.com, where you sleep in log cabins and excellent food is served in the main lodge. The lodge rents canoes and organizes horseback trips. Another source for canoes is **Clearwater Lake Tours** ((250) 674-2121 E-MAIL harvest@wells gray.net. If whitewater rafting appeals, contact **Interior Whitewater Expeditions** ((250) 674-3727 TOLL-FREE (800) 661-7238 WEB SITE www.interior whitewater.bc.ca, which arranges three-hour runs in spring and summer.

CARIBOO-CHILCOTIN

A vast region very much on the map during the Cariboo Gold Rush, Cariboo-Chilcotin now has a number of smaller communities, the main centers being 100 Mile House, Williams Lake, Quesnel, and Bella Coola. Highway 97, once the route followed by the early settlers, remains the main north–south artery. The attractions are mainly natural and much of the rural accommodation is in fishing resorts and on working ranches, which usually offer great food and hospitality. The **BC Guest Ranchers' Association** ((250) 374-6836 TOLL-FREE (800) 435-5622 FAX (250) 374-6640 WEB SITE www.bcguestranches.com, in Kamloops, can supply details. **Cariboo-Chilcotin Coast Tourism Association** ((250) 392-2226 TOLL-FREE (800) 663-5885 WEB SITE www.landwithoutlimits.com, is in Williams Lake, 118A North First Avenue.

100 MILE HOUSE

Travelers along the Cariboo Wagon Road of the 1860s were glad to stop at Bridge Creek House. Here, 100 miles from Lillooet, they found refreshing hospitality. The original roadhouse, renamed 100 Mile House, burned down, but the stop grew to become the center of the South Cariboo and gateway to a vast lake playground. The **South Cariboo Visitor Infocentre** ((250) 395-5353 FAX (250) 395-4085 WEB SITE www.tourism.100mile .com is at 422 Highway 97.

WILLIAMS LAKE

Williams Lake, named for a Shuswap chief, is a logging town with one major attraction (the Stampede) and an excellent museum. The **Visitor Information Centre** ((250) 392-5025 is at 1148 South Broadway Street, off Highway 97.

The **Williams Lake Stampede** ((250) 398-8388 or (250) 392-6585 TOLL-FREE (800) 717-6336 (for tickets) WEB SITE www.williamslakestampede.com lasts four days in late June / early July and has been held since 1919. As it draws great crowds, it's wise to book accommodation in advance. The Stampede is essentially a rodeo, taken very seriously by the participants, with all the traditional Wild West skills on display.

The **Museum of the Cariboo Chilcotin** ((250) 392-7404 WEB SITE www.cowboy-museum.com, 113 North Fourth Avenue, is dedicated to preserving and promoting the heritage of ranching and rodeo and explains the history of the Stampede. The museum includes the British Columbia Cowboy Hall of Fame and works by western artists. At **Scout Island Nature Centre** ((250) 398-8532, Causeway Road, trails cross marshes that attract countless migratory birds.

The **Native Arts & Crafts Shop** ((250) 398-6831, 99 South Third Avenue, is run by the Cariboo Friendship Society, so you can be sure the goods are genuine local handicrafts.

The **Overlander Hotel** ((250) 392-3321 TOLL-FREE (800) 663-6898 WEB SITE www.overlanderhotel .com, 1118 Lakeview Crescent, Williams Lake, is near the airport and offers a range of sightseeing packages, as well as all the usual hotel facilities, including three restaurants (mid-range). The inexpensive **Caesar's Inn** ((250) 392-7747 TOLL-FREE (800) 663-6893, 55 Sixth Street South, is a large downtown hotel with a pub and restaurant.

Williams Lake is accessible from Vancouver by **Air BC** TOLL-FREE (888) 247-2262, **BC Rail** TOLL-FREE (800) 339-8752, and **Greyhound** ((250) 398-7733 TOLL-FREE (800) 661-8747 WEB SITE www .greyhound.ca.

BARKERVILLE

Named for Billy Barker, the first to discover gold here (in 1862), Barkerville is a restored gold-rush town. **Barkerville Historic Park** ((250) 994-3332 WEB SITE www.heritage.gov.bc.ca/bark is open May to September daily from 8 AM to 8 PM. It is possible to visit the rest of the year too, but most places are closed. It offers 125 renovated buildings and a costumed "population," with free walking tours explaining the gold-rush days. You can also (pay to) don period costume and tour the town on a stagecoach. There is accommodation right on the Barkerville site. The **St**. **George Hotel** ((250) 994-0008 TOLL-FREE (888) 246-7690 WEB SITE www.stgeorgehotel.bc.ca is open May to September and has mid-range to expensive rates.

If you're not driving yourself, the only transportation to Barkerville is a shuttle from Quesnel with commentary run by the **Gold Safari Stage Lines** ((250) 994-3463 TOLL-FREE (888) 996-4653 WEB SITE www.barkervilletours.com, which operates May to October.

QUESNEL

Quesnel is a logging town known as the "Gateway to the Goldfields." It is accessible by air, rail and Greyhound, and is worth considering as an en route stop, if only to consult the **Quesnel Visitor Information Centre** ((250) 992-8716 TOLL-FREE (800) 992-4922 WEB SITE www.northcariboo .com, 703 Carson Avenue. The adjacent **Quesnel Museum** ((250) 992-9580 features a hotchpotch of mining, farming and logging antiques and is rated as one of the province's top 10 museums.

BOWRON LAKE PROVINCIAL PARK

The main fame of the Bowron Lake Provincial Park ((250) 398-4414 lies in its spectacular 116-km (72-mile) canoe trip, which makes a circular tour through eleven different lakes, with eight relatively short portages. It takes seven to ten days and there are strategically located campgrounds. The park authorities limit the number of canoes that can start every day to 27, and charge a fee. The circuit is open mid-May to October, and there are no catering establishments, so you must bring/catch your own supplies. Contact **BC Tourism** TOLL-FREE (800) 435-5622 WEB SITE www.Hello BC.com for an information pack and to make reservations. If you don't fancy such a long trek, you can skip the formalities and settle for a day canoeing on Bowron Lake.

Cariboo Mountain Air ((250) 398-743 operates floatplanes from Williams Lake and Quesnel. Otherwise, access is by road (Bowron Lake Road is a 28-km/17-mile stretch of gravel off Highway 26). If you have no car, use the Gold Safari Stage Lines from Quesnel (see BARKERVILLE, above).

PRINCE GEORGE

Prince George is a major lumber town and British Columbia's northern capital. It's a major crossroads if you're heading inland — and large (population 80,000), so it has a good range of facilities. If you wish to learn about logging, the **Visitor Information Centre** ((250) 562-3700 TOLL-FREE (800) 668-7646 WEB SITE www.tourismpg .bc.ca, 1198 Victoria Street, can arrange visits to local pulp mills in July and August.

Port George's main attraction is The Exploration Place at the **Fraser-Fort George Regional Museum** ((250) 560-1612, Fort George Park, Twentieth Avenue and Queensway. The museum covers both the pioneers and the local First Nations people, with hands-on exhibits and the Virtual Voyages SimEx Theatre. The town's other major museum is the **Prince George Railway and Forestry Museum** ((250) 563-7351 WEB SITE www .pgrfm.bc.ca, 850 River Road (May to October, daily 9 AM to 5 PM), a non-profit organization which displays over 60 pieces of early railway rolling stock and old logging vehicles, and nine historical buildings — along with numerous smaller exhibits.

The **Two Rivers Gallery** ((250) 614-7800, 725 Civic Centre Plaza, displays the works of both regional and international artists. The **Prince George Native Art Gallery** ((250) 614-7726, Native Friendship Centre, 1600 Third Avenue (summer only) is a combination gallery and shop specializing in local handicrafts.

There's a reasonable choice of **hotels and motels** (the Visitor Information Centre can provide details) and also a **bed-and-breakfast hotline** ((250) 562-2222 TOLL-FREE (877) 562-2626, which provides advice, a free booking service and shuttles from the train and bus stations.

There are rail connections to Vancouver, Prince Rupert and Jasper. The town stands at the junction of the east–west Highway 16 and the north–south Highway 97.

PRINCE RUPERT

Near the southern tip of Alaska's southeastern panhandle, Prince Rupert is the main gateway for the Queen Charlotte Islands and the Inside Passage (See CRUISE THE INSIDE PASSAGE, page 16 in TOP SPOTS), the beginning of one of the most beautiful valleys in Canada, the Skeena, and the starting point for trips into northwest Canada, Northern British Columbia, the Yukon and Alaska.

Until the last decade, Rupert earned its living from the sea. Now that the fish stocks are depleted, the city is casting about for other ways to sustain its economy. Tourism perhaps. Were it not the rainiest city in Canada (more than 236 cm, or 93 inches, a year), Rupert would be awash with visitors. As it is, many just pass through. However the town is worth a stop. It offers delicious seafood and an excellent regional museum where you can learn about the area's first residents, the Tsimshian and Haida, whose ancestors were here some 10,000 years ago.

GENERAL INFORMATION

The **Visitor Infocentre** ((250) 624-5637 TOLL-FREE (800) 667-1994 WEB SITE www.TourismPrince Rupert.com, Suite 100, 215 Cow Bay Road, organizes interesting guided walking tours around the heritage sites and totem poles in the summer. For information prior to your trip, write to Tourism Prince Rupert, Box 22063, Prince Rupert V8J 4P8.

There is **Internet access** at Java Dot Cup ((250) 622-2822, 516 Third Avenue West. The major **rental car agencies** are located in the Rupert Square Shopping Centre on Second Avenue. Free transfers from these outlets to and from the airport and ferry docks can sometimes be arranged.

WHAT TO SEE AND DO

The **Museum of Northern British Columbia** ((250) 624-3207 WEB SITE www.museumofnorthern bc.com, 100 First Avenue West, is housed in an impressive building constructed to resemble a native longhouse. Inside is a small but excellent collection of Tsimshian, Gitksan and Haida artifacts, including reed baskets, ceremonial dress and carved masks in wood and argillite (a rare black stone found only on the Queen Charlotte Islands, which by law can be carved exclusively by the Haida).

The museum has a number of special programs, including a three-and-a-half-hour **archeological tour** to Laxspa'aws (Pike Island), which

offers a chance to learn about the Tsimshian culture, with visits to archeological digs and historic villages and settlements. The Tsimshian have inhabited the area since before the time of the pyramids in Egypt. The island can be visited only with a guide, so call the museum for details.

Across the street from the museum is the **Carving Shed** — where First Nations carvers can be seen at work on copper, silver, gold, cedar and argillite (June to August, hours vary).

A short walk from the museum will take you to the harbor front and, more specifically, to Cow Bay, the most delightful part of the town. The **Cow Bay Historic District** has souvenir and craft shops, good restaurants and a fishing village atmosphere that the rest of Rupert lacks, being cut off from the waterfront by the railway. The best souvenir **shopping** is here, where native artwork can be found for sale in shops and workshops. This part of town is quite pleasant for strolling and browsing. But bring an umbrella.

The **North Pacific Cannery Village Museum** ((250) 628-3538, 1889 Skeena Drive, is British Columbia's oldest surviving salmon cannery (built in 1889), a national historic site and well worth the short drive along Highway 16 to Port Edward; there's a bus for non-drivers. Tours are given throughout the day, along with a live one-person performance relating stories from an important chapter in the region's history. Visitors can see how the cannery operated and learn about the hundreds of First Nations people, Japanese, Chinese and Europeans who worked and lived here. The cannery is on the scenic Inverness Passage, about 20 km (12 miles) south of Prince Rupert.

Wildlife is also a major attraction, with excellent chances of seeing both grizzly bears and humpback whales. **Khutzeymateen Grizzly Bear Sanctuary** (Canada's only bear sanctuary, designated as such in 1994) is 45 km (30 miles) northeast of Prince Rupert and accessible only by water. The park covers 45 hectares (112 acres) and is home to some 50 grizzlies (as well as black bears, wolves, beavers, river otters and many other creatures). Visitor numbers are restricted, so you must join an official tour (one to ten days) and reservations are required. The **humpback whale** season is mid-July to October and you inevitably see many other marine creatures such as minke and gray whales, orcas, sea lions, seals and dolphins. The only two operators who currently have access into the park are **Sunchaser Charters** ((250) 624-5472 WEB SITE www.citytel.net/sunchaser and **Ocean Adventures Charters** ((604) 815-8382 WEB SITE www.theoceanlight.com.

For whale-spotting trips, try **Vertigo Link Charters** ((250) 627-1853 WEB SITE www.vertigo link.com or **West Coach Launch** ((250) 627-9166 TOLL-FREE (800) 201-8377 WEB SITE www.westcoast launch.com; reservations are required.

WHERE TO STAY AND EAT

Downtown, the **Crest Motor Hotel** ((250) 624-6771 FAX (250) 627-7666, 222 First Avenue West, offers excellent mid-range to expensive accommodation, with a lounge, coffee shop and restaurant at your service.

For an entirely unique experience, stay at the **Inverness Bed & Breakfast** ((250) 628-3375 E-MAIL duggle@well.com, 1889 Skeena Drive, Port Edward (open mid-April to October; inexpensive). It's located within the North Pacific Cannery Village Museum (see above), and breakfast is served at the historic Cannery Café.

For no-frills lodging, the drab but tidy **Pioneer Hostel** ((250) 624-2334 TOLL-FREE (888) 794-9998 FAX (250) 627-7945 WEB SITE www.citytel.net/pioneer, 167 Third Avenue East, has the cheapest sleeps in town; cards accepted, but cash preferred. No smoking or pets. Laundry facilities are available.

If you ask locals where to find the best seafood, they'll undoubtedly recommend **Smile's Seafood Café** ((250) 624-3072, 113 Cow Bay Road, which has been in business since 1934. **Cow Bay Café** ((250) 627-1212, 205 Cow Bay Road, is good too and has a nice view of the harbor. The chef at the **Cannery Café** ((250) 628-3375, 1889 Skeena Drive, in nearby Port Edward, lived and worked at the historic North Pacific Cannery before its closure in the late 1960s. The quaint building is the former mess house for the cannery. Salmon, naturally, is the specialty. Next to the Museum of Northern British Columbia, the moderately priced **Pegleg's Seaside Grill** ((250) 624-5667 WEB SITE www.citytel.net/peglegs, First Avenue East and McBride Street, has a vast menu including everything from seafood to Tex-Mex and daily specials such as a halibut curry. There's a very pleasant deck that looks out over the Pacific Mariner's Memorial Park, with its sailor pointing wistfully out to sea.

HOW TO GET THERE

The **Alaska Marine Highway** links Rupert with the Alaska panhandle, including Skagway, from where there are bus, train and road connections to the Yukon.

BC Ferries ((250) 386-3431 TOLL-FREE (888) 223-3779 WEB SITE www.bcferries.com serves the Queen Charlotte Islands and Port Hardy on Vancouver Island. The ferry docks are at the west end of town on Fairview Road. **Greyhound**, whose station ((250) 624-5090 is at Sixth Street, between First and Second Avenues, has a twice-daily service to Vancouver and Prince George.

The **VIA Rail** station ((250) 627-7589 TOLL-FREE (888) 842-7245 WEB SITE www.viarail.ca is 1033 Waterfront Street. From May to October, the little-known **Skeena** train runs from Jasper in the Rockies to Prince Rupert three times a week. The scenic journey takes two days. Totem (First) Class passengers have access to a panoramic viewing dome. From Prince George, **BC Rail** ((604) 984-5246 TOLL-FREE (800) 339-8752 WEB SITE www.bcrail.com connects south to Vancouver. An overnight stop in Prince George is always necessary.

The airport is on Digby Island, and the ferry/bus connection to downtown takes about 45 minutes. **Air Canada Jazz** TOLL-FREE (888) 247-2262 WEB SITE www.aircanada.com, 112 Sixth Street, Prince George (or contact your local Air Canada office), connects Rupert with Vancouver. Ask about standby flights, as they can sometimes be

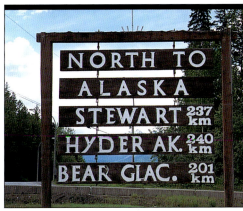

cheaper than the bus or train. **Harbour Air** ((250) 627-1341 TOLL-FREE (800) 689-4234 flies from Seal Cove floatplane base and connects Rupert with many small British Columbian towns.

There's only one road into and out of Rupert: Highway 16, the Yellowhead Highway from Prince George.

THE SKEENA VALLEY

From Prince Rupert, the Yellowhead Highway and the railway line run through a major cleft in British Columbia's Coast Mountains, forming the Skeena Valley. It was once a vital trade and travel link for Tsimshian and interior native bands, whose name for the valley, K'Shian, means "river of mists." One of the most beautiful routes in Canada, the Skeena's fog-shrouded karst mountain scenery is reminiscent of a Chinese silk painting. It is also an excellent opportunity to spot wildlife, such as black bears and bald eagles. Recreational possibilities abound along the valley.

ABOVE: "North to Alaska!" The intersection of British Columbia's Skeena and Cassiar Highways beckons the adventurer to northern British Columbia and beyond. OVERLEAF: On the Queen Charlotte Islands, sea kayaks bear classic Haida designs representing the fauna of the region.

The '**Ksan Historical Village** ((250) 842-5544 TOLL-FREE (877) 842-5518, Hazelton (daily mid-May to mid-October 8 AM to 7 PM), is a replica of an ancient village along the Skeena River, where the Gitksan people lived for thousands of years. Tours take visitors through longhouses where artifacts and multimedia exhibits tell how the clan lived before and after European contact. On display are marvelously complex Chilkat blankets, "button" blankets, woodcarvings including painted spirit masks, totem poles and ceremonial costumes.

THE QUEEN CHARLOTTE ISLANDS

Sometimes called "the Canadian Galapagos" for their ecological uniqueness, the Queen Charlotte Islands, 130 km (78 miles) west of Prince Rupert, form an archipelago of two principal islands, Graham and Moresby, and countless surrounding islets. Most of the islands' 6,000 inhabitants live on Graham Island, in six communities, and about a third of the islands' residents are Haida.

GENERAL INFORMATION

The **Visitor Information Centre** ((250) 559-8316 or (250) 559-8594 FAX (250) 559-8952, Queen Charlotte City, on Wharf Street at the east end of town, opens mid-May to early-September daily 10 AM to 7 PM, and from 10 AM to 2 PM for roughly three weeks either side of the season. It has information on Gwaii Haanas and the islands as a whole, as well as natural history presentations, and sells the useful *Guide to the Queen Charlotte Islands* and detailed maps of the towns. Pick up the free weekly *Islands This Week* to find out what's happening during your stay.

Masset (in the north) also has a **Visitor Information Centre** ((250) 626-3982, 1450 Christie Street, which is open July and August daily 9 AM to 9 PM, and May, June and September 10 AM to 4 PM.

For information specifically on Gwaii Haanas, contact the Superintendent, **Gwaii Haanas National Park** ((250) 559-8818 FAX (250) 559-8366, Box 37, Queen Charlotte V0T 1S0.

WHAT TO SEE AND DO

Visitors are drawn to the Charlottes to see the ancient remnants of the Haida culture and the archipelago's gorgeous wilderness scenery, its rugged west coast and sandy eastern beaches. Kayakers come from all over the world to paddle the waterways and coastline. Scuba divers find a watery paradise on Graham Island's west coast at Rennell Sound, where shore dives are possible from many points along the coastal logging road.

The Charlottes have about 120 km (75 miles) of paved roads, mainly along the shoreline on the east coast of Graham Island. In the northeastern corner of Graham Island, **Naikoon Provincial Park** ((250) 557-4390 protects a wilderness of rainforest, sandy beaches, dunes and bogs. In Old Masset (also called Haida), just to the west of Naikoon, there are many Haida sculptors creating works of art in silver, gold, argillite and wood, as well as prints and woven baskets. You can see the artisans at work here and purchase crafts. On the southern end of Graham Island, in Skidegate, the **Haida Gwaii Museum** ((250) 559-4643, Qay'llnagaay, exhibits Haida totem poles, masks, carvings of silver and argillite, and island wildlife.

From Graham Island a ferry frequently makes the quick 20-minute crossing to Moresby Island. Canada's newest national park, **SGaang Gwaii** (Anthony Island) — a UNESCO World Heritage Site — is located here. This small island features numerous totem poles and is part of **Gwaii Haanas National Park**. For information, call ((250) 387-1642 TOLL-FREE (800) 435-5622. Permission to enter the area (summer only) is given by the Haida Gwaii Watchmen ((250) 259-8225, Box 609, Skidegate, Haida Gwaii V0T 1S0. The office is located at Second Beach, which is just north of Skidegate Landing, along Highway 16. A journey to these sites begins with registration at a Parks Canada Information Office and a 90-minute obligatory orientation session — for details call Parks Canada ((250) 559-8818. The park, which covers the southern two thirds of the Queen Charlottes, is only accessible by boat or plane. There are some 500 archeological and historical sites here, maintained by the Haida Nation. The best way to experience the park is to go for several days, accompanied by an experienced guide. Try **Moresby Explorers** ((250) 637-2215 TOLL-FREE (800) 806-7633 E-MAIL doug @moresbyexplorers.com, 469 Alliford Bay Road, Sand Spit, which runs weekly trips from early-May to late-September and can arrange day trips, or **Queen Charlotte Adventures** ((250) 559-8990 TOLL-FREE (800) 668-4288 WEB SITE www.queen charlotteadventures.com, west end of Queen Charlotte City at Spruce Point Lodge (May to mid-October).

WHERE TO STAY

Most visitors stay and eat in Queen Charlotte, the largest town in the islands, but all of the islands' communities have at least some tourist facilities, including many small bed-and-breakfast places; contact the Visitor Information Centre in Queen Charlotte City (see above) for a list of establishments. Reservations are strongly recommended.

Queen Charlotte Islands — ABOVE: Haida in ceremonial dress. The drum at right bears the image of the killer whale. BELOW: An ancient Haida totem pole greets the dawn on Ninstits Island.

HOW TO GET THERE

Year-round daily air service is available with **Canadian Regional** TOLL-FREE (888) 247-2262 from Vancouver to Sand Spit, as is a floatplane service with **Harbour Air** ((250) 559-0052 from Prince Rupert to Sand Spit and Masset (in the north). **Eagle Cabs** ((250) 559-4461 meet incoming flights at Sand Spit and provide a fixed-rate transfer into Queen Charlotte City. **Rental cars** are available at Masset, Queen Charlotte and Sand Spit.

From Prince Rupert, **BC Ferries** ((250) 386-3431 makes the six-hour crossing daily in summer, three times weekly in winter, docking on Graham Island's south side. (Note that this is an open-sea crossing. Landlubbers may want to bring along their favorite seasickness remedy.) Reservations are strongly recommended.

NORTHERN BRITISH COLUMBIA

The region of Northern British Columbia occupies roughly half of the province, stretching from the Queen Charlotte Islands in the west to Mount Robson Park in the east, from the Yellowhead Highway in the south to the Yukon and Alaska in the north. Three major roads connect the scattered communities: the TransCanada Highway (No. 16), the Alaska Highway (No. 97) and the Stewart–Cassiar Highway (No. 37).

A remote and sparsely inhabited area, Northern British Columbia has much in common with the neighboring Yukon Territory. Despite the logging and mining activities that have dominated the region's economy for over a century, it remains virtually unspoiled — a land of great beauty and seemingly endless bounty. Intrepid travelers come for fishing, hiking through untouched mountain terrain, soaking in hot springs — and for the incomparable solitude.

The **Northern British Columbia Tourism Association** ((250) 561-0432 TOLL-FREE (800) 663-8843 WEB SITE www.northernBCtravel.com is at 850 River Road, Prince George.

A flock of plovers takes to the air.

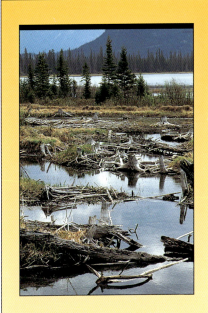

The Canadian Rockies

Straddling the border of Alberta and British Columbia, the Rocky Mountain parks encompass some of the most breathtaking scenery on earth. The area covered by Kootenay, Yoho, Banff and Jasper National Parks, together with Hamber, Mount Robson and Mount Assiniboine Provincial Parks, is recognized as a UNESCO World Heritage Site. Other protected areas in the region include Mount Revelstoke and Glacier National Parks. Together they make up one of the largest protected areas in the world. White mountain peaks and glaciers tower over aquamarine lakes, rivers and waterfalls rush through forested valleys, and wild animals run free.

All the parks present a wealth of opportunities for outdoor enthusiasts, with trailwalking, riding

and mountain biking, climbing, fishing and whitewater rafting. In the winter a thick coat of snow turns it into a skiers' paradise. The weather is unpredictable and changeable, and the higher you are, the colder it is, making warm clothing an essential part of vacation luggage, even in July.

Wildlife abounds, with 69 species of mammals, 277 species of birds, 40 types of fish, 16 amphibians and reptiles and a staggering 20,000 species of insects and spiders. Visitors need not go off the beaten track for glimpses of elk, deer, bighorn sheep and an abundance of clever squirrels. Hikers often spot moose, black bears, grizzlies and mountain goats. Throughout your visit you will be constantly reminded to keep your distance and not to feed the animals, both for their good and for your own. These animals are wild, despite their apparent ease around people. To drive the message home, the park authorities impose heavy fines on those caught feeding animals.

The Rocky Mountains form the backbone and Continental Divide of North America, stretching south for thousands of miles to Colorado. The first sedimentary rocks that make up the vast chain were laid down around 600 million years ago, when a vast sea covered the region. Eventually these sediments built up to form a layer 20 kms (12 miles) thick. One hundred and forty million years ago,

continental drift crushed the rock, forcing mountains to rise of out of the sea, where water and weather ground them into today's magnificent formations. Today, landslides visible on the slopes and heaps of rubble deposited by glaciers and avalanches clearly show the process is far from over.

Parks Canada TOLL-FREE (800) 748-7275 E-MAIL natlparks-ab@pch.gc.ca WEB SITE www.parkscanada.gc.za has several information centers in the region, listed under the relevant headings. For road conditions in all the parks, call ℂ (403) 762-1450. For avalanche information throughout western Canada, call TOLL-FREE (800) 667-1105.

THE BRITISH COLUMBIA ROCKIES

The British Columbia Rockies include four different mountain ranges and several groups of thermal springs, with some superb scenery. Most of the towns are in the southern part of the region, but the major tourist draws are in the north: Glacier, Mount Revelstoke, Kootenay and Yoho National Parks.

For information about the whole region, contact **Tourism Rockies** ℂ (250) 427-4838 TOLL-FREE BROCHURE HOTLINE (800) 435-5622 FAX (250) 427-3344 WEB SITE www.bcrockies.com, 1905 Warren Avenue, Kimberley. Anyone planning an overnight trip into the backcountry must buy a wilderness pass. They're available from any Parks Canada center (addresses listed below).

GLACIER AND MOUNT REVELSTOKE NATIONAL PARKS

Just before it reaches the Rockies, the TransCanada Highway runs through Glacier National Park, a rugged area high in the Columbia Mountains containing hundreds of glaciers, waterfalls and rainforests. This is the birthplace of North American mountaineering, and mountain climbing challenges abound. There are over 20 hiking trails — some short, some aimed at the more adventurous hiker. A number of backpacking trails are easily accessed. The ski season begins in November and lasts almost to June. The spectacular terrain and heavy snowfalls of the Selkirk Mountains combine to produce some of the best ski touring opportunities in North America. Avalanches are a danger here.

Just west of Glacier, the smaller Mount Revelstoke National Park is a favorite destination for mountain bikers and hikers. Ten trails with differing levels of difficulty and great Rocky Mountain scenery make it a popular park. Two of the most accessible hikes consist of boardwalks that lead off into the countryside from Highway 1. The

Visitors to the Canadian Rockies need not get off the beaten track for glimpses of bighorn sheep ABOVE and elk OPPOSITE BOTTOM. A snow-covered Banff church TOP rests below Mount Rundle.

Giant Cedars Trail is a 500-m (one-third-of-a-mile) jaunt through a majestic red-cedar forest, where some of the trees are more than 1,000 years old, and the **Skunk Cabbage Trail** runs 1.2 km (three-quarters of a mile) through towering skunk cabbage patches. You can also drive the 24 km (14 miles) up the **Meadows in the Sky Parkway** (Summit Road) and from the top hike the one-kilometer (half-mile) trail to beautiful alpine meadows.

Nearby on Highway 23, at **Revelstoke Dam** ((250) 837-6211 or (250) 837-6515, there is a visitor center that offers a free tour of the dam. Railway enthusiasts should visit the **Revelstoke Railway Museum** ((250) 837-6060 TOLL-FREE (877) 837-6060 WEB SITE www.railwaymuseum.com, Victoria Road, which charts the construction of the Canadian Pacific Railway and contains several restored steam engines.

Canyon Hot Springs ((250) 837-2420 WEB SITE www.canyonhotsprings.com, on the TransCanada Highway, 35 km (22 miles) east of Revelstoke, were discovered by railway workers at the turn of the last century. Today the waters are channeled to fuel a natural hot tub and a full swimming pool. Swimwear and towels can be rented (May to September).

At Rogers Pass, you'll find the moderately priced **Best Western Glacier Park Lodge** ((250) 837-2126, with a heated outdoor pool and access to 140 km (87 miles) of groomed hiking trails.

The main **Visitor Information Centre** ((250) 837-5345 TOLL-FREE (800) 487-1793 WEB SITE www.revelstokecc.bc.ca, 204 Campbell Avenue, Revelstoke, provides information on the whole area. For information specifically on the parks, visit the **Rogers Pass Center** ((250) 814-5233 or (250) 837-3522, TransCanada Highway, 69 km (41 miles) east of Revelstoke, 72 km (43 miles) west of Golden.

YOHO NATIONAL PARK

Yoho National Park is a land of towering rock walls and thundering waterfalls. Within the park there are 28 peaks over 3,000 m (9,000 ft) high. Once you visit, you'll understand why the Cree natives called this place "Yoho," an expression of wonder and astonishment.

The **Visitor Information Centre** ((250) 343-6783 WEB SITE www.parkscanada.gc.za, just off the TransCanada Highway, Field, can provide all the information you'll need for your visit, including up-to-date news on trail and weather conditions. It is open May to October.

In addition to its scenic attractions, the park is noted for its fossil beds, where the remains of more than 120 species of marine animals from 515 million years ago are the subject of ongoing investigation. **Field** is the administrative and supply center for the park, a compact little village with a history as a railway and mining town.

There are some 400 **hiking trails** in Yoho that lead to glaciated peaks, rolling alpine meadows, deep forests and thundering waterfalls. If you're making a drive-through tour, look for roadside signs pointing the way to the **Spiral Tunnels** viewpoint, where you can watch passing trains corkscrew down a 2.2-percent grade. **Takakkaw Falls** ("magnificent" in Cree), 17 km (10.5 miles) east of Field, are the highest in Canada at 254 m (84 ft). The road is only open late-June to early September and is never suitable for vehicles with trailers. Several popular hiking trails begin here.

With so much natural history and beauty packed into such a small space (1,310 sq km, or 507 sq miles), Yoho is sometimes overburdened

with admirers. Park authorities have established a quota on the number of people who may use the **bus service** ((250) 343-6433 up to **Lake O'Hara**, 13 km (eight miles) from Field. No bicycles are permitted, however there is no limit on the number of people who may hike in.

The **Burgess Shale fossil beds** are among the richest in the world, housing the remains of over 120 marine animals, some 515 million years old. **Walcott's Quarry** and its **Trilobite Beds** can be visited on guided hikes only. The **Yoho-Burgess Shale Foundation** ((250) 343-6006 TOLL-FREE (800) 343-3006 offers earth-science hikes to both sites (July to mid-September, departing from the Yoho Brothers' Trading Post Friday, Saturday, Sunday and Monday mornings at 8 AM). Guided hikes to the **Mount Stephen Fossil Beds** depart every

Banff Avenue — a corridor of commercialism, but the mountains are never out of view for long.

Saturday and Sunday at 10 AM, also from the Trading Post. This hike is somewhat shorter than the Walcott's Quarry hike, but more difficult. It climbs up at a very steep grade and trilobites are everywhere — you have to be careful to avoid stepping on them and crushing them. You must be in good physical condition to undertake either hike. Reservations are required.

Where to Stay and Eat

For accommodation in Yoho, try the delightful **Emerald Lake Lodge** ((250) 343-6321 TOLL-FREE (800) 663-6336 FAX (250) 343-6724 WEB SITE www.crmr.com, eight kilometers (five miles) north of Field, a log cabin surrounded by small

here for lunch, which is served between noon and 4 PM. A number of other **backcountry lodgings** are dotted throughout Yoho. For information, contact the visitor information center.

The **Whiskey Jack Hostel (HI)** ((403) 521-8421 TOLL-FREE (866) 762-4122 FAX (403) 283-6503 WEB SITE www.hihostels.ca, in Yoho National Park, is open mid-June to mid-September and is in an ideal setting about a kilometer (half a mile) from Takakkaw Falls.

When you're in Field, be sure to stop in at the **Yoho Brothers Trading Post** ((250) 343-6030, where you can pick up souvenirs and have one of their great sandwiches of barbecued wild game or salmon.

cottages, all with fireplaces and balconies, alongside a rich turquoise glacier lake. The lodge has a bar, two restaurants and a teahouse, a gym, an outdoor hot tub and a sauna, and offers boating and horseback riding.

The **Cathedral Mountain Lodge & Chalets** ((250) 343-6442 FAX (403) 762-0514 is on Yoho Valley Road in Yoho National Park (mid-May to mid-October; moderate to expensive). Located four kilometers (two and a half miles) east of Field, along the road to Takakkaw Falls, the lodge offers log cabins with fireplaces in quiet wooded grounds along the Kicking Horse River. There is a licensed restaurant and grocery store.

From Takakkaw Falls, you can hike up to the **Twin Falls Chalet** (/FAX (403) 228-7079 (July to Labor Day; reservations are required; mid-range prices include all meals), where there is more cabin accommodation. Day hikers are welcome

KOOTENAY NATIONAL PARK

Lying southwest of Banff and Yoho national parks, the 1,406 sq km (543 sq mile) Kootenay National Park is accessible via magnificent Highway 93, off the TransCanada Highway south of Castle Junction. This was the first major road to cross the Rockies, and it runs right through the park to its southern edge; look out en route for such marvels as the Continental Divide on **Vermilion Pass**, 95 km (60 miles from Radium); **Marble Canyon**, 88 km (55 miles) from Radium (take the 20-minute interpretive walk); and the ochre-tinted **Paint Pots**, three kilometers (two miles) away. The **Visitor Information Centre** ((250) 347-9505 WEB SITE www.parks canada .gc.za, is at 7556 Main Street East, Radium Hot Springs (open May through August).

At the southern edge of the park, **Radium Hot Springs** ((250) 347-9485 TOLL-FREE (800) 767-1611

WEB SITE www.parkscanada.gc.ca/hotsprings features a hot pool (39°C/103°F) and a swimming pool (27°C/84°F); towel and suit rentals are available. Treatments include massage and reflexology.

The town of Radium Hot Springs is 129 km (80 miles) from Banff, and the **Panorama Resort** ((250) 342-6941 TOLL-FREE (800) 663-2929 FAX (250) 342-3395 WEB SITE www.britishcolumbia.com/ski/bcr/panorama.html, Toby Creek Road, Panorama, is a further 20-minute drive. The **Springs at Radium Golf Resort** ((250) 347-9311 TOLL-FREE (800) 667-6444 FAX (250) 347-6299, 8100 Golf Course Road, Highway 93/95, (mid-range), is a year-round destination packed with activities. It has 119 rooms, a restaurant, a lounge and an indoor swimming pool.

laying of the tracks, three workers discovered some hot sulfur springs, and as soon as word of them got out, visitors began to arrive. In 1885, the government created the Rocky Mountain Park around the springs to preserve the area, and in 1888 the Canadian Pacific Railway opened the magnificent Banff Springs Hotel, a summer resort that was the last word in luxury. A beautiful golf course was laid and trips and expeditions were organized for guests, whose every whim was catered to. People came from far and wide, the town developed, the boundaries of the park were expanded and its name was changed to Banff National Park. Today it covers an area of 6,640 sq km (2,600 sq miles).

BANFF NATIONAL PARK

Banff National Park is the most famous of the mountain parks, and the most popular. About 113 km (70 miles) west of Calgary along the TransCanada Highway, Banff has two townsites that attract millions of visitors from around the world: **Banff** and the smaller, more exclusive **Lake Louise** (56 km/35 miles north of Banff). The town of Banff is the park's main center for entertainment, accommodation and restaurants, and is also the starting point for tours and trails into the park.

Banff was the first national park to be established in Canada. The region was explored in 1841 by the governor of the Hudson's Bay Company, but it was in the 1880s, with the coming of the Canadian Pacific Railway, that word of the area's great beauty began to spread. During the

GENERAL INFORMATION

The **Banff Visitor Information Centre** ((403) 762-1550 WEB SITE www.parkscanada.gc.za is at 224 Banff Avenue, and **Lake Louise Visitor Information** ((403) 522-3833 is in Samson Mall, Village Road and Lake Louise Drive, just off the Trans-Canada Highway. They carry maps, pamphlets and brochures, which detail various trips and trails throughout the area. They also give valuable advice on how to protect yourself against attack from animals, on weather conditions and on survival skills. If you're planning on an overnight hiking trip, you must sign in at either the Banff or Lake Louise Information Center.

All quiet at the boat house — OPPOSITE: Inside Maligne Lake Boathouse, guidesman Barry Wood organizes his gear. ABOVE: Lake Louise canoes wait patiently for the spring melt.

Brewster Motorcoach Tours ((403) 762-6767 WEB SITE www.brewster.ca, 100 Gopher Street, Banff, operates a range of excellent bus tours around Banff and Jasper, including day transfers along the Icefield Parkway with connections to the Snocoach up the Athabasca Glacier (see page 139).

WHAT TO SEE AND DO

Banff

Sixteen kilometers (10 miles) beyond the park gates, Banff lies in the Bow River valley, nestling at the base of Cascade Mountain and shadowed by snowy peaks on all sides. It is the hub of the Banff National Park and Canada's favorite year-round resort. You'll

A Victorian wooden building houses the **Banff Park Museum** ((403) 762-1558, 91 Banff Avenue, where you can see old-fashioned displays of stuffed animals and birds from the park — this is the only place where you can study some of them up close. There is also an excellent reference library on the area. The **Natural History Museum** ((403) 762-4652, Clocktower Mall, 112 Banff Avenue, deals with the geological formation of the Rockies and the early life forms that inhabited them. There are audiovisual displays, exhibits on dinosaurs and a model of Sasquatch, the Rockies' version of the abominable snowman.

At the southern end of the town near the Bow River, a fortified log building houses the **Buffalo**

find everything you need here. It is the starting point for scores of trips, some on horseback, some in the bicycle saddle, some on buses, and others tailored for a variety of outdoor pursuits. There are all kinds of walking trails to places that cars cannot reach, and the most timorous to the most intrepid of hikers will all find something to suit them. Unless you are prepared to hike long distances, you will require transportation to take you at least part of the way to many of the top attractions.

The town is small, however. The peak season of July and August draws large crowds and parking becomes a problem — especially along Banff Avenue, the town's busy main street, lined with shops and restaurants. There is a tourist **trolley bus** in season and **horse-drawn carriage tours** ((403) 762-4551 WEB SITE www.horseback.com, Trail Rider Store, 132 Banff Avenue, with a pickup service from most hotels.

Nations Luxton Museum ((403) 762-2388, 1 Birch Avenue, where there are displays on the various First Nations people of Alberta (there are 41 different groups). The **Whyte Museum of the Canadian Rockies** ((403) 762-2291 WEB SITE www .whyte.org, 111 Bear Street, has a gallery devoted to paintings and sculptures of the mountains, as well as exhibits chronicling the human history of the region.

West of downtown, you can see the original hot sulfur spring that first brought tourism to the area. Railway workers discovered the Cave and Basin Hot Springs in 1883. The spa building that surrounds them has been rebuilt in the original 1914 style. The **Cave and Basin National Historic Site** ((403) 762-1566, Cave Avenue, also has interpretive displays and a film on the history of the area. You can enjoy a theraputic dip in the outdoor hot-spring pool (40°C/108°F) and soak up the glorious mountain views at the **Upper Hot Springs Pool** ℂ (403) 762-1515 TOLL-FREE (800) 767-1611 WEB SITE www .parkscanada.gc.ca / hot springs, Mountain Avenue.

About three kilometers (two miles) south of town, next to the Upper Hot Springs is the **Sulphur Mountain Gondola Lift** ℂ (403) 762-2523 WEB SITE www.banffgondola.com, a gleaming, state-of-the-art aerial tramway to the top of Sulphur Mountain (2,285 m / 7,500 ft). There are wonderful 360-degree views of the Bow Valley from the observation deck, along with several hiking trails. The moderately priced Panorama Room offers set dinners featuring salmon and prime rib; the Summit Restaurant serves light meals and snacks.

Northwest of Banff, 28 km (17 miles) along Highway 1A, there's a lovely one-and-a-half-hour hiking trail leading from **Johnston Canyon**. You can extend the hike by a couple of miles into a meadow where there are some deep-colored underground springs known as the **Ink Pots**.

Lake Louise

In 1882, the explorer Tom Wilson became the first European to lay eyes on Lake Louise, proclaiming, "As God is my judge, I never, in all my explorations of these five chains of mountains throughout western Canada, saw such a matchless scene." Lapis-blue Lake Louise, mirroring the 3,464-m-tall (1,154-ft) Victoria Glacier, has been enchanting ever since.

Following the discovery of the springs, the Canadian Pacific Railway built **Banff Springs Hotel** (see WHERE TO STAY, below), a magnificently located resort on pine-covered slopes close to the springs. So great was its success that in 1910 the hotel was rebuilt in Scottish baronial style. Try at least to have a meal there, or take the historical tour.

The other mountains around the town also have hiking trails. One of the more gentle climbs close to downtown is up **Tunnel Mountain** along Tunnel Mountain Drive, where you can see the strange column-like rock formations known as **hoodoos**.

For a different angle on the landscape, take a trip to **Lake Minnewanka**, 11 km (seven miles) west of the town, where **Lake Minnewanka Tours** ℂ (103) 762-3473 run 90-minute cruises across the waters (mid-May to September). They also operate guided fishing trips. Nearby, **Two-Jack Lake** is a popular spot for rowing and canoeing.

The first question most people ask on arriving at Lake Louise is, "Where's the lake?" That's because the village of Lake Louise is located some distance below the actual lake. Most of the amenities are located in the village, along with restaurants and lodging. Up at the lake, the Fairmont Château Lake Louise is piled high along the shore.

The **Samson Mall** is the center of village life, with several retail shops and restaurants. Right next door, at the **Lake Louise Information Centre** (see GENERAL INFORMATION, above), there is an excellent and entertaining interpretive display on mountain formation — a good overview of the fascinating geological history of the Rockies.

There are several options for laid-back **hikes** around the village, the most obvious being the valley-bottom **Riverside Loop** (seven kilometers / four

OPPOSITE: The view from Château Lake Louise.
ABOVE: The elegant Banff Springs Hotel.

and a half miles) along the Bow River and past the old train station. If you want to stretch your lungs a bit, take the four-and-a-half-kilometer (three-mile) footpath from the village to Lake Louise.

Up at the lake the favorite pastime is gazing at the scenery. In winter it is possible to skate on the lake. Once the ice has eventually melted, in early June, there are **canoes** for rent ((403) 522-3511. As you stroll around the shore on the paved footpaths, look among the rocky banks for golden-mantled ground squirrels and Clark's nutcrackers, large gray and black birds with long black beaks. The lake is the starting point for some challenging hikes that lead to the base of the glacier or to a number of other, smaller but equally beautiful glacier-fed lakes.

Of course, you can't miss seeing Château Lake Louise. Though its exterior is an eyesore, the interior is tastefully lavish. The lobby has a lovely lounge with an arched window looking out on the Victoria Glacier.

On the other side of the TransCanada Highway, four and a half kilometers (three miles) from the village, the **Lake Louise Summer Sightseeing Gondola** ((403) 522-3555 WEB SITE www.skilouise .com/summer (June to September) takes you to the top of Mount Whitehorn (2,040 m/6,700 ft), with its teahouse, picnic areas and numerous hiking trails. Fifteen kilometers (eight miles) south of Lake Louise, **Moraine Lake** is another beautiful and improbably colored lake, surrounded by the Wenkchemna Peaks (named after the Stoney native word for "ten"). Until 1989, these mountains were featured on the Canadian $20 bill.

SPORTS AND OUTDOOR ACTIVITIES

Both Banff and Lake Louise have a wealth of **hiking** trails of all lengths. Some are little more than short walks, while others are wilderness expeditions that take several days to complete. Parks Canada produces brochures detailing the trails, and copies of these can be picked up from the information centers. If you're planning an overnight hike into the backcountry, you will need to buy a permit from either an information center or a park warden. There are also numerous **cycling** trails, which must be strictly adhered to. A few companies operate cycling tours, and renting bikes is easy in both towns, including Bactrax ((403) 762-8177, 200 Bear Street, Banff. Adventures Unlimited ((403) 762-4554 TOLL-FREE (800) 644-8888 WEB SITE www .raftbanff.com provides mountain bikes along with activities from rafting and fly fishing to scenic flights. Banff Hummer Tours and Safaris ((403) 760-4867 WEB www.canadianrockies.net, and Banff ATV Tours TOLL-FREE (888) 293-8687 both offer rugged **off-road 4x4 tours** of the remote mountains.

Several companies offer **heli-hiking**, which involves a helicopter trip out to remote spots high on the mountaintops or onto glaciers for some extra-special hiking. If you're interested in **boating** or **canoeing**, there are many beautiful lakes to choose from, most of which have places that rent out a variety of vessels. If you intend to do a spot of **fishing**, and there are some ideal opportunities in both parks, you must get a National Parks fishing license, which can be bought either from an information center or an outfitter. Several places run fishing trips and rent out tackle.

If you plan to do more serious **climbing**, there are several companies which do outfitting and guiding including Mountain Magic Equipment ((403) 762-2591, 224 Bear Street, Banff, and Corax Alpine ((403) 760-0609, Lake Louise.

Rivers throughout both parks offer opportunities for **whitewater rafting**. Among the many companies organizing trips are Canadian Whitewater Adventures TOLL-FREE (888) 577-8118 WEB SITE www.canadianwhitewater.com; Hydra River

Guides ((403) 762-4554 TOLL-FREE (800) 644-8888 WEB SITE www.raftbanff.com, 211 Bear Street, Banff; and **Wild Water Adventures** ((403) 522-2211 TOLL-FREE (888) 647-6444 WEB SITE www.wildwater.com, Fairmont Château Lake Louise.

Horseback riders have a choice of many treks of varying lengths and designed for all abilities. There are several stables in both parks, including Holidays on Horseback ((403) 762-4551 WEB SITE www.horseback.com, 132 Banff Avenue, Banff, and Brewster Lake Louise Stables ((403) 762-5454, Fairmont Château Lake Louise.

Skiing

Banff's nearest slopes are at **Mount Norquay** ((403) 762-4421 SNOW PHONE (403) 762-4421, only five kilometers (three miles) away from town, and the well-equipped **Sunshine Village Resort** ((403) 762-6500 TOLL-FREE (800) 661-1676 SNOW PHONE (403) 760-6543, about 16 km (10 miles) west of the town, where there are ski lifts and more than 60 runs. Sunshine Village comprises a 1960s-era hotel and several restaurants. In summer there are hiking trails that lead through alpine meadows. At Lake Louise, the **Lake Louise Ski Area** ((403) 522-3555 TOLL-FREE (800) 258-7669 SNOW PHONE (403) 762-4766 offers runs of up to eight kilometers (five miles) long, some of the longest runs in the Rockies. In winter, there are also sleigh and sled-dog rides, snowshoeing and icewalks on offer.

NIGHTLIFE AND THE ARTS

Banff's cultural life revolves around the **Banff Centre** ((403) 762-6100 TOLL-FREE (800) 413-8368 WEB SITE www.banffcentre.ca, St. Julien Road, which has a busy program of concerts, plays and films. The **Lux Cinema Centre** ((403) 762-8595,

Skiers at Lake Louise.

229 Bear Street (Wolf & Bear Mall), shows first-run movies. The town is home to prestigious television (June) and film (early November) festivals.

There are several busy bars in Banff, mostly around Banff Avenue, and some in the hotels. Several have live musical entertainment. **Barbary Coast** ((403) 762-4616, 119 Banff Avenue, regularly hosts blues, funk and jazz bands in its upstairs lounge. Celtic and maritime bands are featured at the **St. James's Gate Olde Irish Pub** ((403) 762-9355, 205 Wolf Street. For country and western as well as live rock bands, there's **Wild Bill's** ((403) 762-0333, upstairs at 201 Banff Avenue, which also has line-dancing lessons every Wednesday night.

WHERE TO STAY

Reservations are strongly advised for the summer season in both Banff and Lake Louise. **Banff/Lake Louise Central Reservations** ((403) 762-5561 TOLL-FREE (800) 661-1676 can help you sort out the dizzying options.

Banff

The most renowned hotel in the Rockies is the **Fairmont Banff Springs Hotel** ((403) 762-2211 TOLL-FREE (800) 441-1414 FAX (403) 762-5755 WEB SITE www.fairmont.com, Spray Avenue, overlooking the Spray Valley and surrounded by towering peaks (expensive). It was here that the Canadian Pacific Railway built its first resort hotel in 1882, replacing it by this larger structure in 1928 — with no expense spared. It remains a resort with riding stables, skiing and fishing packages available, along with sports facilities including indoor and outdoor pools and one of the most spectacular golf courses anywhere. At the Solace spa, you can bask in the myriad mineral pools or simply lounge by the fireside while deciding between a frighteningly thorough list of "therapies." However, this massive hotel's very fame works against it: tour groups may receive preferential treatment, and overbooking can be a problem in peak season.

Though the Banff Springs is more famous, many say the magnificently situated, 345-room **Rimrock Resort** ((403) 762-3356 FAX (403) 762-4132 TOLL-FREE (800) 661-1587 WEB SITE www.rimrockresort.com, 100 Mountain Avenue, on the road to the Sulphur Mountain Gondola, is the place to go to do Banff in style, with superlative amenities including a health club and spa. Equally luxurious, but with a rustic Rocky-mountain atmosphere, **Buffalo Mountain Lodge** ((403) 762-2400 TOLL-FREE (800) 661-1367 FAX (403) 762-4495 E-MAIL bmll @telusplanet.net WEB SITE www.crmr.com, Tunnel Mountain Road, has 108 rooms and suites with fireplace, whirlpool and kitchenette. Recent renovations have made this old standby quite popular. Both hotels are expensive.

A number of Banff hotels offer good value at the low end of the expensive price range. The **Banff Park Lodge** ((403) 762-4433 TOLL-FREE (800) 661-9266 FAX (403) 762-3553 WEB www.banff parklodge.com, 222 Lynx Street, is just a couple of blocks from the town's main street, and elegantly decorated throughout. There is an indoor swimming pool, restaurants and a lounge. **Inns of Banff** ((403) 762-4581 TOLL-FREE (800) 661-1272 FAX (403) 762-2434 WEB SITE www.innsof banff.com, 600 Banff Avenue, is an attractive resort, whose 180 rooms have balconies and lots of luxurious touches. It has an indoor and a large outdoor swimming pool, a squash court, a good dining room and lounge, and a Japanese restaurant. The hotel offers special winter ski

ABOVE: The wintery landscape LEFT at Lake Louise, and the Weeping Wall RIGHT along the Icefields Parkway. OPPOSITE: Moraine Lake, a few kilometers east of Lake Louise.

packages. The **Douglas Fir Resort and Chalets** ((403) 762-5591 TOLL-FREE (800) 661-9267 FAX (403) 762-8774 E-MAIL douglasfir@banff.net WEB SITE www.douglasfir.com is a particularly good choice for families with its tangle of indoor water slides. Rustic chalets come with kitchenette, fireplace and patio looking out onto wooded grounds where elk graze.

Banff Avenue is lined for much of its length by hotels, many of them offering excellent mid-range value. One of the most convenient, and only a couple of minutes' walk from the centre, is the **Banff International Hotel** ((403) 762-4895 TOLL-FREE (800) 665-5666 FAX (403) 762-4895 E-MAIL banffih@banff.net, 333 Banff Avenue, with comfortable rooms, a sauna and a Jacuzzi. An-other is the **Ptarmigan Inn** ((403) 762-2207 TOLL-FREE (800) 661-8310 FAX (403) 762-3577 WEB SITE www.banffcaribouproperties.com, 337 Banff Av-enue, with 134 rooms. The **Swiss Village** ((403) 762-4581 TOLL-FREE (800) 661-1272 FAX (403) 762-2434 WEB SITE www.innsofbanff.com, 600 Banff Avenue, has 52 units, and shares the facilities of the Inns of Banff.

Whatever the season, our favorite place to stay is **Eleanor's House** (403) 760-2457 FAX (403) 762-3852 WEB SITE www.bbeleanor.com, 125 Kootenay Avenue, where a friendly host with boundless en-ergy (that's Eleanor) offers the comfort and pri-vacy of an inn (rooms are located in an addition to a private home) in a quiet residential area a few paces of downtown. It is one of many bed-and-breakfast places in Banff. For a full list, contact the tourist office.

The **Banff International Hostel** ((403) 762-4122 FAX (403) 762-3441 WEB SITE www.hostellingintl.ca/alberta, Tunnel Mountain Road, three kilometers (two miles) from downtown, is an attractive build-ing with good facilities and accommodation for 154 people.

Lake Louise

In Lake Louise Village, the **Post Hotel** ((403) 522-3989 TOLL-FREE (800) 661-1586 FAX (403) 522-3966 WEB SITE www.posthotel.com is a lovely alpine-style building with 100 rooms and suites, some of which have lofts and large river-stone fireplaces, while others have self-catering facilities (expen-sive). Suites have generous bathrooms with Jacuzzis and balconies looking out over neatly trimmed lawns, stands of spruce and the sparkling Pipestone River. The hotel has the best dining room in the region. In winter, the Post is the per-fect ski lodge; in summer, it's just plain paradise.

Above the village, overlooking the beautiful ultramarine-blue waters of the lake, the **Fairmont Château Lake Louise** ((403) 522-3511 TOLL-FREE (800) 441-1414 FAX (403) 522-3834 is another historic Canadian Pacific hotel. This hotel adds nothing at all to the scenic beauty of the lake, but

inside there are 510 attractive rooms and suites with spectacular views. The hotel boasts a good restaurant, evening entertainment, riding stables and indoor pools (expensive).

The **Lake Louise Inn** ((403) 522-3791 TOLL-FREE (800) 661-9237 FAX (403) 522-2018 WEB SITE www.lakelouise.com, 210 Village Road, has 232 mid-range to expensive rooms and suites with beautiful views. The inn also has has tennis courts, an indoor swimming pool and a free shuttle to Ski Lake Louise.

Despite its reputation as an exclusive desti-nation, Lake Louise does have a good budget option too. Conveniently located in the village center, the large **Canadian Alpine Centre and International Hostel** (HI) ((403) 521-8421 TOLL-FREE (866) 762-4122 FAX (403) 522-2253 WEB SITE www.hihostels.ca, on Village Road, is jointly run by Hostelling International and the Alpine Club of Canada.

WHERE TO EAT

Banff

Many of Banff's best tables are found in its hotels. You could eat your way through the restaurants at Banff Springs Hotel for two weeks without exhausting the options. The top table here, among several excellent restaurants, is the elegant **Banffshire Club** ((403) 762-1798, with gourmet tasting menus accompanied by the most extensive wine list in Canada, all served in baronial splendor.

The multi-award winning **Dining Room at the Buffalo Mountain Lodge** ((403) 760-4484 TOLL-FREE (800) 663-6336, Tunnel Mountain Road, serves Canadian cuisine, with game a speciality. **The Pines** ((403) 760-6690, at Rundlestone Lodge, 537 Banff Avenue, similarly serves inventive Canadian cuisine with an emphasis on local game. At **Ticino's** ((403) 762-3848, High Country Inn,

415 Banff Avenue, the Swiss-Italian cooking features antipasto of air-dried beef, coppa ham and mountain cheeses, raclette (melted cheese with boiled potatoes, cured meats and pickles) and pasta dumplings. Save room for a *gelato* made from Ticino's specially brewed coffee.

The **Grizzly House** ((403) 762-4055, 207 Banff Avenue, is known for its exotic fondues, some of which feature alligator and rattlesnake. For a more classical approach, there is excellent French cuisine at award-winning **Le Beaujolais** ((403) 762-2712, corner of Buffalo Street and Banff Avenue.

Banff has a multitude of more informal, moderately priced dining spots. **Melissa's** ((403) 762-5511, 218 Lynx Street, is probably the best in town,

---

The spectacular Icefields Parkway links Banff with Jasper following the Continental Divide along a route lined with glaciers, lakes and mountains. OVERLEAF: The Pipestone River tumbles down the mountainside to Lake Louise Village.

serving breakfast as well as salads and sandwiches for lunch and steaks, stews and pasta in the evenings. Downtown, **Coyotes Deli and Grill** ((403) 762-3963, 206 Caribou Street, has lines round the clock for a similar mix of light lunches (pizzas and wraps) and excellent evening meals. Reservations are recommended for both. For good Italian fare try **Giorgio's Trattoria** ((403) 762-5114, at 219 Banff Avenue, which has a warm, intimate atmosphere. If you're craving Chinese, try the **Silver Dragon** ((403) 762-3939, Third Floor, 211 Banff Avenue.

Lake Louise

Canada's highest village has some very high-caliber dining establishments. Most notable, and not

100-year-old log station surrounded by vintage rail cars and gardens. The food is good, if not too imaginative, with Alberta beef and pasta dishes predominating.

HOW TO GET THERE

The nearest major airport to Banff is **Calgary International** (see page 168), 120 km (75 miles) east. There are several car rental companies at the airport, as well as scheduled bus services to Banff and Lake Louise with **Brewster** ((403) 762-6767 TOLL-FREE (800) 661-1152 or the **Banff Airporter** ((403) 762-3330 TOLL-FREE (800) 449-2901 WEB SITE www.banffairporter.com.

to be missed, is the **Post Hotel** ((403) 522-3989, in Lake Louise Village. Many people consider this the best table in the Rockies. Built in 1942 for alpine enthusiasts, the Post offers European cuisine with a California influence. Reserve early to get a window table and a view of the Victoria Glacier. Among the four restaurants at Château Lake Louise is the elegant **Edelweiss Dining Room** ((403) 522-3511, where diners can also revel in glacier views and enjoy Canadian and continental cuisine.

The Samson Mall has a number of inexpensive places to eat, including **Bee Line** ((403) 522-2077, with chicken and takeout pizza by the slice; the small eat-in or takeout café/bakery **Laggans Deli** ((403) 522-2017; and the **Village Grill and Bar** ((403) 522-3879, for a family sit-down dinner. At the end of Sentinel Street is the **Lake Louise Station Restaurant** ((403) 522-2600, in a

You can join the private train tour to Vancouver, the **Rocky Mountaineer Railtours** ((604) 606-7200 TOLL-FREE (800) 665-7245 FAX (604) 606-7250 WEB SITE www.rockymountaineer.com at Banff. In Banff, **Greyhound** ((403) 762-6767 TOLL-FREE (800) 661-8747 WEB SITE www.greyhound.ca operates frequent service to Calgary, Edmonton and Vancouver. The TransCanada Highway (Highway 1) runs through Banff National Park, linking it with Calgary in the east and with Vancouver in the west.

THE ICEFIELDS PARKWAY

Linking Banff with Jasper, the Icefields Parkway is one of the most spectacular drives anywhere, offering a fabulous overview of the two national parks. Built as an emloyment-providing scheme during the Depression, it follows the Continental

Divide along a route lined with glaciers, lakes, valleys and mountains, where wildlife roams — sometimes into the middle of the road, so keep a sharp lookout. Set aside at least a day for traveling the Parkway to allow time to stop and enjoy the views. There is a tollbooth at either end.

Start at the **Lake Louise Visitor Information Centre** (see GENERAL INFORMATION, page 127 under BANFF NATIONAL PARK), which has maps and up-to-the-minute information on road conditions (also available by calling ((403) 762-2266). The Parkway runs north from the TransCanada Highway. Some 16 km (10 miles) along the Parkway north of Lake Louise you'll see the bright waters of **Hector Lake** fringed by dark green forest. Eighteen

with rivers flowing from the icefield to the Arctic, the Pacific and the Atlantic Oceans.

At the foot of the Athabasca Glacier, whose toe stops just short of the Parkway, the **Icefield Interpretive Centre** ((403) 762-6735 has information desks, a restaurant, a café and a museum detailing the geological and human history of the area. From here, **Brewster Snocoaches** ((403) 762-6735 TOLL-FREE (877) 423-7433 WEB SITE www.columbia icefield.com will take you right out onto the glacier for a closer look (mid-May and mid-October). The six-wheel-drive Snocoaches are built especially for traveling on the Athabasca Glacier and surrounding gravel fields. Up on the ice you can walk around and even take a sip of pure glacial water

kilometers (11 miles) further along the road, the glacial waters of **Bow Lake** reflect the surrounding peaks, and a few miles beyond, a trail leads to **Peyto Lake,** where the waters change from green to blue as the year advances — a phenomenon caused by the presence of glacial silt. Other sights along the way include the **Crowfoot Glacier**, **Mistaya Canyon** and the **Weeping Wall**, where melting snow streams down the cliff face at the bottom of Cirrus Mountain. It is most spectacular in June; in winter climbers come from all over to scale the ice.

At the **Sunwapta Pass**, 122 km (76 miles) north of Lake Louise and 108 km (67 miles) south of Jasper town, you enter Jasper National Park. This is the edge of the huge **Columbia Icefield**, 325 sq km (129 sq miles) of glaciers and snow within the Canadian Rockies. This is one of only two areas in the world that form a triple continental divide,

(said to make you youthful). Guided ice-walking tours of the glacier will safely shepherd you over the surface, away from the deep and treacherous crevasses that thread through the ice.

Continuing towards Jasper, there are two spectacular waterfalls. The **Sunwapta Falls**, 175 km (108 miles) north of Lake Louise and 55 km (34 miles) south of Jasper, are reached via a short access road. Further along the Parkway, there's access to the **Athabasca Falls**, tumbling down into a narrow gorge.

Icefield Helicopters ((403) 721-2100 TOLL-FREE (888) 844-3514 WEB SITE www.icefieldheli coptertours.com operate sightseeing tours over the glaciers from Cline River Heliport, a one-hour drive north of Lake Louise.

Along the Icefields Parkway in Jasper National Park — OPPOSITE: The Athabasca Glacier and Num-ti-Jah Lodge ABOVE.

WHERE TO STAY AND EAT

Forty kilometers (25 miles) north of Lake Louise, **Num-Ti-Jah Lodge** ((403) 522-2167 FAX (403) 522-2425 WEB SITE www.num-ti-jah.com nestles in a lovely, isolated spot on the banks of Bow Lake below the Crowfoot Glacier. An old hunting lodge (circa 1898), it comprises 25 comfortable guestrooms and a large restaurant and lounge bedecked with animal pelts and unusual furnishings. Num-Ti-Jah offers cross-country skiing and snowshoeing in winter and horseback riding, fishing and hiking in summer (closed November; mid-range to expensive).

The **Sunwapta Falls Resort** ((780) 852-4852 TOLL-FREE (888) 828-5777 FAX (780) 852-5353 WEB SITE www.sunwapta.com, next to the Sunwapta Falls, 52 km (34 miles) south of Jasper on the Icefield Parkway, is a comfortable, moderately priced resort with accommodation in log cabins, a good if basic restaurant and an excellent gift shop, along with mountain bike and fishing rentals.

The **Athabasca Falls Hostel** (HI) ((780) 852-3215 TOLL-FREE (877) 852-0781 FAX (780) 852-5560 WEB SITE www.hihostels.ca, conveniently near the spectacular Athabasca Falls, has three sleeping cabins and a large dining and recreational building.

JASPER NATIONAL PARK

Jasper sits in a broad valley where the Icefields Parkway crosses the Yellowhead Highway. It is smaller than Banff, with a less spectacular setting, but quieter and considerably less congested during the summer season. The town is the starting point for many excellent hiking trails, riding treks, rafting tours and various other excursions into the beautiful wilderness beyond. Here, wildlife even comes into town, with elk cropping the lawns and wandering the streets.

Jasper National Park, the largest of the Canadian Rockies' mountain parks, was developed later than Banff. In the early nineteenth century the Athabasca River and Pass were part of the overland fur-trading route, and at one time a trading post existed not far from the present town. Apart from these traders and some gold prospectors on their way west, the area was not visited until the national park was created in preparation for the transcontinental railway that was to cross the Rockies at Yellowhead Pass. The railway brought with it visitors, and the opening of the Icefields Parkway in 1940 made Jasper Park even more accessible. Although Jasper is today a major tourist attraction with a thriving ski season, it remains quieter and wilder than its older neighbor.

GENERAL INFORMATION

The **Visitor Information Centre** ((780) 852-6176 TOLL-FREE (888) 773-8888 WEB SITE www.jasper canadianrockies.com and www.parkscanada .gc.za, 500 Connaught Drive, is shared by Parks Canada and the local tourist office for one-stop information. It is necessary to sign in here if you're planning an overnight hike in the park.

WHAT TO SEE AND DO

Before you head out of town to enjoy the scenery, you might want to drop by the **Jasper-Yellowhead Museum and Archives** ((780) 852-3013, Pyramid Lake Road. Historical exhibits detail life in the area when the first European explorers and settlers arrived a century ago. The **Den Wildlife Museum** ((403) 852-3361, downstairs at the Whistler's Inn, 105 Miette Avenue, has over 100 stuffed animals for those who've had little luck seeing the live version. The **Jasper Carriage Company** ((780) 852-3562 offers horse-drawn carriage tours.

The **Jasper Tramway**, which is seven kilometers (four miles) south of Jasper, whizzes you up Whistlers Mountain for panoramic views of the ice field and Mount Robson — the highest mountain in the Canadian Rockies (April to October). It is also possible to walk up from the bottom. Officials estimate that it takes five to six hours, but the record is apparently held by some Royal Marines, who ran it in 26 minutes! **Sun Dog Tours** ((780) 852-4056 TOLL-FREE (888) 786-3641, 414 Connaught Drive, operates regular shuttle services from the town to the tramway, as well as a range of other guided tours and hikes.

Just seven kilometers (four miles) northwest of town, on Pyramid Lake Road, **Patricia** and **Pyramid lakes** are set amid cottonwood forest and make fine places to picnic, boat, ride horses, hike or canoe. The former was the sight of the bizarre *Project Habbakuk*, a wartime scheme to create the ultimate weapon: an unsinkable boat made of ice (needless to say, the project failed). Three kilometres (two miles) east of town, on Lodge Road, **Lake Edith** and **Lake Annette** both have picnic areas, beaches and hiking trails, and Lake Annette has a bike trail. Closer to town still is **Lac Beauvert**, where the famous Jasper Park Lodge (see WHERE TO STAY, below) spreads out along the shore.

To the east of the town lies **Maligne Canyon**, which is reached by the Yellowhead Highway and then Maligne Road, about 10 km (six miles) outside Jasper. The water has worn away the limestone to create this deep, and in parts very narrow, slash across the landscape, which can be explored by means of paths and bridges. Begin your hike

The blue ice of Maligne Falls remains locked in winter's embrace.

along the canyon at the trailhead to the right of the teahouse for maximum drama. Six bridges span the canyon at heights of up to 50 m (150 ft). In winter there are guided ice walks through the canyon (see SPORTS AND OUTDOOR ACTIVITIES, below).

Fourteen kilometers (nine miles) further along Maligne Road lies the mysterious **Medicine Lake**, where the water level changes throughout the year, causing it virtually to disappear during the autumn, when water constantly seeps away through holes in the bedrock; during summer melting snow maintains the water level.

The crowning glory of this trip — some might say of the entire tour of the parks — is **Maligne Lake**, which lies a further 21 km (13 miles) along

Maligne Road. The lake stretches a length of 22 km (14 miles) and the amount of still and motion film that would have been shot here would probably cover that distance several times over. Snowcapped mountains rise up from the deep blue glacial waters, and at its center lies the magical **Spirit Island**; a tiny spit of land — not really an island at all — crowned with trees. A **Maligne Tours boat trip** will take you along the lake and to Spirit Island between mid-May and mid-October; a hefty fare is charged. They also operate shuttle services between Jasper and the lake for those without transport, and rowboats, canoes or kayaks, and rod and tackle rental are all available. Professionally guided fishing trips and fly-fishing lessons can also be arranged. You can make reservations for all of your Maligne Lake activities in Jasper at **Maligne Tours** ((780) 852-3370 TOLL-FREE (866) MALIGNE WEB SITE WWW .malignelake.com, 627 Patricia Street.

For a relaxing treat after a hard day's hiking or skiing, visit the **Miette Hot Springs** ((403) 866-3939, which lie 60 km (37 miles) northeast of the town off Highway 16 on Miette Road (mid-May to mid-October). The springs are the hottest in these mountains.

To the south of the town **Mount Edith Cavell** looms magnificently. For a closer look, take a 30-km (18-mile) trip south of Jasper along Highway 93 and turn onto Highway 93A, a winding access road (open only from June to October) that will bring you to the foot of the mountain. A trail will take you to **Angel Glacier**, a wing-shaped tongue of ice that clings to the northeastern slopes of the mountain. There's another path that will take you into the alpine Cavell Meadows, and further back along the access road a trail leads to **Cavell Lake**.

Brewster Motorcoach Tours ((780) 852-3332 WEB SITE www.brewster.ca operates a range of excellent bus tours around Banff and Jasper, including day transfers along the Icefield Parkway with connections to the Snocoach up the Athabasca Glacier (see page 139).

EXCURSIONS FROM JASPER

Mount Robson Provincial Park makes a nice hour-long trip from Jasper townsite. Following Highway 16, the terrain and scenery are similar to Jasper's, though lusher.

The highest mountain in the Canadian Rockies, Mount Robson towers 4,324 m (12,972 ft) high. After five unsuccessful attempts, Robson was finally scaled in 1913. Certain routes on this forbidding mountain are still considered to be among the worlds' most difficult. Viewing conditions are rarely perfect, as Mount Robson is notorious for bad weather and clouds often obscure the top.

There are good views of the mountain (weather permitting) from the parking lot of the **Mount Robson Visitor Information Centre** ((250) 566-9174, which is open mid-May to early October; there is also a small restaurant here. The park has five hiking trails, ranging from eight-kilometer (five-mile) day hikes to 70-km (44-mile) tramps; a permit is required. For helicopter flights over Mt Robson, call **Robson Helimagic** TOLL-FREE (887) 454-4700. Route information is available at the park information center.

SPORTS AND OUTDOOR ACTIVITIES

You can get a complete list of **day hikes**, the *Day Hiker's Guide to Jasper National Park*, from the Visitor Centre. **Horseback riding** and a dozen other

ABOVE: Rocky Mountain flora — a tiny conifer welcomes spring. RIGHT: Eons of erosion by the rushing water of Maligne Falls dug this deep canyon.

outdoor activities are available at Jasper Park Lodge ((403) 852-3301, which also has an excellent 18-hole **golf** course. Alternatively, contact the Pyramid Riding Stables ((780) 852-RIDE, Pyramid Lake Road, four kilometers (two and a half miles) from Jasper townsite.

With so many lakes, Jasper is a boater's paradise. **Canoeing** is mainly reserved for experienced paddlers, as the mountain waterways are swift and dangerous, but there are several outfitters offering **river rafting** on the Athabasca River, including Jasper Raft Tours ((780) 852-2665 TOLL-FREE (888) 55FLOAT and Maligne Rafting Adventures ((780) 852-3370 TOLL-FREE (866) 625-4463 WEB SITE www.mra.ab.ca, 627 Patricia Street, Jasper. **Motorboating** is allowed only on Pyramid Lake.

There's excellent **skiing** at Marmot Basin ((403) 852-3816 SNOW PHONE (403) 488-5909 WEB SITE www.skimarmot.com, 19 km (12 miles) south of Jasper on Highway 93-93A. Here there are slopes to suit beginners and experts, and cross-country trails sweep through the stunning scenery surrounding Maligne Lake. For information on **ski packages** in the area you can call Ski Jasper ((403) 852-5247 TOLL-FREE (800) 473-8135. Also in winter, the popular **Canyon Icewalks** offered by the Jasper Adventure Centre ((780) 852-5595 TOLL-FREE (800) 565-7547 WEB SITE www.jasperadventurecentre.com, 604 Connaught Drive, take hardy adventurers on ice-climbing and walking trips along the multicolored ice falls at Maligne Canyon. Ice-gripping "super soles" and boots are provided on this three-hour tour. They also offer **snowshoe** and **snowmobile** tours and **dog sledding**, along with a wide range of guided tours, hikes wildlife safaris and other adventure activities. Cold Fire Creek Dog Sledding ((780) 852-5650 WEB SITE www.jasperoutdooradventure.com, 620 Connaught Drive, offers sled rides pulled by huskies up an old trappers' trail in the Small River Valley.

For specialist **birding** or **fishing** tours, **mountain bike**, **boat and canoe rentals**, visit On-Line Sport ((780) 852-3630, 600 Patricia Street. High Country Helicopters ((780) 852-5650, booking c/o Beyond the Beaten Path, 620 Connaught Drive, run sightseeing flights from Jasper/Hinton Airport.

NIGHTLIFE

Jasper is much quieter than Banff, and most people like it that way. What drinking and dancing goes on here tends to take place in the hotel lounges. The **Whistlestop Pub** ((780) 852-3361, at the Whistlers Inn, Connaught Drive and Miette Avenue, has a good selection of local ales and rare scotch, and there's a big-screen television, pool and darts. For a quiet drink in an elegant setting, there's the Jasper Park Lodge's **Emerald Lounge** (with fireplace and entertainment in season) and **Palisade Lounge**, overlooking beautiful Lac Beauvert.

WHERE TO STAY

In splendid solitude, the **Fairmont Jasper Park Lodge** ((780) 852-3301 TOLL-FREE (888) 463-2200 FAX (780) 852-5107 WEB SITE www.fairmont.com unrolls across 365 hectares (903 acres) of wilderness along the milky green Athabasca River and Lac Beauvert to the east of town (expensive). Between the main lodge, cabins and outbuildings, there are 440 rooms and suites — some with fireplaces, all with beautiful views, lots of character, sitting rooms and creature comforts. It has riding stables, luxurious log cabin lodges, five restaurants, four lounges and a famous golf course. It

also offers fishing, boating and skiing packages. Many of the activities offered here can be enjoyed by non-guests as well.

Charlton's Château Jasper ((780) 852-5644 TOLL-FREE IN CANADA (800) 661-9323 FAX (780) 852-4860 E-MAIL info@chateaujasper.com WEB SITE www.decorehotels.com, 96 Geikie Street, tries hard to live up to its expensive bracket prices, but is frankly overpriced. Rooms and suites are very large, but the hotel suffers from ambient noise, and some of the highest-priced rooms look out over a dreary jumble of air-conditioning vents. The dining room has a good reputation, however, and there is an attractive indoor pool.

Lobstick Lodge ((780) 852-4431 TOLL-FREE (888) 8JASPER FAX (780) 852-4142 WEB SITE www.mtn-park-lodges.com, close to the center on the corner of Geikie and Juniper Street, has 139 mid-range to expensive motel units and lots of home-away-from-home comforts; it's an ideal choice for families. Located just opposite the Via Rail station right in the town center, **Whistlers Inn (** (403) 852-3361 TOLL-FREE (800) 282-9919 FAX (403) 852-4993 WEB SITE www.whistlersinn.com, 105 Miette Avenue, is a busy mid-range hotel with 40 nicely furnished rooms and suites. It has friendly staff, an outdoor rooftop hot tub, a cocktail lounge, an excellent restaurant and a busy bar.

Also mid-range in price, the **Athabasca Hotel (** (780) 852-3386 TOLL-FREE (877) 542-8422 FAX (780) 852-4955 WEB SITE www.athabascahotel .com, 510 Patricia Street, has 65 simply furnished rooms, about two-thirds of which have private bathrooms. There's a popular bar, an attractive dining room and a cocktail lounge.

A kilometer (about half a mile) south of the town, nestled along the Athabasca and Miette rivers, **Tekarra Lodge (** (780) 852-3058 FAX (780) 852-4636, off Highway 93A, offers cozy and peaceful self-catering cabins with fireplaces from May to October (inexpensive to mid-range). The **Patricia Lake Bungalows (** (780) 852-3560 FAX (780) 852-4060, five kilometers (three miles) north of Jasper, has 37 tidy, rustic cottages; clumps of aspen and fir dot the banks of an ultramarine lake. The playground and cabins with kitchenettes make this a good place for families (mid-range). **Pyramid Lake Resort (** (780) 852-4900 FAX (780) 852-7007, has 88 rooms, some with fireplaces, and a restaurant that serves seafood and barbecue (mid-range).

The mainstay of the Jasper lodging scene is **home accommodation**, a tradition since the park's early days; you'll see signs posted throughout the residential area. Options range from basic to very comfortable, from full apartments with kitchen to rooms with private or shared bath. Many are self-contained; some provide breakfast. Rates range from very inexpensive to mid-range, depending on facilities. Write to **Jasper Home Accommodation Association** WEB SITE www.visit-jasper.com or www.bbcanada.com, PO Box 758, Jasper, Alberta T0E 1E0, for its annual brochure that provides contact information for the individual homes.

The hostels nearest to the town, both open year-round, are the **Maligne Canyon Hostel** (HI), on Maligne Lake Road, 11 km (six and a half miles) east of town, and the **Jasper International Hostel (HI)** Whistler's Mountain Road, seven kilometers (four miles) to the southwest. The Jasper International offers downhill skiing packages. For both, contact **(** (780) 852-3215 TOLL-FREE (877) 852-0781 FAX (780) 852-5560 WEB SITE www.hihostels.ca, PO Box 387, Jasper, Alberta T0E 1E0.

WHERE TO EAT

The **Caledonia Grill (** (780) 852-4070, Whistler's Inn, 600 Connaught Drive, is an excellent restaurant serving burgers, salads and pasta through-

out the day, alongside delicious Canadian game grills. A little further up Connaught Drive, **Papa George's Restaurant (** (780) 852-3351, at the Astoria Hotel, is another fine restaurant serving imaginative Canadian cuisine. **Something Else Greek Taverna (** (780) 852-3850, 621 Patricia Street, is well loved and well patronized for its mouth-watering traditional dishes. **Prime Rib Village (** (780) 852-8728, at the Tonquin Inn, Juniper Street, between Connaught and Geikie Streets, is the place to go for melt-in-the-mouth Alberta steaks.

You'd never know the modern **Mountain Foods & Café (**/FAX (780) 852-4050, 606 Connaught Drive (directly across from the train station), is

housed in a former dance hall. "Jasper's best bartender" and a pack of friendly locals are two among many reasons to pay a call. Quesadillas, bagels and creative omelets are the specialities here.

Outside the townsite, the **Jasper Park Lodge (** (780) 852-3301 on Lac Beauvert has nine restaurants. The flagship is the four-diamond-award-winning Edith Cavell Dining Room, featuring freshly baked breads and herbs grown in the lodge greenhouse. The cafeteria-style **Maligne Canyon Teahouse (** (780) 852-5565, at Maligne Canyon (open April to October), has a generous salad bar and hot meals that can be enjoyed on chilly days by the hearth or in summer on the terrace; avoid peak hours as this is a favorite pit stop for bus tour groups. The **View Restaurant at Maligne Lake**

OPPOSITE: The Pipestone River at Lake Louise Village. ABOVE : Ice clings to the surface of the Pipestone.

((780) 852-3370 is another good spot run along similar lines. There's a pleasant terrace and the cafeteria serves hot meals, big sandwiches, and homemade breads and pastries.

HOW TO GET THERE

Jasper is 292 km (184 miles) north of Banff along the Icefields Parkway, making Calgary International Airport 412 km (259 miles) away from Jasper. Edmonton International Airport is 350 km (215 miles) away from Jasper along the Yellowhead Highway. If you're aiming for Jasper during the winter you may want to drive via Calgary and Edmonton rather than taking the Icefields Parkway from Banff — winter conditions on this mountain road are sometimes hazardous.

Sun Dog Tours ((780) 852-4056 TOLL-FREE (888) 786-3641, 414 Connaught Drive, operate regular shuttle services to Banff, Lake Louise, Calgary and Edmonton airports, as well as the Jasper Tramway shuttle.

The **VIA Rail** station WEB SITE www.viarail.ca is in the town center along Connaught Drive, and trains run west to Kamloops and Vancouver, eastwards to Edmonton, Winnipeg and beyond, and northward to Prince George and Prince Rupert. The **Greyhound** station ((403) 852-3332 TOLL-FREE (800) 661-8747 WEB SITE www.greyhound.ca shares the train station in the town center, and regular services operate to Vancouver via Kamloops, to Edmonton and to Banff.

The Yellowhead Highway runs through Jasper from Edmonton in the east and to Prince George in the west, also linking with Vancouver via Kamloops.

THE ALBERTA ROCKIES

THE KANANASKIS

The foothill region of Kananaskis Country lies between Calgary and the Rocky Mountains. Several provincial parks, created to take some of the pressure off Banff, protect this area. Along the TransCanada Highway, 106 km (66 miles) west of Calgary and only 21 km (13 miles) east of Banff townsite, the community of **Canmore** is nestled at the base of the Three Sisters Mountain Range. As the nearest town to the Rockies outside the national parks, Canmore is a hive of building activity, with holiday homes, apartments and hotels crowding the hillsides. The **Canmore Information Centre** ((403) 678-5277 is west of town on Highway 1A.

The town center has plenty of shops and eateries, and is a good base for outdoor activities. The Kananaskis region encompasses three provincial parks, including the **Peter Lougheed Provincial Park** ((403) 591-6344, Alberta's largest, with

500 sq km (190 sq miles) of valleys and lakes and hiking trails. Canmore was the sight of the 1988 Olympic cross-country skiing and biathlon events, and the **Canmore Nordic Centre** ((403) 678-2400 still draws skiers in winter and mountain bikers in summer. **Wild Cave Tours** ((403) 678-8819 TOLL-FREE (877) 317-1178 WEB SITE www.canadianrockies .net / wildcavetours conducts year-round tours of the labyrinthine caves under Grotto Mountain, five kilometers (three miles) east of Canmore. There are easier half-day tours and challenging full-day expeditions involving rope work. All participants need to be reasonably fit. **Alpine Helicopters** ((403) 609-1714, Canmore Heliplex, 91 Bow Valley, offers a series of spectacular helicopter flights over the Mount Assiniboine and Gloria glaciers. **Mountain Fly Fishers** ((403) 678-9522 TOLL-FREE (800) 450-9664 WEB SITE www .greendrakefly.com offers guided and self-guided fly-fishing expeditions, including all equipment.

Oh Canada Eh?! ((402) 609-0004 TOLL-FREE (800) 467-2071 WEB SITE www.ohcanadaeh.com, at 125 Kananaskis Way, Canmore, is a lively dinner show, imported from Niagara Falls, where it has been running for years, featuring Mounties, lumberjacks and other jolly Canadian types, with music, dance and a five-course meal.

The resort of Kananaskis Village and the adjacent **Nakiska Ski Area** ((403) 591-7777 and **Kananaskis Country Golf Course** ((403) 591-7272, one of several excellent mountain courses in the area, are reached via Highway 40, south of the TransCanada Highway. The Canmore Nordic Centre and Nakiska Ski Area were 1988 Winter Olympic sites. Kananaskis Village is the departure point for many hiking and cross-country skiing trails. The Kananaskis was also the venue for the 2002 G8 Summit.

Brewster Kananaskis Guest Ranch ((403) 673-3737 FAX (403) 673-2100 WEB SITE www.kananskisguestranch.com, in Seebe, 30 minutes east of Banff, is a charming place with cedar cabins furnished with antiques. The ranch offers its guests horseback riding, canoeing, rafting and golf, as well as a dining room, a cocktail lounge and a whirlpool (expensive).

Pebbles sparkle like flakes of gold in Banff's Bow River.

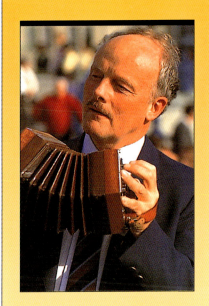

Alberta

ALBERTA

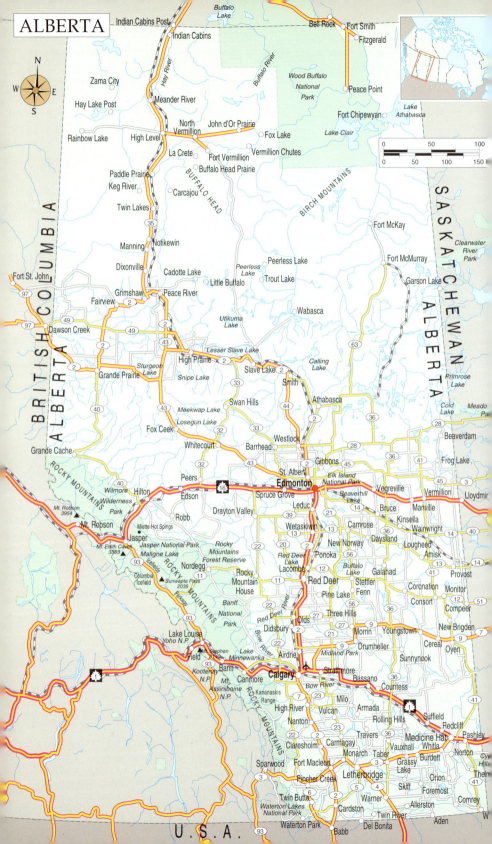

British Columbia (west side)

Saskatchewan (east side)

Alberta

U.S.A. (south)

Buffalo Lake
Indian Cabins Post
Indian Cabins
Bell Rock   Fort Smith
Fitzgerald
Zama City
Hay Lake Post
Meander River
Buffalo River
Wood Buffalo National Park
Peace Point
Fort Chipewyan
Lake Athabasca
North Vermillion   John d'Or Prairie
Rainbow Lake
High Level   Fox Lake
Lake Clair
La Crete   Fort Vermilion   Vermillion Chutes
Paddle Prairie   Buffalo Head Prairie
Keg River
Carcajou   BUFFALO HEAD
Twin Lakes
35
Fort McKay
Manning   Notikewin
Peerless Lake   BIRCH MOUNTAINS
Dixonville   Peerless Lake
Cadotte Lake   Trout Lake   Fort McMurray
Little Buffalo
Fort St. John   Garson Lake
97   Grimshaw   Peace River   Wabasca   Clearwater River Park
Fairview
97   Dawson Creek   Utikuma Lake
49   49
2   43
Lesser Slave Lake   63
High Prairie   2
Grande Prairie   Snipe Lake   Slave Lake   2
Sturgeon Lake   33   Calling Lake
Smith
40   Meekwap Lake   Swan Hills   Athabasca   Cold Lake   Meado Pa
43   Losegun Lake   44   2   36   Primrose Lake
Fox Creek   32   33   Westlock   28   Beaverdam
Grande Cache   Whitecourt   Barrhead   28   41   Frog Lake
Gibbons   45   36
32   St. Albert   Elk Island National Park
Peers   Edson   Edmonton   Vegreville   Lloydmir
Hilton   16   Spruce Grove   Beaverhill Lake   Vermillion
Mt. Robson 3954   Robb   Leduc   14   Bruce   Manville   40
Mt. Robson   Drayton Valley   21   Kinsella   Wainwright
Jasper   Wilmore Wilderness Park   39   Wetaskiwin   13   Camrose   14
Miette Hot Springs   13   New Norway   Daysland   Lougheed
Mt. Edith Cavell 3363   Malabe Lake   22   20   Ponoka   56   Buffalo   Amisk
Jasper National Park   Rocky Mountains Forest Reserve   Red Deer Lake   Galahad   13   14
Columbia Icefield   Nordegg   Lacombe   12   Stettler   41   Provost
93   Sunwapta Pass 2035   11   Red Deer   Pine Lake   Fenn   Coronation   Monitor
Rocky Mountain House   Stettler   Consort
Banff National Park   22   Three Hills   51
Didsbury   27   Compeer
Lake Louise   Morrin   New Brigden
Yoho N.P.   Olds   21   9   Youngstown   7
Field   Lake Minnewanka   22   Drumheller   Cereal
Kootenay N.P.   Airdrie   Midland Park   Sunnynook   Oyen
Banff   Stratmore   9
Canmore   Calgary   Bassano
Mt. Assiniboine N.P.   Bow River   Countess   41
Kananaskis Range   7   Milo   Suffield
High River   23   Armada   Rolling Hills   Redcliff   Pashley
Nanton   Vulcan   Travers   36   Medicine Hat   Whitla   Norton
22   2   Claresholm   Carmagay   Vauxhall   Grassy Lake   Burdett
Sparwood   Monarch   Taber   3   Orion   Thel
Fort Macleod   Lethbridge   Skiff   Foremost   41
Pincher Creek   6   2   Warner   Comrey
Twin Butte   5   Allerston
Waterton Lakes National Park   Cardston   Aden
Waterton Park   Del Bonita
93   Babb   Twin River

U.S.A.

Stretching from the Northwest Territories to Montana, Alberta is bordered by the Canadian Rockies to the west and Saskatchewan to the east. It shares Canada's vast prairie land with Saskatchewan and Manitoba and, covering some 650,000 sq km (250,000 sq miles), is the largest of the three Prairie Provinces. Alberta has a population of 2.8 million, half of whom live in Calgary and Edmonton, leaving vast areas of the province uninhabited.

Alberta has the cowboys, cattle and wide-open spaces that epitomize prairie land, but it is also famous for the magnificent Rocky Mountain landscape of snowy peaks, sweeping slopes and brilliant lakes that characterize the Banff, Jasper and Waterton Lakes National Parks to the southwest. The prairie lands of the southeast offer three different landscapes: in the southeastern corner, an area of arid cattle-raising grassland and badlands is surrounded by a larger wheat-growing belt that in turn gives way to an even larger area of parklands, trees and mixed farming. It is in this last region that the province's major cities, Calgary and Edmonton, are located. The north of the province is a sparsely inhabited region of forests and lakes.

Exploitation of the province's oil and natural gas resources sparked a period of rapid growth and prosperity in the 1970s that carried the cities of Edmonton and Calgary to the fore. Fluctuations in oil and grain prices brought hard times in the 1980s, but these days Alberta is booming again with the fastest-growing economy in Canada. The province remains a producer of beef and grain as well as a major producer of oil and gas, with forestry also playing a role in the economy. The province's endless outdoor opportunities and the stunning scenery of its national parks contribute to a flourishing tourist industry.

The first European to explore the area was Anthony Henday, who acted on behalf of the Hudson's Bay Company. Among those who eased the way for the settlement of the area was Father Albert Lacombe, who founded a mission, schools and churches, and established good relations with the prairie's native population. In 1869 the Hudson's Bay Company sold the land to the government and Alberta became part of Canada's Northwest Territories. Whisky peddlers and fur traders descended on the area, and there followed a period of lawlessness and bloodshed, which continued until the arrival, in 1874, of the North West Mounted Police.

The traders introduced guns to the native tribes, and the ease with which the buffalo could be slaughtered spelled the end of the massive herds that once roamed the prairie and had been the mainstay of the native way of life. With the herds gone, the indigenous people were willing to negotiate treaties. Cultivation of the prairie by the whites began in the 1880s, along with immigration from Europe, Russia and the United States. The province of Alberta was created in 1905; the subsequent world wars and various political upheavals brought more immigrants to the province in search of a new life.

Although the discovery of oil brought Alberta prosperity and wealthy, modern cities, the province has steadfastly retained the spirit of its early ranching days. The picture-book image of the cowboy riding among herds on the plains is not an uncommon sight in the south of the province, while the Wild West is celebrated each year with great gusto in the famous Calgary Stampede and Edmonton's Klondike Days festival.

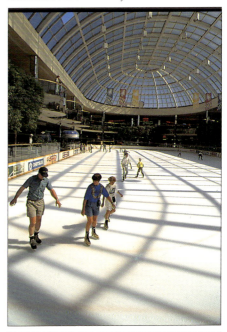

EDMONTON

Alberta's capital city stands on the outer rim of the prairie, right at the center of the province, in the deep valley of the North Saskatchewan River. Shiny modern high-rises testify to the prosperity of this oil town, a wealth that Edmonton seems to have handled wisely. The town is well planned: streets conform to a grid system, underground and sheltered walkways protect citizens from the winter cold, and the riverbanks have been turned into parklands that provide winter and summer recreation.

With a population of 938,000, Edmonton is the sixth largest city in Canada and the northernmost major city in North America. It is Canada's oil capital, with some 2,000 wells within 40 km

The West Edmonton Mall is not just for shopping.

(25 miles) of the city, producing approximately 10 percent of Canada's oil. It deals with all the technological and scientific aspects of the oil industry, having refineries and petrochemical plants, but it leaves the administrative side of the industry to Calgary.

BACKGROUND

In the late eighteenth century, two fur-trading posts were established in the area, one belonging to the Hudson's Bay Company, the other to the rival North West Trading Company. When the two companies merged in 1821, Edmonton House, the fort established in 1795 by the Hudson's Bay Com-

merchants. This period of Edmonton's history is affectionately remembered every year in the town's annual Klondike Days celebrations.

When the province of Alberta was created in 1905, Edmonton, then with a population of 8,000, was elected its capital, much to the disappointment of rival Calgary. It continued to grow rapidly, with a further surge of immigration during the construction of the Alaska Highway. The biggest boom of all started with the discovery of oil in 1947 at Leduc, to the south of Edmonton. The discovery of further oil fields followed, and by 1965 the population had quadrupled. The 1960s and 1970s brought a period of great prosperity and frantic urban development, which

pany, became the trading and administrative center of the northwest and the jewel in the company's crown. From here, the Company traded with the Blackfoot confederacy of warrior tribes who, together with the Cree, then inhabited the land.

In 1870, the Hudson's Bay Company sold the land to the Canadian government, and the area opened to settlers. As elsewhere in Alberta, there followed a wild and lawless period during which the town of 600 inhabitants was incorporated. Law and order finally arrived with the North West Mounted Police in 1874. In 1891 the railroad reached Edmonton, increasing the city's importance as a transportation center and triggering an influx of settlers. The discovery of gold in the Klondike in 1898 brought Edmonton its first boom period, as prospectors flooded to the town to prepare for the long trek, increasing the population to around 4,000 and bringing prosperity to the

declined in the 1980s with the drop in oil prices. The economic mood of the 1990s, however, was decidedly upbeat. Edmonton remains Canada's oil center, but is not wholly dependent on this one commodity. It is also the handling and supply center for the surrounding fertile agricultural area, mineral-rich northern Alberta, and for northern Canada as a whole.

GENERAL INFORMATION

There are visitor centers at all of the major points of entry into the province. For information on Edmonton, contact **Edmonton Tourism Information Centre** ((780) 496-8400 TOLL-FREE (800) 463-4667 E-MAIL gateway@ede.org WEB SITE www .tourism.ede.org, 9797 Jasper Avenue NW. There are three information offices: Gateway Park, 2404 Calgary Trail Northbound SW; downtown at the Shaw Conference Centre, 9797 Jasper Avenue NW; and in the Spruce Grove & District Chamber of Commerce Building, Highway 16A West, one kilometer (half a mile) west of Spruce Grove.

There are many Internet cafés in the city, including the **Bohemia Cyber Café**, 11012 Jasper Avenue, and **Bytes Internet Café**, 1668 Bourbon Street.

Getting Around

Like most Canadian cities, Edmonton's street plan is laid out on a numbered grid, making it easy to find your way around. Avenues run east to west and streets run north to south. Edmonton's **Light Rail Transit (LRT) System** ((780) 496-4611 runs north from the city center to Commonwealth Stadium, the Skyreach Centre and Northlands Park, across downtown from Churchill Station to Grandin Station at 111th Street and then south to the university.

ETS ((780) 496-1600 WEB SITE www.takeETS.com runs an excellent network of city buses. It is possible to buy discounted books of 10 tickets, valid on all city transportation, or passes for a day, month or year. The **Edmonton High Level Street Car** ((780) 496-1464 WEB SITE www.edmonton-radial-railway.ab.ca is a 1920s Japanese streetcar that runs between Old Strathcona and Grandin, with departures every 30 minutes daily 11 AM to 4 PM (until 10 PM during "Fringe").

For tours of Edmonton and the surrounding area, contact either **Magic Time Tours** ((780) 940-7479 or **Out an' About** ((780) 909-8687 WEB SITE www.outanabouttours.com.

WHAT TO SEE AND DO

Edmonton is not a particularly scenic city, but the people are friendly, the local arts and festival scene is humming, and several of the neighborhoods, such as Chinatown and old Strathcona, have real charm. There are plenty of sights to keep visitors happy for a couple of days.

In the heart of the downtown "Arts" area, the **Edmonton Art Gallery** ((780) 422-6223 WEB SITE www.edmonton artgallery.com, 2 Sir Winston Churchill Square, holds a series of temporary exhibitions, based on visiting collections or its own permanent collection of contemporary and historical art. Also on the square are the city's main theater, concert hall, library and city hall. The fountain and plunge pool, used to cool off in summer, becomes a skating rink in winter.

Southwest of the downtown core, the **Alberta Legislature** ((780) 427-7362, 10820 98th Avenue WEB SITE www.assembly.ab.ca, which has free tours daily, is the home of the provincial government. Built between 1907 and 1912, on the site of the original Fort Edmonton, it is a dignified building of yellow sandstone, overlooking the river and surrounded by landscaped grounds

with fountains, pools, formal gardens and lawns. Below ground, the Government Center Pedway links the Legislature building to other government buildings and has an exhibition area with displays about Alberta.

West of downtown, the excellent **Provincial Museum of Alberta** ((780) 453-9100 WEB SITE www.pma.edmonton.ab.ca, 12845 102nd Avenue, is pleasantly situated in parkland overlooking the riverbank. The Wild Alberta gallery recreates the various eco-systems found in Alberta, from the mountains to the prairies or the boreal forests of the north, complete with animal and plant life. The Natural History Gallery covers the geology of the area, its fossils and the days of the

dinosaurs. The compelling Bug Room crawls with live spiders, beetles and other insects. The fascinating Syncrude Gallery of Aboriginal Culture tells the story of the local First Nations people, mainly the Blackfoot and Cree.

The **Odyssium** ((780) 451-3344 WEB SITE www.odyssium.com, 11211 142nd Street, northwest of the city center in Coronation Park, is a suitably spaceship-like building containing Canada's largest planetarium — the Margaret Zeidler Star Theatre — as well as an observatory and a series of fascinating hands-on exhibitions on astronomy and science. The Syncrude Science Stage hosts regular scientific demonstrations; there is also an Imax theater.

Valley Zoo ((780) 496-8787, 134th Street and Buena Vista Road, is a good day out for the kids, with around 100 species of exotic, endangered and native species, a children's zoo, small train, elephant bathing and camel rides.

Over on the south side of the river, close to Macdonald Bridge, the unmistakable **Muttart Conservatory** ((780) 496-8755 WEB SITE www.gov.edmonton.ab.ca/muttart is a botanic garden housed in four striking glass pyramids, three

OPPOSITE: The little steamtrain chugs its way across Fort Edmonton Park. ABOVE: Edmonton's skyline at night.

simulating different climatic zones — tropical, arid and temperate — while the fourth pyramid holds changing displays.

Across the road, on the riverbank, is the departure point for the *Edmonton Queen* ((780) 424-2628 WEB SITE www.edmontonqueen.com (offices at 9734 98th Avenue), a paddlewheel that operates gentle hour-long cruises along the Saskatchewan River, through the heart of the city, from May to October daily.

Still south of the river, a little further west, is the Strathcona, a town that joined with Edmonton in 1912. In the **Old Strathcona Historic Area** ((780) 433-5866, between 99th and 109th Streets and Saskatchewan Drive and 80th Avenue, many of the lovingly restored buildings predate the union. Pick up a walking tour brochure from a Tourism Information Centre and enjoy a stroll along these Victorian streets, now full to the brim with delightful boutiques, coffee shops and restaurants. There's a **Farmers' Market** from 8 AM to 3 PM on Saturday in the old bus barns, 10310 83rd Avenue. **Edmonton Ghost Tours** ((780) 469-3187 WEB SITE www.edmontonghosttours.com (summer Monday to Thursday 9 PM) offers hour-long walking tours of ghostly old Strathcona, departing from the Rescuer Statue next to the Walterdale Playhouse, 10322 83rd Street.

A red brick mansion built in 1911 for the family of Alexander Cameron Rutherford, first premier of Alberta, **Rutherford House** ((780) 427-3995, 11153 Saskatchewan Drive, has been fully restored and furnished in period style. With costumed historical interpreters, it is now open for tours, and serves fine lunches and afternoon tea.

From here, continue west, through the university campus, to **Fort Edmonton Park** ((780) 496-8774 WEB SITE www.gov.edmonton.ab.ca/fort, on the south bank of the river just west of Whitemud Freeway, close to Quesnel Bridge. This ambitious project tells the history of the white settlement of Edmonton in vivid terms, with a detailed reconstruction of the palisaded Fort Edmonton, the 1846 Hudson's Bay Company trading post complete with "inhabitants" who are happy to chat to you about their life as a company employee. There is a re-creation of village life in 1885, before the coming of the railroad; a 1905 street, showing Edmonton as an expanding capital city; and a 1920 street scene showing Edmonton as a prosperous business city. Meticulous attention is given to detail, with schools, churches and offices, as well as shops carrying stock appropriate to the period. To complete the experience you can ride in a restored streetcar, a steam train, a stagecoach or a horse wagon. Special events are held here throughout the year.

Coming back to modern times with a jolt, the **West Edmonton Mall** ((780) 444-5300, at 170th Street and 87th Avenue, is to date the world's largest mall, covering a staggering 500,000 sq m (5.3 million sq ft). The mall is devoted to shopping and recreation, with about 800 stores (including six major department stores), over 110 places to eat, 26 cinemas (including an Imax screen) and several activity-based atttractions — Iceland skating rink; Galaxyland amusement park (with a roller-coaster); Professor Wem's Adventure Gold; an 18-hole mini-golf course; the rooftop driving range Top Flite Skyrange; World Waterpark; a trio of underwater attractions including a 200-species aquarium, submarine rides and performing dolphins; the Playdium video games arcade; and Palace Casino. Like it or hate it, it's there and worth a visit for the experience alone. Some 20 million visitors a year must find it worthwhile.

Smaller city museums include the **Loyal Edmonton Regiment Museum** ((780) 421-9943, 10440 108th Avenue; the **Ukrainian Canadian Archives and Museum of Alberta** ((780) 424-7580, 9543 110th Avenue; the **Telephone Historical Centre** ((780) 433-1010, 10430 83rd Avenue; the **Alberta Railway Museum** ((780) 472-6229, 24215 34th Street; and the **Alberta Aviation Museum** ((780) 451-1175, 11410 Kingsway Avenue.

Festivals

Not to be outdone by Calgary's Stampede celebration, Edmonton introduced **Klondike Days** ((780) 423-2822 WEB SITE www.klondikedays .com, a 10-day knees-up in honor of the 1898 gold rush, with parades, competitions, music, dancing, parties and breakfasting in the open air. This is only one of an action-packed festival calendar that celebrates music (folk, jazz and classical), art, comedy, film, street performance and Edmonton's heritage. Others worth looking out for are the **Edmonton Heritage Festival** ((780) 488-3378 WEB SITE www.edmontonheritagefest .com, **Edmonton Folk Music Festival** ((780) 429-1899 WEB SITE www.edmontonfolkfest.org and **Edmonton's International Fringe Theatre Festival** ((780) 448-9000 WEB SITE www.fringe .alberta.ca, the largest alternative theater festival in North America, with over 140 productions on 30 stages. All three are in August.

In November, come to Edmonton for the **Canadian Finals Rodeo** ((780) 471-7210 WEB SITE www.canadianfinalsrodeo.com, the Canadian end-of-season championship.

EXCURSIONS FROM EDMONTON

Near the town of Devon, and only 15 minutes' drive from West Edmonton Mall, the **Devonian Botanic Garden** ((780) 987-3054 WEB SITE www. discoveredmonton.com/Devonian is one of the finest in North America. Founded by the University of Alberta in 1959, it now covers 32 hectares (80 acres), with a further 44 hectares (110 acres)

of wilderness. Highlights include the breathtaking orchid house and butterfly house, the Japanese Garden, the Desert Garden, the Alpine Garden and, in season, spectacular displays of lilies, irises and peonies.

Elk Island National Park ((780) 922-2950 WEB SITE www.parkscanada.gc.ca/elk, Rural Route 1, Fort Saskatchewan, is a wildlife reserve with unspoiled wilderness of forests and lakes, only 48 km (29 miles) east of Edmonton on Highway 16 (the Yellowhead Highway). Elk, bison, moose and deer roam here, and hundreds of species of birds can be seen. The park has an Information Centre, hiking trails ranging in length from 2.5 to 18 km (1.5 to 11 miles), cross-country skiing trails over rolling terrain and a lake for canoeing and swimming. Camping is permitted throughout the year.

Further east along Highway 16 about 50 km (31 miles) from Edmonton lies the **Ukrainian Cultural Heritage Village** ((780) 662-3640, a reconstruction of an early settlement of Ukrainian immigrants. Ukrainian settlers arrived in Alberta in droves during the 1890s, and contributed greatly to the cultural development of the province. A reception area has exhibitions on the lives of these pioneers and on the story behind their immigration.

Ask the tourist office for details of the many other sites in the area, as well as the 70 golf courses within an hour's drive of the city.

SPORTS AND OUTDOOR ACTIVITIES

The North Saskatchewan River snakes its way east–west through the city, lined on both banks by a long green belt of parkland that stretches

A ride in one of Fort Edmonton Park's horse-drawn wagons.

for nearly 30 km (19 miles). This popular city parkland offers all kinds of facilities, including snack bars and networks of **jogging**, **running** and **cycling** trails. In the winter there are **cross-country skiing** trails here too, as well as at Elk Island National Park.

The city has several professional sports teams: the **Edmonton Oilers** ((780) 451-8000 WEB SITE www.edmontonoilers.com are part of the Canadian National Hockey League, the **Edmonton Eskimos** ((780) 448-3757 WEB SITE www.esks.com play in the Canadian Football League, and the **Edmonton Trappers** ((780) 414-4450 WEB SITE www.trappersbaseball.com play PCL Triple A professional baseball.

WEB SITE www.edmontonopera.come and the **Alberta Ballet Company** ((780) 428-6839 WEB SITE www.albertaballet.com. The **Francis Winspear Centre** ((780) 428-1414 (box office) or (780) 429-1992 (tours) WEB SITE www.winspearcentre.com, 4 Sir Winston Churchill Square, is a 1,928-seat concert hall, now home to the Edmonton Symphony Orchestra. There are also many other theater venues scattered throughout Edmonton, including a couple of dinner theaters. Edmonton holds the **Fringe Theatre Festival** for 11 days in August (see above).

For stand-up comedy with your dinner, try the **Comedy Factory** ((780) 469-4999, 34th Avenue and Calgary Trail North. For jazz, there's

NIGHTLIFE AND THE ARTS

Edmonton is particularly well endowed with theaters and theatrical companies. For the schedule, pick up a copy of one of the free papers such as *Vue Weekly*.

The **Citadel Theatre** ((780) 425-1820 WEB SITE www.citadeltheatre.com, 9828 101A Avenue at 99th Street (Churchill Square), is a major Canadian performing arts center. This impressive glass-and-brick complex houses five theaters, where a variety of first-rate stage and musical productions are performed; there is also a pleasant indoor garden where you can while away some time. The **Northern Alberta Jubilee Auditorium** ((780) 427-9622 WEB SITE www.jubilee auditorium.com, 87th Avenue and 114th Street, is another venue for theater, ballet and concerts. It is home to the **Edmonton Opera** ((780) 429-1000

the **Yardbird Suite** ((780) 432-0428, 10203 86th Avenue, and occasional jazz concerts at the **Northern Alberta Jubilee Auditorium** (above).

The city also has dozens of bars and eateries that double as nightclubs and feature a wide range of music. You can hear rhythm and blues, country, jazz and all sorts of other music at the **Sidetrack Café** ((780) 421-1326, 10333 112th Street, where you can also enjoy some excellent light meals and snacks.

Café Select ((780) 423-0419, 10018 106th Street, is known as the after-theater spot for a quiet drink. The city's biggest patio, at **Earl's Tin Palace** ((780) 448-5822, 11830 Jasper Avenue, is jammed every Friday night before the club scene gets underway.

Try out the beer at Edmonton's own microbrewery, **Brewster's Brewing Company** ((780) 421-4677, at 5820 87th Avenue, or, to get that cow-town feel, down a cold one at **Cowboys Country Saloon** ((780) 481-8739, 10102 180th Street. If that has put you in foot-stomping mood, check out the dancing at **Nashville's Electric Road House** ((780) 489-1330, West Edmonton Mall. If rock is more your scene, head for **The Purple Onion** ((780) 433-9616, 10401 81st Avenue.

Edmonton has five casinos. **Baccarat** ((780) 413-3178, 10128 104th Avenue, downtown, has 300 slot machines, the largest selection of table games in the city, and a 24-hour poker room. Others include the vast **Casino Yellowhead** ((780) 424-9467, at 12464 153rd Street, in northwest Edmonton, and the **Palace Casino** ((780) 444-2112, West Edmonton Mall.

Street, offers excellent accommodation in elegantly furnished, well-equipped rooms, conveniently connected to a major shopping mall. The hotel has two good restaurants, a beautiful lounge set amid an indoor garden, a bar and an indoor swimming pool. The **Westin Hotel** ((780) 426-3636 TOLL-FREE (800) 228-3000 FAX (403) 424-1525 WEB SITE www.westin.ab.ca, 10135 100th Street, is another first-rate hotel, with beautifully decorated and luxuriously furnished rooms and suites, the excellent Pradera Restaurant and an indoor pool.

The **Varscona** ((780) 434-6111 FAX (780) 439-1195 WEB SITE www.varscona.com, 8208 106th Street, is a superbly located boutique hotel in Old

WHERE TO STAY

Expensive to Mid-range

With 198 rooms, it is smaller and more affordable than many of its brethren, but the **Fairmont Macdonald** ((780) 424-5181 TOLL-FREE (800) 441-1414 FAX (780) 428-1566 WEB SITE www.fairmont.com, 10065 100th Street, still has many of the trademarks of the old Canadian Pacific hotels. It also has a superb downtown location overlooking the river, castle-like stone walls, a soaring roof, an elegant lobby, the excellent Harvest Restaurant, charming staff and a full set of services including a business center and an indoor swimming pool.

For something more modern in approach, the **Sheraton Grande Edmonton** ((780) 428-7111 TOLL-FREE (800) 263-9030 FAX (403) 441-3098 WEB SITE www.sheratonedmonton.com, 10235 101st

Strathcona. It has attractive, well-appointed rooms and suites, a 24-hour business center and fitness suite, a ground-floor coffee shop, and evening wine and cheese tasting. Continental breakfast is included in the rate, and there is an arrangement for guests with Sorrentino's excellent Italian restaurant next door.

If you feel like being really frivolous, take one of the themed rooms at the **Fantasyland Hotel & Resort** ((780) 444-3000 TOLL-FREE (800) 661-6454 FAX (780) 444-3294 WEB SITE www.fantasylandhotel.com, 17700 87th Avenue, over in northwest Edmonton in the larger-than-life West Edmonton Mall. There is a Polynesian room, a

Children splash OPPOSITE while adults ABOVE look on at the West Edmonton Mall, the world's largest shopping complex. OVERLEAF: Telephone poles stand single-file across the prairies of eastern Alberta.

Roman room, a Hollywood room, an Arabian room and the intriguingly named Truck room, among others. All have whirlpools, and some steam baths.

Inexpensive to Mid-range

Downtown, the **Edmonton House Suite Hotel** ((780) 420-4000 TOLL-FREE (800) 661-6562 FAX (780) 420-4008 WEB SITE www.maclabhotels.com, at 10205 100th Avenue, has 300 attractive suites with balconies and kitchens, and a very good range of facilities and services that include an indoor pool, an exercise room and a bar. They also offer a free shuttle to the Edmonton Mall. The neighboring **Econo Lodge** ((780) 428-6442 TOLL-FREE IN CANADA (800) 613-7043 FAX (780) 428-6467, at 10209 100th Avenue, is very good value with 73 nicely furnished rooms, a bar and a restaurant.

For accommodation in one of Edmonton's few older establishments, try **La Bohème** ((780) 474-5693, 6427 112th Avenue. Known primarily as a fine French restaurant, it now offers a few charming suites, which, like the service, are continental in style and quite charming. Breakfast is included in the price.

Assistance with bed-and-breakfast accommodation is available through **Alberta's Gem B&B Reservation Agency** (/ FAX (780) 434-6098, 11216 48th Avenue, or the **Bed and Breakfast Association of Greater Edmonton** ((780) 432-7116 TOLL-FREE (866) 432-7116 WEB SITE www.bbcanada.com / associations / bbage.

The **Edmonton International Hostel (HI)** ((780) 988-6836 FAX (780) 988-8698 TOLL-FREE (877) 467-8336 WEB SITE www.hihostels.ca, 10647 81st Avenue, in Old Strathcona, has dormitory beds, family rooms and mountain bike rentals.

WHERE TO EAT

Edmonton's cultural mix makes for a healthy restaurant scene with a wide choice of cuisines. Yet, as a prairie town it has its own specialty: some of the best beef in Canada. You will find concentrations of restaurants in the Old Strathcona district between 101st and 106th streets, the downtown area and the Boardwalk Market at 103rd Street.

The **Hardware Grill** ((780) 423-0969, Jasper Avenue and 97th Street, housed in the historic Goodridge Block, is a consistent award winner, both for its food and wine list. Its attractive decorating keeps with its former life as a hardware store. The delicious, seasonally inspired Canadian cuisine includes specialties such as smoked salmon, venison and cedar-planked salmon. Reservations recommended. The menu is also Canadian, with a European twist, at **La Ronde** ((780) 428-6611, the revolving restaurant at the top of the Crown Plaza Château Lacombe,

10111 Bellamy Hill. Unlike many of its counterparts, it is not only a feast for the eyes: the food and the service are also of a high standard.

La Bohème ((780) 474-5693, 6427 112th Avenue, is housed within an older building close to downtown and is decidedly French in both cuisine and ambiance. You'll find some of the best French fare in town here, and there is a wine cellar to match. Reservations are recommended.

One of the best steak houses in town, **Hy's Steak Loft** ((780) 424-4444, 10013 101A Avenue, is a good place to sample some of the province's first-rate beef. The **Unheardof** ((780) 432-0480, 9602 82nd Avenue, offers set-priced specials featuring excellent international cuisine prepared with fresh ingredients. **The King and I** ((780) 433-2222, 8208 107th Street, in Old Strathcona, serves the best Thai cuisine in town.

Doan's has authentic Vietnamese cuisine at two locations: downtown ((780) 424-3034, at 10130 107th Street, and on the south side ((780) 434-4448, at 7909 104th Street.

There are light meals at the much-loved **VI's** ((780) 454-4300, 13408 Stony Plain Road, where desserts, including homemade pies, are a specialty. The cozy and affordable **Crêperie** ((780) 420-6656, at 10220 103rd Street, is Edmonton's most romantic restaurant, where the French cuisine is country style.

The stylish **Russian Tea Room** ((780) 426-0000, 10312 Jasper Avenue, does indeed serve Russian tea along with wonderful cakes and pastries; it also has a restaurant menu where you'll find traditional Russian dishes. For a very different, trendier style of tearoom, try **Cargo and James Tea** ((780) 433-8152, 10634 82nd Avenue, which offers 120 different types of tea, along with sinful desserts.

HOW TO GET THERE

Edmonton International Airport ((780) 890-8382 WEB SITE www.edmontonairports.com is located 29 km (17 miles) south of the city along Highway 2, and the drive into downtown takes about 30 minutes. The **Sky Shuttle** ((780) 465-8515 runs between some of the big hotels and the airport.

Edmonton lies at the center of what remains of Canada's transnational rail network, with three weekly trains each way connecting with Jasper, Toronto and Vancouver. **VIA Rail** ((780) 422-6032 TOLL-FREE (888) 842-7245, (800) 561-8630 or (800) 561-3949 WEB SITE www.viarail.ca is at 12360 121st Street.

Greyhound ((780) 413-8747 TOLL-FREE (800) 661-8747 WEB SITE www.greyhound.ca, with offices at 10324 103rd Street, operates north to Hay River in the Northwest Territories and Whitehorse in the Yukon Territory, west to Prince Rupert, and south to Drumheller and Calgary. **Red Arrow** ((780) 424-3339 TOLL-FREE IN ALBERTA (800) 232-1958, 10014 104th Street, serves Calgary, Red Deer, Rocky Mountain House and Fort McMurray.

Motorists will find the Yellowhead Highway (Highway 16) — which runs from Winnipeg through Edmonton to British Columbia — easy to join. Highway 2 runs the 514 km (320 miles) from the United States Montana border via Calgary to Edmonton, and continues northwards.

CALGARY

Calgary sprawls over prairie land that seems to stretch ever eastwards. However, the city also lies in the foothills of the Canadian Rockies, and on clear days there are magnificent views to the west over the snow-tipped mountains some 80 km (50 miles) away. Originally a small settlement at the confluence of the Bow and Elbow Rivers, Calgary now has a population of around 877,000 and the city spreads out over a larger area than any other Canadian city. The center has become a high-octane hive of mirrored highrises, malls and other modernities. The climate here is generally dry and sunny with hot summers, and winters that can get bitterly cold but are tempered by the Chinook winds that sweep down from the mountains; they can raise temperatures dramatically within hours and create splendid sunsets.

Calgary is undeniably an oil boomtown, with glittering skyscrapers and busy traffic, but the almost aggressively friendly residents are eager to nurture its former identity as a cow town. Honored guests are "white-hatted" — presented with a white Stetson — as long as they agree to pass on the city's tradition of hospitality to strangers. And, of course, it's almost impossible to think of Calgary without thinking of the Stampede, an annual 10-day festival that seems to get the whole of Canada reaching for cowboy hats and boots.

BACKGROUND

In 1875, the newly formed North West Mounted Police were sent here to restore peace to an area where whisky traders and fur trappers had been cooking up trouble and fanning wars between the natives. They set up a fort at the point where the Bow and Elbow Rivers meet; the commander of police named it after Calgary Bay in his native Scotland. Settlers clustered around the post almost immediately. In 1877 a treaty was signed, without bloodshed, in which the native tribes who roamed the area relinquished the land to the government in return for certain provisions and rights (many of which were neither understood or met in full).

The Canadian Pacific Railway arrived here in 1883, and this, together with the offer of free land to settlers, brought about rapid population growth. The excellent grazing lands of the prairie brought the ranchers and their huge herds from the United States, so the town continued to expand, becoming an important meat-packing center and the hub of the farming and ranching region. By 1891 the population was around 4,000; in 1893 the city was granted a charter.

In 1914, the discovery of oil in the Turner Valley, just southwest of Calgary, brought prosperity to the area, but it was the big strike in Leduc in 1947, soon to be followed by similar discoveries in the Edmonton area, that triggered the meteoric rise in Calgary's fortunes. The city has become the administrative center for Canada's petroleum industry and now over 500 oil and gas companies have their headquarters here. In the late 1960s there began a 20-year period of frantic development, with skyscrapers breaking out like a rash, dramatically changing the face of the city and turning it into a perpetual building site — while the population exploded to around 640,000. Though things quieted down in the 1980s, the city's hosting of the Olympic Games in 1988 brought the area to the world's attention. The 1990s brought yet another surge of development, and Calgary is now second only to Toronto as a Canadian financial center. The city is growing at an astonishing rate, and the visitor information center is as much a welcome wagon as it is a tourist service.

GENERAL INFORMATION

For information on Calgary and the surrounding area, call or drop by **Tourism Calgary** ((403) 263-8510 TOLL-FREE (800) 661-1678 WEB SITE www.tourismcalgary.com, 237 Eighth Avenue SE, Suite 200. There are also year-round visitor centers at Riley & McCormick Western Stores, 220 Eighth Avenue SW and Eau Claire Market, and on the arrivals level at Calgary International Airport.

Getting Around

Sprawling Calgary is divided into northwest, southwest, southeast and northeast sections (NE, SE, SW or NW forms part of all addresses here). The east–west dividing line is Centre Street, while the Bow River separates north from south. Streets follow a grid system, and most of those downtown are one-way. The network of enclosed walkways called "Plus 15s" (because they are a minimum of 15 ft, or 4.5 m, above the ground) makes for a somewhat characterless shopping scene, but provides welcome protection from the bitter winter cold. Just about everything in downtown Calgary — excluding the Stampede grounds — is accessible on foot. Should you want to save some shoe leather, there are good buses and the **C-Train** is free along the Seventh Avenue SW section in the city center.

For sightseeing tours of the city and surrounding area, contact **Exclusive Mountain Transportation and Tours** ((403) 282-3980 WEB SITE WWW .mountaintours.com.

WHAT TO SEE AND DO

Begin your tour of the downtown section with a trip up **Calgary Tower** ((403) 266-7171 WEB SITE www.calgarytower.com, Ninth Avenue and Centre Street South. A high-speed lift will whisk you to the observation deck close to the top of this

funky pedestrian **Stephen Avenue Walk**, with a wide range of cafés, galleries and boutiques, many in restored historic buildings. If you feel like a respite from the concrete jungle, take a detour through the Plus 15 level on Ninth Avenue SW, between Fifth and Sixth Streets, to see the city's extraordinary herd of painted cows. Then head up to the fourth level of the nearby Toronto Dominion Square at 317 Seventh Avenue SW, where you'll find the **Devonian Gardens** ((403) 221-4274, a one-hectare (2.5-acre) indoor water garden, with coi karp pools, waterfalls, sculptures, and some 20,000 local and Californian tropical plants. With a few snack bars and a stage for lunchtime entertainment, this entirely organic

191-m (625-ft) landmark. Opened in 1968, views cover endless prairie land stretching to the east and the magnificent Canadian Rockies to the west. The tower contains the almost statutory revolving restaurant and a café for light lunches. The Olympic flame atop the tower is lit on special occasions.

Over the road, the **Glenbow Museum** ((403) 268-4100 or (403) 777-5506 (24-hour information) WEB SITE www.glenbow.org, 130 9th Avenue SE, is one of Canada's best museums, with a superbly designed Blackfoot Gallery telling the story of the Blackfoot People. Other exhibits cover the development of western Canada, a fine children's museum, local geology, medieval to modern weaponry, an interesting fine art collection, and regular touring exhibitions.

A block north of here, Eighth Avenue between Barclay Mall and Macleod Trail SE becomes the

indoor botanical garden is an ideal place to sit out the long, cold winter.

The **Calgary Science Centre** ((403) 268-8300 WEB SITE www.calgaryscience.ca, at 701 11th Street SW, has star shows, hands-on displays, films, simulators and an outdoor science playground. On the riverbank north of downtown, **Eau Claire Market** ((403) 264-6540, corner of Second Street and Second Avenue, has been attractively revived as one of the city's favorite playgrounds, with trendy coffee shops, cinemas, clubs and an **Imax Theatre** ((403) 974-4629 WEB SITE www.imax-calgary.com. Nearby, **Prince's Island Park**, accessible by footbridge from both banks, is a pleasant, shady island retreat, good for cycling, jogging and picnics.

Fort Calgary Historic Park ((403) 290-1875 WEB SITE www.fortcalgary.com, at 750 Ninth Avenue SE — just east of the city center, at the confluence of the rivers — was the birthplace of the city and site of Fort Calgary, established by the North West Mounted Police in 1875. Set in 16 hectares (40 acres) are an Interpretive Center, the 1875 fort reconstruction and a number of restored historical buildings. Deane House, once the commander's home, is now a restaurant that offers murder mysteries with your dinner. Costumed staff people the garrison effectively.

Cross the bridge to St. George's Island to see the excellent **Calgary Zoo** ((403) 232-9300 WEB SITE www.calgaryzoo.ab.ca, 1300 Zoo Road NE. Here some 300 species of creatures great and small are represented by over 1,200 animals. Spacious environments simulate their natural

Calgary Stampede ((403) 261-0101 TOLL-FREE (800) 661-1260 WEB SITE www.calgarystampede.com, southeast of downtown at 14th Avenue and Olympic Way SE, is where the big events take place during the Calgary Stampede (see THE CALGARY STAMPEDE, below). It's worth a trip even when the Stampede isn't in progress just to see the stunning **Pengrowth Saddledome** ((403) 777-2177, a sports arena with a roof in the shape of a gigantic saddle. While you're there, visit the **Grain Academy** ((403) 263-4594 on the upper floor of the Round-Up Centre, a museum where models and a miniature railway show how grain is transported from the prairies to the Vancouver docks. Other attractions include the

habitats. For those who haven't seen grizzlies in the wild, this is an excellent place to come nose-to-nose with Canada's native wildlife, while the other sections, including the stunning Discovery Africa area, introduce global wildlife to Canadian children. Large **Botanical Gardens** filled with thousands of tropical plants also provide an ideal setting for exotic birds and butterflies. Attached to the zoo is the **Prehistoric Park**, with a group of life-size replica dinosaurs set in a prehistoric landscape.

There's more wildlife at the **Inglewood Bird Sanctuary** ((403) 269-6688, Ninth Avenue and Sanctuary Road SE, about two and a half kilometers (one and a half miles) from the zoo, a 32-hectare (79-acre) forested reserve on the west bank of the Bow River with over 250 species of birds and 300 species of plants. The Visitor Center offers information and natural history courses.

Country Music Hall of Fame ((403) 290-0702 and Calgary's largest **casino**.

For a full reconstruction of life in pioneer times and other periods of Calgary's history, head for the largest "living-history" village in Canada, **Heritage Park Historical Village** ((403) 259-1900, 16 km (10 miles) southwest of town at the Glenmore Reservoir (open mid-May through September daily, weekends only in October; the admission charge includes an old-fashioned pancake breakfast, served 9 AM to 10 AM). Many original buildings have been brought here from various parts of Alberta, and an early-1900s village has been reconstructed with a working bakery, a mill, a newspaper office, stocked-up stores and

Costumed interpreters talk shop OPPOSITE at Heritage Park's turn-of-the-twentieth century village. ABOVE: Calgary's Old City Hall, a survivor amongst the modern skyscrapers.

housing. You can enjoy the antique midway rides, take a trip on a restored steam train or go out onto the reservoir aboard an old sternwheeler called the **SS** *Moyie*. There are also plenty of places to snack or dine here.

Continuing south along the Macleod Trail, then left along Bow Bottom Trail SE, you'll come to **Fish Creek Provincial Park** ((403) 297-5293, which spreads out along 10 km (six miles) of river valley. This park is a wildlife sanctuary but is also where people come simply to escape from city life. There is an Archeological Interpretive Centre, a magnificent colony of great blue heron and a swimming lake. In winter there's cross-country skiing and ice-skating.

The impressive facilities Calgary built for the 1988 Winter Olympics are still in use. The **Canada Olympic Park** ((403) 247-5452 WEB SITE www.coda .ab.ca/COP, a 10-minute drive west of downtown along the TransCanada Highway, was the main site for free-style skiing, ski jump, luge and bobsleigh events. Explore the site for yourself or join a guided tour (11 AM, 1 PM and 3 PM; highly recommended). A ski lift takes you to the top of the course from where you can gaze down the 90-m (295-ft) ski jump tower and see the courses from the perspective of the Olympic athletes who tackled them. The **Olympic Hall of Fame and Museum** has three floors stacked with Olympic memorabilia, photographs, films and a hands-on Discovery Centre. You can also take the Bobsleigh Bullet — a winter or summer bobsleigh ride (no children under 14), go mountain biking or try out the skateboard park. In winter, there is skiing (downhill and cross-country) and skating on offer.

Other small museums in the city include the self-explanatory **Calgary Police Interpretive Centre** ((403) 268-4566, Second Floor, 316 Seventh Avenue, which offers a chance to play detective; the **Firefighters Museum** ((403) 246-3322 WEB SITE www.firefightersmuseum.org, 4124 11th Street SE; the **Spaceport** ((403) 717-7678 WEB SITE www .calgaryspaceport.com, at Calgary Airport, with

space-related exhibits, including a shuttle simulator; the **Museum of the Regiments** ((403) 974-2853, 4520 Crowchild Road SW, about Canadian military history; the **Naval Museum of Alberta** ((403) 242-0002 WEB SITE www.naval museum .ab.ca, a bizarre addition to this landlocked province, which has apparently provided many sailors to the Canadian navy; the **Aero Space Museum of Calgary** ((403) 250-3752 WEB SITE www .asmac.ab.ca, with aviation and space memorabilia; and **Korite Minerals** ((403) 287-2026 WEB SITE www.korite.com, which sells locally made jewelry and offers tours of its jewelry workshops, where Alberta's homegrown specialty gem, the rainbow-hued ammolite predominates.

The Calgary Stampede

Like most Canadian cities, Calgary's calendar is crammed with festivals and celebrations, but they all pale to insignificance beside the Calgary Stampede, a 10-day celebration of Calgary's Wild West days, billed as "The Greatest Outdoor Show on Earth." It takes place every July and has been going on since 1912. Everyone gets into the spirit of it, donning Stetsons, jeans and boots. There is a big parade with dancing in the streets, while hearty breakfasts are served up around town. Calgary's nightlife percolates, too, with all sorts of special events. Southeast of the town at Stampede Park there are bands, more dancing, food, livestock shows and the real business of the Stampede: the rodeo and the chuck-wagon races. For the professional cowboys who take part in the rodeo and make their living from the sport, this is serious business, with big prize money awaiting only the first-prize winner in each of seven main events. Visitors need to reserve their tickets and accommodation well in advance. For details of the event contact the **Calgary Stampede** ((403) 261-0101 TOLL-FREE (800) 661-1260 WEB SITE www.calgarystampede.com, Box 1060, Station M, Calgary T2P 2K8.

EXCURSIONS FROM CALGARY

Calaway Park ((403) 240-3822 WEB SITE www. calawaypark.com, 10 km (six miles) west of Calgary on the TransCanada Highway (mid-May to mid-October, days and hours vary), is a family amusement park with 27 rides and other attractions. **Cochrane**, 25 km (16 miles) west of Calgary, is a favorite spot for trail rides and canoe trips on the Bow River. Its western-style buildings house some interesting local arts and crafts and one of the best ice-cream shops in Canada.

SPORTS AND OUTDOOR ACTIVITIES

The city has over 400 km (250 miles) of pathways for **cycling**, **hiking**, **jogging** and **in-line skating** along the riverbanks, through the pleasant Prince's Island Park and Fish Creek Provincial Park. Calgary Parks and Recreation Information Service ((403) 268-3888 publishes an excellent map, available from bookshops and newsagents. They can also give you information on the city's 17 **skating** rinks, including the lagoon at Bowness Park and the covered speed-skating track at the Olympic Speed Skating Oval ((403) 220-7954 at the University of Calgary.

In winter, the **downhill ski slopes** at the Olympic Park are open to the public, and there's **cross-country skiing** at Fish Creek Provincial Park. It is also possible to try **bobsleigh** and **luge runs**, summer and winter, and skateboarding at

Spruce Meadows ((403) 974-4200 WEB SITE www.sprucemeadows .com, 18011 14th Street SW, hosts world-class **show jumping** four times a year; Race City Motorsport Park ((403) 272-7223 WEB SITE www.racecity.com, 11550 68th Street SE, offers a variety of high octane **motor-sports** on three tracks; the AAA affiliate **Calgary Cannons Baseball Club** ((403) 284-1111 WEB SITE www.calgary cannons.com, play at the Burns Stadium; and the **Calgary Stampeders Football Club** ((403) 289-0258 WEB SITE www .stampeders.com, play at the McMahon Stadium. The Saddledome is the home of the **Calgary Flames** ((403) 777-2177 WEB SITE www.calgaryflames.com, the city's National Hockey League team.

Olympic Park. In summer, the Olympic Park uses the ski runs as a **mountain bike** course (ride the ski lift to the top and zigzag your way down) and rents bikes and helmets. Shaw Millennium Park ((403) 268-1696 has North America's largest park for **skateboarding** and **in-line skating**.

For **horseback riding**, Happy Trails Riding Stable ((403) 251-3344 in Fish Creek Park, gives lessons and also operates guided or unguided trail rides.

The Bow and Elbow Rivers are popular for **canoeing**, particularly at Bowness Park ((403) 288-5133, at 48th and 90th Street NW. There's world-class **fly-fishing** and trout fishing in the section of the Bow River between Carseland and east Calgary. Lists of the many places to fish along these rivers are available from information centers, along with details of the 40-odd **golf courses** in the Calgary area.

NIGHTLIFE AND THE ARTS

For entertainment listings, check the local daily and weekly newspapers, especially the Friday *Herald*, and the *Sun*. Several large hotels have nightclubs and offer a variety of entertainment.

Calgary's cultural life centers around the excellent **Epcor Centre for the Performing Arts** ((403) 294-7455 WEB SITE www.theartscentre.org, 205 Eighth Avenue SE, which has five performance spaces including the Jack Singer Concert Hall, home to the Calgary Philharmonic Orchestra. The Alberta Ballet Company performs at the **Jubilee Auditorium** ((403) 297-8000 WEB SITE

OPPOSITE: In the Badlands, a Richardson's ground squirrel packs in the peanuts. ABOVE: Calgary's Olympic Park — the main site for the 1988 Winter Olympics — is now enjoyed year-round by skiers, bobsledders and mountain bikers.

www.jubileeauditorium.com, 1415 14th Avenue NW. The **Pumphouse Theatre** ((403) 263-0079, 2140 Ninth Avenue SW, features a variety of theatrical performances during its September to June season. Concerts and dramatic works, both classical and contemporary, are also presented at the **University of Calgary Theatre** ((403) 220-4900, 2500 University Drive NW.

Jubilations Dinner Theatre ((403) 249-7799 WEB SITE www .jubilations.ca, 1002 37th Street SW, serves down-home music and comedy with dinner, while the **Stage West Theatre Restaurants** ((403) 243-7077 WEB SITE www.stagewestcalgary .com offers a mix of musicals, comedy nights and celebrity cabaret.

Calgary has hundreds of bars and clubs, many of which regularly put on live music.

Jazz and blues can be enjoyed at **Kaos Jazz and Blues Bistro** ((403) 228-9997, 718 17th Avenue SW, or at **McQueen's** ((403) 269-4722, 317 10th Avenue SW. Local and touring alternative bands can be seen at various venues in Calgary, such as **The Night Gallery** ((403) 266-5116, 1209B First Street SW, which is primarily known for its theme nights, often with live bands. For country and western try the **Ranchman's Restaurant** ((403) 253-1100, at 9615 Macleod Trail South, where there's also beer swilling and dancing; or **Coyote's** ((403) 263-5343, 1088 Olympic Way SE, where there are free two-step lessons on Tuesday and Wednesday nights. The relatively quiet, older neighborhood of **Kensington**, centered on Kensington Road and 10th Street NW, is a good area for restaurants, pubs, bars and nightlife.

Calgary also has several casinos, including Alberta's largest, the **Stampede Casino** ((403) 261-0422 at Stampede Park.

WHERE TO STAY

Expensive

Downtown, the **Fairmont Palliser Hotel** ((403) 262-1234 TOLL-FREE (800) 441-1414 FAX (403) 260-1207 WEB SITE www.fairmont.com, 133 Ninth Avenue SW, was built by the Canadian Pacific Railway in 1914. With its pillars, stately staircases and crystal chandeliers, the Fairmont remains an oasis of old-fashioned splendor in this city of steel high-rises. It provides for just about every comfort. There are exercise facilities, a splendid dining room, a café and a lovely bar.

For a more modern kind of elegance there's the centrally located **Calgary Marriott** ((403) 266-7331 TOLL-FREE (800) 228-9290 FAX (403) 262-8442 WEB SITE www.marriott.ca, 110 Ninth Avenue SE, located within the Convention Centre complex. It is luxurious without being brash, and the service echoes this quality with its understated excellence. Rooms and suites have all kinds of special features, and there's an indoor pool and garden, two dining rooms and a bar with live entertainment.

Also downtown, the **Westin Hotel** ((403) 266-1611 TOLL-FREE (800) 937-8461 FAX (403) 265-7908 WEB SITE www.westin.com, 320 Fourth Avenue SW, offers modern luxury with 525 attractive bedrooms and suites, and a bevy of complimentary touches. The hotel lobby is large and sumptuously decorated, there is a beautiful indoor swimming pool, and the hotel has several excellent dining spots — including the city's famous Owl's Nest restaurant.

The **International Hotel of Calgary** ((403) 265-9600 TOLL-FREE IN WESTERN CANADA (800) 661-8627 TOLL-FREE (800) 637-7200 FAX (403) 265-6949 WEB SITE www.internationalhotel.ca, 220 Fourth Avenue SW, is a modern high-rise that exudes luxury. It has 250 attractive suites with balconies, and facilities include a health spa, a gym, a restaurant and a piano bar.

Located in a leafy residential area, northwest of the city center, **A Good Knight Bed & Breakfast** ((403) 270-7628 TOLL-FREE (800) 261-4954 FAX (403) 284-0010 WEB SITE www.goodknight .com, 1728 Seventh Avenue NW, is a luxury bed and breakfast offering a happy combination of homespun style and soothing comforts. The decor is quaint in the extreme — the teddy bear collection is astounding. While two of the three individually decorated rooms are smallish, the third is quite spacious with a cathedral ceiling, king-size bed and jet bath. For other bed and breakfasts, contact the **Bed & Breakfast Association of Calgary** ((403) 277-0023 FAX (403) 295-3823 WEB SITE www.bbcalgary.com.

The **Homeplace Guest Ranch & Trail Rides** (/FAX (403) 931-3245 TOLL-FREE (877) 931-3245 WEB SITE www.homeplacerance.com, Rural Route 1, Priddis, just outside the city's southern perimeter is a guest ranch. Rooms come with private bathrooms, family meals are provided, and riding lessons, fishing and cross-country skiing are on offer.

Mid-range

The centrally situated **Sandman Hotel (** (403) 237-8626 TOLL-FREE (800) SANDMAN FAX (403) 264-2656 WEB SITE www.sandmanhotels.com, 888 Seventh Avenue SW, has 300 attractively furnished rooms, some with good views, all kinds of comforts and conveniences, and an excellent range of facilities. There's a fitness center, a glass-roofed swimming pool and a coffee shop / restaurant. The downtown **Hawthorn Hotel & Suites (** (403) 263-0520 TOLL-FREE (800) 661-1592 FAX (403) 298-4888 WEB SITE www.hawthorn calgary.com, 618 Fifth Avenue SW, is good value for families, with 300 one- or two-bedroom suites with kitchens. The hotel also has laundry facilities, a fitness center, a sauna and steam room, an outdoor pool and a dining room.

In northwest Calgary there is a motel strip along Banff Trail, near the point where Crowchild Trail crosses the TransCanada Highway. Along this strip, the **Quality Inn-Motel Village (** (403) 289-1973 TOLL-FREE (800) 661-4667 FAX (403) 282-1241 WEB SITE www.qualityinnmotelvillage.com, 2359 Banff Trail NW, has one of the best ranges of facilities, with a poolside dining room, cocktail lounge and 100 suites and rooms, all with telephones and televisions.

Inexpensive

The appealing **Lord Nelson Inn (** (403) 269-8262 TOLL-FREE (800) 661-6017 FAX (403) 269-4868, at 1020 Eighth Avenue SW, downtown, has 55 rooms and suites with private bathrooms, refrigerators, televisions and telephones. There are also some bridal and executive suites. The hotel has a warm and attractive lobby, a dining room and bar.

There is another cluster of hotels and motels along Macleod Trail near Stampede Park. The **Elbow River Inn & Casino (** (403) 269-6771 TOLL-FREE (800) 661-1463 FAX (403) 237-5181, at 1919 Macleod Trail SE, sits on the banks of the Elbow River, connected by an underpass walkway to Stampede Park. All 75 rooms have bathrooms; some have kitchenettes. There is a dining room with pleasant riverfront views, and a full breakfast is included in the rates. The **Quality Hotel (** (403) 243-5531 TOLL-FREE (800) 361-3422 FAX (403) 243-6962 WEB SITE www.quality hotelcalgary.com, 3828 Macleod Trail SW, has nicely appointed rooms and suites, meeting facilities, an indoor pool, shops, a bar, a cocktail bar and a dining room that lays on a generous buffet. The **Econo Lodge South (** (403) 252-4401 TOLL-FREE (888) 559-0559 FAX (403) 252-2780 WEB SITE www.econolodgesouthcalgary.com, 7505 Macleod Trail South (inexpensive to mid-range), is set in pleasant grounds and has 73 good-sized rooms and suites with bathrooms — some with kitchenettes — and an indoor pool, a sauna and a laundry.

The **University of Calgary (** (403) 220-3210, 2500 University Drive NW, also offers some good-value accommodation during the summer months, and may have a few rooms available during term-time.

The **Calgary International Hostel (HI) (** (403) 521-8421 TOLL-FREE (866) 762-4122 FAX (403) 266-6227 WEB SITE www.hihostels.ca, 520 Seventh Avenue SE, near Stampede Park, has six- to eight-bed dormitory rooms.

WHERE TO EAT

La Chaumière ((403) 228-5690, 139 17th Avenue SW, offers traditional French cuisine prepared to

gourmet standards and excellent service in a charming, intimate setting. Reservations advised. The **Owl's Nest (** (403) 266-1611, Westin Hotel, 320 Fourth Avenue SW, is one of Calgary's best-known and finest dining spots. It is a splendidly decorated place serving continental cuisine, with the region's excellent beef featuring largely on the menu.

Oh Canada ((403) 266-1551, Nexen Building, 815 Seventh Avenue SW, serves excellent Canadian cuisine and a wide range of Canadian wines. In summer you can sit on the pleasant park-side patio. There is also excellent Canadian cuisine at the elegantly casual **River Café (** (403) 261-7670, Prince's Island Park, which also offers a patio for outdoor eating in the warmer months. **Caesar's (** (403) 264-1222, 512 Fourth Avenue SW, is one of the oldest steak houses in town, all dark wood and dim lighting, with melt-in-your-mouth steaks and lush desserts.

Informal and inexpensive places abound: **4th Street Rose (** (403) 228-5377, 2116 Fourth Street SW,

OPPOSITE: One of the Royal Tyrrell Museum's Jurassic monsters. This scale model shows an Albertosaurus, one of the dinosaurs that once walked the badlands. ABOVE: Home on the range — a latter-day monster haunts the streets of Calgary.

is a trendy place serving healthy California fusion cuisine, with seafood, Asian dishes and salads. There are several other eateries around this section of Fourth Street. **Wildwood** ((403) 228-0100, 2417 Fourth Street SW, is a fashionable micro-brewery serving excellent Rocky Mountain cuisine in its upstairs dining room. You'll find another such cluster of restaurants along 17th Avenue SW.

Calgary's **Chinatown**, the second largest in Canada, begins at the downtown end of the Centre Street Bridge and extends across the river. There are plenty of Asian restaurants to choose from, some of which serve dim sum. Among the best known and most popular is the **Silver Dragon** ((403) 264-5326, 106 Third Avenue SE.

How to Get There

The **Calgary International Airport** ((403) 735-1372 WEB SITE www.calgaryairport.com, 17 km (10.5 miles) northeast of downtown, is one of the busiest in Canada, and the gateway for all Rocky Mountain tours. The **Airport Shuttle Express** ((403) 509-4799 operates a 24-hour, door-to-door service from any address in Calgary. The **Calgary Airporter** ((403) 531-3909 runs every 30 minutes from 6 AM to 11:30 PM, picking up from seven downtown hotels.

The only way to get here by rail is on the *Rocky Mountaineer*, which arrives from Vancouver three times a week May to October (see RIDE THE LEGENDARY RAILS, page 11 in TOP SPOTS).

The main bus station is at Eighth Avenue SW and 16th Street, a 30-minute walk from the city center. A free shuttle connects with the C-Train during the day. **Greyhound** ((403) 265-9111 TOLL-FREE (800) 661-8747 WEB SITE www.greyhound.ca operates bus services to Calgary from all directions. **Red Arrow** ((403) 531-0350 TOLL-FREE IN ALBERTA (800) 232-1958, 205 Ninth Avenue SE, serves Edmonton, Red Deer and Fort McMurray.

The TransCanada Highway (Highway 1) runs through Calgary, linking it with British Columbia to the west and Saskatchewan to the east.

West of Calgary, the TransCanada Highway runs through Banff National Park and on through Glacier National Park in British Columbia.

Highway 2 runs north from the United States–Montana border to Calgary, continuing on to Red Deer, Edmonton and beyond. Calgary is 244 km (151 miles) north of the United States border, 128 km (80 miles) east of Banff, and 294 km (176 km) south of Edmonton.

SOUTHERN ALBERTA

The area south of Calgary, skirting the divide between the Rockies and the Prairies, is quite beautiful — built-up (by Canadian standards) with lots of pretty, small farming villages and towns. There is plenty here to keep visitors exploring for days, including several dude ranches in the neighborhood for those who fancy their chances wrangling cows. Ask the tourist office in Calgary for details.

If you want to see how it was done by the professionals, the **Bar-U Ranch National Historic Site** ((403) 395-2212 TOLL-FREE (800) 568-4996, 15 km (nine miles) south of Longview along Highway 2, 100 km (62 miles) south of Calgary, which is open daily May to October. It was first established in 1882 and is one of few of the old ranches in the province to survive. The visit involves a video and exhibits and an hour-long guided tour around Ranch Headquarters. There are 35 historic buildings, workshops, a general store and Roadhouse, peopled by costumed interpreters.

The **Head-Smashed-In Buffalo Jump** lies 165 km (102 miles) south of Calgary along Highway 2 and Secondary Highway 785. For over 5,000 years, indigenous people stampeded herds of buffalo to their deaths over the edge of this steep cliff. These hunts were an important part of the native culture, involving hundreds of men, precise planning and religious rituals. The hunt would provide food, hides and bone. Archeological digs at this UNESCO World Heritage Site have uncovered bones, village sites and First Nations artifacts. The **Head-Smashed-In Buffalo Jump Interpretive Centre** ((403) 553-2731 WEB SITE www.head-smashed-in.com is a seven-level complex built into the cliff; it describes the culture of the Plains native people, in particular the Blackfoot, and the business of the hunt itself through films, displays and guided walks of the site.

The smallish town of **Fort Macleod**, 16 km (10 miles) to the southeast, is the site of the first North West Mounted Police post in Alberta, named after their first commander, Lieutenant Colonel James Macleod. This force (now the Royal Canadian Mounted Police) was formed in 1873 to enforce law and order on the whiskey traders in the west. They arrived here in 1874 after a grueling march from Manitoba. The **Fort Macleod Museum** ((403) 553-4703 WEB SITE www.nwmpmuseum.com, 219 25th Street, is a reconstructed police post with displays about the way of life of the Mounties, the province's pioneers and the native people. The town center contains many old buildings and has been declared a Provincial Historical Area. Drop by the **visitor booth** ((403) 553-2500 for information on self-guided tours.

On Highway 2, about 55 km (33 miles) south of Fort Macleod, **Cardston** was founded by Mormon pioneers in 1887, and is home to the first Mormon Temple built outside the United States, which dates from 1923. The **Visitor Centre** ((403) 653-1696 WEB SITE www.town.cardston.ab.ca, 348 Third Street West (open from May to September) depicts the history of the town and settlers. The **Remington-Alberta Carriage Centre** ((403) 653-5139 WEB SITE www.remingtoncentre.com, 623 Main Street, has North America's largest collection of over 200 carriages, wagons and sleighs.

In the far south of the province, the lower peaks of **Waterton Lakes National Park** ascend abruptly from grasslands of the extreme southwestern corner of Alberta — giving rise to the park's sobriquet "the place where the mountains meet the prairie." Waterton Lakes is situated along the Montana–Alberta border where it joins the United States' Glacier National Park as the world's first "International Peace Park," founded in 1932. The region's unique geological history has been recognized as UNESCO World Heritage Site. It is also part of the Trail of the Great Bear, a scenic corridor stretching from Yellowstone National Park in Wyoming the whole way up to Banff and Jasper in the Canadian Rockies.

Accommodation and visitor services are located in the townsite of **Waterton Park**, and the **Parks Canada Visitor Centre** ((403) 859-2445 or (403) 859-2224 is just north of the townsite, on Highway 5.

Though only 525 sq km (189 sq miles) in area, Waterton Lakes contains scenery as wondrous as any of the bigger Canadian Rockies parks, as well as abundant recreational activities. Backpackers and hikers come here to enjoy the park's 225 km (135 miles) of trails, and there are motorboating and boat tours on Upper Waterton Lake, and canoeing at the marina and on Cameron Lake. An almost constant wind blows across Upper Waterton Lake, averaging 32.5 km/h (19.5 mph), making windsurfing a top draw. Scuba divers can explore the wreck of a sunken paddle steamer in Emerald Bay. Picnicking, tennis, bicycling and swimming round out the summer activities. Winter access is restricted by road closures, but skiing, snowshoeing and waterfall ice climbing are all popular activities.

For accommodation in the area, see Calgary listing, page 166.

CANADIAN BADLANDS

The strange, lunar-like landscape of the badlands, characterized by gullies and deeply carved canyons, was once a subtropical marshland roamed by dinosaurs. Today it is home to the world's second richest fossil beds (after China's Gobi Desert).

Start your tour at the **Infocentre** ((403) 823-6300, 703 Second Avenue West, in the small city of **Drumheller**, 140 km (84 miles) northeast of Calgary. Its newest attraction is a 25-m (80-ft)

T-Rex ((403) 823-8100 TOLL-FREE (866) 823-8100 WEB SITE www.dinosaurvalley.com, which you can climb up to survey the valley from a platform in its mouth. Children will probably also appreciate a trip to **Reptile World** ((403) 823-8623, 1222 Highway 9, South Drumheller, which has some 85 species of reptile, some of which visitors can handle. Every July, a **passion play** is performed in an outdoor amphitheatre overlooking the town: for details call ((403) 823-2001 or go to WEB SITE www.canadianpassionplay.com.

About six kilometers (four miles) northwest of Drumheller, the superb **Royal Tyrrell Museum** TOLL-FREE (888) 440-4240 WEB SITE www.tyrrellmuseum.com, contains the largest exhibition of

OPPOSITE: Calgary's nighttime skyline rides the Saddledome, home of the city's National Hockey League team, the Flames. ABOVE: Public art in downtown Calgary.

dinosaurs in the world and presents theories about evolution up until the appearance of man, with over 35 complete dinosaur skeletons, hands-on displays and a variety of special programs. You can watch museum technicians at work behind a glass window, chipping away a millimeter at a time at huge stone-encrusted skeletons. The curators are clearly aware of the aesthetic as well as the scientific interest of the fossils, and offer displays emphasizing the myriad patterns and colors of petrified organisms, such as delicate million-year-old seed ferns, swirling ammonites, and rainbow-hued ammolite, a gemstone that is unique to Alberta. The star exhibit at the Tyrrell is the Burgess Shale blacklight presentation where

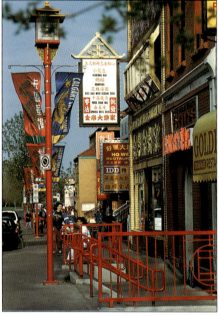

you can see the oldest known multi-cellular marine animals at 12 to 20 times their actual size. There are multilingual audio-guides available for taking a self-guided tour (see also WALK WITH THE DINOSAURS, page 12 in TOP SPOTS).

The museum is situated in **Midland Provincial Park**, and a trail system gives you the chance to walk through the grounds where exposed fossils are often found. But remember that Alberta has strict laws preserving the province's heritage. All fossils are the property of the people of Alberta; collecting is permitted only outside the provincial parks. The museum's Day Digs program gives you the chance to go out and **dig for dinosaurs** with trained technicians, and do the actual work of excavating.

Drumheller is also the starting point of the **Dinosaur Trail**, a 48-km (29-mile) circular driving route taking you to various places of interest

in the area and offering some good views of the badlands. The *Visitors Guide to the Drumheller Valley* lists 30 separate stop-offs.

Though mainly commercial and an attempt to capitalize on the dinosaur theme, the Dinosaur Trail is a fun jaunt through the badlands history and geography. You can take an all-terrain vehicle ride through **Horsethief Canyon**, cross the Red Deer River on the 1913-vintage **Bleriot Ferry**, which works on a pulley system, traverse the **Rosedale Swinging Suspension Bridge**, visit the tumbleweed town of **Rosedeer**, and drop in to the **Last Chance Saloon**, where wagon wheels and elk horns decorate the façade and bullet holes riddle the interior.

On Highway 10, shortly after the hamlet of Cambria (don't blink), turn left into the **Hoodoos Provincial Recreation Area**. These bizarre rock formations were created by 10,000 years of wind and rain erosion; protective caps of hard sandstone prevent the pillars from eroding as quickly as the surrounding rock. Cross-sections of the region's geological history, the hoodoo's shale base was once the floor of an ancient sea, now some 73 million years old; the sandstone above this was deposit by swamps and streams in the dinosaur era, 70 million years ago.

Those who have caught the dinosaur bug may want to extend their journey to the **Dinosaur Provincial Park** ((403) 378-4342 or (403) 378-4344 (tour reservations) FAX (403) 378-4247 WEB SITE discoveryweb.com/aep/parks/dinosaur, which is 140 km (87 miles) southeast of Drumheller. Take Route 56 to Brooks then Highway 873, then follow the signs. This area of the Red Deer Valley badlands, also a UNESCO World Heritage Site, is one of the most extensive dinosaur graveyards in the world, and throughout the park skeletons are on view exactly in the position that they were discovered. So extensive are the remains that they say you're never more than two feet from a fossil here. In the park you can visit the **Royal Tyrrell Museum Field Station** ((403) 378-4342 (open year-round, with interpretive programs daily mid-May to early September), where you can see the paleontologists working on finds. You can also explore the interpretive display here, and take a bus tour or guided walk of the park.

For accommodation, try the **Canadian Badlands Bed and Breakfast Association** ((403) 823-5889 FAX (403) 823-7040 E-MAIL taste@telusplanet .net WEB SITE www.dinosaurvalley.com.

ABOVE: Calgary's Chinatown is the second-largest in Canada. OPPOSITE: A Plains Indian in full regalia.

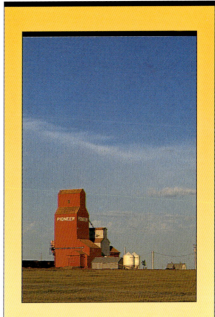

Saskatch-ewan

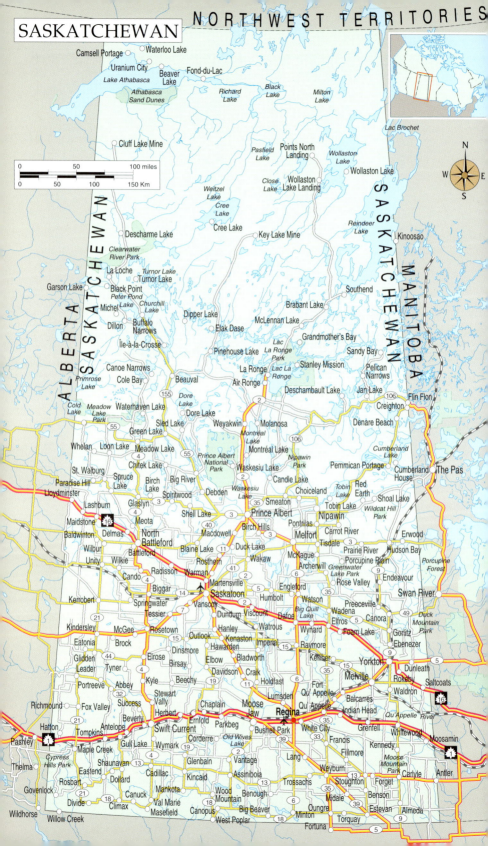

Situated between Manitoba in the east and Alberta in the west, Saskatchewan contains the largest area of Canada's three Prairie Provinces. When, in 1858, John Palliser led an expedition through the southwestern part of the province, he deemed the land unsuitable for agriculture, but subsequent irrigation proved his assessment wrong, turning Saskatchewan into North America's largest wheat-growing region. More than 50 percent of Canada's crop is produced here, while the grasslands of the south have made good cattle-raising country. The mineral wealth of the province has also proved profitable; oil is now an important part of the economy. The favorable summer weather and hundreds of parks attract outdoors lovers, making the tourist industry a newer strand in an economy that is rapidly growing.

Scenically, Saskatchewan has become a byword for the endless, treeless plains that in the minds of many typifies the word "prairie." This is unfortunate and somewhat unfair. In the south of the province, the lunar-like landscape of the badlands, a mixture of semiarid grasslands and rocky desert, occupies a large semicircular portion of the prairie. This section is surrounded by the vast, flat, treeless wheat-growing belt in which the provincial capital of Regina lies. Beyond that strip, the outer section of the prairie, known as the parkland, is an area of gently rolling hills and trees, threaded by the North and South Saskatchewan Rivers.

Beyond the prairie, Prince Albert National Park stands at the edge of the remote North Country, a wilderness of forests and marshlands, crisscrossed with a latticework of lakes and rivers, much of which is Canadian Shield country. Here the roads peter out, and it is very sparsely populated. These wide-open spaces, ideal for fishing, canoeing and whitewater rafting, attract adventurers and urban refugees. In all, the province has some 100,000 jewel-blue lakes for fishing and recreation, 200,000 hectares (five million acres) of protected provincial and national parkland, as well as green valleys and acres of boreal forest.

Saskatchewan has a population of about a million, with a surface area of 651,900 sq km (251,700 sq miles), leaving a lot of empty space. The citizens of the province's two major cities, Regina and Saskatoon, revel in the opportunities provided by their parklands. The relaxed character of the people masks a fighting spirit and a willingness to work together for the common good that has brought them through some very difficult times. They are also unafraid of change: in 1944 Saskatchewan elected the first Socialist government in North America and embarked upon a series of innovative social programs. The people are proud of their pioneering past, which they commemorate in many museums — Saskatchewan has the highest number of museums per capita of all the provinces. There are frequent reminders of the remarkable contribution made by the North West Mounted Police in the development of the area, and also of the bitter Northwest Rebellion that once shook the province and still seems to send out shock waves.

Saskatchewan has a colorful history. The first white man to explore the territory was Henry Kelsey in 1690, acting on behalf of the Hudson's Bay Company. Trading posts were then established in the region, and throughout the nineteenth century the fur trade flourished here. As a result, the Métis people came into being, children of French fathers and native mothers who lived the native way of life but followed Roman Catholicism. Often well educated by local standards of the time,

they became a crucial link between Canada's two, vastly differing societies.

In 1870, the Canadian government, seeing the area's agricultural potential, bought the land from the Hudson's Bay Company and began to negotiate treaties in preparation for the settlement of the area. The government advertised free land to settlers, and ranchers began to move their herds into the southwest. In 1873 the North West Mounted Police were formed to enforce law and order in the Northwest Territories. But it was the coming of the Canadian Pacific Railway in 1882 that began to reel in settlers from the United States, Britain and Continental Europe.

The arrival of the settlers caused great consternation among the Métis, who stood to lose rights to the lands they already inhabited. As their

A vehicle decorated for Regina's Buffalo Days.

pleas to the government went unheeded, they turned to the leadership of a young man named Louis Riel. They set up their own provincial government in an attempt to establish their rights, but the English Métis did not lend their support to this faction, and conflict arose between Riel's people and some of the settlers. An attempt was made on Riel's life; Riel had one of the settlers killed. The Métis were eventually granted some land for settlement, but Riel was forced into exile. In 1885, when the Métis and the natives again found themselves about to be dispossessed, Riel returned to lead them in the Northwest Rebellion, dubbing himself "Prophet, Infallible Pontiff and Priest King."

ince continued steadily, along with prosperity and growth. The Depression of the 1930s hit the province particularly hard, and to add to the misery, 10 years of drought brought crop failure, creating a depressing brown landscape dotted with starving cattle. The 1990s ushered in a period of great economic growth and with the start of the new century, the region is thriving.

REGINA

Saskatchewan's capital is one of Canada's sunniest cities and, as befits its name, Regina rises regally from the center of the flat prairie wheat fields. With the Canadian Pacific Railway and the Trans-

This was a bitter conflict that ended with a hopeless but noble stand at Batochem, the ill-armed rebels facing the Gatling guns of the government troops. Riel surrendered, was brought to trial in Regina. Opinion was divided, as many believed his cause to be a just one that highlighted the French–British conflict in Canada, but Riel was found guilty of treason and hanged in November of that year.

Subsequently, the Métis did receive the land rights they had sought, but the death of Riel had far-reaching political repercussions. To this day it remains an emotive subject, his name symbolic in the French–English conflict and the ongoing First Nations struggle for land rights. Saskatchewan does much to keep the memory alive, and in Regina the trial of Riel is reenacted every year.

In 1905 Saskatchewan was incorporated, with Regina as its capital, and immigration to the prov-

Canada Highway running through the city, it is the financial, industrial and agricultural center of Saskatchewan, with a population of around 200,000. It has a healthy cultural life with a good number of theater and dance companies, as well as Canada's oldest symphony orchestra and one of her top concert halls. Regina is home to Canada's only training academy for the Royal Canadian Mounted Police, which adds a splash of red and some ceremonial pomp, while the city's museums afford visitors a fascinating window on the province's past.

Once a miserable, muddy and unpromising site along the banks of the Wascana Creek, Regina has been transformed into a serene, dignified city of parklands and well-considered public facilities. The Wascana Centre, a pleasant parkland of trees and gardens surrounding a manmade lake, is the core of the city and home to several of its major attractions.

BACKGROUND

When the Canadian Pacific Railway was planning its route across the plains, the government, realizing that the erstwhile capital of the Northwest Territories would be nowhere near the railway, entered into discussions with the Canadian Pacific Railway to decide on a site for a new settlement that would lie along the line. The place they settled upon was far from being an obvious choice. It lay along the banks of an almost dried-up creek, with only a few stagnant pools remaining — an area that varied from being too muddy to being too dusty. The Cree had used the banks for slaughtering buffalo and drying the skins, and because of the large numbers of buffalo skeletons there, they had given it the inauspicious name Oskana — meaning "Pile of Bones." However, settlement was soon under way, and in 1882 the first train chuffed into the station and Princess Louise, wife of Canada's governor-general, bestowed upon it the more dignified name of Regina, in honor of her mother, Queen Victoria.

The North West Mounted Police set up headquarters here, and in 1885 Regina became the focus of attention when, following the Northwest Rebellion, it was the scene of the trial of the Métis leader, Louis Riel.

When the province of Saskatchewan was incorporated in 1905, Regina became its capital city and immigrants began to flood in. Gradually the problems of the location were solved: the creek was dammed to create an artificial lake, the surrounding parkland was landscaped, the dignified Legislative Building was planned, and present-day Regina began to take shape.

GENERAL INFORMATION

Tourism Regina ((306) 789-5099 TOLL-FREE (800) 661-5099 extension 277 FAX (306) 789-3171 E-MAIL info@tourismregina.com WEB SITE www.tourism regina.com, Highway 1 East (TransCanada Highway), is found on the eastern edge of the city. It is open year-round, daily in summer, Monday to Friday only in winter. For information on the whole province, contact **Tourism Saskatchewan** ((306) 787-2300 TOLL-FREE (877) 237-2273 WEB SITE www .sasktourism.com, 1922 Park Street.

The **Saskatchewan History and Folklore Society** ((306) 542-2317 TOLL-FREE (800) 919 9437 organizes heritage bus tours of both the city and the province.

WHAT TO SEE AND DO

Along the banks of Wascana Creek lie several parks, but Regina's pride is the **Wascana Centre** ((306) 522-3661 WEB SITE www.wascana.sk.ca, made up of six interlinked parks covering 930 hectares (2,300 acres) in the heart of the city. Once a muddy area with an uncertain water supply, settlers dammed the creek here to create Wascana Lake and a water reserve. It is now one of the largest urban parks in North America — a beautiful green space with shady trees and vivid flowerbeds. From the pleasant marina on the lakeshore, you can take a ferry over to Willow Island, a lovely spot for a picnic. With canoeing, sailing, boating, windsurfing and many picnic areas, it is a place of recreation; the art gallery and science center also make it a place of culture and education. The **Devonian Pathway** ((306) 777-7803, an eight-kilometer (five-mile) jogging and cycling track winds along the Wascana Creek from Rotary Park, off Albert Street Bridge, to AE Wilson Park in the northwest.

On the western side of the park stands the stately domed **Legislative Building** ((306) 787-5357 WEB SITE www.legassembly.sk.ca, built between 1908 and 1912 in the style of the English Renaissance Revival, lavishly decorated within, and set in pleasant gardens. Tours can be arranged around the huge library, the Legislative Chamber and the art galleries on the lower levels. Nearby, **Government House** ((306) 787-5717 WEB SITE www.iaa.sk.ca/govhouse, Dewdney Avenue at Connaught Street (Tuesday to Sunday 10 AM to 4 PM), served as the residence of the lieutenant-governors between 1891 and 1945. The rooms have been beautifully restored and contain period furnishings.

Over on the north bank of Wascana Lake, the **Royal Saskatchewan Museum** ((306) 787-2815 WEB SITE www.royalsaskmuseum.ca, at corner of College Avenue and Albert Street, is a low building built in Tyndall stone and decorated with a frieze. This museum provides an excellent introduction to the flora and fauna of the whole province, with dioramas of various regions, complete with wildlife and sound effects adding to the realism, and displays on wildlife biology. The Earth Sciences Gallery traces the province's geological history and features some hands-on displays, while another gallery deals with Native American history.

Close by, the **Mackenzie Art Gallery** ((306) 522-4242, WEB SITE www.mackenzieartgallery.sk.ca, Albert Street and 23rd Avenue, began as a private collection bequeathed to the University of Regina. It now includes both contemporary and older works from a variety of countries, but with an emphasis on Canadian art. It is open daily, with evening hours on Wednesday and Thursday; admission is free. Every August a theater company reenacts the trial of Louis Riel here from court transcripts; it never fails to stir up controversy.

Regina's skyline as seen from the Wascana Centre.

Also on the north shore of the lake, the old city power station has been converted into the **Saskatchewan Science Centre** ((306) 522-4629 TOLL-FREE (800) 667-6300 WEB SITE www.sciencecentre.sk.ca, at the corner of Winnipeg Street and Wascana Drive. Still growing, this exciting center has an Imax cinema and planetarium alongside hands-on exhibits about physics, genetics and human life, the Living Planet, geology and meteorology, and space. Its coverage of Olympic sports includes Nordic skiing, alpine skiing, the biathlon, bobsled and figure skating. There are also live demonstrations on anything from cryogenics, lasers or sound, as well as a gift shop and a restaurant.

Museum ((306) 780-5838 WEB SITE www.rcmpmuseum.com, is off Dewdney Avenue West. The museum traces the colorful history of the Mounties and the vital role they played in Canada's development — a role that far exceeds that normally fulfilled by a police force. Archival material, uniforms, weaponry, artifacts and a wealth of memorabilia recall the famous and grueling march that the newly formed force made through the west to establish law and order, along with other key events in the force's history. Curiosities on display include Chief Sitting Bull's tobacco pouch, while some exhibits add a lighter touch, such as the Hollywood representations of those who "always get their man." Guided tours are available.

Also within the Wascana Centre, the **Saskatchewan Centre of the Arts** ((306) 565-4500 (information) or (306) 525-9999 (tickets) TOLL-FREE (800) 667-8497 WEB SITE www.centreofthearts.sk.ca, Lakeshore Drive, contains two theaters, the larger of which serves as an excellent concert hall, where you can hear the Regina Symphony Orchestra, Canada's oldest continuously operating symphony orchestra. The center presents operas, theatrical productions, dance and music. Nearby, on the lakeshore, the **Waterfowl Park** ((306) 522-3661 is home Canada geese, swans, pelicans and many other species. There's a naturalist on hand to answer questions, an information center, a gift shop and a small art gallery. Guided tours are available.

To the north of the Wascana Centre, the famous Royal Canadian Mounted Police, or Mounties, have their training academy. The **RCMP Centennial**

For those who enjoy parades and military drills, the boisterous **Sergeant Major's Parade** takes place weekdays at 1 PM, and from July to mid-August the colorful **Sunset Retreat Ceremony** draws the crowds on Tuesday evenings, when the flag is lowered.

EXCURSIONS FROM REGINA

Seventy-one kilometers (44 miles) west of Regina along the TransCanada Highway lies **Moose Jaw**, Saskatchewan's fourth largest city. For information, visit **Tourism Moose Jaw** ((306) 694-1882 TOLL-FREE (866) 693-8097 E-MAIL tourism.moosejaw @sk.sympatico.ca WEB SITE www.citymoosejaw.com, 99 Diefenbaker Drive. The **Moose Jaw Trolley Company** ((306) 693-8537 runs sightseeing tours on a restored 1920s passenger trolley bus from May to October.

A prosperous railroad and industrial center, Moose Jaw was renowned in the Roaring Twenties as a haven for American bootleggers. The **Tunnels of Moose Jaw Tours** ((306) 693-5261 WEB SITE www.tunnelsofmoosejaw.com, 18 Main Street North, show you how the network of underground passages beneath many of the downtown buildings was used to smuggle liquor during the prohibition era. To keep on the sybaritic theme, visit the **Temple Gardens Mineral Spa Hotel and Resort** ((306) 694-5055 WEB SITE www.temple gardens.sk.ca, 24 Fairford Street East. This is Canada's only geothermal mineral spa, with indoor and outdoor pools fed by naturally heated therapeutic spring water.

his neighbors considered him mad, he never received the funding to finish the ship during his lifetime; he died in an asylum.

Another of the four Western Development museums lies in **Yorkton**, 187 km (116 miles) northeast of Regina along Highway 10 (for the two others, see WHAT TO SEE AND DO, page 184 under SASKATOON). Yorkton is a major distribution center with a population of around 16,000 and some decent accommodation on offer. For information, contact **Tourism Yorkton** ((306) 783-8707 TOLL-FREE (877) 250-6454 WEB SITE www.touryorkton.com, at the junction of Highways 9 and 16. Their offices are open Monday to Friday 8 AM to 7 PM, Saturday and Sunday 8 AM to 5 PM.

Another of the city's principal attractions is the huge **Western Development Museum** ((306) 693-5989 WEB SITE www.wdm.ca, 50 Diefenbaker Drive at the junction of the TransCanada Highway and Highway 2. There are four Western Development museums in Saskatchewan, each dealing with a different area of provincial history. This branch covers the history of transportation, with displays on aviation, the railway, land and water transportation. Exhibits include vintage cars and aircraft, an old Canadian Pacific Railway train, a reconstructed railway station, wagons and old snowmobiles.

The **Sukanen Ship Pioneer Village and Museum** ((306) 693-7315 is open daily 9 AM to 5 PM from late-May to mid-September. It covers 16 hectares (40 acres), and includes a number of historic houses and the *Dontanien*, an ocean-going ship, built on the prairies by Finn Tom Sukanen. Sadly,

The Yorkton **Western Development Museum** ((306) 783-8361 WEB SITE www.wdm.ca, Highway 16 on the west side of town, depicts daily life in Saskatchewan during the eighteenth and nineteenth centuries, with displays of tools and machinery both old and new, along with recreated interiors of early homes, reflecting the style of the various ethnic groups, such as the Plains natives, the English, French, Ukrainians and Swedes. In late May or early June, you can catch the **Yorkton Short Film and Video Festival**.

The **Qu'Appelle Valley** cuts through the prairie from Lake Diefenbaker, northwest of Regina up to the Manitoba border to the east, a route that stretches across roughly two-thirds of the province. This long, green valley of trees and lakes was

OPPOSITE: Pinning down enthusiasm for Buffalo Days. ABOVE: The Legislative Building in Regina.

a favorite place for fur traders and natives, offering welcome respite from the prairie and a valuable source of wood. Today it is as green as ever, lined with parks, villages, resorts and several excellent golf courses. Route 10 from Regina will bring you to **Fort Qu'Appelle**, 70 km (43 miles) away, which is a good place to buy local crafts. In this stretch of the valley there is a series of lakes that provide excellent fishing (license required) and swimming, boating and water-skiing.

WHERE TO STAY

Expensive to Mid-range

For first-class accommodation in older surroundings, try the **Hotel Saskatchewan Radisson Plaza** ((306) 522-7691 TOLL-FREE (800) 333-3333 WEB SITE www.hotelsask.com, 2125 Victoria Avenue, Regina (expensive), a stately building dating from 1927 and the city's only AAA four-diamond hotel. The public areas have an old-fashioned grandeur, while the 215 generously proportioned rooms and suites are furnished in modern style, with many creature comforts. The Royal Suite has indeed housed royalty. There is a cocktail lounge and a restaurant.

The **Regina Inn Hotel and Convention Centre** ((306) 525-6767 TOLL-FREE (800) 667-8162 FAX (306) 525-3630 WEB SITE www.reginainn.com, 1975 Broad Street, Regina, is a top-rank modern hotel and convention center in the heart of downtown. It has 235 rooms and suites, all with balconies, and good facilities. There is a business center, a fitness center with a massage therapist on-call, two attractive dining spots and a dinner theater. There are similarly high standards at the **Ramada Hotel and Convention Centre** ((306) 569-1666 TOLL-FREE (800) 667-6500 FAX (306) 525-3550, WEB SITE www.saskramada.com, 1818 Victoria Avenue, Regina, which has particularly attractive public areas and 250 well-equipped rooms and suites, a lovely indoor swimming pool and fitness center, a business center, a restaurant and a pub. Both have rooms ranging from inexpensive to expensive.

Inexpensive

Situated downtown, the **Chelton Suites Hotel** ((306) 569-4600 TOLL-FREE (800) 667-9922 FAX (306) 569-3531, 1907 Eleventh Avenue, Regina, has 56 large rooms and suites, attractively decorated and equipped with refrigerator, microwave and wet bar. A restaurant, a friendly atmosphere, and prices that vary from inexpensive to mid-range make this good value.

The **Plains Hotel** ((306) 757-8661 TOLL-FREE (800) 665-1000 FAX (306) 525-8522, downtown at 1965 Albert Street, Regina, has 60 rooms with bathrooms and television. There's a pub and a dining room. Slightly to the north of the center, the **Inntowner Motor Inn** ((306) 525-3737 TOLL-FREE (800) 667-7785 FAX (306) 525-5548, 1009 Albert

Street, Regina, has 43 good size rooms with television, some with queen-size beds, and the hotel has a dining room and a coffee shop.

Close to Wascana Park, the **Turgeon International Hostel (HI, IYHF)** ((306) 791-8165 TOLL-FREE (1-800) 467-8357 FAX (306) 721-2667 E-MAIL hihostels .sask@sk.sympatico.ca WEB SITE www.hihostels.ca, 2310 McIntyre Street, Regina, is a restored heritage house with lots of character, offering dormitory-style rooms, good self-catering facilities, a laundromat, and a lovely old sitting room. The hostel closes for the month of January.

WHERE TO EAT

Regina has many good restaurants, considering the size of its population. If you want to trawl the menus before deciding, head down to South Alberta Strip, home to many of the more upmarket establishments; to Victoria Avenue East, which

has a wide variety of well-known chains; or to the Cathedral District, for funkier, more individual eateries.

The **Diplomat** ((306) 359-3366, 2032 Broad Street, is one of Regina's most elegant restaurants. Seafood and steaks, prepared expertly, are complemented by an excellent wine list. **Danbury's Contemporary Cuisine** ((306) 525-8777, 1925 Victoria Avenue, downtown, is one of Regina's newer restaurants, with a bar and a cigar lounge. **The Creek in Cathedral Bistro** ((306) 352-4448, 3414 Thirteenth Avenue, in the Cathedral district, offers that ideal mix of fine dining in an intimate but casual atmosphere. **Park Place Restaurant and Fine Dining** ((306) 522-9999, 3000 Wascana Drive, next to the marina in Wascana Park, offers seasonal products. **Heliotrope** ((306) 569-3373, 2204 McIntyre Street (Fourteenth Avenue), a pleasant brick house with a fireplace, serves vegetarian food with global influences.

HOW TO GET THERE

Regina Airport ((306) 761-7555, 5201 Regina Avenue, is seven kilometers (four miles) southwest of the city center. It's about a 10- to 20-minute ride to downtown. For airport transportation contact **Triple B/Regina Airport Shuttle Services** ((306) 537-9767.

Greyhound TOLL-FREE (800) 661-8747 WEB SITE www.greyhound.ca buses run from Regina to Saskatoon where connections can be made with **VIA Rail** TOLL-FREE (888) 842-7245, (800) 561-8630 or (800) 561-3949 WEB SITE www.viarail.ca. Buses also run to Calgary and Vancouver, Winnipeg, Toronto and Montréal. The bus station ((306) 787-3340 is close to downtown at 2041 Hamilton Street.

The two main highways into Regina are the TransCanada Highway (Highway 1), which runs

Royal Canadian Mounted Police at their training academy in Regina.

east and west of the city, and Highway 6, which runs from the United States Montana border through the town, continuing northwards beyond Melfort. Highway 11 from Saskatoon links with Highway 6 just north of Regina, then runs into the city center.

SOUTHERN SASKATCHEWAN

In the southwest corner of Saskatchewan, and stretching into southern Alberta, **Cypress Hills Interprovincial Park** ((306) 662-5411 WEB SITE www .cypresshills.com, Highway 21, comes as something of a surprise. This lush green area of forests, hills, valleys, lakes and streams rises out of

WEB SITE www.parkscanada.pch.gc.ca, 55 km (34 miles) southwest of Maple Creek along Highway 21. The site is open daily mid-May to mid-October 9:30 AM to 5:30 PM. The fort, restored inside and out, depicts the tough living conditions faced by the men. The interpretive center has films and displays on the fort and the history of the police force. Among their more difficult tasks was that of trying to persuade Chief Sitting Bull and his 5,000 braves to return to the United States after they had fled here following their defeat of Custer at Little Big Horn.

A bus from the fort will take visitors to **Farwell's Trading Post**, where costumed guides help recreate the lawless days of the whisky traders.

the prairie plains to heights of almost 1,500 m (5,000 ft) — making this the highest point of land between Labrador and the Rocky Mountains. There are pine forests (mistaken by the French explorers for cypresses, hence the name), rare flowers, birds and other wildlife. One area of the park is set aside for a resort with campsites, cabins, hiking trails, riding stables, tennis courts, golf courses and a beach.

This is also an area of historical significance. In 1873 it was the scene of a massacre, when some Montana wolf hunters who mistakenly believed the Assiniboine were responsible for stealing their horses killed a group of Assiniboine. The illegal whisky trade had played its part in the affair, and the massacre spurred the creation of the North West Mounted Police. In 1878 they set up headquarters at Fort Walsh, now the center of the **Fort Walsh National Historic Site** ((306) 662-2645

SASKATOON

Saskatoon, a small, pleasant city of around 220,000 people, sits in the center of the prairie parkland, an area of trees and farmland north of the wheat-growing belt and south of the forested northern wilderness. The South Saskatchewan River runs northeast to southwest through the city, crossed by several bridges and lined by parks and trails offering peaceful retreats and recreation. The wide downtown streets have a mix of old and new buildings, most of them low-rise.

Saskatoon was founded as a temperance colony in 1882 by a group of Methodists from Ontario. They christened it after the purple berries that grew plentifully in the area. Temperance seems to have been unpopular, however, for at the turn of the century there were only 113 inhabitants, and even the coming of the railroad in 1890 didn't tempt new settlers here. Eventually, in the early 1900s, the agricultural potential of the area began to attract settlers from Europe and the Ukraine, and in 1906 the city was incorporated. A year later the University of Saskatchewan was founded here.

The city offers visitors a variety of accommodation, several interesting eateries and a warm, friendly welcome, making it a good stopover if you are on your way to the wild North Country. The University of Saskatchewan campus, the city's largest employer, dominates the east bank of the river. The university has been at the forefront of medical technology development, and is home to Canada's largest science project — the Canadian Light Source

the east–west dividing line. Several galleries and shops downtown sell **arts**, **crafts** and **antiques**, and some other outlets can be found on the east side of the river, particularly along Victoria and Broadway Avenues.

The **Meewasin Valley Trail** is made up of 21 km (13 miles) of jogging, cycling, hiking or cross-country ski trails, which meander through landscaped parkland and natural areas along the city center riverbanks. The **Meewasin Valley Centre** ((306) 665 6887 WEB SITE www.meewasin.com, 412 Third Avenue South, has a variety of entertaining hands-on exhibits about the history of Saskatoon. One of the most distinguished landmarks on the west bank is the **Delta Bessborough**

Synchrotron. In spite of that, the city has still not quite shaken off the aura of a frontier town.

GENERAL INFORMATION

Tourism Saskatoon ((306) 242-1206 TOLL-FREE (800) 567-2444 FAX (306) 242-1955 WEB SITE www.tourismsaskatoon.com, Old Canadian Pacific Railway Station, 305 Idylwyld Drive North, provides information on the city and the province.

WHAT TO SEE AND DO

The downtown core, along the west bank of the South Saskatchewan River, is a fairly small area, so many of the main attractions are within walking distance of one another. The city is built on a grid system, with Twenty-second Street dividing it into north and south, while Idylwyld Drive forms

Hotel, a 1930s railway hotel built in the grand château style favored by the railway companies of that time. Nearby **Kiwanis Park** is a popular picnicking spot.

A little further north along the riverbank, the **Ukrainian Museum of Canada** ((306) 244-3800 WEB SITE www.umc.sk.ca, 910 Spadina Crescent East, preserves the culture of the peasant immigrants who settled in the region during the late nineteenth and early twentieth centuries, with displays of costumes, arts and crafts, artifacts, textiles and photographs documenting the history of their immigration. The gift shop sells Ukrainian cookery books, arts and crafts.

Continuing towards the north along the riverbank, the modern **Mendel Art Gallery and**

OPPOSITE: The campus of Saskatoon University. ABOVE: Bison roam at the Forestry Farm Park and Zoo in Saskatoon.

Civic Conservatory ((306) 975-7610 WEB SITE www.mendel.ca, 950 Spadina Crescent East, has a permanent collection of contemporary and older works from Europe and Canada, and also hosts visiting exhibitions. The building contains a small but pleasant conservatory and an interesting gift shop. From the wharf behind the Mendel, you can catch the 45-minute **Shearwater Boat Cruise** ((306) 549-2454 WEB SITE www.shearwatertours.com along the river. There are hourly departures from noon to 6 PM during the summer only.

Looking across the river from the gallery you'll see the attractive gray-stone buildings of the **University of Saskatchewan** ((306) 966 4343 WEB SITE www.usask.ca. Tours of the campus start from Place Riel Campus Centre; places of interest here include the **Museum of Natural Sciences and Geology** ((306) 966-4399, the **Museum of Antiquities** ((306) 966-7818 (closed mid-December to mid-January), and the **Little Stone School House** ((306) 966-8384 (open May to August daily), Saskatoon's first schoolhouse and oldest public building, dating from 1887. Admission is free for all of these museums. The university's **Diefenbaker Canada Centre** ((306) 966-8384 is a museum, art gallery and research center in Canadian studies, named after Canada's thirteenth prime minister.

The **Western Development Museum** ((306) 931-1910 WEB SITE www.wdm.ca, 2610 Lorne Avenue South (take bus No. 1 from Second Avenue downtown), is one of Saskatoon's two major tourist attractions and one of four such museums in Saskatchewan (the others are in Yorkton and Moose Jaw — see EXCURSIONS FROM REGINA, page 179 under REGINA — and in North Battleford — see below), each devoted to a different aspect of the province's history. This museum brings "Boomtown 1910" to life in an impressive indoor reconstruction of an entire street of that year, complete in every detail. Care has been taken to represent the period not only in visual terms but also in smells and sounds. As you stroll along the wooden sidewalks, past the horse-drawn buggies and automobiles, you can peruse the remedies on display at the pharmacy, look in the windows of the stores, and even see a silent movie at the picture house. The street also has a fully equipped Chinese laundry, bank, railway station and school. Other areas of the museum have collections of old cars, aircraft and farming equipment. There's also a display on the mail order services that were an important part of life for many families until quite recently.

Saskatchewan's railway heritage comes to life at the **Saskatchewan Railway Museum** ((306) 382-9855 WEB SITE www.geocities.com/saskrail museum, West on Highway 7 and two kilometers (just over a mile) south on Highway 60 (open 1 PM to 6 PM mid-May through June and September Saturday and Sunday; July to August Wednesday to Sunday; tours at other times by arrangement).

This museum has a variety of diesel locomotives, streetcars, rolling stock, railway buildings and other railway artifacts, and offers rides on operating railway motor cars.

The **Saskatchewan Science Centre** ((306) 791-7927 WEB SITE www.sciencecentre.sk.ca, 2903 Powerhouse Drive, is a entertaining, interactive science museum with plenty of hands-on games and experiments and an IMAX cinema (phone for program details).

Wanuskewin Heritage Park ((306) 931-6767 WEB SITE www.wanuskewin.com, RR 4, five kilometers (three miles) north of Saskatoon, off Highway 11, is open May to mid-October daily 9 AM to 9 PM, with cultural demonstrations from 11 AM to 3 PM and dance performances at 2 PM. In fall and winter, it opens Wednesday to Sunday 9 AM to 5 PM. This is a fascinating museum complex built around the ongoing archeological excavation of 19 ancient Indian sites. You can walk the trails and observe archeological digs in progress, including living areas, teepee rings, bison jumps and other remnants of the Northern Plains peoples who once inhabited the area. At the amphitheater there are performances by native dancers and storytellers, while at the outdoor activity area visitors can learn how to build a teepee, bake *bannock* or tan a moose hide. The main exhibition halls feature artifacts, interactive computer displays, multimedia shows exploring the archeology and culture of the Plains peoples and contemporary art. Overnight tipi stays are possible.

Eight kilometers (five miles) northeast of downtown, along Attridge Drive, lies the **Saskatoon Forestry Farm and Zoo** ((306) 975-3382 WEB SITE www.city.saskatoon.sk.ca/org/leisure/facilities/zoo.asp. This pleasant verdant area houses around 300 animals and birds, most of them indigenous to North America. There are recreation areas (including cross-country skiing in winter), picnic and barbecue facilities, making it a nice spot for a family outing.

EXCURSIONS FROM SASKATOON

Batoche National Historic Site ((306) 423-6227 lies 88 km (55 miles) northeast of Saskatoon along the banks of the South Saskatchewan River. Take Highway 11 from Saskatoon, turn onto Highway 312 at Rosthern, then north onto Highway 225. This site is a must for anyone interested in the history of the Northwest Rebellion. Batoche was the site of a major Métis settlement in the nineteenth century, and the headquarters of Louis Riel's Provisional Government, set up to fight for the lands of the Métis people. At the park you can tour four battlefield areas and view a film at the Interpretive Center, which also has displays on the Métis culture and the rebellion. Altogether, the park pays a moving tribute to Métis people and their plight. It is open mid-May to September 9 AM to 5 PM.

There are more entertaining history lessons in store at the two communities of **Battleford** and **North Battleford**, which lie either side of the North Saskatchewan River, 140 km (87 miles) northwest of Saskatoon. The most direct route is along the Yellowhead Highway (Highway 16) to North Battleford. Battleford, to the south, was once the capital of the Northwest Territories, but lost its status when the Canadian Pacific Railway laid their line further south. It was also the site of a North West Mounted Police fort, built in 1876, and at **Fort Battleford National Historic Site** ((306) 937-2621 WEB SITE parkscanada.pch.gc.ca/parks/saskatchewan/fort_battleford, Central Avenue, you can see the restored fort, fitted with authentic artifacts and furnishings. Within the palisades there are five buildings, including the Officers' Quarters, the Commanding Officer's Residence and the Barracks. The Interpretive Center provides some good displays on the 1885 rebellion. Open daily May to October, 9 AM to 5 PM.

Across the bridge, North Battleford, created when the Canadian National Railway ran its line along the north shore of the river, contains another **Western Development Museum** ((306) 445-8033 WEB SITE www.wdm.ca, junction of Highways 16 and 40. This one takes the "Heritage Farm and Village" as its theme, with extensive displays of agricultural equipment and techniques, as well as a reconstruction of a small village, vintage 1925, including pioneer homes, a Ukrainian Orthodox church and a railway station. It is open daily May to September 9 AM to 5 PM, October to April from Wednesday to Sunday, 12:30 PM to 4:30 PM.

Protecting a slice of northern coniferous forest and wildlife at the center of Saskatchewan, **Prince Albert National Park** ((306) 663-4522 TOLL-FREE RESERVATIONS (888) 333-7267 FAX 306-663-5424 WEB SITE www.parkscanada.gc.ca/Parks/Saskatchewan/Prince_albert, lies 200 km (124 miles) north of Saskatoon and 60 km (36 miles) north of Prince Albert. It is a preserve of lakes, streams, hills and forest — where coyotes, black bears, elk, moose, beavers and many other creatures roam free. In addition to canoeing it offers its visitors hiking trails ranging from easy walks to backpacking hikes several days long; there is cross-country skiing in winter. Although the park is open year-round, the Information Center only opens mid-May to early September daily 8 AM to 8 PM; an Interpretive Center opens daily July to September.

Just inside the eastern entrance of the park are **Waskesiu Lake and townsite**. With accommodation of all descriptions, cafés and shops, it makes an excellent base from which to explore the park. Waskesiu has a beach, golf course, tennis courts, stables and boat rentals, and you can take a leisurely cruise along the lake aboard a paddlewheel. The **Nature Centre** ((306) 663-4509, (which is open daily June to September) gives interesting and entertaining presentations on the park, telling the story of Grey Owl, the self-styled naturalist who lived in the park during the 1930s and spoke out for the cause of conservation. There's an interactive exhibit on the boreal forest and its inhabitants; guided walks are available.

WHERE TO STAY

Expensive to Mid-range
The **Delta Bessborough** ((306) 244-5521 TOLL-FREE (800) 268-1133 FAX (306) 653-2458 E-MAIL bessales@deltahotels.com WEB SITE www.deltabessborough.ca, 601 Spadina Crescent East, Saskatoon, is Saskatoon's most distinguished hotel, built in the grand

château style of railway hostelries and set in attractive gardens overlooking the river. The hotel retains its 1930s splendor while incorporating modern conveniences, including an indoor swimming pool, a Japanese steak house, a bistro, a pleasant lounge, a coffee shop and business facilities. There are 225 rooms, all slightly different but quite spacious with old-style furnishings. Also on the riverbank, the **Radisson Hotel Saskatoon** ((306) 665-3322 TOLL-FREE (800) 333-3333 FAX (306) 665-5531 WEB SITE www.radisson.com/saskatoonca, 405 Twentieth Street East, Saskatoon, is a relatively new 18-story building with an ornate lobby and 291 well-decorated rooms and luxury suites. Among the excellent range of recreational facilities are two indoor water slides and several dining spots.

There is superb fishing to be found in the many lakes of central Saskatchewan.

The **Sheraton Cavalier** ((306) 652-6770 TOLL-FREE (1-800) 325-3535 FAX (306) 244-1739 WEB SITE www.sheratonsaskatoon.com, 612 Spadina Crescent East, Saskatoon, is a modern downtown hotel with 249 comfortable standard and executive rooms and all the facilities you could wish for. There are recreational features for the whole family, including a pool, two indoor water slides, a sun deck, an attractive dining room, a café and a nightclub.

Close to the airport, the **Saskatoon Inn** ((306) 242-1440 TOLL-FREE (1-800) 667-8789 FAX (306) 244-2779 WEB SITE www.saskatooninn.com, 2002 Airport Drive, Saskatoon, has 250 sumptuously decorated rooms with sitting areas, a lovely courtyard filled with tropical plants, a pleasant indoor pool and whirlpool, a smart restaurant and a more casual dining spot. There's nightly entertainment and dancing in the hotel lounge.

At Prince Albert National Park, the **All Season Waskesiu Lake Lodge** ((306) 663-6161 FAX (306) 663-6144, 175 Lakeshore Crescent, Waskesiu Townsite, is a comfortable lodge and convention center. Despite its name, it is only open May to mid-October.

Inexpensive

The **Senator Hotel** ((306) 244-6141 FAX (306) 244-1559, 243 Twenty-first Street East, Saskatoon, downtown, was built in the early 1900s and still retains a rather grand style throughout. Its 45 rooms are all slightly different but with the same modern amenities. The dining room has lots of character and there is an English-style pub. Also centrally located, the **Park Town Hotel** ((306) 244-5564 TOLL-FREE (800) 667-3999 FAX (306) 665-8697, 924 Spadina Crescent East, Saskatoon, has recently renovated and attractive rooms with televisions and telephones, and an indoor pool.

There's no hostel in Saskatoon, but the **Patricia Hotel** ((306) 242-8861 FAX (306) 664-1119, 345 Second Avenue North, Saskatoon, is just as inexpensive. It's located a couple of blocks from the bus depot, on the corner of Twenty-fifth Avenue.

For details of **farm vacations** and **bed and breakfast** accommodations, contact the Saskatchewan Country Vacation Association ((306) 731 2646 FAX (306) 731 2768 E-MAIL scva@canada.com WEB SITE www.scva.ca, 1308 Fifth Avenue North, Saskatoon, S7K 2S2.

WHERE TO EAT

This is prairie land and consequently there are some excellent steak houses in town. Of them all, the best is probably **Carver's** ((306) 652-8292, Sheraton Cavalier Hotel, 612 Spadina Crescent East. It has warm decor, modern art, excellent service and mouthwatering steaks for moderate to expensive prices. An excellent alternative is **John's Prime Rib House** ((306) 244 6384, 401 Twenty-first Street East.

The splendid Delta Bessborough Hotel (see above), houses two reliable restaurants: the **Samurai Japanese Steak House** and the **Garden Bistro**. You'll find elegant continental dining at the Quality Hotel's **R.J. Wiloughby** ((306) 665-7576, 90 Twenty-second Street East.

St. Tropez Bistro ((306) 652-1250, 238 Second Avenue South (moderate) is a pretty and popular spot. **Fuddruckers** ((306) 955-7777, 2910 Eighth Street East, serves good homemade hamburgers, and **Calories** ((306) 665 7991, 721 Broadway Avenue, is a friendly bistro with particularly good desserts (both inexpensive).

HOW TO GET THERE

Saskatoon International Airport is a 10- to 20-minute drive west of downtown.

The **VIA Rail terminal** TOLL-FREE (888) 842-7245 or (800) 561-8630 WEB SITE www.viarail.ca is at the western edge of the city on Chappell Drive; a five-minute walk to the downtown bus. The **Greyhound** bus station ((306) 933-8000, 50 Twenty-third Street East, handles services between Saskatoon and Regina, Winnipeg, Calgary, Edmonton and Jasper.

If **driving** from Regina, you'll arrive on Highway 11; from Manitoba in the east or Alberta in the west, you'll probably need to take the Yellowhead Highway (Highway 16), which becomes Idylwyld Drive within the city limits. If you're driving from Prince Albert National Park or Lac La Ronge Provincial Park further to the north, you need to take Highway 2 and pick up Highway 11 south of Prince Albert, which will bring you to the northern edge of Saskatoon.

NORTHERN SASKATCHEWAN

About 150 km (95 miles) north of Prince Albert National Park lies **Lac La Ronge Provincial Park** ((306) 425-4234 TOLL-FREE (800) 772-4064 (open year-round) with 340,500 hectares (841,035 acres) of lakes and forests. Over 100 lakes, including the huge Lac la Ronge, plus waterfalls and rapids, make this an ideal place for canoeing and fishing. Accommodation can be found in the town of La Ronge on the southwestern edge of the lake, along with agencies offering canoeing and camping trips.

Northeast of Prince Albert National Park, **Meadow Lake Provincial Park** ((306) 236-7680 is a strip of parkland surrounding a string of lakes. Like Prince Albert, it is an area of forests, lakes and rivers that marks the transition between the northern Saskatchewan wilderness and the prairie parkland area. Visitors enjoy beautiful lakeside beaches and wildlife, and can hike, canoe and fish. There are campsites and cabins for rent, tennis courts and stables and, in the winter, cross-country skiing trails.

Images of life on the prairies.

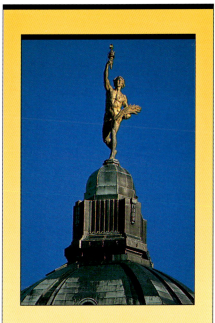

Manitoba

In 1612, Englishman Thomas Button sailed into Hudson Bay and spent the winter at the mouth of the Nelson River. He came in search of the fabled Northwest Passage to the Orient. Although disappointed at coming up against the mass of mid-Canada, the area turned out to be a hunter's paradise, teeming with furry animals and cut by rivers brimming with fish. In 1668, the ketch *Nonsuch* sailed from England to Hudson Bay and returned laden with furs. As a result, the Hudson's Bay Company was formed and was granted the vast territory, then known as Rupertsland, by Charles II. Trading posts were established around the province.

French trappers were the first white settlers in the prairie, the fathers of the Métis race, a half-French, half-Indian people who followed the Catholic faith but led the native way of life. The fur trade continued to flourish and eventually the French posts were surrendered to the British. With the success of trade and transportation, the province began to open up, threatening the Métis way of life.

In 1870, the Hudson's Bay Company sold its land to the Dominion of Canada, which immediately surveyed the area in preparation for land allotment to new settlers. The Métis people rose in defense of their land rights and, under the leadership of the young Louis Riel, they set up their own provisional government. As a result, a small area around the Red River Valley was declared the province of Manitoba, with land allocated to the Métis. In 1870 Manitoba was incorporated into the Dominion of Canada.

The coming of the Canadian Pacific Railway in the 1880s heralded a period of great change, bringing with it immigrants from Ontario, Iceland, Eastern and Western Europe and the Ukraine. By 1912 the ever-growing province had been extended to its present-day boundaries, farming was flourishing, and good communications increased the province's supply lines, thus strengthening the economy.

Often referred to as Canada's "keystone province" because of its central position, Manitoba stretches across a vast 650,088 sq km (251,000 sq miles), between Saskatchewan to the west and Ontario to the east. Rivers and lakes cover about one-sixth of its land. It has a population of just over one million.

Agriculture — primarily wheat, cereals and cattle — continues to play an important role in the province's economy. Food processing and manufacturing are the province's main industries, and the rich mineral deposits of the Canadian Shield form the basis of several others. However, of the three Prairie Provinces, Manitoba has the smallest portion of prairie land, its wheat belt only in the southwest corner. Beyond the prairies lie the great lakes of Winnipeg, Manitoba and Winnipegosis;

beyond them a vast, rugged, rocky wilderness of forests, bogs and more lakes stretch northwards to the subarctic coastline of Hudson Bay. With the Northern Lights and polar bears of Churchill, over 100,000 lakes, the desert-like landscape of Spruce Woods Provincial Park, and numerous parks offering escape routes into the wilderness, there is a lot more to Manitoba than farms.

Outdoor enthusiasts can paddle broad and wild rivers, hike through a variety of terrain, ride horse trails, learn many winter sports and participate in wildlife-spotting safaris: black and polar bears, bison, lynx, moose, badgers, golden eagles and beluga whales are among the possible sightings. The climate, however, is a limiting factor. Summer temperatures sometimes run upwards of 30°C (86ºF), while in winter they can drop to -20°C (-4°F). Snow and blizzards chill to the bone, even in southerly Winnipeg.

WINNIPEG

Halfway across Manitoba, at the very center of Canada, the city of Winnipeg, Manitoba's only major city, rises out of the prairies like a mirage, so far is it from any other city. It lies at the junction of the Assiniboine and Red Rivers, 2,093 km (1,300 miles) west of Toronto, and 572 km (355 miles) east of Regina, connected by rail and the TransCanada Highway. Around 667,000 people live in western Canada's oldest city — over half the entire population of the province.

Winnipeg is a very likeable, fairly cosmopolitan place. Its nucleus is, and always has been, the junction of Main Street and Portage Avenue, streets that stretch out for miles across the prairie, following the direction of the city's two rivers. It has pleasant parks, lovely riverside walks, wealthy suburbs with old mansion houses, and at the northeastern end of the city an old area of warehouses and depots reminds visitors of its early importance as a distribution center. The buildings along the wide, flat downtown streets testify to a policy of urban development that has respect for the city's stately older buildings, while remaining unafraid of change and innovation.

The corner of Portage Avenue and Main Street has benefited from such innovation, with an underground mall and walkways now offering shelter from what is billed as the windiest spot in Canada. Winnipeggers seem to take pride in their ability to withstand the bitterness of their long winters. The combination of harsh weather and Winnipeg's isolation from other urban centers may be why it has created such a rich cultural scene for itself. It boasts the world-famous Royal Winnipeg Ballet, a widely acclaimed symphony orchestra, the Manitoba Opera, the excellent Manitoba Theatre Centre and one of the country's finest museums, the Manitoba Museum.

Another enriching factor in Winnipeg's cultural life is the diverse ethnic mix of its population. It started out with a mixture of Indians, British, French and Métis, but the coming of the Canadian Pacific Railway added more to the mix. Chinese came as laborers working on the construction of the railway, then came other Western and Eastern Europeans, Ukrainians, Mennonites and Icelanders. The various nationalities tended to settle in ethnic-based communities around the city, and though this arrangement has to a large extent broken down, certain districts still retain a strong cultural identity. The downtown area has a sizable Chinatown, while the St. Boniface district to the east of the river has a large French-speaking community, and the southern part of town generally tends to be British in origin. Each August the city celebrates its rich ethnic mix with Folklorama: the world's largest multi-cultural event of its kind (see FESTIVE FLINGS, page 35).

Maybe the city's isolation and self-sufficiency underlies its strong character. Even the cityscape, with its cut-stone buildings, huge stockyards, warehouses and mansion-like houses, has solidity and a sense of security about it. Winnipeggers are themselves a resilient bunch, proud of their city, with an intense loyalty binding them to it wherever they wander.

BACKGROUND

Once a region where Cree, Ojibway and Assiniboine roamed, change began when the first white man arrived in 1738. He was a French explorer and fur trapper, Pierre Gaultier de la Verendrye, who established Fort Gibraltar near the confluence of the Red and Assiniboine Rivers. The fur trade flourished, albeit with a good deal of friction between rival factions. In 1812 the Hudson's Bay Company gave land in the Red River valley to Lord Selkirk, allowing him to establish a Scottish settlement and supply center for the traders.

Regular flooding and pestilence made a difficult start for the Scottish Highlanders who came here in search of a more prosperous life, but slowly they began to farm the area. For the Métis people, who lived by hunting buffalo, the settlement and farming of the area was a threat to survival, and in 1816 they attacked the settlement, killing 20 of the Scots in what has become known as the Seven Oaks Massacre. The colony faltered, but continued to grow slowly. A commercial center developed around the junction of the two rivers, with river and road transportation linking it to the United States.

In 1870 the province of Manitoba was created, and by 1873, the city of Winnipeg was incorporated. The Canadian Pacific Railway arrived in 1886, sparking the rapid expansion of the city and bringing in large numbers of immigrants. The agricultural industry flourished, strengthening Winnipeg's position as a distribution center and financial capital. Today it has a thriving manufacturing industry, and the city remains a major financial and distribution center with a large Commodity Exchange. The junction of Portage Avenue and Main Street, shadowing the two old trade routes, remains at the center of the city's financial district.

GENERAL INFORMATION

At The Forks waterfront complex (next to the Johnston Terminal), you can visit the huge **Explore Manitoba Centre** ((204) 945-3777 TOLL-FREE (866) 626-4862 WEB SITE www.travelmanitoba.com, where exhibits and travel counselors will help you sort through your options. Information on camping in Manitoba's provincial parks can be obtained from **Manitoba Conservation** ((204) 945-6784 TOLL-FREE (800) 214-6497.

For information specifically about Winnipeg, there is **Tourism Winnipeg** ((204) 943-1970 TOLL-FREE (800) 665-0204, 279 Portage Avenue, with a second location at the **Winnipeg International Airport** ((204) 982-7543 TOLL-FREE (800) 665-0204 WEB SITE www.tourism.winnipeg.mb.ca.

WHAT TO SEE AND DO

The **Exchange District** ((204) 942-6716 WEB SITE www.exchangebiz.winnipeg.mb.ca, a national historic site, lies at the very heart of Winnipeg, a 20-block area stretching from Portage Avenue and Main Street to the Manitoba Museum. Guided walking tours are offered June to September, Tuesday to Sunday at 11 AM and 2 PM.

The **Market Square**, at King Street and Bannatyne Avenue, is the hub of Winnipeg's visual arts activities, with numerous galleries and studios in historic buildings. There are shops, trendy restaurants, market stalls selling arts and crafts, and street entertainment during the summer months. This is also the location of the Fringe and Jazz Festivals, and a lively nighttime spot when the theaters, clubs and restaurants open up.

On the edge of the Exchange District, at Main Street, stand several significant buildings, including the **Centennial Concert Hall** ((204) 949-3950 (information), (204) 949-3999 (box office) or (204) 986-6069 (tours). Another is the excellent **Manitoba Museum** (until recently the Museum of Man and Nature) ((204) 956-2830 or (204) 943-3139 (24-hour recorded information) WEB SITE www.manitobamuseum.mb.ca, 190 Rupert Avenue. Consistently among Canada's "Top Ten Museums," this splendidly presented establishment is devoted to the province's geology, nature, history and culture. Realistic dioramas of Manitoba's various natural regions combine sight, sound and

smell, and a gallery focuses on the prairie lands, with reconstructions of pioneer dwellings and displays describing the native way of life. Highlights include a gallery devoted to the Hudson's Bay Company and the *Nonsuch*, a full-scale and seaworthy replica (which can be boarded) of the ketch that left London in 1668 for Hudson Bay. Within the museum are a 280-seat **Planetarium** ((204) 943-3139 and the hands-on **Science Centre** ((204) 956-2830.

Close by stands the **Ukrainian Cultural and Educational Centre (Oseredok)** ((204) 942-0218, 184 Alexander Avenue East. This old building houses an art gallery and museum containing archives and changing exhibitions on the history and culture of the Ukrainian people, the second largest group of immigrants to settle in the province. Many of the refugees brought with them smuggled documents, which now form the most complete archive about the country outside the Ukraine itself. Exhibits include samples of embroidery, ceramics, carving, costumes and the delicately painted Easter eggs called *pysankys*.

Moving south along Main Street, opposite the railway station there's a tiny park in which you can see **Upper Fort Garry Gate**, all that remains of the early nineteenth-century Hudson's Bay Fort. To the east along Broadway, another Winnipeg landmark carries on the name — **The Fort Garry**, a château-like hotel built by the Grand Trunk Railway in 1913.

Behind the station, 5.5-hectare (13.6-acres) **Forks National Historic Site** ((204) 983-6757 WEB SITE www.parkscanada.pch.gc.ca / forks has interpretive displays about the region's history, heritage entertainment — Parks Events Hotline ((204) 983-6757 — and riverside pathways.

Next to the historic site, sharing the riverside promenade, is **The Forks** ((204) 943-7752 WEB SITE www.theforks.com, a sprawling complex of renovated railway buildings and parkland. There's a lively public market in a former stable, a skating rink in winter and Johnston Terminal — with shops, restaurants, a viewing tower, an outdoor stage, a railway museum, a children's theater and **Manitoba Children's Museum** ((204) 924-4000 WEB SITE www.childrensmuseum.com, a state-of-the-art, hands-on space that appeals equally to adults. Seven galleries cover history, science, nature, technology — and hockey. Kids can climb aboard a vintage steam engine or try out a fully functioning television studio.

The **Splash Dash Water Bus** ((204) 783-6633 offers a dock-to-dock service on the Red and Assiniboine Rivers (May to October daily 7 AM to sunset, with departures from The Forks every 15 minutes). It also rents canoes for individual river trips.

The magnificent **Legislative Building** ((204) 945-5813, Broadway and Osborne Street, is an excellent example of neoclassical architecture, designed by English architect Frank Worthington

Simon and built in 1919. This H-shaped structure is made of fossil-rich Tyndall limestone. Atop its dome stands the recently re-gilded figure of the **Golden Boy**, symbolically facing north. He holds the torch of economic progress in one hand and carries a sheaf of wheat in the other to symbolize agriculture. The work of French sculptor Charles Gardet the statue has become the symbol of the city. The building is set in lovely grounds dotted with statuary honoring the city's various ethnic groups with depictions of some of their distinguished countrymen, including Louis Riel. The interior of the building is also quite spectacular; guided tours allow visitors a look at the Legislative Chamber (hourly tours July through Labor Day daily, 9 AM to 6 PM).

South of Broadway, take a look at what high-tech meant to the late Victorians at the **Dalnavert Museum** ((204) 943-2835, 61 Carlton Street, a house that was built for the son of John A. Macdonald, Canada's first prime minister. It is a red brick building that was built with indoor plumbing and electric lighting, and was fitted with all kinds of household gadgetry.

The superb **Winnipeg Art Gallery** ((204) 786-6641 WEB SITE www.wag.mb.ca, 300 Memorial Boulevard, is housed in an unmissable wedge-shaped building. It has a varied collection of international art, but is most famous for the world's largest collection of contemporary Inuit works of art (over 9,000 pieces), which are exhibited in continually changing displays. Cultural events are often staged in the roof garden.

Across the Red River, the **St. Boniface** district is home to the oldest French-speaking community in Canada. French traders lived in the area from 1738 when Pierre Gaultier de la Verendrye arrived. In 1819, following the building of a church here, a French community began to develop that included French Canadians and Métis. The 1906 City Hall, 219 Provencher Boulevard, now houses a tourist information center and gallery with works by francophone artists.

St. Boniface Cathedral, 190 Cathedral Avenue, is a modern structure built among the ruins of an earlier cathedral that burned down in 1968. In the old cemetery lies the body of Louis Riel, who was executed following the defeat of the Northwest Rebellion. *In Riel's Footsteps* is a 45-minute play staged in the cemetery July to August, Wednesday to Sunday at 2 PM and 7 PM, Saturday and Sunday at 4 PM too — French and English versions alternate, so check.

Next to the basilica stands Winnipeg's oldest building, an oak structure dating from 1846, which was a convent for the Grey Nuns who arrived here from Montréal. It now contains the **St. Boniface Museum** ((204) 237-4500, 494 Taché Avenue, which has a large collection of artifacts belonging to the Métis and other early settlers,

including some Louis Riel memorabilia. Also in the area is the **Church of the Precious Blood**, an interesting modern structure that is shaped like a tipi.

At the southern edge of the city you can visit **Riel House** ((204) 257-1783, 330 River Road (mid-May to early-September, daily 10 AM to 6 PM), which stands close to the river in St. Vital. It was the home of the Riel family, although Louis Riel never lived here. It has been restored to the year 1885, when Riel was executed, and bilingual tours and exhibits offer glimpses into Métis life of the period.

Moving eastwards, a striking glass pyramid houses the **Royal Canadian Mint** ((204) 257-3359, 520 Lagimodière Boulevard, which produces coins for Canada and over 30 foreign nations: it's estimated that a quarter of the world's population carry coins minted here. Guided tours (by appointment only; English and French) show you the processes and high-tech equipment involved in making money, but the product is out of reach!

Assiniboine Park ((204) 986-3130, 2355 Corydon Avenue, accessible by footbridge over the Assiniboine River from Portage Avenue, west of the city — about 11 km (seven miles) from downtown — is a 153-hectare (378-acre) park with the Leo Mol sculpture garden, an English garden with a statue of Queen Victoria, and the Lyric outdoor theater. There's a Winnie-the-Bear statue (the beloved Pooh was named after a Canadian bear in the London Zoo named Winnepeg, but the Disney Corporation has the copyright on the name "Winnie-the-Pooh") and an attractive old pavilion ((204) 888-5466, with an art gallery containing the only known E. H. Shepard oil painting of Winnie. The park also contains a **zoo** ((204) 986-6921, with around 1,700 animals of over 300 species, many indigenous, and a **conservatory** ((204) 986-5537, a small but delightful spot filled with orchids and other flowers.

The **Fort Whyte Centre for Family Adventure and Recreation** ((204) 989-8355 WEB SITE WWW .fortwhyte.org, 1961 McCreary Road, has 215 hectares (600 acres) of land in Winnipeg's southwest corner. Here the natural habitat of the province's lakes and rivers has been recreated in and around several former cement quarries — you can canoe on the lakes, see (usually) a 40-strong herd of bison, and feel a bear's fur. Self-guided nature trails and an interpretive center tell all about it.

Excursions from Winnipeg

Lower Fort Garry ((204) 785-6050 TOLL-FREE (877) 534-3678, about 32 km (20 miles) north of Winnipeg along Highway 9 (mid-May to Labor Day daily 9 AM to 5 PM), was built by the Hudson's Bay Company in the 1830s and is the only remaining stone fort of that era in North America. It has been carefully restored and visitors can see the various living quarters, the fur loft and the governor's residence, as they were when the fort functioned as an important trading post. Before you begin your tour of the buildings, watch the background film shown in the reception center. Inside the compound, costumed "workers" demonstrate crafts in the various workshops. In the grounds you'll see a restored York boat, a vessel designed for transporting furs.

The **Mennonite Heritage Village** ((204) 326-9661 WEB SITE www.mennoniteheritagevillage .mb.ca lies 61 km (38 miles) southeast of Winnipeg. To get there from Winnipeg, take Highway 1 to Highway 12 North, and watch for signs just north of Steinbach. This living museum runs a

working mill and has Mennonites demonstrate their nineteenth-century crafts. The Mennonites who settled in Manitoba came from Russia in the 1870s and 1880s, and this heritage village presents a colorful picture of their way of life. The sect is totally committed to pacifism and has been persecuted because of its beliefs. The Livery Barn Restaurant serves traditional Mennonite food and the general store sells traditional goods.

The *Prairie Dog Central* ((204) 832-5259 WEB SITE www.vintagelocomotivesociety.mb.ca is an early twentieth-century steam train that takes you on a delightful 45-km (28-mile), two-and-a-half-hour trip to **Warren**. It leaves from Inkster Junction, just north of Inkster Boulevard (with free bus service from The Forks) at 10 AM and 3 PM every Sunday from May to September; in July and August there are Saturday trips too.

SPORTS AND OUTDOOR ACTIVITIES

There are **hiking** trails and **cycling** paths in the city parks (details available from information centers) and several **skating** rinks throughout Winnipeg. When the snow comes, there's also **snowmobiling** at Birds Hill Provincial Park, about 32 km (20 miles) northeast of the city.

There's excellent **fishing** in the province, as you would expect with so many lakes, but you need to venture outside Winnipeg. The tourist information centers can help you on where to go and how to get there, and with details of the many **canoe** routes for which the province is famous.

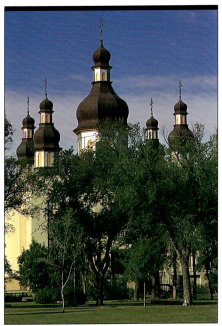

NIGHTLIFE AND THE ARTS

Winnipeg has a lively nightlife. To find out what's going on, check the entertainment listings that appear in the daily *Winnipeg Free Press* and the *Winnipeg Sun*. Hotels and other places distribute the free *Uptown*, a weekly arts and entertainment paper, and there's a useful monthly publication, *Where Winnipeg*.

The theater season in Winnipeg is really under way between September and early May, but in July the **Manitoba Theatre Centre (MTC)** ((204) 942-6537 (box office), 174 Market Avenue, promotes the 11-day **Fringe Theatre Festival** E-MAIL fringe@mtc.mb.ca, as well as staging a variety of comedy and serious drama throughout the

ABOVE: Part of the façade of the Legislative Building LEFT and the towers of the Ukrainian church at the Ukrainian Cultural and Educational Centre RIGHT.

theater season. Nearby, the smaller **MTC Warehouse Theatre** ((204) 956-1340 or (204) 942-6537 (box office) stages experimental productions.

There are several other companies scattered around town, including the **Prairie Theatre Exchange** ((204) 942-5483, Portage Place Shopping Centre, and the **Rainbow Stage** ((204) 780-7328, which specializes in musicals. In summer, productions are staged at the outdoor amphitheater in Kildonan Park. The most cherished and famous of Winnipeg's cultural institutions is the **Royal Winnipeg Ballet**, which performs a program of classical and modern works at the **Centennial Concert Hall** ((204) 956-0183 (information) or (204) 956-2792 (box office), Room 101, 555 Main Street (season October to May), and also gives a free open-air performance on the Lyric Stage in Assiniboine Park in the summer. The acclaimed **Winnipeg Symphony Orchestra** ((204) 949-3950 (information) or (204) 949-3999 (box office) (season September to May) and the **Manitoba Opera** ((204) 942-7479 (information) or (204) 780-3333 (box office) (season November to May) also perform at the Centennial Concert Hall. Also with a November to May season, **Winnipeg's Contemporary Dancers** ((204) 452-0229 are famous for pushing the boundaries of modern dance. They perform at different venues. The **Manitoba Theatre for Young People** ((204) 942-8898, The Forks, offers productions October through March that are aimed at children and teenagers. For summer visitors, varied entertainments are presented at the Festival Park outdoor **Scotiabank Stage** ((204) 942-6302 WEB SITE www.theforks.com.

A mixture of jazz, folk, and classical music can often be heard at the **Winnipeg Art Gallery** ((204) 786-6641 WEB SITE www.wag.mb.ca, 300 Memorial Boulevard.

You'll find rock and other live music playing at various bars and clubs in the town, often in hotel lounges. The **Palomino Club** ((204) 772-0454, 1133 Portage Avenue, is a country music hangout. **Pyramid Cabaret** ((204) 957-7777, 176 Fort Street, offers top local and national bands, as well as DJs covering a wide variety of styles.

Winnipeg has a lively and rapidly changing club scene, especially in the Exchange District, and two **casinos**, with a common TOLL-FREE number (800) 265-3912 and a common WEB SITE www.casinosofwinnipeg.com. Both operate Monday through Saturday 10 AM to 3 AM, Sunday from noon. Nobody under 18 is admitted. **Club Regent** ((204) 957-2700, 1425 Regent Avenue West, is set-up as a Disney-type jungle with ersatz palm trees, beasts and temples on all sides, as well as a genuine walk-through aquarium with a small shark and less fearsome creatures. **McPhillips Street Station** ((204) 957-3900, 484 McPhillips Street, has a less-striking decor but incorporates the **Millennium Express** ((204) 957-3900 TOLL-FREE (800) 265-3912,

a mind-blowing 3D combination ride/history/entertainment. In addition to these attractions and the usual mass of gaming tables, both casinos feature Vegas-style live entertainment, restaurants and lounges.

WHERE TO STAY

Expensive

The **Delta Winnipeg** ((204) 942-0551 TOLL-FREE (800) 268-1133 FAX (204) 943-8702, 350 St. Mary Avenue, is part of a recently renovated complex that connects with the Convention Centre. The 390 pleasant rooms include several suites. Facilities include indoor and outdoor pools and a good range of services, a choice of restaurants within the hotel and several more inside the complex.

The **Fairmont Winnipeg** ((204) 957-1350 TOLL-FREE (800) 441-1414 FAX (204) 949-1486, 2 Lombard Place, one of the city's top-rated hotels, is in the

very center of town. Service is excellent, there are 340 luxurious rooms and guests have the use of an indoor swimming pool, a choice of restaurants, a café and in-house entertainment.

For some old-style grandeur, go to **Hotel Fort Garry** ((204) 942-8251 TOLL-FREE (800) 665-8088 FAX (204) 956-2351, 222 Broadway. This castle-like hotel was built by the Grand Trunk Railway in 1913 and has undergone extensive but careful renovation to preserve its original splendor. There are 240 elegant rooms and suites and two beautiful dining rooms. A full breakfast is included in the rate.

The **Sheraton Winnipeg** ((204) 942-5300 TOLL-FREE (800) 463-6400 FAX (204) 943-7975, 161 Donald Street, is another top downtown hotel, located close to the Convention Center. It has an indoor pool, a sundeck, and nightly entertainment. Some rooms are mid-range. Their **Just Off Broadway** restaurant specializes in regional cuisine.

Mid-range

The **Radisson Winnipeg Downtown** ((204) 956-0410 TOLL-FREE (800) 333-3333 WEB SITE WWW .radisson.com/winnipeg.ca, 288 Portage Avenue, is a downtown high-rise hotel with 272 rooms above its multistory parking facility. The rooms are smart and have good views. The service is first-rate and amenities include a recreation center with indoor swimming pool, sauna, whirlpool and exercise room, and a business center with secretarial services and free Internet access.

For accommodation with lots of character and excellent service, book in at the **Ramada Marlborough Hotel** ((204) 942-6411 TOLL-FREE (800) 667-7666 FAX (204) 942-2017, 331 Smith Street, in the town's financial district. This Victorian Gothic building has a grand interior of vaulted ceilings, stained glass and polished wood. The rooms and

Feathers for sale in the Old Market Square.

suites are stylish, with modern conveniences, and the hotel has a restaurant, an English pub and a coffee shop.

Canad Inns TOLL-FREE (888) 332-2623 (central reservations) WEB SITE www.canadinns.com, have half a dozen establishments scattered around town. They are big, new and spotlessly clean, with pools and waterslides for the kids and good-quality family restaurants. One is attached to the Club Regent Casino. Some rooms are inexpensive.

Inexpensive

The **Charter House Hotel** ((204) 942-0101 TOLL-FREE (800) 782-0175 FAX (204) 956-0665, 330 York Avenue, is a good downtown choice. It has 90 rooms

(some with balconies), a very good steak house and an outdoor swimming pool.

The **Ivey House International Hostel** ((204) 772-3022 FAX (204) 784-1133, 210 Maryland Street, is located in a turn-of-the-twentieth-century residence within walking distance of the city's cultural attractions. It's open year-round.

The *Bed & Breakfast of Manitoba* listing is available from the information centers or **Manitoba Bed and Breakfast** ((204) 661-0300 WEB SITE www.bedandbreakfast.mb.ca, 893 Dorchester Avenue. If a rural retreat appeals, get in touch with the **Manitoba Country Vacations Association (MCVA)** (/FAX (204) 776-2176 E-MAIL ffamfarm @escape.ca WEB SITE www.countryvacations.mb .ca, c/o Ernest Fraser, Box 93, Minto R0K 1M0. The tourist information centers can also tell you about campgrounds in the region.

WHERE TO EAT

Winnipeg's diverse ethnic mix makes for some exciting dining, and there is a surprisingly large number of restaurants for a city of its size.

Expensive

The restaurant **529 Wellington** ((204) 487-8325, 529 Wellington Crescent, is unashamedly the priciest place in town — but worth it. The elegant uncrowded surroundings, superb service and connoisseurs' wine list match the quality of the superb steaks. Excellent jumbo prawns and fresh Atlantic lobster also feature on the menu.

Wasabi ((204) 774-4328, 588 Broadway, is a top Japanese establishment, the funkiest sushi bistro in town. Don't miss the soft-shell crab. **Fusion Grill** ((204) 489-6963, 550 Academy Road at Lanark Street, takes a lot to beat it if you enjoy the imaginative use of spices. Fresh local ingredients prepared in a way that reflects the city's mixed ethnic influences are delicious enough to attract many well-known clients, as well as "normal" folk who enjoy the simple bistro atmosphere.

Moderate to Expensive

Dubrovnik Restaurant ((204) 944-0594, 390 Assiniboine Avenue, is in a large Victorian house on the riverbank, with a charming interior and many original features. Some beautiful examples of Yugoslavian crafts adorn the walls. The food is continental with Yugoslavian specialties, and it is delicious.

Tre Visi ((204) 949-9032, 173 McDermot Avenue, is a comfortable but elegant California/ modern-Italian restaurant with a great wine selection to accompany brilliant salads and wonderful dishes made with fresh ingredients.

Moderate

Earls ((204) 989-0103, 191 Main Street, is a popular rendezvous with a wide-ranging good-quality menu, reasonable prices and a pleasantly casual ambiance. The **Dim Sum Garden** ((204) 942-8297, 277 Rupert Avenue, lives up to its name, with over a hundred delicious choices of authentic Cantonese-style dim sum brought round on carts.

Mona Lisa ((204) 488-3687, 1697 Corydon Avenue, is the place for classic Italian pizzas, excellent pastas and the like. It's family-oriented with a casual atmosphere. **Stella's Café and Bakery** ((204) 453-8562, 166 Osborne Street, is a great place for brunch, with excellent quiches and other baked goods, but it's always busy, so get there early. **Rae and Jerry's Steak House** ((204) 783-6155, 1405 Portage Avenue in the west end of the city, is a popular 1950s-style steak house that includes chicken and fish dishes on its menu. Prices vary between inexpensive and moderate.

If you like Vietnamese food, try **Nhu Quynh** ((204) 786-1182, 510 Sargent Avenue, which offers rice-flour pancakes wrapped round blanched vegetables and delicious sauces. Again, it's moderate to inexpensive.

Inexpensive

The north end of town has a plethora of delis and cafés that make for some interesting and enjoyable dining. **Alycia's Restaurant** ((204) 582-8789,

559 Cathedral Avenue, serves homemade Ukrainian food in cozy surroundings decorated with traditional arts and crafts. This is a place where Winnipeggers hang out. Both **Oscar's Deli** ((204) 947-0314, 175 Hargrave Street, and **Simon's Delicatessen** ((204) 589-8269, 1322 Main Street, are well-established Jewish delicatessens open into the small hours.

Mrs. Mike's Burgers ((204) 237-3977, 286 Taché Avenue, opens only in summer for outdoor dining or takeaway. It is Winnipeg's oldest burger joint, and consistently popular as it is both good and very cheap. The two **Soup Pierre** TOLL-FREE (888) 7687, 238 Portage Avenue, and ((204) 453-7687, 651 Corydon Avenue, offer a large selection of homemade soups, some vegetarian, and sandwiches. You can eat in or take away.

Winnipeg's **Chinatown** lies to the north of the Exchange District, stretching between James and Logan avenues and covering an eight-block area. You'll find good-value Chinese restaurants here.

How to Get There

Winnipeg International Airport ((204) 987-9402, is approximately 10 km (six miles) northwest of downtown, about a 20-minute drive away, but allow longer during rush hours. An airport shuttle runs between the airport and some of the big hotels. Apart from Air Canada, the only scheduled airlines covering the city are **Westjet** ((403) 444-2552 TOLL-FREE (800) 538-5696 WEB SITE www.westjet .com (within Canada) and **Northwest Airlines** TOLL-FREE (800) 447-4747 or (800) 225-2525 WEB SITE www.nwa.com (primarily from Minneapolis).

The **VIA Rail** station ((204) 949 1830 TOLL-FREE (888) 842-7245 WEB SITE www.viarail.ca is downtown at 123–146 Main Street. Trains run to Vancouver via Kamloops, Jasper, Edmonton and Saskatoon. From the east the line runs into Winnipeg from Toronto, while VIA Rail runs the *Hudson Bay* train to Churchill via Dauphin, The Pas and Thompson.

The bus station is downtown at 487 Portage Place. **Greyhound** ((204) 783-8857 TOLL-FREE (800) 661-8747 WEB SITE www.greyhound.ca operates buses to and from this terminal. **Grey Goose Bus Lines** ((204) 784-4500, 301 Burnell Street, links Winnipeg with other towns in Manitoba.

Winnipeg is quite isolated, so if you're driving, the chances are that wherever you're coming from (unless it's the airport), you'll have quite a long drive. The TransCanada Highway (Highway 1) runs through the city, linking it with Toronto, 2,093 km (1,300 miles) to the east, and Calgary, 1,359 km (844 miles) to the west. Minneapolis in Minnesota is 734 km (456 miles) from Winnipeg via Interstate 94 and Interstate 29 in the United States, becoming Highway 75 in Manitoba.

ELSEWHERE IN MANITOBA

WHITESHELL PROVINCIAL PARK

Nature sets the stage for all kinds of outdoor pursuits in this large wilderness park (272,090 hectares / 672,334 acres) close to the Ontario border, 144 km (89 miles) east of Winnipeg. It is Canadian Shield country, an area rich in clear, deep lakes, rushing rivers, forest, sandy beaches and wildlife — ideal for hiking, mountain biking, canoeing, horseback riding, fishing and all kinds of water sports in summer. In winter these give way to cross-country skiing, ice fishing, skating, snowmobiling and snowboarding. Areas of the park have been developed for tourism and offer such things as shops, a golf course, tennis courts and small museums about local features. Specific points of interest include centuries-old aboriginal petraforms, a goose sanctuary, a fish hatchery, a lily pond and rock tunnels through which canoes can pass.

LAKE WINNIPEG

This vast lake lies to the north of Winnipeg and is lined with sandy beaches, making it an excellent place for relaxation and water sports. Grand Beach, on the eastern shore, is one of North America's best for swimming, windsurfing and fishing, with powdery sand, dunes up to eight meters (26 ft) high and a lagoon crowded with waterfowl.

The **Visitor Centre** is operated by the **New Iceland Heritage Museum** ((204) 642-4001, which focuses on Icelandic settlement in the area and inter-cultural history.

The fishing town of **Gimli** (meaning "paradise" in Norse mythology) has the largest Icelandic community outside Iceland. It stands on the western shore of the lake, 90 km (56 miles) north of Winnipeg. Back in the 1870s, Icelanders came to the area in search of a new volcano-free home. They found that this area could offer them a good living through fishing and farming, and for a time the region was an independent country known as New Iceland. The community of Gimli retains a strong Icelandic identity and culture, and in August it celebrates the **Icelandic Festival**, a celebration of sports, music, parades, art and traditional food.

Hecla/Grindstone Provincial Park ((204) 378-2945, Riverton, encompasses a collection of islands in Lake Winnipeg. These islands are wildlife preserves and a bird-watcher's delight, while hikers, fishermen, canoeists and winter sports enthusiasts also find much to enjoy here. Hecla Island is accessible by car, and at its northern end the **Gull**

Winnipeg's skyline.

Harbour Resort and Conference Centre ((204) 279-2041 TOLL-FREE (800) 267-6700 WEB SITE www .gullharbourresort.com, offers recreation facilities, attractive accommodation and good Icelandic hospitality without marring the natural beauty of the island. The hotel is open year-round.

RIDING MOUNTAIN NATIONAL PARK

Riding Mountain National Park is an outdoor playground 248 km (154 miles) northwest of Winnipeg, on the highlands of a prairie escarpment. The resort town of **Wasagaming**, on the shores of Clear Lake, offers a variety of accommodation and extensive recreational facilities, but the area remains largely unspoiled, with 60 species of mammal, including bison, moose, elk, whitetailed deer, black bears and beaver inhabiting the parkland. In the winter there are cross-country skiing trails through the park.

The **Visitor Centre** in Wasagaming ((204) 848-7275 or 7272 TOLL-FREE (800) 707-8480 E-MAIL RMNP_Info@pch.gc.ca will provide guides, maps and information, as well as offering films and other worthwhile educational aids.

On the outskirts of Wasagaming, the **Elkhorn Resort & Conference Centre** ((204) 848-2802 WEB SITE www.elkhornresort.mb.ca/www.rci.com, has chalets and suites, a nine-hole golf course and organized horseback riding treks. Prices vary from mid-range to expensive.

Rather less hectic is **Riding Mountain Guest Ranch** ((204) 848-2265 E-MAIL wildlifeadventures @mts.net WEB SITE www.wildlifeadventures.ca, Lake Audy, a peaceful spot run by animal lovers Jim and Candy Irwin, whose guests are made to feel part of the family. Horseback riding in the park and canoeing on the lake that laps at their front lawn are among the activities arranged to work off the excellent food, while less strenuous pursuits include billiards, board games, books, a sauna, and bear-watching from a comfortable "hide" (an old school bus). A great place to really get away from it all and relax. Many guests become friends and regular visitors.

CHURCHILL

The small town of Churchill lies on the southwestern shore of Hudson Bay at the estuary of the Churchill River, and is one of the few places in the north accessible from the south by rail or air. It is one of the world's largest grain-handling ports, with huge grain elevators looming overhead, but it has become an international tourist destination because of its substantial natural attractions. Although weather conditions are very difficult here, with snow during most of the year creating a sparse, subarctic vegetation, the wildlife draws visitors.

Churchill is the world capital for **polar bear watching**, especially during October and early November, when migration is at its height and the bears are regularly seen wandering around the outskirts of town.

Tundra Buggy Tours ((204) 675-2121 TOLL-FREE (800) 544-5049 operates specially built buggies that take visitors out on bear-spotting safaris on the tundra. Half-day tours run July through September, full-day tours October and early November.

This is also one of the best places on earth to see the **Northern Lights** in their full glory: they are visible for around 190 nights a year! Their appearance is determined by the weather but you would be unlucky not to see them if you were to stay for more than a couple of nights any time from October through April. At this time they may well be visible from other parts of the province: March is the peak in the north, a little later in the south.

The town is not without a summer attraction, too: from July through mid-August **beluga whales** congregate at the mouth of the Churchill River, and there are daily tours in a hydroplane-equipped boat to listen to these most vocal whales with **Sea North Tours** ((204) 675-2195 WEB SITE www.cancom.net/seanorth.

The **Eskimo Museum** ((204) 675-2030, in downtown Churchill, has an excellent collection of Inuit artifacts, including walrus tusks carved with scenes from mythology and everyday life.

Calm Air ((204) 778-6471 TOLL-FREE (888) 225-6247 WEB SITE www.calmair.com, 90 Thompson Drive, runs flights between Winnipeg and Churchill year-round, at least once a day.

There's also the option of a two-night **VIA Rail** journey from Winnipeg. In peak seasons (July, and mid-September to mid-November) there are three trains a week in each direction. For information, contact VIA Rail ((506) 857-9830 TOLL-FREE (888) 842-7245 WEB SITE www.viarail.ca, 146-123 Main Street, Winnipeg R3C 1A3.

OPPOSITE: Waterfowl and moose share the unspoiled beauty of Riding Mountain National Park.

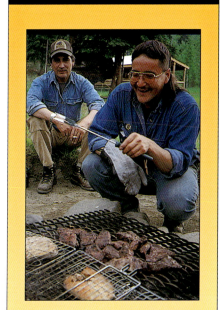

The North

One could argue that all of Canada is the north. But, for Canadians, "true north" is that vast stretch of country that extends from the 60th parallel to beyond the magnetic North Pole. This North occupies a special place in the national mythology, forming a significant part of the identity of all Canadians — despite the fact that most of them have never been there. Northerners, for their part, call the rest of Canada "the outside." The Yukoners' history is as closely linked to that of Alaskans as to their fellow Canadians, and the Inuit majority of the northeast shares a common culture with the native peoples of Greenland.

Two-thirds of this varied landscape constitutes the Northwest Territories and Nunavut — a land of giant lakes, treeless tundra and the hardy Dene, Inuit and other native groups who have thrived in this rugged environment for thousands of years. This is the least densely populated area in the world, with Canada's highest concentration of aboriginal peoples (60 percent). Following decades of land-rights negotiations, on April 1, 1999, the former Northwest Territories was divided. The new border extends north from the Manitoba–Saskatchewan frontier for 500 km (310 miles), veers northwest for 1,050 km (650 miles), hooks back east 500 km (310 miles) to 110 degrees latitude, then cuts dead north to the Arctic Ocean. The territory east of this border has been named Nunavut (which means "our land" in Inuktitut), and includes those islands in Hudson Bay, James Bay and Ungava Bay that are not within Manitoba, Ontario or Quebec. The lands west of the new border will remain the Northwest Territories until a new name is chosen.

To the west of the Northwest Territories is the Yukon, distinguished from the rest of the North by its indigenous populations, its climate, its geography and its history. Aside from its cultural and geographical differences, the Yukon is also more accessible than Nunavut and the western Northwest Territories, primarily because of its transportation infrastructure. On the whole, the Yukon tends to attract more hikers and paddlers, while Nunavut and the Northwest Territories attract hunters and fishermen, though all three territories offer excellent opportunities for hiking, boating, fishing and hunting.

For the traveler who wishes to explore the North, several aspects of northern travel should be borne in mind. The first is that this is a vast, vast land. "The Canadian north," writes Pierre Berton, "is so big that you could drop the state of Texas or the British Isles in here and never notice either of them." Thus, you will want to choose a specific area to explore, depending on your interests, rather than trying to "do" the North. Second, a trip to Canada's North will probably require

The Northwest Territories — A hiker surveys the Mackenzie Mountains.

more than the usual amount of advance preparation and will certainly demand a significantly greater outlay of money.

Be aware that mosquitoes and changeable weather are major issues in the northern summer. A bug jacket over your T-shirt during the day will be as important as a sweater in the evening.

If you intend to do any wilderness hiking or paddling, you should obtain accurate and timely information about conditions to be expected and advise a friend or relative, and the nearest Royal Canadian Mounted Police detachment, where you are going and when you will be back.

Many of the Yukon's roads are now widened, straightened and paved, but major gravel roads

still exist. In the Northwest Territories highways are mainly all-weather gravel roads. Keep your headlights on at all times.

With the exception of Whitehorse in the Yukon Territory, northern communities are not under the 911 emergency system (see HEALTH AND SAFETY, page 244 in TRAVELERS' TIPS).

THE YUKON TERRITORY

In the far northwest corner of Canada, a rough triangular boundary defines the Yukon Territory's 483,450 sq km (174,000 sq miles). Bordered by British Columbia to the south and the Northwest

Skookum Jim ("skookum" means handsome), one of the discoverers of Bonanza Creek, where the gold was "thick between the flaky slabs, like cheese sandwiches." The discovery touched off the 1896 gold rush.

Territories to the east, the northern tip of the triangle is cut through by the Arctic Circle and ends at the Beaufort Sea, home to musk oxen, polar bears and beluga whales. Frozen wilderness defines the Yukon's southern boundary as well, where the largest non-polar ice caps in the world are suspended over the saw-toothed mountains of Kluane National Park. In between all of this frozen water is a semi-arid land that, if it were not so far north, would be a desert.

The Yukon's dry climate and long hours of sunshine come as a surprise to many visitors. Dawson City's temperature may drop below -50°C (-58°F) in January, but easily rises to 35°C (100°F) in July. Each year thousands of hectares burn in raging forest fires, which are closely monitored but generally allowed to take their own course.

Over 1,000 species of flowering plants have adapted to ice, wind and fire to thrive in the territory. Fireweed — so named because it is the first plant to revegetate land cleared by fire — is the Yukon's official flower, seen blazing along the roadways all summer long. Only a few hardy trees, such as spruce and lodgepole pine, poplar, birch and willow, are able to tolerate the growing conditions, and tend to be smaller and spindlier than their southern relatives. Wildlife flourishes, with 278 bird and 61 mammal species, and 27 species of freshwater fish.

The Yukon's 33,000 human inhabitants are also a ruggedly adaptable bunch. Situated 2,720 km (1,700 miles) from Vancouver and over 1,400 km (900 miles) from Edmonton, and hemmed in by lofty mountains to the south, they are extraordinarily isolated from the rest of Canada. In fact, Yukoners feel stronger ties with their Alaskan neighbors than they do with Canadians. Yukoners live in one of the earth's last frontier lands: a place full of hardship and opportunity. As you might expect, most love and revere the outdoors, even though two-thirds of them live in the capital city of Whitehorse.

The Yukon has much to offer visitors: the ancient cultures of the region's First Nations peoples, still alive in communities from Whitehorse to Old Crow; historic sites linked to the era of one of the world's greatest gold rushes; wilderness areas where barely a trace of human existence can be found; and some of the most splendid mountainscapes in Canada.

BACKGROUND

Until around the 1800s the region now known as the Yukon was occupied exclusively by bands of Gwitch'in, Kaska, Tagish, Tutchone and Teslin Hän natives — hunters and nomads who, in springtime, gathered into larger groups for fishing.

Beginning in the eighteenth century, Russian explorers began trading with the area's indigenous

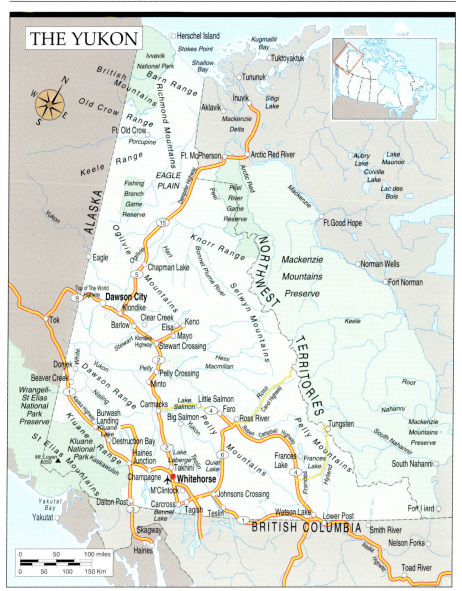

THE YUKON

populations. Then, in 1825, the explorer Sir John Franklin anchored off the Yukon's Arctic coastline. The Hudson's Bay Company moved into the interior in the 1840s, and United States traders arrived after Russia sold Alaska to America in 1867.

Prospectors began to trickle into the Yukon in the 1870s, following a trail of gold strikes along the Rockies that had begun in California in 1849 and had continued into the interior of British Columbia. By 1882 there were 50 miners in the Yukon Valley searching for and finding small but promising amounts of gold. By the early 1890s the number had grown to nearly 1,000, centered on the community of Forty Mile, near present-day Dawson City.

In 1896, a white prospector, George Washington Carmack, and his native brothers-in-law, Skookum Jim and "Dawson" Charlie, found gold — lots of it — in Rabbit Creek. Carmack brought word back that the rocks of Rabbit Creek had gold "thick between the flaky slabs, like cheese sandwiches." The three men staked their claims and Carmack renamed the creek "Bonanza." The gold rush was on.

Thousands of people poured into this remote corner of Canada, most arriving by way of Skagway, Alaska, and the upper Yukon River. These stampeders had to pack enough provisions to last out the year, haul them over the White or Chilkoot

Pass, and then build a boat at the foot of Lake Bennett to carry them the remaining stretch to the Klondike gold fields near Dawson City. In the spring of 1898, Mounties counted 28,000 men and women in 7,000 makeshift boats leaving the shores of Lake Bennett bound for the Klondike. Amidst this hullabaloo, the town of Dawson was born.

Within a few years Dawson was left in the sawdust as gold seekers moved on to Nome, Alaska, where yet another big strike had been found. Gold mining in the Yukon continued (and continues today), but from 1913 onwards, the Yukon's economy shifted to other minerals, such as silver and lead at Keno Hill in the central Yukon. The construction of the Alaska Highway

Whitehorse became a stopping point for the stampeders clawing their way north to Dawson City. In 1900, the White Pass & Yukon Railway was completed, with its terminus in Whitehorse, and the settlement began to take shape. The building of the Alaska Highway through its backyard gave the town a further boost. In 1942, the population jumped from 500 to around 8,000, although it fell back to about 3,000 in 1955. Today, Whitehorse, the territorial capital since March 1951, has a population of about 23,000.

If someday there are cities built on Mars, they'll probably look like parched and pragmatic Whitehorse. It's about as homely as cities come, but it grows on you — and quickly. Many are the stories

and the Canol pipeline and road brought new mineral exploration activity as well as bringing people, services, industries and tourists to the Yukon. With the highway came permanent non-native settlers, who finally outnumbered Yukon's aboriginal peoples.

Though the Yukon contains some 30 percent of Canada's natural resources, current low prices for precious metals, along with the cost of extraction, have put most mining operations in mothballs. In recent years, mining has been supplanted by tourism as the Yukon's leading industry.

WHITEHORSE

A little over 100 years ago, Whitehorse was just a stop on the Southern Tutchone and Tagish peoples' seasonal round of hunting and fishing. As the Klondike gold rush peaked in 1897–98,

of people who "came for a few days and stayed 20 years." But no matter the length of your stay, you'll discover that Whitehorse is a friendly town with fine, hot, dry summers with daylight lasting long into the evenings. Everything you need for moving on into the remoter stretches of the territory is available here. There are plenty of historic buildings in the downtown area and some worthwhile museums to explore.

General Information
Your first stop should be the **Yukon Reception Centre** ((867) 667-3084 FAX (867) 393-6351 E-MAIL yktour@yknet.ca WEB SITE www.writeyukon.com, Hanson Street and Second Avenue (daily mid-May to mid-September, 8 AM to 8 PM). They have stacks of information about the city and the territory, as well as interactive kiosks, video presentations and helpful staff.

Another source of information is the **City of Whitehorse** ((867) 668-8660 WEB SITE www.city .whitehorse.yk.ca, 2121 Second Avenue.

The **Whitehorse Public Library** ((867) 667-5239, 2701 Second Avenue, has Internet access. There are plenty of Interac and Plus system **ATMs** in Whitehorse, Dawson City, and Watson Lake, but Cirrus system ATMs are rare — try the **Bank of Montréal** ((867) 668-4200, located at 111 Main Street, Whitehorse.

What to See and Do
Though Whitehorse extends over an area of 413 sq km (162 sq miles), the downtown is small and easy to get around. The center, laid out around

Main Street, has four blocks of stores and an almost-bustling pace.

Begin your explorations at the **Yukon Historical & Museums Association** ((867) 667-4704, Donneworth House, 3126 Third Avenue. June through August, they run a 45-minute **historical walking tour**. The **Yukon Conservation Society** ((867) 668-5678, 302 Hawkins Street, offers a variety of guided nature hikes in the Whitehorse area. These are suitable for all ages and are free.

In the territory's heyday, over 200 sternwheelers steamed up and down the Yukon River and its tributaries. Now only a few of these majestic ships are left, and the SS *Klondike* is the only one to have been restored to its earlier splendor. The **SS *Klondike* National Historic Site** ((867) 667-3910, near the downtown core at the Robert Campbell Bridge offers an excellent interpretive tour and video (May to September).

"Oh, for some of that gold," writes a wistful British Columbian in the guest register at the **MacBride Museum** ((867) 667-2709, First Avenue and Wood streets. This log structure with a sod roof houses an array of gold nuggets — each with its distinctive form — taken from a spectrum of Klondike creeks. Hands-on exhibits allow visitors to get a sense of the weight of gold (it's 19 times more dense than water) and see a prospector's sluicebox in action. Other exhibits cover archeology, culture, history, natural history and transportation.

The **Old Log Church Museum** ((867) 668-2555, 303 Elliot Street, is just that: a log cathedral erected by the pioneers and containing exhibits about them, whaling and First Nations culture — don't miss *The Bishop Who Ate His Boots*.

Below the White Horse Rapids Dam you can see Chinook salmon completing the word's longest salmon migration at the **Whitehorse Fishway** ((867) 633-5965 (open daily in summer). This manmade fish ladder, located at the end of Nisultin Drive in suburban Riverdale, allows spawning salmon to bypass the dam on their annual upstream migration. The migration takes place in late July and August.

Whitehorse has its share of boutiques and corner pocket malls to browse in. The **Indian Craft Shop** ((867) 667-7216, 504 Main Street, across from the Gold Rush Inn, is a family-run operation selling First Nations arts and crafts. Nancy Huston, owner of **Midnight Sun** ((867) 668-4350 WEB SITE www.midnightsunyukon.com, 205C Main Street, has made it her mission to find and market Yukon art and crafts, herbal teas, local jams and jelly, pottery and prints as well as seventeenth-century First Nations trading beads made into works of art and jewelry. The Jetsons-style sign of **Murdoch's Gem Shop** ((867) 667-7716, 207 Main Street, is a downtown landmark. On display are "Klondike Kate's diamond belt" and the Yukon's largest selection of gold nugget jewelry.

Several interesting sights are located outside of the downtown area. **Whitehorse Transit** ((867) 668-8394 makes the rounds, but it is probably worth renting a car. The **Yukon Art Centre** ((867) 668-8575, Yukon Place at Yukon College, is the best place in the territory to see art. Exhibits in this beautiful gallery showcase Yukon artists, both native and non-native, as well as internationally recognized visual artists.

While you're on campus, you can find out if there is a prospector in your past at the **Yukon Archives** ((867) 667-5321 TOLL-FREE (800) 661-0408 E-MAIL yukon.archives@gov.yk.ca. Besides genealogical research, archive staff will help you find out more about any aspect of Yukon history.

The Kluane Range, west of Whitehorse — You don't have to go far outside of town to find wide open spaces.

The archive has a file of ready-made historical photos, which get our vote as the best-value souvenirs in the territory. Choose from portraits of handsome Skookum Jim or that Yukon iconic image — toilers on the Chilkoot Trail — and many others.

On the drive up Two mile Road, on the corner of Fourth Avenue, look for the **spirit houses**, a cluster of small, brightly colored shelters. This is a First Nations burial ground (and thus not to be disturbed).

Continuing onto the Alaska Highway from the Yukon College area, head for the airport, where there are two more very good museums. The **Beringia Interpretive Centre** ((867) 667-8855

Next to the Beringia Centre is the **Yukon Transportation Museum** ((867) 668-4792 WEB SITE www.yukontransportmuseum.homestead.com, 30 Electra Crescent. In such a remote area, the history of European settlement is in many ways the history of transportation. The museum takes you on a fascinating historical journey from snowshoes and moose-skin boats to dogsleds, stagecoaches, pioneer aircraft, railroads, riverboats and finally the military vehicles that helped build the Alaska Highway. There's a very good film about the building of the White Pass & Yukon Railway.

A soak at **Takhini Hot Springs** ((867) 633-2706 WEB SITE www.takhinihotsprings.yk.ca, 27 km (17 miles) north of Whitehorse, off the Klondike

WEB SITE www.beringia.com, Milepost 915, weaves together First Nations creation myth and hard scientific evidence to tell the story of Beringia, the land bridge created during the last Ice Age along which the first inhabitants of North America migrated from Asia. On this continent-sized land bridge, woolly mammoths and giant beavers as big as black bears roamed during the Pleistocene Age. The exhibits present the paleontological and archeological evidence of the age alongside Tlingit native stories about a great flood and how the clever Crow created the world. Fossilized remains include the five-kilograms (11-lb) tooth of a woolly mammoth, dioramas showing the flora and fauna of the age, and skeleton models of giant beavers and sloths. It was the gold rush that led to the discovery of this mother lode of Ice age fossils, released from the permafrost by prospectors digging for gold.

Loop Road (late-May weekends; June to mid-October, daily), is surprisingly refreshing on a scorching Yukon summer's day. Suit rental and lockers are available. There is also horseback riding. In winter there are cross-country ski trails and a toboggan hill.

During the gold rush, hundreds of stampeders smashed their crude boats attempting to run the Whitehorse Rapids, which once raced through **Miles Canyon**, five kilometers (three miles) south of the city. The canyon's frothing water reminded the prospectors of horses' manes, giving the capital city its name. Now that the Whitehorse Dam has tamed the water, the canyon offers a pleasant float.

You can take a two-hour Yukon River cruise on the **MV** *Schwatka* ((867) 668-4716, Miles Canyon Road off the Alaska Highway South, accompanied by a narration about those wilder times (June to early September); reservations recommended. **Gold Rush Float Tours** ((867) 633-4836, First Avenue (May to September) takes passengers through Miles Canyon on a two-and-a-half-hour narrated trip on a quaint (but seaworthy) craft that is a replica of the stampeders' rafts. The boat makes a stop at Canyon City, where recent excavations have turned up remnants of stampeder encampments, as well as remains of early native use.

Excursions from Whitehorse

With First Nations tourism rapidly changing and growing, contact **Yukon First Nations Tourism Association** ((867) 667-7698/9 FAX (867) 667-7527 E-MAIL yfnta@yknet.yk.ca WEB SITE www.yfnta.org, to find out about the latest offerings.

along, the **Carcross Desert** is actually a former sandy lakebed, where winds have formed dozens of dunes. At Carcross, the friendly staff at Tourism Yukon's **Visitor Reception Centre** ((867) 821-4431, the Old Train Depot, will help orient you to the tiny native town, where log cabins line the unpaved streets.

Before the gold rush, Carcross (originally Caribou Crossing), at the foot of Lake Bennett, was a seasonal hunting and fishing camp for the Tagish. During the stampede, the Tlingit displaced them. The Tlingit who now live here are descendants of the tribe that once traveled and traded across the Chilkoot Trail and became renowned as porters when the gold rush was on. Sites in the tiny town

Not far from Whitehorse a couple of First Nations camps welcome visitors. a 45-minute drive from Whitehorse **Kwaday Dan Kenji (Long-Ago Peoples)** ((867) 667-6375, Indian Way Ventures, Box 33031, Whitehorse Y1A 5Y5, is located on the Alaska Highway two kilometers (just over a mile) south of Champagne (May to October 9 AM to 7:30 PM). This family-run enterprise is a traditional First Nations camp where you can also enjoy hot tea and fresh *bannock*, fried biscuits. (See also LISTEN TO ANCIENT VOICES, page 16 in TOP SPOTS.)

The **Carcross Loop** is a wonderful drive offering lovely scenery, along with gold rush and native history. Head out of Whitehorse south along the Alaska Highway, then take the Klondike Highway south. You'll shortly reach one of the most photographed scenes in the territory, **Emerald Lake**, whose turquoise hue is caused by decomposed shells suspended in the water. Further

include the **New Caribou Hotel**, built in 1900 and the oldest in the Yukon, and the historic **Old North West Mounted Police Barracks**, now a curio shop.

You can retrace your route from Carcross back to Whitehorse or head east along Tagish Road through the village of Tagish and reconnect with the Alaska Highway to complete the loop. The distance from Whitehorse to Carcross is 74 km (47 miles).

Sports and Outdoor Activities

Many people come to the Yukon for its world-class **river running**. Resources are legion, but start by contacting the Yukon Canoe and Kayak Club

OPPOSITE: Indigenous mountain goats graze at a Whitehorse wildlife preserve. ABOVE: At Silver City near Kluane National Park you can ramble among the decaying shanties and mining equipment of this boom-and-bust silver mining encampment.

((867) 633-5642 E-MAIL adventure@bear.yk.net. Canoes, kayaks, mountain bikes and camping gear can be rented from Kanoe People ((867) 668-4899 E-MAIL info@kanoepeople.com, which also offers guided or unguided tours, and fishing trips. Up North ((867) 667-7035 WEB SITE www.upnorth.yk.ca, 103 Strickland Street, also rents equipment and offers guided and unguided tours year-round — using snowmobiles and snowshoes in winter. Nahanni River Adventures ((867) 668-3180 TOLL-FREE (800) 297-6921 WEB SITE www.nahanni.com runs guided trips for beginners and experts on the Tatshenshini, Yukon, Nahanni and other northern wilderness rivers. Tatshenshini Expediting ((867) 633-2742 WEB SITE www.tatshenshiniyukon.com, 1602 Alder Street, organizes guided whitewater rafting trips on the Tatshenshini and the Alsek, and rents rafts and canoes.

The area around Whitehorse is great for **fishing**. A sport-fishing license (available at sporting-goods stores) is required, even to catch the odd grayling. There are strict regulations governing seasons, sizes and weights. Guided fly-fishing trips for two or three people are offered by Fly-Fishing Adventures ((867) 667-2359 E-MAIL fish yukon@polaris.ca, which also rents boats and equipment.

If you are in the Yukon in the spring or winter, take a **dogsledding trip** with Walden's Guiding and Outfitting ((867) 667-7040 or Blue Kennels (/FAX (867) 633-2219 or (867) 634-2750 WEB SITE www.bluekennels.de.

Several operations offer a full menu of activities from guided outdoor adventures to cultural trips: Arctic Outdoor Recreation (/FAX (867) 668-7766 WEB SITE www.arcticoutdoor.com offers a variety of small-group guided tours in summer and snowmobile tours in winter; activities include canoeing, hiking, heli-hiking and dog-sledding.

AAA–Big Bear Adventure Tours ((867) 633-5642 WEB SITE www.helloyukon.com has canoeing, kayaking, hiking, rafting, fly/drive and bicycle tours, and rents out bicycles and campers.

Nightlife

Nightlife in Whitehorse centers around cold glasses of excellent Chilkoot Brewery ale, sipped late into the sunlit night on "The Deck" at the **Yukon Mining Co.**, High Country Inn (see WHERE TO EAT, below). Another favorite gathering spot is the small terrace at **Sam 'n' Andy's** (see WHERE TO EAT, below). But before you've earned the right to kick back with the rest of Whitehorse's night creatures, you must see *Frantic Follies* at the Westmark Whitehorse Hotel ((867) 668-2042 WEB SITE www.franticfollies.com. From Dawson City to Beaver Creek, every town in the Yukon will implore, if not order, you to see its "variety" show. Most of them are to be avoided, but the Whitehorse show is a happy exception. The follies pack

in plenty of physical comedy, pulled off, in general, with flair, and the Robert Service recitations are truly funny. Even locals go at least once a year to see the new talent and get their fix of high-kicking showgirls. There are nightly performances. Make reservations, as seats are often filled with tour groups.

Where to Stay

Easily the most luxurious accommodation north of the 60th parallel, **Hawkins House** ((867) 668-7638 FAX (867) 668-7632 E-MAIL cpitzel@internorth .com, 303 Hawkins Street (mid-range to expensive), is a painted-lady-style Victorian mansion in downtown Whitehorse. Fortunately, the interior is much more soothing. Rooms are small, but lovingly decked out in warm wood tones and packed with all the comforts you could ask for, including queen-sized beds, en-suite baths, sinks, refrigerators and balconies.

In the heart of downtown, the **Westmark Whitehorse Hotel** ((867) 393-9700 TOLL-FREE (800) 544-0970 FAX (867) 668-2789 WEB SITE www.westmarkhotels.com, 201 Wood Street (mid-range), is the largest hotel in the Yukon, with 181 spacious, nicely furnished and well-decorated rooms. Following renovation in 2001, there is now a full range of amenities.

The **Edgewater Hotel** ((867) 667-2572 TOLL-FREE (877) 484-3334 FAX (867) 668-3014 WEB SITE www.edgewaterhotel.yk.ca, 101 Main Street, is a small, vintage hotel at the end of Main Street, overlooking the Yukon River. The 20 rooms are cozy and come equipped with extra-long beds and air conditioning.

A casual atmosphere, spacious rooms, full breakfast, complimentary snacks in the kitchenettes, laundry facilities and a host who will always go out of her way to make her guests' stay as carefree as possible are all trademarks of the **Four Seasons B&B** ((867) 667-2161 TOLL-FREE (877) 735-3281 FAX (867) 667-2171, 18 Tagish Road (mid-range). The house is located in a quiet residential area, a 15-minute walk from downtown and hillside hikes. It's wheelchair accessible and open year-round. It is typical of accommodation on the list of **Select Reservations** ((867) 393-2420 WEB SITE www.selectrez.com, an agency specializing in good-value good-quality accommodation throughout the northwest of Canada. It also arranges complete itineraries, free of charge.

Haeckel Hill Bed & Breakfast ((867) 633-5642 FAX (867) 633-5630 E-MAIL bear@yknet.yk.ca is at the foot of Haeckel Hill in the rural suburb of Porter Creek, a five-minute drive from downtown (mid-range). It makes an excellent base for day hiking and exploring the hilly countryside and forest trails; the proprietors are also tour operators who can arrange hiking, bicycling and river trips. Rooms are sunny and comfortably furnished in white pine with a clean, uncluttered northern European touch.

Whitehorse has no hostel, YMCA, or university dormitory housing, and camping is at a premium, with hundreds of Canadian college students coming north to supply labor for the Yukon summer tourist season. Bargain hunters traveling in groups of three or four can sometimes make arrangements with bed-and-breakfast establishments.

Where to Eat

Hearty fare is served in Yukon restaurants; steak and seafood are featured on many menus. Arctic char, Alaska king crab and Yukon or Taku River salmon are some of the local delicacies. You'll also find a variety of ethnic eateries with good, if not authentic, cuisine.

Locals and savvy tourists alike all seem to agree that the **Cellar Dining Room** ((867) 667-2572, Edgewater Hotel, 101 Main Street, is the best restaurant in Whitehorse. You'll pay top dollar for the excellent prime rib, Alaska king crab or lobster and prawns served in the plush lower-level dining room. The same great food is served in a more casual atmosphere — and for less money — in the upstairs **Gallery**.

Considering how far "north of the border" they are, **Sam 'n' Andy's Tex Mex** ((867) 668-6994, 506 Main Street, serves fairly good Mexican food. The admittedly overpriced pitchers of margaritas continue to draw the locals to the small, friendly terrace each evening.

At the inexpensive **Pasta Palace** ((867) 667-6888, 209 Main Street, the proprietors don't bother with atmosphere, but concentrate on serving some of the tastiest and best-value meals in the city. In addition to pasta, there is an extensive selection of appetizers. Service is prompt and friendly. Another excellent pasta and pizza place is **Georgios Cuccina** ((867) 668-4050, 208 Jarvis Street, so popular that the owners have just opened a second restaurant in Skagway, Alaska.

Known locally as "The Deck," the **Yukon Mining Co.** ((867) 667-44714051, High Country Inn, Fourth Avenue, is the place to go for an excellent cold one from the local Chilkoot Brewery and one of Heinz's juicy barbecued burgers. Also on the menu is a range of seafood, pasta and salads, and surprisingly good sushi on certain nights.

There are several roasters in Whitehorse serving excellent coffee, such as the homey **Midnight Sun Coffee Roaster** ((867) 633-4563, 4168C Fourth Avenue, which also has great muffins and cookies. Another "must" on the Whitehorse scene is the **Alpine Bakery** ((867) 668-6871, 411 Alexander Street, where you can purchase long-lasting expedition bread for your hiking or boating trip. The Alpine has a reputation for being not only the best bakery in the Yukon, but one of the best in the country. If you have a sweet tooth, try **The Choco-**

late Claim ((867) 667-2202, 305 Strickland Street, for a variety of snacks (not all sweet), including handmade chocolates.

How to Get There

The **Whitehorse International Airport** is seven kilometers (five miles) from downtown, on a hill above the city. There are direct flights from the United States and **Condor Airlines** TOLL-FREE (800) 524-6975 E-MAIL reservations_usa@condor .de operates charters twice weekly from Frankfurt, Germany, during the summer. Additional international connections may be added as the Yukon becomes a more popular destination for Europeans.

A roadside marker denotes the international boundary between the United States and Canada.

Most people still fly in via a Canadian city. Daily services are available through Calgary, Vancouver and Edmonton on **Air Canada** TOLL-FREE (888) 247-2262 WEB SITE www.aircanada.ca and the North's major airline **Air North** ((867) 668-2228 WEB SITE www.airnorth.yk.net, which also links Whitehorse to Alaska (Juneau and Fairbanks), Dawson City and Inuvik. Flying to the Yukon is appallingly expensive. During certain seasons it is possible to arrange one-way charter flights to Vancouver or other Canadian cities for much less than the regular airline fare.

Coming from British Columbia, motorists enter the Yukon via the **Alaska Highway** (Highway 1) or the **Stewart-Cassiar Highway**, which connects with Highway 1 near the Yukon–British

Columbia border. From Alaska, Highway 1 leads from Fairbanks into the southwest corner of the territory. Those heading to Dawson City from Alaska can pick up the **Taylor Highway** (Highway 5) at Tok, Alaska, and from there connect with the **Top of the World Highway** (Highway 9) which leads to Dawson City. From Skagway, travelers can also follow in the footsteps of the gold-rush stampeders by trekking the **Chilkoot Trail** (see SKAGWAY, ALASKA, below); or they can reach the Yukon by car via the **Klondike Highway** (Highway 2).

If you wish to travel by bus, **Greyhound (** (867) 667-2223 TOLL-FREE (800) 661-8747 WEB SITE www.greyhound.ca offers a daily service from Vancouver. The trip takes 40 hours. **Alaskon Express** TOLL-FREE (800) 343-7373 WEB SITE www.whitepassrailroad.com runs four to six trips per day, from mid-May until late September.

SKAGWAY, ALASKA

Described in 1898 as nothing more than "a spot of wet, mossy earth at the foot of a high mountain on the seashore," Skagway, Alaska, is one of the primary routes to the Yukon. The name, incidentally, means, "place of the north wind." A popular destination in itself, Skagway is swamped throughout the summer with short-term visitors: some 450,000 cruise-ship passengers pass through each season. Most of the 2,000 or so people who

FREE (800) 544-2206 has regularly scheduled services from Skagway to the Yukon communities of Carcross, Whitehorse, Haines Junction and Beaver Creek. Tickets may be booked at any Gray Line Office. Cheaper fares are to be had on the **Alaska Direct Bus Lines (** (867) 668-4833 or (907) 277-6652 TOLL-FREE (800) 770-6652, 125 Oklahoma Street, Anchorage, Alaska, which also runs through the Yukon, serving Whitehorse, Haines Junction, Burwash Landing and Beaver Creek.

But the most scenic way to get to the Yukon is via the Alaska State Ferries along the **Inside Passage** (see CRUISE THE INSIDE PASSAGE, page 16 in TOP SPOTS). Passengers can debark at Haines, Alaska, and follow Haines Road (Highway 3) up to Haines Junction where it connects with the Alaska Highway; or they can get off at Skagway, Alaska, where they can journey over the White Pass by train. The **White Pass & Yukon Railway (** (907) 983-2217

work in Skagway are not residents, but come up only for the summer tourist season. Only about 800 live here year-round. A day is certainly enough time to rest up from your ferry trip, get a feel for the place and make your onward connections to the Yukon.

General Information

The overburdened **Convention and Visitor Bureau (** (907) 983-2854 FAX (907) 983-3854 E-MAIL infoskag@aptalaska.net has town and trail maps and offers information on all travel and accommodation needs.

What to See and Do

The United States Park Service has done an admirable job of preserving the historical district of this boom-and-bust town, but behind the boardwalks and authentic false-fronted buildings, there are only a few attractions, eateries and hostelries of good quality. Skagway's historical district is essentially a show for the passengers of the giant luxury cruise ships that dock by the threes and fours in its small harbor. Much of downtown Skagway constitutes the **Klondike Gold Rush National Historic Park**, which also encompasses the White Pass and Chilkoot Trail (as well as Pioneer Square in Seattle, Washington). The Park Visitor Centre ((907) 983-2991, Second Avenue and Broadway offers films, ranger talks and a worthwhile **walking tour of the historic district** (May to September daily 8AM to 6PM).

Dozens of operators — with mottoes such as "Why pay more?" — offer **sightseeing tours**

around and about town. Take your pick. The one stand-out in the crowd is the **Skagway Street Car Company** ((907) 983-2908, whose costumed interpreters take you around in a shiny yellow 1920s-vintage limousine.

For those who did not arrive in Skagway via boat, book a taste of the Inside Passage on a **boat tour** to Haines or Juneau. **Chilkat Cruises** ((907) 766-2100 TOLL-FREE (888) 766-2103 operates a daily scheduled ferry shuttle service; **Goldbelt Inc.** ((907) 789-4183 TOLL-FREE (800) 478-3610 runs the catamaran *Alaskan Dream* on day-long round-trip cruises to Juneau.

And don't worry — Skagway is not under attack; it's only helicopters and planes giving **flight-seeing tours** to Mendenhall Glacier. You can hardly miss **Temsco Helicopters** ((907) 983-2900 WEB SITE www.temscoair.com, near the harbor, or **Skagway Air Service** ((907) 983-2218.

They also have flight-seeing tours of the spectacular Glacier Bay.

Skagway has two locally owned art and craft shops: **Inside Passage Arts** ((907) 983-2585, with Southeast Alaska native arts alongside hand-carved silver jewelry created by the store's owners, and **Inhofe's Carvers Gallery** ((907) 983-2434, which sells the work of the owner and his protégés. Both are on Broadway. The rest of Skagway's shops are not noteworthy, running the gamut from expensive jewelry stores to trinket shops brimming with big-eyed seal T-shirts.

Excursions from Skagway

For many travelers, the sole reason for passing through Skagway is to access the famed 53-km-long (33-mile) **Chilkoot Trail**, a difficult three- to five-day hike that follows the route of the stampeders. It begins near the Dyea townsite northwest of Skagway. You must obtain a backcountry permit from the National Park Service. Only 50 hikers per day are allowed to cross into Canada via the trail. Because of this quota, it may be necessary to obtain your permit as early as six months in advance if you wish to hike the trail in peak season (from mid-July to mid-August). Contact the **Klondike Gold Rush National Historic Park** ((907) 983-9224 or (907) 983-2921 FAX (907) 983-9249 E-MAIL KLGO_Ranger_Activities @npsgov, Box 517, Second and Broadway, Skagway, Alaska 99840.

Where to Stay and Eat

The historic **White House Bed and Breakfast** ((907) 983-9000 FAX (907) 983-9010 E-MAIL white hse@aptalaska.net, Eighth and Main (mid-range), on a quiet street far enough away from Broadway, provides escape from the hubbub but is close enough for convenience. The **Skagway Inn** ((907) 983-2289 FAX (907) 983-2713 E MAIL stay@skag wayinn.com, Seventh and Broadway (inexpensive to mid-range), is a good choice if you want to be in the center of the historic district. It's a European-style inn with cozy rooms decorated to commemorate "the girls" of Skagway's gold-rush days. Bathrooms are shared. For budget travelers, the **Skagway Home Hostel** (/ FAX (907) 983-2131, Third Street and Main, has dormitory accommodation as well as inexpensive private double rooms.

It's difficult to make recommendations for restaurants in Skagway, whose dining establishments have begun to suffer from their success. On the ground floor of the Skagway Inn is **Olivia's** ((907) 983-2289, where Caesar Salad is prepared at your table. Its reputation as the best restaurant in town is probably deserved, but standards are

The 1898 Klondike gold rush— "Tenderfeet" labor over the Chilkoot Pass from Dyea, Alaska, to Lake Bennett, British Columbia. ABOVE: A seasoned prospector, or "sourdough."

lamentably low here; nevertheless, reservations are recommended.

The next best bets are both on the waterfront, by the small boat harbor. **Stowaway Café** ((907) 983-3463 is consistently good — it has a day menu (wraps, great soup and freshly-baked bread) and an evening menu (Cajun style: steak, fish, pasta, salad). **Skagway Fish Company** ((907) 983-3474, as the name suggests, concentrates on seafood, notably chowder and fish and chips. It has different chefs, so the standard of cuisine can vary, but there's always a great atmosphere.

The **Golden North Hotel** ((907) 983-2451, Third Street and Broadway, has a restaurant with a delightful terrace, but service is slow. Also on

Broadway (No. 315), the very popular **Sweet Tooth Café** ((907) 983-2405 is your best bet for a hearty breakfast. You can count on good solid food here, but be sure to arrive before the morning ferry passengers alight. They'll be hungry.

How to Get There

Skagway can be reached year-round via the **Alaska Marine Highway** (ferry) ((907) 627-1744 or (907) 627-1745 TOLL-FREE (800) 642-0066 from Bellingham (Washington); Prince Rupert (British Columbia); and Wrangell, Petersburg, Sitka, Juneau and Haines (Alaska). **Skagway Air Service** ((907) 983-2218 makes daily connections from Juneau and Haines. Road routes to Skagway from the Yukon are the

ABOVE and OPPOSITE BOTTOM: Alaska State Ferries' MV *Matanuska* plies the Inside Passage. TOP: A Dawson cabin sports the traditional moose antler and knotty pine admorments.

Alaska and Klondike Highways. From Skagway, the Klondike Highway takes you over the White Pass to the Yukon's capital city of Whitehorse. For bus service, **Rival Highway Tours** ((867) 667-7896 connects Whitehorse to Skagway via Carcross and Fraser, British Columbia. Before the highway there was the **White Pass & Yukon Railway** ((907) 983-2217 TOLL-FREE (800) 343-7373 WEB SITE www.whitepassrailroad.com.

KLUANE NATIONAL PARK

Tucked in the southwest corner of the territory, a two-hour drive from Whitehorse, Kluane (pronounced kloo-*ahn*-ee) National Park is the jewel of the Yukon, a designated UNESCO World Heritage Site. These 22,015 sq km (8,500 sq miles) of glaciers, marshes, lakes and mountains are unsettled and virtually untouched. There are no ski lifts in Kluane waiting to whisk you to the top of a mountain, no teahouses at the end of the trail. "Kluane," said a transplanted Swiss couple we met there, "is the Swiss Alps without all the people." The Matterhorn of this alpine land is **Mount Logan** (6,050 m/ 19,849 ft), Canada's highest peak and the second highest mountain in North America. It is part of the St. Elias Mountains, which include six other peaks over 5,000 m (16,000 ft).

Much of the reserve's wilderness has been the homeland of the Southern Tutchone people for thousands of years. Many of the trails follow traditional paths of these First Nations people, who still use them. The Champagne and Aishihik First Nations have a constitutional right to hunt and fish in the park and are co-managers of Kluane.

Because the park is undeveloped, much of the interior is only accessible to experienced alpinists (or those with the money to take a flight-seeing tour, see below). Despite this, parts of Kluane are accessible. Rafting, fishing in crystal-clear waters and wildlife watching are the chief activities.

General Information

Kluane has two visitor reception centers, staffed mid-May to mid-September. The **Kluane Park Visitor Reception Centre** ((867) 634-7207 or (867) 635-2345 FAX (867) 634-7208 provides literature, information and maps. Within the same facility is the territorial **Yukon Visitor Reception Centre** ((867) 634-2345. The **Sheep Mountain Visitor Centre** ((867) 841-5161, km 1707 Alaska Highway, runs an interpretive program through the summer months, with guided hikes and presentations. Haines Junction is the place to stock up on provisions, and the public library has the only public **Internet access** for miles around.

What to See and Do

You don't have to be a mountaineer to enjoy the many kilometers of trails throughout the park's

front ranges. The best time of year for hiking is mid-June to mid-September, when temperatures range between a high of 28°C (82°F) and a low of 0°C (32°F). All overnight trips into Kluane require registration at one of the visitor reception centers, where you can also find out how to avoid sneaking up on a bear (to begin with, always make noise as you are walking). The trailhead for the short hike to St. Elias Lake Trail is 60 km (38 miles) south of Haines Junction on Haines Road. The trail leads through wood and meadow to backcountry camping along a lake visited by loons. The Auriol Trail (15 km, or nine miles) is a popular overnight loop. The trailhead is seven kilometers (four miles) south of Haines Junction on Haines Road.

Kluane is also a wonderful place for paddling. You can rent a canoe, kayak or raft and strike out on your own, or you can hook up with an outfitter (see below).

Just east of the Sheep Mountain Visitor Centre, look for the scenic viewpoint marker for the turnoff (to your left) for Silver City, a ghost town located five kilometers (three miles) down a gravel road. It's a worthwhile side trip, where you can ramble among the decaying shanties and mining equipment.

The only way to get a good look at the St. Elias Mountains, short of mounting a major expedition, is to take a flight-seeing tour with one of the local operators — such as **Trans North Helicopters** ((867) 668-2177, on the Alaska Highway east of the Sheep Mountain Visitor Centre. The helicopters will take you to the spectacular Kaskawulsh Glacier, part of the world's largest non-polar ice field. Or you can arrange a heli-hiking trip.

Haines Road is a gorgeous drive leading into an uninhabited corner of British Columbia before arriving at Haines, Alaska. At its highest point, the road cuts across a grand plateau guarded by glaciated mountains. Numerous creeks pass through the region, and this area has some of the continent's best river trips (see below).

Outfitters

Paddlewheel Adventures ((867) 634-2683 WEB SITE www.paddlewheeladventures.com, across from the Kluane Park Visitor Centre, has canoe and mountain bike rentals, guided tours, heli-hikes, fishing, and does bookings for a variety of other tours, including whitewater rafting, flight-seeing, horseback riding and llama hikes.

The Tatshenshini Wilderness Area provides some of the best river running in the world. **Tatshenshini Expediting** ((867) 633-2742 E-MAIL tatexp@polarcom.com, 1602 Alder Street, Whitehorse, is one of the Yukon's longest established rafting and kayaking companies. They offer a range of adventures from one-day paddling trips along the Tat to the full 11-day Tatshenshini and Alsek river-rafting experience — this is the one

that draws people from all over the world, not only for its challenging rapids but for its unparalleled scenery. They also rent boats and all necessary equipment.

Where to Stay and Eat

In Haines Junction, the **Raven Hotel** ((867) 634-2500 FAX (867) 634-2517 E-MAIL kluaneraven @yknet.ca, 181 Haines Road (inexpensive to moderate), has comfortable rooms with direct-dial telephones, en-suite bathrooms and television. Smoking is prohibited. The restaurant (expensive) is among the best in the Yukon. Rooms at the **Alcan Motor Inn** ((867) 634-2371 FAX (867) 634-2833 E-MAIL alcan@yknet.yk.ca are of surprisingly

high quality given the appearance of the building and office. Standing at the junction of the Alaska Highway and Haines Road, few motels can compete with its stunning views of the snow-capped Kluane Mountain Range.

One of the best ways to explore the region is to stay at **Dalton Trail Lodge** ((867) 634-2099 FAX (867) 634-2098 WEB SITE www.daltontrail.com (moderate to expensive), nestled at the base of the St. Elias Mountains on Dezadeash Lake. Activities run from horseback riding to canoeing, hiking, fishing for trout, salmon and Arctic grayling, mountain biking, river rafting, tennis and flight-seeing. Visitors can opt for full-fledged, guided excursions or relaxed day-long forays into Kluane. The lodge has canoes stationed at many of the lakes and its own gold claim on Kimberly Creek where visitors can pan for nuggets and learn about placer mining. All meals are included

DAWSON CITY

At a latitude of 64°4' north, Dawson City is a place of strange contradictions. Once the largest metropolis north of San Francisco, it now has a year-round population of less than 2,000. One of the

OPPOSITE and ABOVE: Kluane National Park — The St. Elias Lake Trail, "bear country."

most northerly of Canadian towns, it is also one of the hottest. In June you can watch the sun sink below the horizon at 1 AM and stick around to see it come back up three hours later. The town's beer halls are loaded with frontier character, but it also lovingly preserves the cabins of two famous literary men, Robert Service and Jack London.

Dawson's gold-rush atmosphere is what draws most visitors. Large portions of the town are part of a registered historical area administered by Parks Canada and the Klondike Visitors Association. Many of the buildings are authentic gold-rush era structures and the rest are good reproductions. The streets remain as they were in 1898, unpaved and lined by boardwalks. Museums, tours, pan-

ning for gold, gambling, old-time music, riverboat rides and can-can girls are all part of the fun.

Yet there is much more to Dawson City than Golden Age revelry. Visitors who take a moment to look beyond the gold-rush glitter will also find a welcoming native community composed of descendants of the region's original inhabitants. Outdoor enthusiasts will find abundant opportunities for hiking, fishing, paddling and more, while motorists can enjoy some wonderfully scenic drives.

Background
The first wave of stampeders to arrive in Dawson City were totally unprepared for what lay ahead. In the winter of 1897, there was not enough food to go around and fearful prospectors began to

Yukon flora and fauna — ABOVE: Lichens flourish in an alpine meadow. OPPOSITE: A felled tree offers evidence of beavers.

panic and hoard; candle and lamp oil was in short supply, leaving 3,000 of 6,000 inhabitants without light for the season — when daylight lasts only from 10 AM to 2 PM. Two thousand people were unsheltered or living in tents.

Despite its rough start, Dawson City prospered. At the height of the gold rush, it had a population of around 30,000, making it one of the biggest cities west of Winnipeg. Between 1897 and 1904, it is estimated that over $100 million in gold was recovered from the Klondike and its tributaries, which covered an area of around 64 sq km (40 sq miles). It was a small pocket of land that glittered with gold, yet only a handful of prospectors went home millionaires. Tens of thousands were disappointed: by the time they reached the gold fields, all of the best claims had been staked.

After the stampede, the population of Dawson City began to decline almost immediately. Many prospectors were soon discouraged and were lured by reports of other gold discoveries (e.g., Nome, Alaska in 1899). By 1906 the most easily worked placer mines (containing gold that is found loose in sand and gravel as opposed to "lode" gold that occurs in hard rock) were finished, leaving claims to be mined by large companies using huge and expensive dredges. The employment offered by these dredging companies kept Dawson City alive for the next 50 years. These days the little town of 2,000 year-round residents thrives on tourism.

General Information
For orientation, stop by the excellent **Yukon Visitor Reception Centre** ((867) 993-5566 WEB SITE www.dawsoncity.org and www.dawsoncity.info .com, Front and King Streets (open mid-May to mid-September). The building is a replica of the Alaska Trading Company building. **Parks Canada** ((867) 993-7200 maintains a counter here as well, where you can purchase a Parks Pass — worth the price if you're planning to visit more than three of their sites. For trip planning, you can contact the park service by writing to: The Superintendent, Klondike National Historic Sites, Box 390, Dawson Y0B 1G0. The public library, in the school across from the post office, Fifth Avenue, has free **Internet access**; however, there is usually a long waiting list (we're talking days). It's better to shell out a few dollars to check your e-mail at **Grubstake Pizza & Sub Shop** ((867) 993-6706, Second and King Streets, or **Klondike InfoTech** ((867) 993-5539, in a little house on Third Avenue across from the liquor store.

What to See and Do
Interesting **walking tours** through the historic downtown area are given by costumed interpreters and depart from the Visitor Information Centre (mid-May to mid-September three times daily).

You can rent an audiotape in English, French or German, for a self-guided walking tour.

On the riverbank near Queen Street, you can see an old, grounded sternwheeler, the **SS Keno**. Built in 1922 to ply the Stewart River around the mining hamlets of Mayo and Keno, it was the smallest in the Yukon fleet. Because of its diminutive size, the *Keno* was the first to break through the winter ice to Dawson — a welcome sight after long months without fresh vegetables. Tours of the newly restored boat are offered by the **SS Keno National Historic Site** ((867) 993-5462.

A few blocks from the river, the **Dawson City Museum** ((867) 993-5291, Fifth Avenue at Church Street (mid-May to mid-September), features some 25,000 artifacts associated with the history of the gold rush. Exhibits on the native Hän, who populated the area before the gold rush and who still live here, are lackluster. Silent films of the period, unearthed during a 1978 restoration project, are the best part of the museum's offerings.

The **Robert Service Cabin**, Eighth Avenue between Mission and Hanson, is a two-room log structure in which the poet lived between 1909 and 1912. Actor Tom Byrne performs a daily recitation of the life and works of the "Bard of the Yukon" — who wrote such classics as *The Shooting of Dan McGrew* and *The Call of the Yukon* (call Parks Canada ((867) 993-7200 for performance times).

Further south, on Eighth Avenue between Fifth and Grant, is the **Jack London Cabin** ((867) 993-6317 (mid-May to mid-September 11 AM to 3 PM), where the writer lived briefly. Though his time in the Yukon was short, he collected the materials here for such classics as *White Fang*, *The Snow Wolf* and *The Call of the Wild*.

Souvenir shoppers should not miss the **Dawson Trading Post** ((867) 993-5316, Front Street, a gold mine for those on the lookout for the unusual. The **Klondike Nugget and Ivory Shop** ((867) 993-5432, Front and Queen streets, has the Yukon's signature souvenir gold-nugget and mastodon-ivory jewelry.

Dawson nightlife retains some of the frontier, whoop-it-up flavor of its heyday. The diminutive and beautifully restored **Palace Grand Theatre** ((867) 993-6217, Third and King Street, was built in 1899 from materials that once made up two steamboats. Parks Canada restored the theater in 1962, and now offers guided tours in the summer. The theater is also home to the much-vaunted *Gaslight Follies*. If you feel you must see the show, tickets are available at the Historic Post Office. It's safe to say that your evening might more wisely be spent elsewhere, say at **Diamond Tooth Gertie's Gambling Hall** ((867) 993-5575, Fourth Avenue and Queen Street. At least here you'll have fun wasting your money. Minors are not admitted. The gaudy pink **Westminster Hotel** ((867) 993-5463, 975 Third Avenue, is the home of the "Pit" beer

parlor, which offers live music. It's very popular, stocked with local character and frequented by residents partying by day and night.

Excursions from Dawson City

A hike or drive up to **Midnight Dome** is another requisite of the Dawson City experience. Dawson sits at the foot of this mountain, and the summit affords views of the gold fields, Yukon River valley, Dawson and the Ogilvie Mountains. Go up for the late-night sunset.

If you'd like to go with a group, contact **Gold City Tours** ((867) 993-5175, Front Street, across from the SS *Keno* riverboat. They also take sightseers out to the Bonanza Creek gold fields, and

on a 12-hour trip via bus along the Dempster Highway to the Arctic Circle and back.

The twin-deck *Yukon Queen* takes passengers from Dawson City to Eagle, Alaska, a distance of 174 km (108 miles). The daylong cruise includes two meals and a stopover in Eagle. Book well in advance at Gray Line Yukon ((867) 993-5599, Front Street near the visitor center.

Dawson City has some wonderful river excursions where you can meet and learn about the regional aboriginal cultures. **Ancient Voices Wilderness Camp** ((867) 993-5605 FAX (867) 993-6532 E-MAIL avwcamp@dawson.net (see LISTEN TO ANCIENT VOICES, page 16 in TOP SPOTS), has an evening barbecue with drumming and storytelling, as well as accommodation, adventure packages and programs including wilderness survival, arts, crafts and women's workshops. **Fishwheel Charter Service** ((867) 993-6857 runs two-hour historical and cultural tours, where you can see a traditional aboriginal method of fishing. *Bannock* and tea are included in the trip. **River of Culture** ((867) 993-5482 arranges travel on an authentic Yukon paddle wheeler to Moosehide Island, to learn about the Hän Hwëch'in people.

The gold fields lie just south of Dawson City, in the hills and creeks along the Klondike Highway. Though the rush is long over, you can pan for gold — success guaranteed — at **Claim 33** ((867) 993-5303, Bonanza Creek Road. But what's the fun in noodling around in a trough laced with gold flakes? Far better to roll up your sleeves and take your chances in a creek. **Goldbottom Mining Tours** ((867) 993-5023 runs escorted trips to

the Klondike area. Floating in manmade ponds, the dredges scooped, sifted and spewed out creek gravel, creating huge, caterpillar-shaped mounds of tailings.

The best way to get an idea of the extent of the gold fields is to take an aerial tour with **Trans North Helicopters** ((867) 993-5494. They also offer **heli-hiking** in the nearby Tombstone and Ogilvie mountains. The helipad is on the Klondike Highway, half a kilometer (about one quarter mile) south of Dawson City.

One hill over from Dredge No. 4, **Bear Creek** was for 60 years the home of the Yukon Consolidated Gold Corporation. This dredge support camp was where the gold ore was milled and

an authentic placer mining operation where you'll see a gold processing demonstration and get an hour of gold panning in the creek — rubber boots, pan and shovel provided. They are located at Goldbottom and Hunker creeks, 30 km (19 miles) south of Dawson City and 15 km (just over nine miles) up Hunker Creek Road from the Klondike Highway.

After the first wave of individual prospecting, companies moved into the Yukon and began large-scale mining with dredges. Until it sank in the 1960s, **Dredge No. 4** ripped 22,000 grams of gold out of the ground each day. The largest wooden-hulled dredge ever built, it is now an historical monument located 13 km (eight miles) south of Dawson City on Bonanza Creek Road; call Parks Canada ((867) 993-7200 for information. This dredge and others like it are responsible for the eerie, apocalyptic look of the landscape in

melted down into bullion. This Parks Canada site has 65 buildings to tour, illustrating the history of large-scale mining. The turnoff for Bear Creek is 16 km (10 miles) south of Dawson City, off the Klondike Highway (June to mid-September).

Where to Stay

The **Aurora Inn** ((867) 993-6860 FAX (867) 993-5689 WEB SITE www.wildandwooly.yk.net, Fifth Avenue and Harper Street (mid-range to expensive), has spacious, sunny rooms with a contemporary Scandinavian look. Scandinavian breakfast is served at an additional moderate cost. Rooms come equipped with data ports and television. The two suites have Jacuzzi baths. **Downtown Hotel** ((867) 993-5346 TOLL-FREE (800) 661-0514

Dawson City — OPPOSITE: A sunny seciton of the city's wooden sidewalks. ABOVE: The "Pit" at the Windsor Hotel is a popular night spot.

FAX (867) 993-5076 WEB SITE www.downtown
.yk.net, Second and Queen Streets, is one of
Dawson's two central year-round hotels. The
rooms are comfortable and modern (mid-range).

The **Westmark Klondike Inn** ((867) 993-5542
TOLL-FREE (800) 544-0970 or (800) 999-2570 WEB SITE
www.westmarkhotels.com, Fifth Avenue and
Harper Street, is part of the northern chain (mid-
range). It focuses most of its energies on the many
bus tours that its parent company brings to Dawson
City, but rooms for independent travelers are sometimes available. Nondescript but reliable, the **Triple
J Hotel** ((867) 993-5323 TOLL-FREE (800) 764-3555
or (800) 661-0405 FAX (867) 993-5030 WEB SITE www
.triplejhotel.com has a hotel, a motel and small cabins with kitchen units (inexpensive to mid-range).
All units have private bath. The main hotel building, right next to Diamond Gertie's Casino, includes
a restaurant and lounge with a terrace.

The First Nations-owned and operated **Bear
Creek Bed & Bannock** ((867) 993-5605 or (867)
993-6765 FAX (867) 993-6532 E-MAIL kormendy
@yknet.ca offers inexpensive to mid-range bed
and breakfast accommodation in Bear Creek, a
quiet subdivision 10 minutes from Dawson. Traditional First Nations arts and crafts are on display. Guests have use of a kitchen, living room and
dining area, and there are laundry facilities and
a large deck.

The **Bunkhouse** ((867) 993-6164 FAX (867) 993-
6051 WEB SITE www.bunkhouse.ca, Front and Princess Streets, has clean, affordable accommodation,
including rooms with shared bath, or suites with
private baths (inexpensive to moderate).

Dawson has the Yukon's only Hostelling-In-
ternational-affiliate the **Dawson City River Hostel** ((867) 993-6823 WEB SITE www.yukonhostels
.com, directly opposite Dawson across the Yukon
River. To get there, take the free 24-hour ferry from
Front Street to West Dawson; the hostel is located
150 m (164 yds) upstream from the landing site.
The hostel's season coincides with the ferry's: usually mid-May to late-September. It has a kitchen
and offers bike and canoe rental and a free lift to
the bus depot for the Whitehorse bus. The Alaska
Shuttle bus stops at the hostel.

Where to Eat
Good dining can be found in the local hotels,
most notably the Downtown Hotel's atmospheric
Jack London Grill and Sourdough Saloon ((867)
993-5346.

The best restaurant in Dawson City, however,
is **Marina's** ((867) 993-6800, Fifth Avenue between
Princess and Harper. The pasta is heavenly. It can
fill up quickly with hungry bus tour groups, so
you may want to arrive a bit early for dinner.
Klondike Kate's ((867) 993-6527, King Street
and Third, is housed in an authentic gold-rush-
era building. The extensive menu features ethnic

dishes such as gyros, falafel, wraps, seafood, sandwiches and domestic and imported beers. The
breakfast special is one of Dawson's best buys.

Along the riverfront, **River West Food &
Health** ((867) 993-6339, Front Street, has sand-
wiches, salads and soups to take out or to eat in.
The coffee is good.

How to Get There
You can fly from Whitehorse to Dawson City on
Air North ((867) 668-2228 WEB SITE www.airnorth
.yk.net. If you're driving from Alaska, you'll take
the **Taylor** and **Top of the World Highways** from
Chicken to Dawson City. The **Klondike Highway**
runs from Skagway, Alaska, through Carcross,
Whitehorse, and on to Dawson. The section of the
highway from Whitehorse to Dawson City is
537 km (333 miles) and the road is excellent.

The bus service between Whitehorse and
Dawson is provided by **Dawson City Courier/
Taxi** ((867) 993-6688 (in Dawson City) or ((867)
393-3334 (in Whitehorse).

YUKON HIGHWAYS

The Top of the World Highway
The Top of the World Highway (Highway 9) is a
scenic drive that begins just across the Yukon River
and leads 105 km (64 miles) to the border, where
it connects with the historic Taylor Highway
(Highway 5). The trip begins with the free automobile and passenger ferry ((867) 993-5441,
which operates 24 hours a day (closed for servic-
ing Wednesday mornings 5 AM to 7 AM.) Expect
long lines in peak months.

This road began as a pack trail connecting
Dawson City with Sixtymile and other neighboring mining communities. After crossing the Yukon
River, the 175-km (110-mile) highway climbs rapidly above the tree line and meanders along
mountain ridges with good views of the surrounding countryside. Moving on into Alaska, the Taylor Highway leads north to Eagle or south to Tetlin
Junction and the Alaska Highway. The border area
is a good place to spot rough-legged hawks, red-
tailed hawks, merlins and kestrels during spring
and fall migrations.

The Alaska Highway
Hastily constructed as a military route during
World War II, the Alaska Highway (Alcan) is now
a tourist route to the northern frontier. As much
a pilgrimage route as a road, it attracts thousands
every year, many of them retirees behind the
wheel of their brand new RVs.

TOP: A motorboat ride up the Yukon River is a
chance to spot wildlife such as moose and black
bear. BOTTOM: Permafrost plays havoc with house
foundations. These days, pilings that can be
raised and lowered stablize the city's buildings.

The Alaska Highway (Highway 1) starts at Dawson Creek, British Columbia, and travels northwest for 2,452 km (1,520 miles), ending in Fairbanks, Alaska. Along the way it cuts through the southwest corner of the Yukon. Until almost the end of the twentieth century, sections of the road were unpaved. It is now entirely paved, though you will likely find some rough spots, as construction crews only have the precious summer months to upgrade and maintain the road.

First stop along the Canadian portion of the Alaska Highway is the "Gateway to the Yukon," **Watson Lake** (population: 1,700). Tourism Yukon operates the **Visitor Reception and the Alaska Highway Interpretive Centre** ((867) 536-7469 at the junction of the Robert Campbell and Alaska highways. The town is home to the **Northern Lights Centre** ((867) 536-7827, which in summer puts on daily shows about the aurora borealis; in winter you may be lucky enough to see the real thing.

Stop at mile 1,021 to look at the **Sign Post Forest**, which was started by an American soldier in 1942 and continues to grow — there are currently over 48,000 signs and you can add to them.

The next, long stretch of road travels through Teslin, a largely Tlingit town where there is a **Tlingit Heritage Centre** ((867) 390-2529, and then skims past Whitehorse, after which the highway skirts Kluane National Park. Spreading south from Alcan, the snow-covered **Icefield Ranges** can be seen behind the rugged Kluane Ranges. This is the most scenic part of the route. Plan to take your time.

As the Kluane Ranges taper off, you'll come to **Burwash Landing,** a tiny native village (population: less than 100) that overlooks Kluane Lake. Here you'll find the very worthwhile **Kluane Museum of Natural History** ((867) 841-5561 (mid-May to mid-September). It has the Yukon's best natural history display, along with fine exhibits of Southern Tutchone garments, tools and weapons, and fossils. The museum has a stock of videos, which they will play on demand.

The last Canadian stop on the Alcan is **Beaver Creek** (population: 129), the westernmost community in Canada. Like many other small Yukon and Alaskan towns, it began as a settlement during the construction of the road. It is situated 30 km (18 miles) south of the Alaskan border. There's a **Visitor Reception Centre** ((867) 862-7321, on the Alaska Highway. Directly across the street you'll find the **Westmark Inn Beaver Creek** ((867) 862-7501 TOLL-FREE (800) 544-0970 FAX (867) 862-7902. The hotel has 174 rooms, a dining room, dinner theater, recreation room, mini-golf, a recreational vehicle park, a laundry, a convenience store and a gas station. Unfortunately the only superlatives we can bestow on this Westmark are that it has the tiniest bathtubs we've ever encountered, as well as the thinnest walls.

The Klondike Highway

The Klondike Highway (Highway 2) is a scenic, paved road leading from Skagway, Alaska, north through Whitehorse and on to Dawson City. About 180 km (112 miles) north of Whitehorse and 360 km (224 miles) south of Dawson, the village of **Carmacks** is located on a traditional First Nations trading site. In 1892, George Carmacks (later part of the group that precipitated the gold rush) established a small trading post here. The gravel-paved **Robert Campbell Highway** (Highway 4) intersects the hamlet, going on to Faro, Ross River and various mining operations, and provides an alternative to the Alcan between Whitehorse and Watson Lake, through remote spectacular wilderness. If you need to break the drive from Whitehorse to Dawson City, you can bed down at the **Carmacks Hotel** ((867) 863-5221 FAX (867) 863-5605 E-MAIL hotelcar@yknet.yk.ca.

The Dempster Highway

The start of the Dempster Highway (Highway 5) lies 40 km (25 miles) south of Dawson City. From here, this famed trek runs north 735 km (456 miles) to Inuvik, Northwest Territories, near the Arctic Ocean. The most northerly public road in Canada, the Dempster offers beautiful scenery, especially in early autumn when the tundra plants take on fall colors and migrating caribou are more easily seen.

Driving the Dempster Highway is no more difficult than traveling any other gravel road: Some precautions must be taken, however: the **Northwest Territories Visitor Centre** ((867) 993-6167, Front Street, Dawson, across the street from the Dawson visitor center, is the place get information on traveling the Dempster and on visiting the Northwest Territories. For information on road conditions, call TOLL-FREE (800) 661-0750.

The **Klondike River Lodge** ((867) 993-6892, Klondike and Dempster Highways, is the place from which to launch your trip up the Dempster Highway. Operated by the Gwitch'in Tribal Council, the lodge includes parking for recreational vehicles, a restaurant, a car wash and a grocery store.

THE NORTHWEST TERRITORIES AND NUNAVUT

A vast frontier covering an area nearly half the size of the United States and one-fifth of Canada (1,994 million sq km or nearly 770 million sq miles), the Northwest Territories and Nunavut form the North American continent's last true wilderness: a "don't miss" experience for those who love outdoor activities in totally unspoiled — and spectacular — surroundings.

At Ancient Voices Wilderness Camp, a moosehide is stretched on a rack for tanning.

The approximately 1,367,000 caribou that roam the land far outnumber the population of 67,500 Dene, Athapaskan, Inuit, Inuvialuit, Métis and Europeans who call these territories home. These two territories have the world's lowest population density, averaging one person for every 100 sq km (39 sq miles).

In the eastern areas, the Inuit (singular Inuk) form a majority of the population. Although their traditional culture has suffered from contact with Anglo-European settlers, they remain a strong cultural force, and in recent decades have won significant victories in the fight to preserve a way of life that is intimately tied to the land. Their land-rights negotiations finally led to the partitioning, on April 1, 1999, of the old Northwest Territories into today's eastern Nunavut and western Northwest Territories. Although twenty-first-century amenities are encroaching, the basic lifestyle is still much as it has been for centuries, and the local people see few enough visitors to retain a welcoming attitude to those who do make it their way.

Inuit / Inuvialuit art is becoming increasingly popular. Pangnirtung is famous for prints, and Cape Dorset for prints and carvings. The Inuit carvings and paintings come in many different styles. Yellowknife is a great place to shop for genuine arts and crafts — but beware of fakes as some shops do sell Taiwanese copies. Such things as co-op tags and artists' names identify the genuine articles. Prices are not cheap.

With all that wilderness to spare, wildlife is a major feature of the region, from migratory birds to beluga whales, grizzly bears and caribou. In the Northwest Territories alone, there are four national parks, three bird sanctuaries and the Mackenzie Bison Sanctuary. Two of the national parks are designated UNESCO World Heritage Sites: Wood Buffalo, which overlaps the Alberta border, and Nahanni, which is in the southeast near the Yukon border. The other reserves are all in the north and inaccessible by road.

Much of Nunavut's area consists of islands, on many of which there are nature reserves. Auyuittuq National Park, on Baffin Island, easily accessible from Pangnirtung or Clyde River, is popular with hikers, while more adventurous visitors might want to try some ice climbing.

Outdoor activities are ubiquitous, largely based on the necessity to employ non-road-using forms of transportation: from dog-sledding and snowmobiling in winter, to hiking, rafting and canoeing / kayaking in summer. Sport fishing and hunting are also options.

Winter provides an excellent chance to see the Northern Lights, as they are visible for some 190 nights a year. Be prepared to stay three or four nights to ensure you have clear skies. In summer, the long, long days are warm and sunny.

For the adventurer, the Northwest Territories and Nunavut offer incomparable scenic wonders, along with abundant wildlife, world-class fishing, and opportunities to visit and learn from the native inhabitants. However, you do need to plan your trip in advance, and confirm accommodations and guide services before departure. In much of the area, transportation is limited to airplanes, snowmobiles and all-terrain vehicles (ATVs), as there are no roads linking many communities. Dog teams are still used in winter and boats travel during warmer months, when the ice comes off the water.

GENERAL INFORMATION

If you hear the call of the North, advance planning is essential. Your first response should be to get in touch with the government tourism agencies: **Northwest Territories Tourism** ((867) 873-

5007 TOLL-FREE (800) 661-0788 WEB SITE www.nwt travel.nt.ca., Box 610, Yellowknife X1A 2N5, and **Nunavut Tourism** ((867) 979-6551 TOLL-FREE (866) 686-2888 WEB SITE www.nunavuttourism.com, Box 1450, Iqaluit, Nunavut X0A 0H0.

Many northern communities have **regional and local visitor centers** offering information and assistance, as well as interpretive displays on the local culture and history. In communities that don't have visitor centers, you can usually get assistance at the community center and from hotel staff.

Recommended (if not indispensable) publications include *The Nunavut Handbook* (Marion Soubliere, ed., Nortext Press), *NWT Explorers' Guide* (a free annual publication produced by Northwest Territories Tourism and available from them) and *The Milepost* (Vernon Publications). Nunavut Tourism also publishes a free annual Travel Planner.

NORTHWEST TERRITORIES

Northwest Territories' capital, **Yellowknife**, is the only sizeable town in the area, with a population of some 18,000. It was founded on gold fever and is now North America's richest source of diamonds. If you feel like a taste of the wilderness without actually leaving behind all the trappings of civilization, this could be the place for you.

A visit to the **Prince of Wales Northern Heritage Center** ((867) 873-7551 WEB SITE www.pwnhc .learnnet.nt.ca (daily 10:30 AM to 5:30 PM, with shorter hours in winter), is a "must." It offers dioramas and hands-on exhibits about the flora, fauna and human history of the region — and also supports local artists. There are several art galleries in town.

The Dempster Highway runs from just east of Dawson City to Inuvik in the Northwest Territories.

There are some excellent eating places in Yellowknife: whichever you choose, make sure you sample the local dishes featuring caribou, musk-ox and Arctic char, you can do so at most restaurants in town. The **Wildcat Café**, across from the Prospector Bed and Breakfast is one of our favorites. This was the Yukon's first restaurant, built in the 1940s. It's a one-room log cabin, small and cozy, with good food and a great atmosphere, so it remains one of the most popular venues in Yellowknife.

Tours by road, air and water are available, including excursions to nearby Dene and Dogrib communities, which maintain a largely traditional lifestyle.

adventures.com, Box 1410, Vashon, Washington 98070, USA, runs trips suitable for wildlife enthusiasts. In July it visits Wager Bay to see the bears, caribou and (probably) beluga whales.

Nunavut is also the site of the **North Magnetic Pole**, which is difficult to pinpoint, as it moves a few kilometers east every year — there's nothing to be seen, but it's of interest to scientists and does great things with compasses. Most people heading for the North Pole set off from the community of Resolute.

Inuktitut is far and away the most common language once you're out of Iqaluit, and hiring an Inuktitut-speaking guide is sensible (though not compulsory), both to ensure that you get

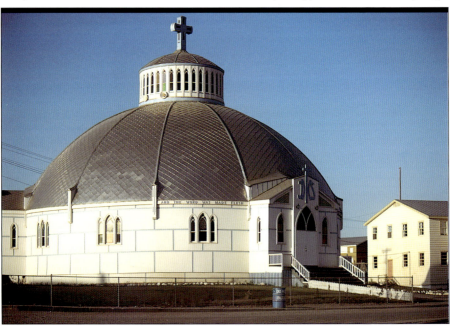

NUNAVUT

Baffin Island is easily the largest of Nunavut's islands, and home to the capital, **Iqaluit** (population approximately 6,500), as well as several different wildlife reserves.

On King William Island, Gjoa Haven is named for Amundsen's ship — the first to traverse the elusive **Northwest Passage**, which evaded many explorers and actually goes past communities in this Kitikmeot region. A self-guided trail commemorates the marine explorers.

Wager Bay, in the Kivalliq region (the mainland area to the northwest of Hudson Bay), is increasingly on tourist itineraries, thanks to its concentration of polar bears, which can be seen in the offshore waters during the summer. **International Wildlife Adventures** ((206) 463-1943 TOLL-FREE (800) 593-8881 WEB SITE www.wildlife

around safely and to act as an interpreter in the small settlements, where little English or French is spoken. Quite apart from the practical considerations, it's great hearing the old stories about the days before outsiders made a noticeable impact (about 50 years ago) and having somebody knowledgeable explaining the culture.

WHERE TO STAY

There's a reasonably wide range of accommodation in Yellowknife. Choice in Iqaluit is more limited, but the town does have a good selection of bed-and-breakfast establishments as well as some hotels.

A number of lodges in wilderness settings offer great accommodation, good food and aboriginal experiences. There is some commercial accommodation, including home-stays, in all the settlements. Camping may be the only option in some areas — though *not* recommended in winter. Ask the tourism agencies for possibilities in the specific areas you intend to visit.

For modern comforts, try the **Château Nova** ((867) 873-9700 TOLL-FREE (877) 839-1236 WEB SITE www.chateaunova.com, Box 4401, Fiftieth Avenue, Yellowknife, which is conveniently situated for both the Old Town and the downtown areas. The 60 high-standard rooms are equipped with voice mail and complimentary high-speed computer ports. Room service is available, and there's an airport shuttle. Facilities include a restaurant, a bar, valet laundry, and a fitness center and a business center (expensive).

an attractive complex of log buildings in a natural setting on the edge of Inuvit — within walking distance of downtown, and a courtesy vehicle is available for a couple of hours at a time. All rooms have satellite television and phones. Some cabins have phones. Breakfast is available every day except Saturday. Smoking is permitted only in outside areas, but pets are welcome. The owners raise and run dog teams and rent kayaks (mid-range).

The best hotel in Iqaluit is the **Frobisher Inn** ((867) 979-2222 FAX (867) 979-0427 E-MAIL info @frobisherinn.com WEB SITE www.arctic-travel .com / frobisher, Box 4209, Astro Hill Terrace, Iqaluit. Centrally located, there are executive and business suites as well as ordinary rooms (smok-

A good year-round bet is the **Prospector Bed and Breakfast** ((867) 920-7620 FAX (867) 669-7581 WEB SITE www.theprospector.net, Box 400, 3506 Wiley Road, on the historic waterfront (with seaplane docking for fly-in guests), in the heart of old Yellowknife, opposite the historic Wildcat Café. There's a choice of individual bedrooms, studios or suites, and each floor has an outdoor deck from which to watch the Northern Lights in winter and activities on the Great Snake Lake in summer. There's a good restaurant / grill, with mining and aviation memorabilia, where the menu includes northern fish and wild game. The atmosphere is relaxed and the hosts are happy to recommend what to see and do in the area. Breakfast is included in the mid-range rates.

The **Arctic Chalet** ((867) 777-3535 FAX (867) 777-4443 WEB SITE www.arcticchalet.com, Box 1099, 25 Carn Street, Inuvik, is also open year-round. It's

ing and non-smoking) with bath, room service and coffee-making facilities. Amenities include a good licensed restaurant, Internet access, voice mail, cable television and airport transfers (expensive).

Self-catering facilities are excellent at the **Capital Suites** ((867) 975-4000 FAX (867) 975-4070 E-MAIL thecapital@urbco.com, Box 2510, Aiviq Street, Iqaluit. On offer are fully furnished and accessorized studio and corporate suites, in the center of downtown, with satellite television, voice mail, jacks, telephones and security systems (mid-range to expensive).

Inuvik, the town that stays up all summer — OPPOSITE: Our Lady of Victory Church is often called the Igloo Church. ABOVE: A downtown street is backlit by the midnight sun.

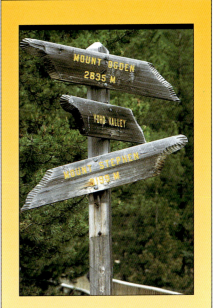

Travelers'
Tips

The best tip we can offer any traveler is to get on the Net, do your homework and get a good travel agent. In a world where fares, schedules, even routes are changing hourly, access to the latest information can only help to ensure an economical and hassle-free vacation.

GETTING THERE

BY AIR

Almost all of the major international airlines fly to Canada, but Air Canada has more flights to more Canadian cities than any other airline. Also, as you would expect, Air Canada has an extensive network of domestic airlines linking cities within Canada (see GETTING AROUND, below). Contact numbers for **Air Canada** are as follows: TOLL-FREE IN CANADA (888) 247-2262 TOLL-FREE IN THE UNITED STATES (800) 268-0024 IN AUSTRALIA ((02) 9286-8900 IN NEW ZEALAND ((09) 379-3371 IN THE UK ((0870) 524-7226 WEB SITE www.aircanada.ca.

Other major airlines offering flights to Canada from the United States include **American Airlines** TOLL-FREE (800) 433-7300 IN THE UK (0845) 778-9789 WEB SITE www.aa.com; **Delta** TOLL-FREE (800) 221-1212 TOLL-FREE IN THE UK (0800) 414-767 WEB SITE www.delta.com; **United** TOLL-FREE (800) 241-6522 IN THE UK (0845) 8444-777 WEB SITE www.ual.com; **Northwest** TOLL-FREE (800) 447-4747 WEB SITE www.nwa.com; **US Airways** TOLL-FREE (800) 428-4322 IN THE UK (0845) 600-3300 WEB SITE www.usairways.com; and **WestJet** ((403) 444-2552 TOLL-FREE (888) 937-8528 WEB SITE www.westjet.com.

Other major airlines offering flights to Canada from Europe include: **Air France** TOLL-FREE IN CANADA (800) 667-2747 TOLL-FREE IN THE US (800) 237-2747 IN THE UK ((0845) 084-5111 IN FRANCE ((08) 2032-0820 WEB SITE www.airfrance.com; **British Airways** TOLL-FREE (800) AIRWAYS IN THE UK ((0845) 773-3377 WEB SITE www.britishairways.com.

BY RAIL

Amtrak TOLL-FREE (800) 872-7245 WEB SITE www.amtrak.com, the United States passenger railway system, has several routes serving Canada's east coast and one route serving the west coast. In the west, Amtrak connects Seattle, Washington, with Vancouver, British Columbia.

BY ROAD

There are 13 principal border-crossing points where the American highway system connects directly with the Canadian. Crossing into Canada by car is usually a quick, simple matter, although in peak season you might want to avoid the busier crossing points such as Detroit–Windsor and Niagara Falls. Once in Canada, no matter where you've crossed, you are only a short drive from the TransCanada Highway.

Greyhound TOLL-FREE (888) 842-8747 WEB SITE www.greyhound.ca is the only company operating a cross-border service, but it has such a huge route system that you should have no difficulty in getting to most points in Canada from virtually anywhere in the United States. It also has a hugely complicated system of fares, discount fares, seasonal rates, unlimited-travel passes, including the 7- to 60-day Canada Pass.

BY WATER

There are several **car-ferries** operating to Canada from points in the northeastern and northwestern United States. For address details see BY FERRY, page 237 under GETTING AROUND.

Although there is no regular passenger ship service between Europe and Canada, some **cargo lines** leaving from European ports accept passengers. Accommodations on board are usually comfortable and food plentiful if plain. Costs are less per day than they are on luxury cruise liners, but the trip is longer, so this option is not for those in a hurry. (The trip from Le Havre, France, to Montréal, for example, takes 18 to 20 days.) For information on freighter travel, contact your travel agent or **Freighter World Cruises** ((626) 449-3106 TOLL-FREE (800) 531-7774 WEB SITE www.freighterworld.com, 180 South Lake Avenue, Suite 335, Pasadena, California 91101-2655.

For more information about cruise ships that ply the west coast see TAKING A TOUR, page 41 in YOUR CHOICE, and CRUISE THE INSIDE PASSAGE, page 16 in TOP SPOTS.

ARRIVING AND LEAVING

United States citizens require only proof of citizenship to enter Canada (passport, birth certificate, voter registration card or naturalization certificate). United States residents who are not citizens must show their Alien Registration Receipt Card. Nationals from all other countries need a full valid passport, with at least six months' validity. United States, European, Australian and New Zealand nationals do not require a visa; those of other nationalities should check in advance.

Travelers crossing the border with children should carry identification for them (passport or birth certificate), as Canadian and United States Customs and Immigration are taking measures to reduce parental and other kinds of child abduction. Children traveling with one parent or adult should bring a letter of permission from the other parent, the parents or legal guardian. Divorced parents with shared custody rights should carry legal documents establishing their status.

Customs

Customs regulations are similar to those in most countries, including the usual restrictions on bringing in meats, plants and animals. Items intended for personal or professional use do not have to be declared, and you are allowed up to 200 cigarettes or 50 cigars, and 1.5 liters of wine or 1.1 liters of spirits or 8.5 litres of beer duty-free. The minimum drinking age is 18 in Québec, Manitoba and Alberta, and 19 in all other provinces.

You can bring in gifts up to $60 per gift in value. There are no currency restrictions.

Personal hunting and fishing equipment may be brought in duty-free as well, but all firearms and ammunition must be declared and a written description of each item, including serial numbers of guns, must be provided. Certain non-firearm weapons are also prohibited. Details of Customs regulations are available from Customs Canada ((204) 983-3500 TOLL-FREE (800) 461-9999 WEB SITE www.ccra-adrc.ga.ca.

If you are planning on purchasing furs or other animal products (e.g., antlers) check with your country's customs regulations to find out which animals are considered endangered and cannot be imported. The same consideration applies to Inuit art, which may be made of whalebone or mastodon ivory, neither of which can be brought into the United States or the United Kingdom.

Taxes

Provincial and federal taxes are added to the published price of all goods. With federal GST of 7 percent and provincial sales tax of up to 15 percent, this can add significantly to the price. Alberta makes a great play of the fact that it is the only province in Canada with no provincial sales tax.

As a visitor to Canada, you can claim a **tax refund** for some of the tax you pay on accommodation, as long as you stay less than one month in that accommodation. In addition, you may claim a tax refund for certain goods you take home. Look for the "Tax Refund for Visitors" brochure at Visitor Information Centres, ask for it at your hotel front desk, or write the Visitor Rebate Program, Revenue Canada, Summerside Tax Centre WEB SITE www.ccra-adrc.ga.ca, 275 Pope Road, Suite 104, Summerside, Prince Edward Island C1N 6C6.

EMBASSIES AND CONSULATES

Foreign Representation in Canada

Australian High Commission ((613) 236-0841 WEB SITE www.ahc-ottawa.org, Suite 710, 50 O'Connor Street, Ottawa K1P 6L2. There are consulates in Toronto and Vancouver.

Irish Embassy ((613) 233-6281, 130 Albert, Ottawa K1P 564.

New Zealand High Commission ((613) 238-6097 FAX (613) 238-5707 WEB SITE www.nzcottawa.org, Metropolitan House (suite 727), 99 Bank Street, Ottawa K1P 6G3, and consulates in Toronto and Vancouver.

South African High Commission ((613) 744-0330 FAX (613) 741-1639, 15 Sussex Drive, Ottawa K1M 1M8. Consulates in Montréal and Vancouver.

United Kingdom High Commission ((613) 237-1530 WEB SITE www.britainincanada.org, 80 Elgin Street, Ottawa K1P 5K7. There are also consulates in Calgary, Halifax, Montréal, Québec City, St John's, Toronto, Vancouver and Winnipeg.

United States Embassy ((613) 238-5335 TOLL-FREE (800) 529-4410 WEB SITE www.usembassy.state.gov, 490 Sussex Drive, Ottawa, Ontario K1N 1G8. There are American consulates in Calgary, Halifax, Montréal, Québec, Toronto, Vancouver and Winnipeg.

Canadian Representation Abroad

Australia: Canadian High Commission ((02) 6270-4000 FAX (02) 6273-4081 E-MAIL cnbra@dfait-maeci.gc.ca, Commonwealth Avenue, Canberra ACT 2600. There are consulates in Melbourne, Perth and Sydney.

Ireland: Canadian Embassy ((01) 417-4100 FAX (01) 417-4101 E-MAIL cdnembsy@iol.ie, 65 St. Stephen's Green, Dublin 2.

New Zealand: Canadian High Commission ((04) 473-9577 FAX (04) 471-2082 E-MAIL wlgtn@dfait-maeci.gc.ca, Third Floor, 61 Molesworth Street, Thorndon, Wellington.

South Africa: Canadian High Commission ((012) 422-3000 FAX (012) 422-3052 E-MAIL pret@dfait-maeci.gc.ca, 1103 Arcadia Street, Hatfield 0028, Pretoria. There is also an office in Cape Town and a consulate in Durban.

All aboard! A railway station, though it may be small, is never far away.

United Kingdom: Canadian High Commission ((020) 7258-6600 FAX (020) 7258-6333 E-MAIL Ldn@dfait-maeci.gc.ca, located in Macdonald House, 1 Grovenor Square, London WIK 4AB; Consular and Passport Services ((020) 7258-6600 FAX (020) 7258-6533, Canada House, Pall Mall East, London SW1Y 5BJ. There are consulates in Belfast, Birmingham, Cardiff and Edinburgh.

United States: Canadian Embassy ((202) 682-1740 FAX (202) 682-7726 E-MAIL wshdc-outpack @dfait-maeci.gc.ca, 501 Pennsylvania Avenue NW, Washington DC 20001. There are consulates in Atlanta, Boston, Buffalo, Chicago, Detroit, Los Angeles, Miami, Minneapolis, New York, San Francisco and Seattle.

TOURIST INFORMATION

Rather than having a central source of information for all of Canada, each of the provinces maintains a bureau that dispenses information on subjects of interest to tourists. In the GENERAL INFORMATION sections of the preceding chapters we have listed the local agencies; here, then, are the provincial tourism offices for western Canada.

Travel Alberta ((403) 427-4321 TOLL-FREE (800) 661-8888 FAX (403) 427-0867 WEB SITE www.travel alberta.com, 17811-116th Avenue, Edmonton, Alberta T5S 2J2.

Tourism British Columbia ((250) 356-6363 TOLL-FREE (800) 663-6000 FAX (250) 356-8246 WEB SITE www.hellobc.com, Third Floor, 1803 Douglas Street, Victoria, British Columbia V8W 9W5.

Travel Manitoba ((204) 945-3777 TOLL-FREE (800) 665-0040 WEB SITE www.travelmanitoba.com,

Seventh Floor, 155 Carlton Street, Winnipeg, Manitoba R3C 3H8.

Northwest Territories Arctic Tourism ((867) 873-7200 TOLL-FREE (800) 661-0788 FAX (867) 873-4059 E-MAIL arctic@nwttravel.nt.ca WEB SITE www .nwttravel.nt.ca, Box 610, Yellowknife, Northwest Territories X1A 2N5.

Nunavut Tourism ((867) 979-6551 TOLL-FREE IN NWT (800) 491-7910 FAX (867) 979-1261 WEB SITE www.nunatour.nt.ca, PO Box 1450, Iqaluit, Nunavut X0A 0H0.

Tourism Saskatchewan ((306) 787-2300 TOLL-FREE (800) 667-7191 FAX (306) 787-5744 E-MAIL travel.info@sasktourism.com WEB SITE www.sask tourism.com, 1922 Park Street, Regina, Saskatchewan S4P 3V7.

Tourism Yukon ((867) 667-5340 FAX (867) 667-3546 E-MAIL vacation@gov.yk.ca WEB SITE www.tour yukon.com, Box 2703, Whitehorse, Yukon Y1A 2C6.

NATIONAL PARKS

National parks are federally administered, but locally supervised by park information centers. These are excellent sources of information, and are the place to pickup permits for fishing or backcountry camping. Interpretive talks, exhibits on flora and fauna, nature walks with park naturalists and reports on weather and road conditions are often also part of the package.

Drivers must pay a modest entry fee to all national parks, usually purchased from a roadside booth at the park boundary. A day pass is valid from the day of issue until 4 PM the following day. It is also possible to buy an excellent-value 12-month National Parks Pass to 27 national parks, or a Discovery Package that also includes 67 national historic sites. They are sold at park gates and information centers, over the Internet, or by telephoning **Parks Canada** ((819) 997-0055 TOLL-FREE (888) 773-8888 (trip planning) E-MAIL parks _webmaster@pch.gc.ca WEB SITE www.parkscanada .pch.gc.ca, 25 Eddy Street, Hull, Québec K1A 0M5.

Parks Canada also runs a wide range of campgrounds within the parks, ranging from the fully serviced to the most basic. Advance booking is strongly recommended in high summer. To do longer trails and go wilderness camping, you will need to buy a daily or annual Wilderness Pass ((780) 852-6177. For additional information and reservations, contact Parks Canada or the local parks offices listed in each chapter.

GETTING AROUND

BY AIR

The country's major carrier, **Air Canada** TOLL-FREE IN CANADA (888) 247-2262 TOLL-FREE IN THE UNITED STATES (800) 268-0024 IN AUSTRALIA ((02) 9286-8900

IN NEW ZEALAND ((09) 379-3371 and IN THE UK ((0870) 524-7226 WEB SITE www.aircanada.ca and its regional partners handle the bulk of the middle- and long-distance air traffic. Dozens of local independent carriers connect the remaining dots on the map. Thus there are very few places in Canada, even the remote islands, that are not accessible by air. The principal regional carriers not owned by Air Canada include: **Air Labrador** ((709) 896-6730 WEB SITE www.airlabrador.com, serving the Maritime Provinces; **Air Transat** TOLL-FREE (800) 388-5836 WEB SITE www.airtransat.com, with connections between the major cities; and **WestJet** ((403) 444-2552 WEB SITE www.westjet.com, with a wide range of flights to major cities and throughout western Canada.

By Bus

Where there's a way, there's a willing bus to take you just about anywhere you want to go in Canada. Greyhound Canada has a nationwide route system, and there are five or six large regional companies that reach into the nooks and crannies Greyhound misses. Bus service is frequent, quick and inexpensive, whether it's intercity or cross-country. The 5,000-km (3,000-mile) trip from Montréal to Vancouver, for example, takes about 69 hours. Greyhound offer various passes, some covering Canada, and some the whole of North America. For detailed information contact **Greyhound Canada** ((403) 265-9111 TOLL-FREE (800) 661-8747 WEB SITE www.greyhound.ca. Other, more local bus companies are listed in the HOW TO GET THERE sections of city listings.

By Car and Motorhome

Canada, only slightly less than the United States, is a driver's dream. The highway system may not be as sprawling as in the United States, but it doesn't have to be, since most of the places visited by tourists and natives alike are within easy driving distance of the TransCanada Highway. The gasoline may not be as cheap as in the United States, but it's far cheaper than in Europe.

The major car-rental firms are represented across the country, including: **Avis** TOLL-FREE IN CANADA (800) 272-5871 TOLL-FREE IN THE UK (0870) 606-0100 TOLL-FREE IN THE US (800) 230-4898 WEB SITE www.avis.com; **Hertz** TOLL-FREE IN CANADA (800) 654-3001 TOLL-FREE IN THE UK (0870) 840-0084 TOLL-FREE IN THE US (800) 854-3131 WEB SITE www.hertz.com; **Alamo** TOLL-FREE (800) 462-5266 TOLL-FREE IN THE UK (0870) 599-4000 WEB SITE www.alamo.com; **Budget** TOLL-FREE (800) 527-0700 TOLL-FREE IN THE UK (0870) 156-5656 WEB SITE www.budget.com; **Holiday Autos** TOLL-FREE IN THE UK (0870) 400-4400 WEB SITE www.holidayautos.com; **National Car Rental** ((954) 320-6600

TOLL-FREE (800) 227-7368 WEB SITE www.nationalcar.com; and **Rent-a-Wreck** TOLL-FREE IN CANADA (800) 327-0116 TOLL-FREE IN THE US (800) 944-7501 WEB SITE www.rentawreck.ca.

If you are planning to rent a car in the summer, it's a good idea to reserve before you leave home. In order to rent a vehicle in Canada, you must be at least 25 years old and you must have a credit card.

Perhaps you had in mind something a bit larger. Each year, hundreds of travelers hit the backroads of Canada in rented motorhomes (recreational vehicles) and truck campers. This is the American equivalent of a "caravan," especially attractive for those who want to explore Canada

as a family or group of friends. In order to rent an RV, you must have a driver's license (that you've held for more than one year) and be at least 25 years old. It is strongly recommended that you reserve your RV several weeks prior to departure. Contact your travel agent for information and reservations.

By Ferry

There are both car and passenger ferry services available on most of Canada's major lakes and rivers, as well as between the mainland and the offshore islands, and Canada and the United States. Ferries across the St. Lawrence and to Vancouver Island don't require reservations, but other

OPPOSITE: A "trembling aspen" near Athabsca Falls in Alberta. ABOVE: Winter in Canada is a time for bundling.

ferries should be booked in advance — well in advance if you are taking a car with you.

Information on ferry transportation within various regions is listed under HOW TO GET THERE in the relevant chapters.

In Western Canada, **Alaska Marine Highway System** ((907) 465-3941 or (907) 272-7116 TOLL-FREE (800) 642-0066 WEB SITE www.dot.state.ak.us/amhs, Box 25535, Juneau, Alaska 99802-5535 USA, operates between Bellingham, British Columbia, and Skagway, Alaska, via the Inside Passage, with several stops en route.

BC Ferries ((604) 444-2890 TOLL-FREE IN BRITISH COLUMBIA (888) 223-3779 FAX (250) 381-5452 WEB SITE www.bcferries.com, 1112 Fort Street, Victoria,

British Columbia V8V 4V2, links Vancouver with Vancouver Island, Port Hardy, Prince Rupert, the Queen Charlotte Islands, the Gulf Islands and various southern British Columbia ports.

Victoria Clipper ((206) 448-5000 FAX (206) 443-2583 WEB SITE www.victoriaclipper.com runs services from Victoria to Seattle and the San Juan Islands.

Black Ball Transport ((250) 386-2202 FAX (250) 386-2207 WEB SITE www.northolympic.com/coho operates ferries between Victoria and Port Angeles, on the Olympic Peninsula.

BY RAIL

Canada's main passenger rail carrier is the government-owned **VIA Rail** ((514) 871-6000 (headquarters) TOLL-FREE (888) 842-7245 WEB SITE www.viarail.ca, 3 Place Ville-Marie, Suite 500, Montréal,

Québec H3B 2C9. The VIA Rail network was cut back severely but there are still regular services between the major cities, and it is still possible to make the transcontinental journey by train, although the southern route has been closed. For more on train travel, see RIDE THE LEGENDARY RAILS, page 11 in in TOP SPOTS.

VIA Rail issues the **Canrailpass**, which makes possible substantial savings by allowing 12 days of coach-class travel over a 30-day period. Prices are $423 (low season) and $678 (high season). Sleeping cars are also available, but must be reserved at least a month in advance during the May to October high season. The pass must be purchased prior to arrival in Canada. There are several other passes on offer, such as the **Corridorpass**, for use only in the Eastern cities.

In the west, some services are operated by **BC Rail** ((604) 984-5246 TOLL-FREE (800) 339-8752 FAX (604) 984-5505 E-MAIL passinfo@bcrail.com WEB SITE www.bcrail.com.

For United Kingdom information and bookings for VIA Rail, BC Rail and the *Rocky Mountaineer*, contact **Leisurail** ((0870) 750-0222 WEB SITE www.leisurail.co.uk, 12 Coningsby Road, Peterborough PE3 8XP.

BY LOCAL TRANSPORTATION

Taxis can always be found at airports, railway stations and major hotels. They can also be hailed in the street fairly easily in the larger cities; elsewhere they can be ordered by telephone. Rates are quite reasonable by American or European standards, and a tip of 15 percent or so is normal. In some provinces not all the taxis have meters, making it advisable to agree on the fare before beginning a journey.

Most major cities have good bus networks. If you choose to travel by bus, be sure to have the exact fare with you, as bus drivers do not carry change — or buy a pass. Details are given under each city chapter.

DRIVING

You will be able to drive on a valid national driver's license for three months, however, it is recommended that you get an international driving permit (see WHAT TO TAKE, below). Any standard United States car insurance policy is valid in Canada; get a Canadian Non-Resident Inter-Provincial Motor Vehicle Liability Insurance Card from your insurance company. All other nationals must take out insurance for a minimum of $200,000 ($50,000 in Quebec and the Northwest Territories).

If the car you're driving is not registered under the name of one of the drivers or one of the passengers, bring written proof that you have permission from the owner to take the car into Canada.

Travelers' Tips

The driving regulations will be familiar to anyone used to driving in the United States or in continental Europe: drive on the right and pass on the left, vehicles approaching from the right have the right-of-way at intersections, the use of seat belts is compulsory, and driving under the influence of alcohol will incur stiff penalties. In Newfoundland, Prince Edward Island, Québec, Ontario, Manitoba, the Yukon, Northwest Territories and Nunavut, radar detectors are illegal even if not in use.

The speed limit on highways is 100 km/h (60 mph), on smaller roads 80 km/h (50 mph), and in towns 80 km/h down to 50 km/h (30 mph). You must stop if you come upon a school bus with its red lights flashing. You may turn right at a red

In the event of an accident, you should get to a telephone and dial the operator ("0"), who can connect you with the police and emergency services. Members of automobile clubs affiliated with the Canadian Automobile Association (the American Automobile Association and most European automobile clubs are) should bring their membership cards along with them, as they are entitled to membership benefits. For more information contact the **Canadian Automobile Association** ((613) 247-0117 FAX (613) 247-0118 WEB SITE www .caa.ca, 1145 Hunt Club Road, Ottawa, Ontario K1V 0Y3; the **American Automobile Association** TOLL-FREE (800) 564-6222 WEB SITE www.aaa.com; the **United Kingdom Automobile Association**

light (except in Québec) if you stop first and make sure the road is clear. Some provinces require drivers to keep headlights on for periods after dawn and before sunset. In the Yukon, the law requires drivers to keep headlights on at all times when using territory highways. Pedestrians have the right of way at all intersections without stoplights and at crosswalks. Note: Fines for traffic offenses in Québec are much harsher there than elsewhere in Canada.

There are plenty of 24-hour service stations flanking the major highways, while those in town tend to close around 9 PM (7 PM in small towns, and all day on Sundays). Gasoline (or petrol) is sold by the liter (one liter equals about one quart; there are 3.8 liters to the gallon). Gas is a good deal more expensive than it is in the United States, but cheaper than in Europe. Most stations take credit cards, and most are now self-service.

((0870) 600-0371 WEB SITE www.the-aa.com; or the **Royal Automobile Club** ((0800) 092-2222 WEB SITE www.rac.co.uk.

ACCOMMODATION

When it comes to accommodation in Canada, one is spoiled for choice. Wherever you go in Canada, you will find places to stay that appeal to every taste and suit every budget. If luxury and comfort are your priorities, there are deluxe hotels to rank with any in the world. If convenient locations while driving are important, there are motels in every price range sprinkled along the nation's

OPPOSITE: A steam-powered clock keeps Pacific Standard Time in Vancouver's Gastown district. ABOVE: Sir Wilfred Laurier (1841–1919), the first French-Canadian prime minister of Canada, appears on Canada's five dollar bill.

main roads and highways. If economy is the paramount consideration, you will be able to get rooms at a YMCA, YWCA, university, or hostel in all but the most remote spots — and sometimes even there (see BACKPACKING, page 26 in YOUR CHOICE). If conversation and "character" count alongside economy, there is bound to be a bed and breakfast nearby to fit the bill.

If rustic charm is what you're looking for, there are delightful country inns spread across the country. If you want to get into serious rusticity, there is no better way than to stay on one of the hundreds of working farms and ranches that offer accommodation as well as hearty meals and healthy activities (see SPECIAL INTERESTS, page 39 in YOUR CHOICE). If you just want to get away from it all and hunt or fish or think about the human condition, there are some wonderful lodges in remote wilderness areas where Nature starts at your front door.

If you will be staying in one place for a longish period, particularly with children or in a group, you will get both privacy and savings (on food) in an efficiency apartment in one of Canada's many apartment hotels.

CAMPING

There are thousands upon thousands of campgrounds throughout Canada, of every size and description. Many are in the national and provincial parks, some are municipally owned, others are privately run. Most are open from May until late September, with campsites costing from $10 to $20. Facilities usually include toilets, showers, a laundry, picnic tables, campfire sites and power hookups for recreational vehicles. The fancier ones will also have a shop and a restaurant. Generally speaking, the privately run campgrounds will have more amenities and will be more expensive, while the public ones in the national and provincial parks will be more scenically situated.

As most campgrounds are run on a first-come, first-served basis, during the high season — July and August — it's a good idea to start looking for a site no later than mid-afternoon.

There are three **nocturnal nuisances** that can thoroughly spoil a camping vacation if you come unprepared. The first is that familiar bane, the mosquito. Bring plenty of insect repellent, as well as a tent fitted with a mosquito net. The second nuisance is scavenging animals — often, in Canada, bears. These creatures can be discouraged by never keeping food in or near the tent (unless it's in the car), and by always disposing of uneaten food and washing up the dishes immediately after meals. No leftovers, no problems. Third, even in midsummer, the temperature at night can suddenly drop, leaving you shivering unless you have brought enough warm clothing.

For lists of campgrounds write to the provincial tourism office in the area you plan to visit or contact Parks Canada (see NATIONAL PARKS, above).

PRICES

We have deliberately avoided giving exact restaurant and accommodation prices. This is because we have learned that the only thing you can absolutely depend on in this business is that the prices will have changed before the ink is dry (sometimes, surprisingly, for the better — as special offers and new types of discounts are introduced). We have therefore confined ourselves to price categories where hotels and restaurants are concerned. Hotels in the **expensive** category, for example, will generally charge over $150 a night for a double room; **mid-range** hotels will charge between $75 and $149; **inexpensive** hotels will charge less, sometimes much less.

At restaurants listed as **expensive** you can expect to pay more than $50 per person for a meal, excluding wine; **moderate** restaurants will charge between $25 and $50; **inexpensive** ones will cost you less — sometimes, again, much less. When hotels or restaurants fall at either of the two extremes — very expensive or very inexpensive — we have so indicated.

Another word about prices: All the prices given in this book, and the categories outlined above, are in **Canadian dollars**. Most travel guides tell you to remember that the Canadian dollar is worth about 20 percent to 30 percent less than the American dollar. My advice is precisely the opposite: forget that the Canadian dollar is worth less. Don't translate; think in United States dollars. This is because all the prices quoted in Canada are exclusive of the layers of taxes that are added later — sales taxes, goods and services taxes, even "taxes on taxes," as one hotel owner wanly pointed out to me. So by the time your bill is added in Canadian dollars, it will come to almost exactly the original, untaxed figure in American dollars. If you keep in mind this one simple trick, you will know a real bargain when you see one.

BASICS

BUSINESS HOURS

Business hours are generally more or less from 9 AM to 6 PM, Monday through Friday, with late-night shopping in some stores until 9 PM on Thursday and Friday. Most shops and stores are also open Saturday and some local stores, especially during the summer, are open on Sunday from noon until 5 PM. Stores may have longer hours in summer months.

CURRENCY

Canadian currency resembles American currency in every important respect except value. The coins are in the same denominations and go by the same names (penny, nickel, dime, etc.), the paper notes are of uniform size (but in different colors according to value). There are no longer $1 and $2 bills. Instead there is the $1 "loonie" coin, nicknamed the after the bird that appears on it, and the $2 "toonie."

At press time the **exchange rate** was: US$1 to C$1.54; UK£1 to C$2.38; and €1 to C$1.52. Should you wish to be precisely *au courant*, visit the Uni-

license), although the larger denominations will not always be welcome in places like restaurants that don't like being used as banks.

In general, however, we recommend floating through Canada on a raft of plastic: your bank debit or credit card. All Canadian financial institutions have automatic teller machines (ATMs), and you'll find ATMs located in large and small shopping centers, airports, train stations and even many gas stations and corner stores. Before you leave home check with your bank to be certain your ATM card is on the Plus or Cirrus network; they can also provide you with a booklet listing networks worldwide on which your card with operate.

versal Currency Converter WEB SITE www.xe.net/currency, or check your local newspaper. American dollars are widely accepted, but using them introduces an unnecessary complication into a transaction, as well as an unnecessary discourtesy.

As in all countries with hard currencies, the banks offer the best exchange rates — much better than hotels, for example. Normal banking hours are Monday to Friday 10 AM to 3 PM. Trust companies and credit unions tend to have longer hours and may also be open on Saturday morning. Most major credit cards are accepted anywhere you are likely to go — including American Express, MasterCard, Visa, Diners Club, Enroute and Carte Blanche; consequently you are advised to carry a minimum of cash. If you prefer using non-plastic money, take it in the form of travelers' checks. They can be cashed everywhere, with the proper identification (e.g. passport, driver's

ELECTRICITY

The electric current is 110–120 volts AC, the same as in the United States, and the sockets only take American-type plugs with two flat prongs.

PUBLIC HOLIDAYS

National holidays include: New Year's Day, Good Friday, Easter Monday, Victoria Day (Monday nearest May 24), Canada Day (July 1), Labor Day (first Monday in September), Thanksgiving (second Monday in October), Remembrance Day (November 11), Christmas Day (December 25), Boxing Day (December 26).

ABOVE: Goldie greets guests arriving by floatplane at Eagle Nook Ocean Wilderness Lodge bordering the Pacific Rim National Park.

In addition to the national holidays, each territory and province has its own local holidays, many on the first Monday in August.

TIME

Canada is divided into six time zones, including Newfoundland's own, typically quirky, time zone, which is only a half-hour ahead of Atlantic Standard Time in the Maritime Provinces. The other four time zones correspond to, and are continuations of, the four United States time zones: Eastern Standard Time, Central Standard Time, Mountain Standard Time and Pacific Standard Time.

Atlantic Standard Time is four hours behind Greenwich Mean Time, so when it is 8 PM in London, it is 4 PM in the Maritimes (4:30 PM in Newfoundland). Québec and all of Ontario to the east of Thunder Bay are on Eastern Standard Time, five hours behind GMT. Manitoba and the eastern half of Saskatchewan are on **Central Standard Time** (GMT minus six); the rest of Saskatchewan, Alberta and northeast British Columbia are on **Mountain Standard Time** (GMT minus seven). All of British Columbia west of the Rockies is on **Pacific Standard Time**, eight hours behind GMT.

All of Canada — with the mysterious exception of eastern Saskatchewan — observes Daylight Savings Time from the first Sunday in April, when the clocks are put forward one hour, until the last Sunday in October.

TIPPING

In general, you should tip more or less 15 percent — more if the service is outstanding, less if it is not so good. Tip porters $2 a bag, chambermaids $2 a day — rounding off the total upwards in deserving cases, downwards in undeserving ones.

WEIGHTS AND MEASURES

Canadians, like just about everybody else in the world except their American neighbors, rely almost exclusively on the metric system.

To make life easier for those not yet numerate in metrics, we have devised our own rough-and-ready (and of course approximate) system for making instant conversions on the spot. It is not only simple, but easy to memorize, so long as you remember that the colloquial term "a bit" here represents one-tenth of whatever it is next to. Thus: a meter equals a yard and a bit; a kilometer equals a half-mile and a bit; a kilogram equals two pounds and a bit (500 grams equals 1 lb and a bit); a liter equals an American quart and a bit.

For converting to degrees Fahrenheit, simply double the figure you are given in Celsius and add 32, topping it up by a couple of degrees when you get above 20°C. The temperature you come up with won't be precisely accurate, but it will be close enough. Note that when temperatures descend into the negative numbers the two scales begin to converge, thus: -40°C equals -40°F. (This may seem like an arcane piece of knowledge, but remember, this is Canada.)

COMMUNICATION AND MEDIA

MAIL

Although main post offices in Canada may open as early as 8 AM and close as late as 6 PM on weekdays, and some are open on Saturday mornings, you can avoid disappointment by going between 9 AM and 5 PM, Monday to Friday. In fact, you can avoid post offices altogether for most purposes, as stamps can be bought at hotels and from vending machines in airports, railway stations, shopping centers and drugstores. Letters and postcards can be mailed at most hotels' front desks or at any red mailbox.

If sending mail to a Canadian address, be sure to include the postal code. Also, we are told by the postal authorities that every year there are some Americans who think it is just as good to use American stamps as Canadian ones. It's not. Following are **postal abbreviations** for the provinces and territories: Alberta AB, British Columbia BC, Saskatchewan SK, Manitoba MB, New Brunswick NB, Newfoundland and Labrador NF, Northwest Territories NWT, Nunavut NT, Nova Scotia NS, Ontario ON, Prince Edward Island PEI, Québec QP, Yukon Territory YT.

If you want to **receive mail** in Canada, you can have mail sent to you $c/_o$ General Delivery at the mail post office in the town or city where you wish to pick it up. But remember that it must be picked up within 15 days or it will be returned to sender. If you have an American Express card, or traveler's checks from American Express or Thomas Cook, you can have mail sent to you at any office of either company. It should be marked "Client Mail," and it will be held for you for as long as a month. Telegrams are handled by CN/CP Telecommunications, while most good hotels now have Internet and fax facilities available for guests' use.

TELEPHONES

The Canadian telephone system is completely integrated with that of the United States, which means that it is efficient and economical, and that no international codes are necessary for calls between the United States and Canada. As in the United States, for information on local telephone numbers dial 411; for information on long-distance numbers dial 1-555-1212. For calls requiring operator assistance — such as long-distance personal or collect calls, or for emergency calls — dial "0."

To place a long-distance call within the same area code, dial 1 + the number you are calling. To place a call outside your area code, dial 1 + area code + telephone number. Do the same for dialing toll-free numbers. For direct dialing of overseas calls, dial 011 + country code + city code + telephone number.

Calls placed in the evening or on the weekend are less expensive, although any call from a hotel will incur a (usually steep) surcharge. There are public telephones just about everywhere; they only accept Canadian quarters, and/or prepaid phone cards.

We have made an effort to provide the specific geographic limitations of the toll-free numbers listed in this book when this information was available. Generally speaking, TOLL-FREE refers to numbers available throughout North America, whereas limitations to Canada, the United States, or a specific province are indicated. TOLL-FREE IN WESTERN CANADA means just that: you can use this number in British Columbia, Alberta, Saskatchewan, Yukon and Manitoba, but will not get through if you dial from elsewhere.

THE INTERNET

Canada is wired. Just about everywhere you go, you will find a bookstore, café or public library offering access to the Internet for a nominal fee (and sometimes free). If you've signed up for one of the free global e-mail accounts such as HotMail or Yahoo before leaving home, then you are wired, too.

We found that most libraries offered access, but that actual availability varied greatly because of lack of equipment and high demand. Many hotels have access points now. If that doesn't work, ask around for the latest cybercafé where you can settle down with a coffee and get warming news from home.

The Internet is also becoming a powerful tool for researching and planning trips. Most organizations, hotels, and tour operators listed in this book have home pages on the **World Wide Web**. We have listed web addresses where we could find them, but with new web sites coming online faster than we can type, if the address is not there, you may be able to find it via a simple search on your web browser (e.g., Netscape Navigator™ or Microsoft Internet Explorer™).

Web sites are of varying quality. Some are quite useful, allowing you to retrieve information quickly, make contact via e-mail direct from the site, or even make a reservation at the touch of a button. Others will have you pulling your cyber hair out. All the provinces and major cities now have excellent tourism web sites with detailed links to other local sites, listed along with the office addresses throughout the book. The prize for the best we have discovered in writing this edition goes to the city of Saskatoon, whose web site is a joy to use and filled with useful, up-to-date information.

RADIO AND TELEVISION

We are tempted to say that if you are in Canada you shouldn't be indoors, and leave it at that. We are further tempted to say that if you do find yourself indoors in North America, you certainly shouldn't be watching television. It's difficult to convey the feeling of dull despair that comes over you when you contemplate a galaxy of up to 40 television channels — not one of which is shining brightly enough to engage your attention for more than a few minutes.

If it's any consolation, though, you are better off watching television in Canada then in the United States, simply because you have a choice of programs aside from the American ones (which nonetheless predominate even in areas beyond the reach of American stations). Its precarious finances notwithstanding, the CBC (Canadian Broadcasting Corporation) manages to produce some worthy programming of its own, while the French-language channels serve up the occasional treat. But don't be surprised when you switch channels to escape Teenage Mutant Ninja Turtles only to be confronted with *Popeye et son fils*.

The Canadian radio dial, like the American, features end-to-end music — classical, pop, rock, country, jazz — interspersed with talk shows, phone-ins, and news.

NEWSPAPERS AND MAGAZINES

Canadian journalism, too, closely resembles its American counterpart. With the exception of the *Globe and Mail*, which is published in Toronto, the newspapers are all local papers. Certainly, some big-city papers such as the *Toronto Star* are national,

Posing for the folks back home at Maligne Canyon, Jasper National Park, Alberta.

even international, in stature; but their main emphasis remains on coverage of their own communities. This enlightened parochialism benefits the visitor not only by providing a useful introduction to topics of local interest, but also by providing, through its listings and advertisements, a comprehensive guide to local events and entertainment. So don't neglect this valuable resource whenever you arrive in a new place.

All of the larger newsagents in Canada have shelves that are identical to the ones you would expect to find in comparable shops in the United States — except that in addition to all the American newspapers and magazines you get the Canadian ones as well.

HEALTH AND SAFETY

You really haven't much to worry about in Canada, because health hazards are few and healthcare is excellent. It can be expensive, though, so visitors should check to make sure that they are either covered for Canada by their existing health insurance or take out full travel insurance. An excellent medical emergency policy, which also includes personal travel insurance, is available from the **Europ Assistance Group** through its affiliates in a dozen or so countries, including the United Kingdom ((01444) 442-365 FAX (01444) 416-348, Sussex House, Perrymount Road, Haywards Heath, West Sussex RH1 IDN. A similar policy, similarly priced, is offered by **Wexas International** ((020) 7589-3315 E-MAIL mship@wexas.com, 45-49 Brompton Road, Knightsbridge, London SW3 1DE.

Another wise precaution is to carry a card in your wallet giving your blood type and listing any allergies or chronic conditions (including the wearing of contact lenses) that might affect treatment in an emergency. Also take a letter from your doctor detailing any prescriptions for ongoing medication, and a copy of your glasses prescription, in case you need to replace them.

Beyond that, it's always a good idea to have insect repellent with you, because in summer Canada has plenty of insects to repel, especially black flies and mosquitoes. A sunscreen lotion is also advisable, as the Canadian sun has a burning power out of all proportion to its heating power.

Emergency fire, ambulance, and police services are usually reached by dialing 911. For other emergencies or for areas not serviced by 911 (e.g., the Northwest Territories and Nunavut), you should contact the operator by dialing "0." In the Yukon Territory, only Whitehorse operates a 911 emergency call system. For the rest of the territory, dial Royal Canadian Mounted Police ((867) 667-5555, or for medical assistance ((867) 667-3333. Yukon communities also have local police and medical emergency numbers, which you can

get a list of from a visitor information center when you begin your trip.

CRIME

Crime? What crime? Canada may well be the most law-abiding of the world's industrialized nations. Violent crime isn't exactly unheard of, but it's not heard of very often. Most streets in Canada's cities are as safe at night as they are in the daytime.

All this law-and-orderliness notwithstanding, one should still take sensible basic precautions here: leave valuables in the hotel safe; lock your hotel room and car; don't leave valuable items visible in your car when unattended; don't carry all your cash and cards with you when you go out; use a handbag with a shoulderstrap slung diagonally and a zip, or put your wallet in an inside pocket, to avoid pickpockets; don't go for late-night strolls through questionable areas. In short, exercise your common sense, secure in the knowledge that Canadians can be counted on to exercise their common decency.

DISABLED TRAVELERS

In general, Canada is extremely well set-up for disabled access. Information may be obtained from the **Canadian Paraplegic Association** (CPA), National Office ((613) 723-1033 FAX (613) 723-1060 WEB SITE www.canparaplegic.org, 1101 Prince of Wales Drive, Suite 230, Ottawa, Ontario K2C 3W7, who will be able to offer general advice and refer you to the various provincial organisations. In the United Kingdom, contact **Tripscope** ((0845) 758-5641 E-MAIL tripscopesw@cablenet.co.uk or the **Holiday Care Service** ((01293) 774-535 E-MAIL holiday.care@virgin.net WEB SITE www.holidaycare.org.uk for details.

WHEN TO GO

The decision of when to go will depend on what you are going for, and by now you should have a pretty good idea of what each region has to offer at what time of the year.

Generally speaking, the seasons in Canada's more temperate climes divide up as follows: winter occupies most of the long stretch from November to the end of March, summer occurs in June, July, and August, while the "shoulder" seasons of spring and autumn are largely confined to April through May and September through October.

The most temperate climate in all of Canada belongs to southern British Columbia, where mild summers fade gently into mild winters. In Vancouver, for example, the temperature seldom rises above 21°C (70°F) in summer, and seldom dips below freezing in winter. You will, however, need to take an umbrella: in December and January alone, meteorologists count on seeing 42 days of rainfall, an average that drops to about seven days in July and August.

Once you are east of the Rockies, the climate abruptly changes. The Prairie Provinces of Alberta, Saskatchewan, and Manitoba are known for their climatic extremes. In all three provinces you will find summers that are hot and sunny, though punctuated by the occasional thunderstorm, followed almost immediately by winters that are very cold and generally dry. To give you some idea of the extremes of weather to be encountered in the Canadian prairies, in Saskatchewan temperatures of 45°C (113°F) have been recorded in summer and temperatures of -57°C (-70°F) in winter.

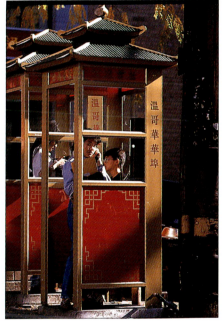

Not surprisingly, weather conditions in the Far North are more extreme than those in the southern provinces. But some visitors are surprised to find out that northern summers can be hot. With the sun out as much as 24 hours a day (above the Arctic Circle), the temperature can reach a balmy 31°C/88°F. But even in July, you should be prepared for cool weather and take sweaters and a fall jacket.

Average monthly temperatures for five western Canadian cities are as follows:

Calgary
January	-10°C/14°F
April	4°C/39°F
July	16°C/61°F
October	6°C/43°F

Inuvik
January	-29°C/-20°F
April	-14°C/7°F
July	14°C/57°F
October	-8°C/18°F

Vancouver
January	3°C/37°F
April	9°C/48°F
July	17°C/63°F
October	10°C/50°F

Whitehorse
January	-18°C/0°F
April	0°C/32°F
July	14°C/57°F
October	1°C/34°F

Yellowknife
January	-28°C/-18°F
April	-7°C/19°F
July	16°C/61°F
October	1°C/34°F

In the North, daylight hours are an important seasonal factor. Average daylight hours for seven northern Canadian cities are as follows:

	DEC	JUNE
Cambridge Bay	0.0	24.0
Dawson City	4.2	21.1
Inuvik	0.0	24.0
Iqaluit	4.5	20.8
Rankin Inlet	4.5	20.8
Whitehorse	5.4	19.1
Yellowknife	6.5	20.0

WHAT TO BRING

To choose what to pack think not about the desirability of having a particular article with you at any given time, but the undesirability of *not* having a particular article with you when you really need it. On that principle, here is our list of things you should never leave home without. On the other hand, you can buy anything you need in Canada, so unless you are going into the remote back country, you won't have any problems.

At the top of the list, by a wide margin, is a Swiss Army knife (or, to put it another way, two knives, two screwdrivers, a bottle opener, a can opener, a corkscrew, a toothpick, tweezers, nail file and scissors). We would also throw in a miniature flashlight and a small travel alarm clock. You will need an adapter and/or transformer if you plan to bring electrical appliances that don't run on 110 volts or don't have an American-style plug.

Because even the most minor physical irritations or afflictions can ruin a trip if they strike at the wrong time (which is the only time they strike), we would be sure to include a small first-aid kit with such items as lip balm for chapped lips, aspirin, anti-diarrhea tablets, antiseptic ointment, a few bandages and a few packets of tissues (which

A phone booth in Vancouver's Chinatown.

can also serve as toilet paper in an emergency). Resealable ziplock plastic bags come in handy when traveling — not least when you have items that you want to keep apart, or you want to segregate items that are damp or dirty or might be inclined to leak.

If you are planning to travel by air and you want to take a Swiss Army knife, or anything else that might conceivably be considered a "weapon" — even a nail file or scissors — be sure to pack it in the luggage you intend to check in. You don't want to be mistaken for an armed passenger, and security these days is tight. On the other hand, if you are taking any battery-powered gadgets — shavers, cassette players, etc. — carry them with you on the airplane or take the batteries out before pack-

as your passport, driver's license, extra travelers' checks, etc. It's just another way of ensuring that any loss causes only a temporary inconvenience.

When it comes to clothing, toiletries, jewelry and gadgetry, it's up to you to decide what and how much you want to take. Canadians are very casual in their dress, so there is no need to take formal or semiformal wear beyond what your taste and your expected engagements require. There is, however, a need to take some warm clothing — a sweater or two perhaps, the odd woolen or corduroy garment, and a windbreaker — because even in summer, even in the hottest spots, it can turn quite cool in the evenings, especially if you happen to be on or near the water.

ing them; airline security personnel get understandably jumpy when unidentified objects with batteries in them show up on their X-ray screen.

Be sure to take with you lists of the numbers of all travel documents, cards and checks you will be carrying, along with any telephone numbers included on them. This will greatly facilitate their quick replacement if lost. Also, take photocopies of your passport and any travel tickets: duplicates are issued more speedily if people can see a copy of the original — much more speedily in the case of tickets or refunds. It is a good idea to get an international driver's license, obtainable from your automobile club, so that you can keep your home driver's license tucked away in a safe place. Always leave your inessential credit cards behind when you go on a trip, and of those you take with you carry only a couple in your wallet: any others should be tucked away in the same safe place

LANGUAGE

Canada's two official languages are English and French, although the province of New Brunswick is the only officially bilingual area in the country. There are also some 53 native languages spoken. Though French is the official language of the province of Québec, English is the mother tongue of 18 percent of the population of Québec, and is widely spoken, particularly around Greater Montréal.

RECOMMENDED WEB SITES

Web sites are listed throughout the book alongside address and telephone numbers. This list adds a few particularly useful or interesting sites without direct connections to sights or associations within the book.

Sympatico www.sympatico.ca. This is a comprehensive site, operated by Bell Canada, with all things Canadian and more. It's very well organized, easy on the eye, and an excellent place to start research on the country in any category. The travel sections are especially good.

Universal Currency Converter www.xe.net/currency. A nifty way to find out what your dollar or euro is worth against any other currency, in real time.

Travelocity www.travelocity.com. The best choice for straightforward air travel fare search and booking. Sign-up for automatic updates on air routes of your choosing. When the rate drops by $50 or more, you'll be notified via e-mail

Where Magazine www.wheremagazine.com. These are locally edited, ad-oriented destination magazines. The web site is useful and attractive. You can order magazines from the site, or browse information on a number of Canadian cities, including Toronto, Winnipeg and Vancouver.

North American Bear Center www.bear.org. Everything you've ever wanted to know about bears.

Mooseworld www.mooseworld.com. And about moose …

Whales www.cetacea.org or www.whaleslife.com. … and about whales.

Rec.Travel Library — Canada www.travel-library.com/north_america/canada/index.html. A homespun and rather out-of-date site that has plenty of information, including personal advice and a list of answers to frequently asked questions about traveling in Canada. Strong on links to many other Canadian sites.

Lost Moose, the Yukon Publishers www.yukonweb.com/business/lost_moose/. These publishers specialize in northern literature, including the legendary *Lost Whole Moose Catalog.*

National Archives www.archives.ca. In English and French, this site contains written records, artwork, photographs and maps that document the history of Canada and the workings of its government.

Canadian Yellowpages www.yellowpages.ca. This is a fairly well organized tool for address and telephone searches. It also offers classified ads, pictures of Canada and links to other sites.

RECOMMENDED READING

ATWOOD, MARGARET. *Alias Grace.* Doubleday, 1997.

BACKHOUSE, FRANCES. *Women of the Klondike.* Whitecap Books, 1995.

BERTON, PIERRE. *The Mysterious North.* Toronto: McClelland and Stewart, 1956. *The Klondike Fever.* New York: Carroll and Graf, 1958.

BERTON, LAURA BEATRICE AND PIERRE BERTON. *I Married the Klondike.* Toronto: McClelland and Stewart, 1996.

BROOK, STEPHEN. *Maple Leaf Rag.* London: Pan Books, 1989.

CRAVEN, MARGARET. *I Heard the Owl Call My Name* and *Again Calls the Owl.* Laureleaf, 1993.

DRISCOLL, CYNTHIA BRACKETT. *One Woman's Gold Rush: Snapshots from Mollie Brackett's Lost Photo Album 1898–1899.* Kalamazoo: Oak Woods Media, 1996.

GALE, DONALD. *Shooshewan, Child of the Beothuk.* Breakwater Books, 1988.

HARDY, ANNE. *Where to Eat in Canada 2002-2003.* Oberon Press.

MACKAY, CLAIRE. *The Toronto Story.* Toronto: Annick Press, 1990.

MACKAY, DONALD. *Flight from Famine: The Coming of the Irish to Canada.* Toronto: McClelland & Stewart, 1990.

MACLENNAN, HUGH. *Papers.* Calgary: University of Calgary Press, 1986.

MALCOLM, ANDREW H. *The Canadians.* New York: Times Books, 1985.

MCNAUGHT, KENNETH. *The Penguin History of Canada.* London: Penguin Books, 1988.

MILEPOST (THE), 54th edition. Bellevue, Washington: Vernon Publications, 2002.

MORGAN, BERNICE. *Random Passage.* Breakwater Books, Ltd., 1992.

MORTON, DESMOND. *A Peculiar Kind of Politics.* Toronto: University of Toronto Press, 1982.

MORTON, WILLIAM L. *The Canadian Identity.* Madison: University of Wisconsin Press, 1973.

PATTERSON, FREEMAN. *The Last Wilderness: Images of the Canadian Wild.* Vanier, Ontario: Canadian Geographic Society, 1991.

PROULX, E. ANNIE. *The Shipping News.* New York: Simon & Schuster, 1994.

RABAN, JONATHAN. *Passage to Juneau: A Sea and its Meaning.* Vintage Books, 2000. Veteran British travel writer retraces Captain Vancouver's 1792 voyage up the Inside Passage.

RICHLER, MORDECAI. *The Apprenticeship of Duddy Kravitz.* London: Penguin Books, 1991. Broadsides. London: Vintage Books, 1991. Papers. Calgary: University of Calgary Press, 1987.

SKOGAN, JOAN. *The Princess and the Sea-Bear and Other Tsimshian Stories.* Polestar Press, 1990.

SOUBLIERE, MARION, Ed. *The Nunavut Handbook: Traveling in Canada's Arctic.* Iqaluit, NWT: Nortext Press, 1998.

WATERMAN, JOHATHAN. *Arctic Crossing: A Journey through the Northwest Passage and Inuit Culture.* New York: Knopf, 2001.

WELLS, E. HAZARD AND RANDALL M. DODD, editor. *Magnificence and Misery: A Firsthand Account of the 1897 Klondike Gold Rush.* Garden City, New York: Doubleday & Company, 1984.

Treading the Athabasca Glacier while a springtime snow falls in Canada's Rockies.

Quick Reference A–Z Guide
to Places and Topics of Interest

Photography Credits

All photographs taken by **Robert Holmes** and **Nik Wheeler**, with the exception of the following:

David Henry: pages 5 *right*, 7 *right*, 11, 12, 13, 14, 20, 21, 22, 24, 25, 26, 27 *top*, 28, 30, 32, 34 *top and bottom*, 35, 39, 40 *top*, 41, 42, 43, 45, 51, 59, 64, 67, 71, 83, 100, 101, 108, 120, 121, 122, 123 *bottom*, 125, 126, 127, 132 *right*, 137, 140, 142, 143, 144, 145, 147, 163, 164 *left*, 165, 167, 170, 233, 236, 241, 243.

Laura Purdom: pages 3, 15, 17 *top and bottom*, 19 *top and bottom*, 31, 38, 40 *bottom*, 113, 148, 203, 208, 210, 211, 213, 216, 217 *top and bottom*, 218, 219, 220, 221, 222, 223, 225 *top and bottom*, 227, 246.

Adina Tovi: Front cover.

Banff/Lake Louise Tourism Bureau: 123 *top*.

Dewitt Jones: pages 23, 36, 37, 46 *bottom*, 50, 62, 65, 99, 115, 117 *top and bottom*.

Emonton Tourism: page 157.

Yukon Archives: Claude Lidd Collection: 53, Skookum Jim Oral History Collection: 206, McBride Museum Collection: 214, Vancouver Public Library Collection: 215.